Research Methods
FOR MEDIA AND COMMUNICATION

To
Ashan and Chinthaka

Research Methods
FOR MEDIA AND COMMUNICATION

Niranjala Weerakkody

OXFORD
UNIVERSITY PRESS
AUSTRALIA & NEW ZEALAND

OXFORD
UNIVERSITY PRESS

Oxford University Press is a department of the University of Oxford.
It furthers the University's objective of excellence in research,
scholarship, and education by publishing worldwide. Oxford is a registered
trademark of Oxford University Press in the UK and in certain other
countries.

Published in Australia by
Oxford University Press
253 Normanby Road, South Melbourne, Victoria 3205, Australia

National Library of Australia Cataloguing-in-Publication data

Weerakkody, Niranjala Damayanthi.
Research methods for media and communication / Niranjala Weerakkody.

ISBN 978 0 19 556044 2 (pbk)

Includes index.
Bibliography.
Mass media–Research–Methodology.
Communications–Research.

302.23072

Edited by Pete Cruttenden
Cover design by studio overture
Text design by Leigh Ashforth, watershed art & design
Typeset by Leigh Ashforth
Proofread by Bruce Gillespie
Indexed by Puddingburn Publishing Services
Printed in Hong Kong by Sheck Wah Tong Printing Press Ltd

Contents

Preface

The aim of this book is to provide teachers and students with an easy-to-read and concise overview of the various aspects and processes related to carrying out research in media and communication, and to introduce them to the quantitative and qualitative data collection methods most commonly used in the discipline. In this endeavour, I have examined the various theories and perspectives, and consulted numerous existing publications by various authors, as indicated in the References section at the end of the main text. In addition, I have incorporated my own observations and practical examples from everyday life that illustrate the concepts covered in the book. I have also used a large number of case studies—both classic ones well known in the field and those based on my own research and personal experiences. These are drawn from across the world and based on contemporary and current events, with special reference to the Asia–Pacific region.

SOME CLARIFICATIONS

Each chapter will include a few exercises for the reader to work on their own. These are listed as 'Try this…'. They give you an opportunity to check how well you have understood the concepts covered in that chapter and examine their practical applications.

The 'Handy Hints' included throughout the book provide, in very simple language, concise definitions or explanations of terms and processes covered in the book.

I have also endeavoured to make this book user-friendly and have avoided introducing too many situations where complex 'number crunching' is required; however, the simple statistics used in the book should already be familiar to the readers from high school mathematics.

In every chapter, the book also discusses the various applications of these research methods in the professional practices of journalism, media and communication (for example, production of media texts) and public relations—widening the scope of the book and its utility beyond the classroom.

THE STRUCTURE OF THE BOOK

The book consists of fifteen chapters divided into five parts. Each chapter is designed to serve as a topic or week's reading for a course unit. At their discretion, individual instructors may like to select the required number of chapters (for example, 12 or 13) as topics to be covered in a semester-long unit.

PART 1

Part 1 is a general introduction that consists of seven chapters dedicated to: the research process (Chapter 1); theoretical paradigms and concepts (Chapter 2); choosing a topic and writing scholarly and non-scholarly research reports (Chapters 3 and 4); research ethics (Chapter 5); and the issues related to sampling (Chapter 6) and measurement (Chapter 7). I have listed them in the order in which I teach the subject, but individual teachers may like to re-order them in a sequence more suitable to their needs and preferences. For example, in Part 1 some of you may like to cover 'From Choosing a Topic to Writing Scholarly Reports' (Chapters 3 and 4) before introducing 'Theoretical

Paradigms and Concepts' (Chapter 2). One could also begin teaching the semester with 'Research Ethics' (Chapter 5) and then teach 'Choosing a Topic and Writing Scholarly Reports' (Chapters 3 and 4) before addressing 'The Research Process' (Chapter 1) and 'Theoretical Paradigms and Concepts' (Chapter 2) depending on your student cohort (professional students rather than scholars) and your own preferences.

The book does not cover the more sophisticated statistical tests under 'Measurement' (Chapter 7) or 'Analysing Data' (Chapter 15), because few beginning researchers in media and communication tend to carry out data analyses more complex than frequencies and cross tabulations. Inclusion of more advanced statistical aspects is beyond the scope of the book because it has to cover a wide area in moderate depth.

PART 2

The two chapters in Part 2 are devoted to quantitative research approaches and examine the data collection methods of 'Survey Research' (Chapter 8) and 'Content Analysis' (Chapter 9) in detail.

The chapter on surveys examines the functions, applications, design and administration of surveys; selection of populations and samples; and issues of reliability, validity, generalisability and measurement. The chapter on content analysis discusses the applications and functions of content analysis and the differences between manifest and latent content; procedures followed in conducting content analyses; and the design and preparation of coding instruments. The advantages and disadvantages of content analysis are also examined.

PART 3

Part 3 consists of three chapters examining the qualitative research approaches of 'Research Interviewing' (Chapter 10), 'Focus Groups' (Chapter 11) and 'Field Studies', including participant observation (Chapter 12). Each of these chapters details how the method is used to collect data; their advantages and disadvantages; and research design, data collection, analysis and reporting.

Note: some of you may wish to introduce qualitative methods (Part 3) before the quantitative methods (Part 2). However, it may be necessary to cover Sampling (Chapter 6) and Measurement (Chapter 7) from Part 1 before introducing the individual data collection methods—be they quantitative or qualitative—included in Parts 2 and 3.

PART 4

The two chapters of Part 4 examine the other research approaches—'Case Study Research' (Chapter 13) and 'Textual Analysis' (Chapter 14). Case studies are discussed in detail to clarify the differences between teaching and research case studies that appear to confuse many. The procedures followed in conducting case studies, such as using methodological triangulation or multiple methods of data collection, are discussed along with their advantages, disadvantages and reporting methods.

Chapter 14 on 'Textual Analysis' is a highly summarised overview of the research method from the points of view of semiotics, genres, narratives, post-structuralism, discourses and ideologies. Please note that this topic area is so wide that separate books are written on it, while individual semester-long course units devoted to the subject are offered at many universities. The chapter has a comprehensive 'Further reading' list that will allow the reader to examine the topic in more depth, if they so desire.

PART 5

Part 5 consists of a single chapter on 'Analysing Data' (Chapter 15) and discusses in detail the most commonly used and specific data analysis method of 'grounded theory' or pattern coding (for qualitative data). It also simply introduces the computer software of SPSS and Excel (for quantitative data) and NVivo and NUD*IST (for qualitative data). In other words, the chapter only provides an overview of the functions of these software, rather than serve as a 'how to' tutorial. Again, the 'Further reading' list provides sources where such training may be available on line.

GLOSSARY

Due to limitations in word length, the book does not include a glossary of terms, but it is provided as part of the online resources for the unit (see below). However, the book's index is a convenient guide for locating definitions of keywords and technical terms discussed in the book, if you wish to do so.

ONLINE RESOURCE CENTRE

The online resources of the unit include the glossary of terms, and qualitative and quantitative data sets that may be useful to carry out practice exercises in data analysis. The URL of the online resource centre is www.oup.com.au/orc/weerakkody.

The instructor's manual   The online instructor's manual includes materials to be used as group exercises for tutorial classes and the answers to the questions posed in these exercises. Some of them may be used in examinations as structured and/or unstructured essay questions.

The instructor's manual also includes detailed instructions on how the data analyses (manually rather than using computer software) should be carried out by students using the data sets provided as online resources.

FEEDBACK

This book is the result of the two decades of media and communication research and teaching experiences of the author. However, I do not expect it to be perfect. As users and the final judges, please feel free to provide feedback or comments on any matter that is relevant to you, and indicate any shortcomings, queries or suggestions for improvements that can be addressed and disseminated to other users if necessary, via the online resources.

So have fun and stay in touch.

Niranjala Weerakkody
Geelong, Vic, Australia.
email: nina.weerakkody@deakin.edu.au

Acknowledgments

I would like to thank the many individuals who both directly and indirectly contributed to the writing and timely completion of this book. Lucy McLoughlin of Oxford University Press was instrumental in getting the book proposal approved and thereafter guided me in drafting the early chapters. She was succeeded by the equally efficient Karen Hiderbrandt as Publishing Editor, who saw the project through to its completion. Anita Castanho served as publishing assistant during the production process with Pete Cruttenden patiently and meticulously editing the manuscript while Rachel Saffer handled the Online Resources. Tim Campbell supervised the overall production process. My thanks go to all.

My gratitude is also extended to the nine anonymous reviewers of the book proposal for their encouragement and valuable feedback; Danielle Smalley of the University of Technology Sydney and Keith Hainsworth of Deakin University for their input on the applications of the various research methods in the practice of public relations; the two anonymous reviewers and Keith Hainsworth for their insightful feedback on the draft manuscript; David Ritchie, Tony Chalkley, Geoff Humble and Hayley Grey, fellow members of the teaching team of the undergraduate unit 'Researching media: Texts, audiences and industries' at Deakin University for their support and feedback; and all past students of the unit for their feedback to help fine-tune the unit's and thereby this book's content.

To Professors Montague Kern and Robert W Kubey of Rutgers University: thank you for being the best teachers and mentors, and going beyond your call of duty to help me over the years. I sincerely hope to 'pay it forward'.

I would like to acknowledge a wonderful teacher, Professor Karen Tracy, who taught me my first unit in research methods in communication at Temple University, and Professor Hartmut Mokros of Rutgers University for imparting his in-depth knowledge of qualitative research methods. Thank you both for the inspiration.

To my family: my mother Muriel, Lakshman, Ashan, Chinthaka, Shelton, Winnie, Kumar, Vino, Sudharma, Leel, Chaminda, Yajeeve, Thiran and Thushara; and to the memory of my father Lionel, who always encouraged me to do my best.

To my friends: Yvonne Schack, Jim McGrath, Arundathi, Bodhini, Chandi, Chandra, Elsie, Eva, Gitanjali, Harshini, Jamilah, Janette, Jythmi, Kathleen, KC Lee and Phil, Kokila and Bernard, Lorraine, Marsha, Po Suan, Priyani, Pushpa, Rani, Rina, Ruchika, Sarina, Shoshi, Shylaja, Sithara, Susan and the 'Spice Girls' (of Deakin University) for their emotional support and staying in touch—most of them across the globe and spanning decades. Thank you for everything.

Part

1

General Introduction

1 The Research Process

Two questions are often asked by students tackling research **methods** for the first time.

o Is research methods a difficult **subject** to learn where you will have to 'crunch a lot of numbers' and learn a lot of difficult statistics?

o Do you still need to learn research methods if you are not planning to do postgraduate study, or become a university teacher or a professional researcher?

Well, even though you may not realise it, you are already familiar with most of the basic statistics and number-crunching skills involved in media and communication research discussed in this book, and you learned them in high school!

You are no stranger to research either. As members of the public, we often receive telephone calls, mail or emails asking us to take part in surveys and we sometimes do. On any given day, newspapers, radio or TV will report on findings of various research, including polls on the popularity of politicians, political parties or issues. The ratings for various TV programs or media outlets are regularly reported in the media and they will decide whether or not your favourite TV program will remain on air.

A theme often debated about in society is the negative effects of various media technologies—such as TV, mobile phones and the internet—or their content on youth, children or society at large, advocating various remedies. All these are linked to research findings.

This is not all. Every time we carry out a Google search on a topic of interest to us, or look up the telephone directory or a library's catalogue, we participate in a research act.

Furthermore, almost every country in the world carries out a census of its inhabitants at regular intervals. Australia does so every five years and the last one was held on 8 August 2006 (www.census.abs.gov.au). The census data collectors make a conscious effort to collect the completed census forms from every household or residence in the country, and include the homeless as much as they can. Since 1970 every baby born in the State of Victoria, Australia, has had a drop of blood collected from its heel to be tested for congenital disorders.

In other words, it is very difficult for an individual not to be a part of, hear about or be affected by research and their findings or be some kind of a researcher themselves. As we live in a media-saturated world, research related to media and communication becomes especially relevant to us.

Research and critical thinking

The study of research methods also helps develop our critical thinking and evaluation skills allowing us to gather and examine information in a more intelligent manner. Critical thinking refers to making value judgments (deciding what is right or wrong) as well as learning how best to make those judgments.

Now that we have explained why you should study research methods, this chapter examines the:

o   different types of research

o   relationship between **theory**, research and practice

o   research process

o   research methods, **methodologies**, **theoretical perspectives** and epistemologies

o   **qualitative** and **quantitative** research methods.

WHY STUDY MEDIA AND COMMUNICATION RESEARCH METHODS? Case Study 1.1

The popular science fiction writer Isaac Asimov (1920–1992) explained why everyone should know about **science** (Asimov, 1980 cited in Singleton et al. 1993). We can extend his argument to the study of research and research methods in media and communication.

Asimov argued that everyone needs to know about science even if they are not scientists or are not planning to become one. He used the analogy of sports fans required to know and understand the rules of the game, even if they could not play it at a professional level (or at all), in order to follow and enjoy what is going on during the sporting action.

Accordingly, a member of the public, a policy maker, professional practitioner or any student interested or involved in media and communication should be able to follow and understand how its research is done, and what is being researched and reported, even if they cannot or do not carry out any formal research themselves.

TYPES OF RESEARCH

The two most common types of research examined in this book are:

1   basic (pure, public or academic) research
2   applied (private or sponsored) research.

BASIC RESEARCH

Basic research is concerned with 'discovering' knowledge for the 'sake of knowledge' to improve our understanding of the world, and is carried out for academic purposes. For example, the Australian Research Council (ARC) grants awarded for pure research are named 'discovery projects'. Findings of academic research are made 'public' in academic journals and other publications.

Academic research takes a theoretical and scholarly approach, is carried out at a pace set by the researcher, and is cheaper to conduct as the overheads are borne by the researcher's organisation, such as a university or research institute.

APPLIED RESEARCH

Applied research is more concerned with practical applications and problem-solving functions. These can relate to the professional practices of journalism, media policy making or public relations. Often sponsored or funded by industry or other groups and organisations for specific purposes, their results are not always be made public (therefore private) or in their entirety. The ARC grants awarded for applied research are named 'linkage grants', recognising the 'links' between academic research and industry.

Sponsored research has to follow the timeline set by the funding body and can be expensive, especially if it involves the hire of independent consultants or commercial research companies.

Overlap between academic and sponsored research However, today pure and applied research often overlap because academic research may have practical applications and sponsored research can add to knowledge just as pure research does. Many academics are involved in both pure and applied research. Equally, many corporations, private research consultants and research companies or other organisations (for example, the Australian telecommunications giant Telstra, international media research companies AC Nielsen and Arbitron media, various government departments and the Parliament of Australia Library) employ trained scholars with Masters degrees or Doctoral qualifications, who are familiar with and use the relevant theories, research methods, data collection and analysis procedures of basic research.

Try this ...

Search for journal articles on databases like Communication and Mass Media Complete, EBSCO Host or other similar databases subscribed to by your library. You can use up to three keywords in your search. For example, to search for any research articles on the 'Effects of video game violence on children' you may use, 'video games', 'violence' and 'children' as your keywords.

Alternatively, visit your library's periodical section and search a few current issues of journals in communication and mass media—such as the *Journal of Communication*, *Mass Media and Society*, *Journalism and Mass Communication Quarterly*, *Australian Journal of Communication*, *Asian Journal of Communication* and *European Journal of Communication*—to search for an article that reports the findings of a research project of your choice. You can use this article for the exercises/discussions in later chapters.

Examine the following:

- Is this article based on pure or applied research or both?
- Why do you think so?
- What is the rationale (reason or importance) for the research given by the author/s?

When carrying out research, we need to base it on applicable theories to provide the research with a suitable context.

WHAT IS A THEORY?

Littlejohn (1989) defines a theory as a way of explaining or understanding a phenomenon: a theory is the theorist's conceptualisation of a systematically observed set of events (p. 2). Heath and Bryant (2000) see theories as 'maps' that guide us from where we are to where we want to be, in an organised and efficient manner. A theory describes, explains and predicts a phenomenon and sometimes suggests how it may be controlled. (However, this control is applicable mostly to the natural world rather than the social world due to the latter's complexity and our inability to control all the relevant factors involved.)

TYPES OF THEORIES

Theories can be of three types: **personal theories**, **scholarly theories** and **common sense theories**.

> **Handy Hint**
>
> A 'theory' is used to explain what happens in society and what we do in 'practice'. This means we cannot have one without the other, challenging the argument that those in professional practice do not need to learn about theory!

PERSONAL THEORIES

We use personal theories in our everyday communication. We develop these ourselves and do not question or test them to see whether or not they are correct. Most of these personal theories are subjective, often culture-bound and have no rational basis. Once formed, they are difficult to change even in the face of evidence that refutes them, because we are personally attached to them.

Personal theories: we all have them

The most common forms of personal theories are superstitions, biases, prejudices and 'old wives' tales' that we hold on to.

For example, 'Do not walk under a ladder!' is a popular superstition and so is the fear of number '13' in some societies.

EXAMPLE 1.1

SCHOLARLY THEORIES

In contrast to personal theories, scholarly or social scientific theories are the result of scholarly research involving systematic observation and inquiry, analysis, generalisation and prediction. Examples include Boyle's law in physics and Newton's laws of motion.

Normative theories, which are also scholarly theories, suggest ways to improve everyday or professional practice. **Working theories**, on the other hand, are at an exploratory stage—still under examination or development.

COMMON SENSE THEORIES

Common sense theories are based on what we know to be true from experience. Common sense theories are different from personal theories, because common sense theories can be scientifically proven to be correct while personal theories cannot.

Common sense theories: cooking the sour vegetable

In traditional cooking of a very sour vegetable, it would be common practice or a common sense theory to add a locally available substance, without realising or knowing that the substance contains a base that reacts with the acid in the vegetable to neutralise it.

EXAMPLE 1.2

THE CRITERIA OF A GOOD THEORY

The strength of a theory is judged by its **scope**, power, appropriateness, **heuristic value**, validity, utility, generalisability, internal consistency, parsimony, falsifiability, and ethical and moral responsibility (Littlejohn, 1989):

- *Scope* means it is comprehensive or inclusive, where its explanation is general enough to cover a range of events—not just a single observation or situation.
- The more general a theory is, the more *powerful* it will be.
- A theory must also be *appropriate* (suitable or be able to do its job). For example, a theory about behaviour is not appropriate for examining meaning-making.
- A theory should also have *heuristic value*, where it can generate research and take our knowledge further.
- The validity of a theory refers to its *accuracy*, importance and *utility* (practical value).
- A theory should also be *generalisable* where it can be applied to other situations.
- *Internal consistency* means it should be logical, reasonable and not contradictory (that is, where one part of the theory is contradicted by other parts or their explanations).
- A theory must also be *parsimonious* where its logical explanations are simple (that is, short and sweet).
- It should also be *falsifiable* (able to be proven wrong) when faced with changed times, circumstances and contexts because if it cannot be disproved, it probably cannot be proved either.
- Last of all, a good theory must be *ethical and morally responsible* where it should not justify acts such as crime, fraud, discrimination, oppression, torture or murder.

THEORY, RESEARCH AND PRACTICE

Heath and Bryant (2000) see theory, research and practice as interrelated, because 'without research findings, theory is mere speculation' (p. 5). Theory poses the questions that methodology tries to answer in a research study (Donohew & Palmgreen, 2003: 112). Applied research uses theory and research findings to improve the effectiveness of communication and related practices. For example, advertising, public relations, journalism, media management, and media policy and regulation carry out research to examine the state of affairs of a phenomenon at a given time and propose measures to improve the situation.

Case Study 1.2   LINKS BETWEEN THEORY, RESEARCH AND PRACTICE:
BILL CLINTON'S 1992 US PRESIDENTIAL CAMPAIGN

Most political campaigns are based on scholarly research findings (even if the research may be sponsored) that examine the 'pulse' of the voting public. For example, *research* carried out during the early stages of the 1992 US presidential campaign of Bill Clinton found that voters were worried about health care, education and the economy.

Using the theory that voters decide on a candidate who best addresses one's own concerns (that is, issue proximity), his campaign designed the catchy slogan 'It's the economy, stupid!' and Clinton promised to address education and health care reform, if elected.

This indicates how *research* and *theory* shaped the *practice* of designing a political campaign strategy.

Source: Wikipedia (2008).

Now that we have established the relationship between theory, research and practice, let's examine the research process in detail.

THE 'WAYS OF KNOWING'

There are four approaches to 'how we end up believing/knowing what we believe/know' that are commonly agreed upon in a given discipline. They are **tenacity**, **authority**, **intuition** and science (Donohew & Palmgreen, 2003: 19).

TENACITY

Tenacity refers to long-held, taken-for-granted beliefs that are difficult to change even when presented with evidence that contradicts our beliefs, such as stereotypes, superstitions or prejudices, and other personal theories.

AUTHORITY

Our beliefs could also be based on authority of the source of the information that's seen as established knowledge or 'truths' and considered reliable; for example, religious scriptures, TV news, lifestyle gurus or even teachers, parents and elders.

INTUITION

Intuition is the third approach that sees truth as obvious, self-evident or based on common sense knowledge. (See common sense theories, above.) However, this approach assumes that if people used open-minded discussions based on democratic principles, they could find the correct answer to a given problem. (Note that this can be true only if all other factors such as power relationships and resources between people are equal.)

Unfortunately, even in democratic contexts, power relations and various power strategies come into play and the majority or the more powerful view generally gets accepted, rather than an absolute 'reason' or the 'right' view winning the day.

In Australia, for example, matters related to values (for example, stem cell research) or questions of policy (for example, adoption of digital TV in Australia) have seen the various stakeholders participating in the debate possessing such unequal power and resources that a truly democratic reasoning process fails to take place. The decisions are ultimately made in favour of those with the most resources and power, allowing them to get their views across and influence the decision makers. At the same time, what is 'right' or 'wrong' in a given situation or context can also be subjective.

SCIENCE

The fourth approach explaining 'how we believe/know what we believe/know' is related to science and the **epistemology** of **objectivism** (explained later in this chapter). Communication researchers who use this approach adopt the methods of the physical sciences to verify facts and beliefs. They begin with a research question or a problem to be examined, propose a solution in the form of a theory (which is a prediction that the proposed solution is correct) and test the prediction with systematic observations using our five senses.

The main advantage of this scientific process is that it has inbuilt checks and balances including standardised procedures to minimise, detect and correct any errors in the research process (Donohew & Palmgreen, 2003: 20).

THE RESEARCH PROCESS

The research process undergoes three basic stages:

1 A researcher begins a project out of curiosity and the need to answer the following questions to provide valid and reliable answers:

- What is (this)?
- If then, what (else)?
- Why (is it so)?
- What if (something was different)?

2 The next stage relates to making observations or data collection, based on the theoretical and research traditions applicable to the question and using specific data collection methods that fit those traditions.

3 The third stage sees the researcher analyse the observations or data to reach the study's conclusions, which will be used to come up with the answers and theories that will try to describe, explain and evaluate the observations (Littlejohn, 1989).

This means the researcher must first consider the following elements of the research process (explained in detail below) (Crotty, 1998: 1):

- What knowledge does this research provide? What will be the characteristics of this knowledge? How would others see this research? This is the epistemology to be used in the study.
- What 'assumptions about reality' do I make in the process? These assumptions are linked to the theoretical perspective or approach used in the research.
- What methodology governs my choice and use of these methods? (Why am I using them instead of others?)
- What methods of data collection should I use?

EPISTEMOLOGIES, THEORETICAL PERSPECTIVES, METHODOLOGIES AND METHODS

Crotty (1998: 2) examines how the four elements of methods, methodologies, theoretical perspectives and epistemologies are used in research and how they relate to each other. The following discussion attempts to clarify the relationships between them. In broad terms these follow a linear path:

epistemologies⟶theoretical perspectives⟶methodologies⟶methods

EPISTEMOLOGIES

Epistemology is 'a way of understanding and explaining how we know what we know' (or believe in) (Crotty, 1998: 4). This relates to our 'ways of knowing'.

The term 'epistemology' generally refers to the 'theory of knowledge' embedded in the theoretical perspective used and thereby in the methodology and methods of data collection selected for a specific research study. In other words, the methods, methodology, theoretical frameworks and epistemologies used in a given research study are interconnected.

Epistemology and the discipline of communication   Let's examine the concept of epistemology from the perspective of the social sciences and as applied to the discipline of communication and related areas such as media studies, journalism and public relations.

For example, an epistemology used in a research project on media effects guides the researcher to examine 'how we can examine the communication's effects on audiences' or society at large using different theoretical frameworks, methodologies and data collection methods (Donohew & Palmgreen, 2003: 17).

THEORETICAL PERSPECTIVES

The theoretical perspective used in a given research study provides a context for it. It is linked to the methodologies and data collection methods used in the study. The most commonly used theoretical perspectives in communication and related disciplines are:

- **positivism**
- **interpretivism** (which includes symbolic interactionism, phenomenology and hermeneutics)
- **systems theory**
- **critical theory**, feminism, **postmodernism**, **functionalism** and **post-structuralism** (Crotty, 1998: 4).

Some of these theoretical perspectives most commonly used in media and communication research will be discussed in Chapter 2.

METHODOLOGIES

The methodology used in a research study is its strategy, plan of action, process or design that shapes how we choose and use a given data collection method. In other words, the methodology we decide to use in a study tells us which data collection method/s may be used and is shaped by what we want to achieve from the research (Crotty, 1998).

The most commonly used research methodologies in communication and related disciplines are:

- **experimental research**—to examine behaviours of people in a controlled setting (not covered in this book)
- **survey research**—to gather information about people and their opinions (Chapter 7)
- **ethnography**—to observe people in their natural, uncontrolled settings (Chapter 11)
- **grounded theory**—to systematically analyse observations or data gathered in **field studies**, and depth or focus group interviews (Chapter 14)
- **content analysis**—to examine how different issues or people are portrayed in media messages (Chapter 8)
- **action research**—to help the powerless find means of solving their problems and be empowered to fight for social justice (Chapter 2)
- **discourse analysis**—to examine how a given topic or subject gets 'talked about' in media messages or in everyday language (Chapter 14).

METHODS

Methods refer to the various data collection and analysis techniques, practices and procedures used in research. Methodologies are selected based on what the research project aims to examine. For example, to examine what people think about a particular TV program, we can carry out a **survey questionnaire** with viewers, interview its fans, conduct **focus groups**, observe fans when they watch the program in groups (as **participant observations** or field studies) and examine the content of the message via a content analysis or **textual analysis** to see what it is about. Each of these could generate either qualitative or quantitative data. (These concepts are examined further in later chapters.)

TYPES OF EPISTEMOLOGIES

'Episteme' means science and epistemology means the 'science of science'. It deals with the nature of knowledge and the ways of gaining knowledge (Sarantakos, 2005). The main epistemologies from social science research applied to and most often used in communication and media-related research are objectivism, **constructionism** and **subjectivism**.

The epistemology the researcher uses serves as the foundation of the research project. As the epistemology is related to the theoretical framework, methodology and methods used, it defines how we carry out the research and present the findings (Crotty, 1998).

OBJECTIVISM

Objectivism supports the theoretical frameworks of positivism and postpositivism and uses the methodology of quantitative research and statistical data analysis. Objectivism is the most used epistemology in the natural sciences such as physics and chemistry (Crotty, 1998).

> **Handy Hint**
>
> Objectivism believes in the existence of an 'absolute' and 'objective reality' and an 'absolute truth' (Sarantakos, 2005). It also argues that meanings and meaningful reality exist whether we know about them or not.

EXAMPLE 1.3 Objectivism: 'meaning' in the deep Amazon rainforest

According to objectivism, a rare, undiscovered plant growing deep in the Amazon rainforest has an existence and a meaning related to what that rare plant means. We will be able to identify it as 'rare' and 'a plant' once we get to see it (discover it).

In other words, objectivism assumes that that there is an 'objective reality' or 'truth' out there—it is just a matter of our 'discovering it'.

Objectivists extend the same argument to ethnographic research involving an unknown culture, which is already there even if no one knows about its existence (Crotty, 1998). According to objectivism, the rare plant and the undiscovered culture both have their own meanings embedded in them, waiting to be discovered.

Objectivism believes that our research subjects (such as individuals, groups, organisations or cultures) are already in possession of their own values and understandings of their world and that with systematic (and objective) research we can uncover these objective truths and meanings (Crotty, 1998).

CONSTRUCTIONISM

Constructionism, on the other hand, takes the position that there is no objective reality or truth 'out there' and that reality is socially constructed. Things that exist outside our experience and consciousness (whose existence we do not know about) have no meaning for us until we come into contact with them (become aware of their existence) and make meanings of them. Constructionism sees knowledge as obtained through means other than our five senses. Meaning does not exist until someone's mind engages with it (Sarantakos, 2005; Crotty, 1998).

Note that constructionism is not the same as *constructivism* even though they are often used interchangeably. Constructivism refers to a theory about how people learn and is related to a way of looking at (or a paradigm for) teaching and learning. It involves individuals asking questions and finding answers via exploration and assessment of what they already know to improve their understanding in a process of interactivity, collaboration and negotiation with others. Constructivism argues that people construct their own understanding and knowledge of the world through their experiences and by reflecting on those experiences. In other words, when a person comes across something new, he or she will compare it with his or her previous knowledge or understanding of related matters. Then the person will either change or add on to what he or she already believes or knows about it or discards the new information as not applicable to him or her, depending on the situation (Educational Broadcasting Corporation, 2004).

For example, tourists who observe a familiar plant from their homeland in the country being visited will touch, smell, taste, closely examine and explore, as well as make inquiries from locals and others, to see if it is the same plant or one either related or unrelated to it.

Constructivism sees knowledge as dynamic and ever changing with our experiences (Educational Broadcasting Corporation, 2004).

In contrast, constructionism refers to 'constructing reality' or making sense of the world around us. We make interpretations or meanings of things based on our culture and history as well as personal experiences. As each person is unique in terms of his or her life experiences—even within the same family or culture—different people and people at different times in history will make different interpretations or meanings of the same 'reality' (event, issue or phenomenon).

For example, slavery was legal in the USA until the 1860s, even if it is almost universally illegal today. When legal, it was seen differently by Abolitionists (those who opposed slavery) and slave owners.

Constructionism: a car is not just a car ... the many 'meanings' of the automobile

EXAMPLE 1.4

Consider an automobile as an example of the social construction of different meanings of the same 'reality'. A car can mean different things to different people, including its owner, users and others, based on each person's values, beliefs, interests, culture, life experiences and lifestyles, plus demographic factors such as age, sex, income, geographic location, education and profession. However, these different meanings will be made within the context of their group's culture and history.

In other words, a car to a poor person from a remote village in a developing country means something different from what it means to an affluent person from an urban area in the developed world. Even in the developed world, owning an automobile is very much different today from 50 years ago.

At the same time, one person may see a car as indicating the owner's affluence or success (for example, the owner has 'made it' to be able to afford that model or make), vanity (showing off), family situation (a station wagon for a family with young children), profession (a tradesperson may drive a 'ute' or utility vehicle for work purposes), 'foolishness' (to have spent so much on a fancy car), mental status (going through a 'mid-life crisis'), extravagance (buying something they can ill afford), lifestyle (racks for bicycles or surf boards) or attitude (based on how the car is maintained). For another, an automobile will simply be a means of getting from A to B, while others may not bother to make any meanings of it or even realise it has 'meanings'.

How meanings are made　Individuals are socialised by their culture or group as to what something may mean and how and under what conditions to use it. (For example, a person from a thrifty family may have been raised or socialised to go for practicality in an automobile rather than as an expression of affluence.) But different members from the same group or culture can assign different meanings to the same thing due to their individuality and/ or unique or different life experiences. Each of these interpretations will indicate the uniqueness of each person and the 'culture' and 'history' to which he or she belongs.

SUBJECTIVISM

The epistemology of subjectivism is the one embedded in the theoretical frameworks of structuralism, post-structuralism (see Chapter 14) and postmodernism, and uses qualitative research methods.

　　The '**object**' is passive as it does not make any contribution to the generation of meaning or 'constructing reality'. 'Meaning' belongs to the subject and comes from anything but interaction between the object and the subject.

　　In other words, the meaning-making is carried out exclusively by the 'active' subject. The subject will import meanings (on to the object) from elsewhere (Crotty, 1998: 9).

EXAMPLE 1.5　Subjectivism: buying designer clothes and name brand goods

Those who buy designer clothes or brand name goods do so because they (the 'subjects') have already imposed a 'meaning' on the 'objects' of these clothes and brand name goods having taken these meanings from, for example, advertising or their social group. The clothes and the goods have no role to play in the matter.

A word of caution　When using a mix of epistemologies in a given research project, one needs to be careful to avoid using both objectivist and constructionist or subjectivist approaches in the same project, because their assumptions are contradictory. That is, while objectivism argues that there is an objective reality or meaning 'out there', the other two say there is not. In other words, one needs to be consistent when working with epistemologies.

　　Table 1.1 provides a list of various epistemologies, theoretical frameworks, methodologies and methods that are commonly used in media and communication research (and in this book).

TABLE 1.1   Epistemologies, theoretical perspectives, methodologies and methods most often used in communication and media related research

Elements of the research process	Examples
Epistemologies	Objectivism, constructionism, subjectivism
Theoretical frameworks	Positivism, systems theory, interpretivism (includes symbolic interactionism, phenomenology and hermeneutics), critical inquiry, post-structuralism, and functionalism
Methodologies	Survey research, ethnography, grounded theory, action research, **evaluation research**, discourse analysis, textual analysis, **feminist research**
Methods of data collection (quantitative, qualitative or mixed)	Quantitative — questionnaires, sampling, measurement, scaling, statistical analysis, content analysis Qualitative — participant and **non-participant observation** or field studies, **depth interviews**, focus groups, **life histories**, **narrative analysis**, **genre analysis**, **pattern coding**, **semiotic analysis**, discourse analysis, **cultural studies**, biographical studies, **ideological analysis** Mixed — **case studies, archival analysis**

Source: adapted from Crotty (1998: 5); Merrigan & Huston (2004: 10, 12); Walter (2006).

APPLICATIONS OF EPISTEMOLOGY, THEORETICAL PERSPECTIVES, METHODOLOGIES AND METHODS IN RESEARCH PROJECTS

When the four elements of epistemology, theoretical frameworks, methodology and method of the research process are correctly applied to a project, they help make sure that the research is sound and will provide convincing outcomes. The four elements can also justify the methods and methodologies used, and help the researcher to analyse the research process by identifying the theoretical assumptions embedded in the study, which helps evaluate its worth (Crotty, 1998).

The epistemology used in a study indicates the researcher's assumptions about the nature of knowledge and what knowledge is being sought in the research (Sarantakos, 2005: 29; Crotty, 1998: 10). The relevant theoretical perspective used indicates the point of view the researcher will be using in the study. The methodology tells researchers what research design to use, where to focus the research activity and how they should recognise and collect relevant data and observations using the various data collection methods (Sarantakos, 2005: 30).

The following are examples of research studies falling under each of the three epistemologies of objectivism, constructionism and subjectivism.

EXAMPLES OF THE THREE EPISTEMOLOGIES APPLIED IN RESEARCH PROJECTS

Case Study 1.3

1   How do Australian teenagers watch their favourite TV program (for example, *Gilmore Girls, Heroes, Supernatural, House, City Homicide, Neighbours, Home and Away* or *CSI*) and interpret its meanings?

This study can be carried out as follows:
- epistemology—for example, constructionism
- theoretical perspective—for example, symbolic interactionism

Case Study 1.3

- methodology—for example, ethnography
- method—for example, participant observation/interviews.

2   What do Australians know and think about digital TV? Who has already adopted it, plans to adopt it or does not want to adopt it and why? What are the factors affecting the adoption of the technology?

   This project can be represented as follows:

- epistemology—for example, objectivism
- theoretical perspective—for example, positivism

- methodology—for example, surveys
- method—for example, statistical analysis

3   How does Australian broadcast TV cover women's sports?

   This project can be carried out as follows:

- epistemology—for example, subjectivism
- theoretical perspective—for example, critical inquiry/feminist theory
- methodology—for example, feminist research
- method—for example, content analysis/ textual analysis of media texts.

Source: adapted from Crotty (1998: 4–5).

Try this ...

Examine the research article you have already selected for the earlier exercise or discussion. Identify the epistemology that has been used in the study, even if not mentioned or specified by the author/s.

Handy Hint

Quantitative methods fall under the objectivist/positivist umbrella and qualitative methods under constructionist/ subjectivist research.

   However, quantitative methods are sometimes used in non-positivist research.

Research methods as well as research data can be labelled as qualitative or quantitative. We now examine them in more detail.

QUANTITATIVE VS QUALITATIVE RESEARCH METHODS

Quantitative research methods provide data that are numerical or can be 'counted'. Surveys and content analysis are the quantitative research methods commonly used in media and communication.

   Qualitative research methods, on the other hand, generate data that are embedded in their context and are non-numerical; for example, texts, opinions, depth interviews, focus groups and field studies.

   The distinction between qualitative and quantitative research occurs at the methods level and not at the theoretical perspective or epistemological levels.

   In the past, each school of thought used to consider the other as less worthy or credible. North America was considered strong on quantitative methods and the United Kingdom and Australia on qualitative. Today, the old argument about qualitative and quantitative research being polar opposites of each other is no longer valid.

   Many communication and media researchers are proficient in both and often use them in combination in the same research project when they use multiple methods.

   For example, Just and colleagues (1996) used depth interviews, focus groups and surveys, with sophisticated statistical analyses carried out with the survey data, in their landmark research on the 1992 US presidential campaign.

   In the past, ethnographic research was classified as quantitative (under the empiricist/ positivist paradigms) even though they are now considered qualitative (under the interpretivist paradigm), indicating how things may change over time (Crotty, 1998).

Let us briefly examine the main characteristics of quantitative and qualitative research.

Quantitative research methods

Quantitative research methods:

- are considered to be objective.
- assume that reality is objective, simple, tangible and 'out there'
- are to be discovered and perceived through our five senses, the same way by each individual, who is governed by universal laws or standard procedures.

Quantitative research:

- examines the cause–effect linkages between the variables observed
- has methods that are considered to be value free and carried out under strict rules
- uses data that are mathematical and are subjected to extensive statistical data analysis.

The quantitative researcher:

- is passive during the research process
- maintains a distance from the subjects under study
- keeps away from 'reality' as reality is studied from the outside.

In quantitative research:

- closed methods of data collection (for example, surveys) and a fixed research design are used
- methods used are agreed upon before the study begins
- a 'still picture' of the world is obtained
- the quantitative (numerical) data are analysed only after the data collection has been completed (Sarantakos, 2005)
- findings are generalised beyond the subjects studied, under conditions of random sampling and other factors (Sarantakos, 2005: 47).

Qualitative research methods

In contrast to quantitative research, qualitative research methods:

- consider reality to be subjective, problematic, holistic (has many facets) and a social construct rather than an absolute 'truth'
- do not provide cause–effect linkages between variables
- are value laden (carry the values of the researcher) and influenced by the researcher
- are not conducted under strict rules the way quantitative methods are
- have data that are mostly verbal and will be analysed as such, without stripping them from their original context
- produce findings that are not generalisable beyond the sample or subjects studied (Sarantakos, 2005: 47).

The qualitative researcher:

- is placed close to the reality he or she is hoping to capture and studies reality from the inside
- is active, and the researcher and the research subject/s or participants are equal partners in an interactive process

- makes his or her own interpretations of the data collected, rather than subjecting them to statistical analysis.

Qualitative data collection methods:

- are open and the research design is flexible
- use naturalistic methods (data collected in their natural setting) to capture the 'world in action' rather than frozen (as would be in an experimental study)
- use data analysis that is carried out both during and after the data collection is completed (Sarantakos, 2005).

Summary

Research epistemologies decide how we conduct research. Therefore, it is necessary to identify the epistemology and the theoretical perspective one hopes to use when examining a research question or phenomenon, which in turn helps the researcher to choose the most suitable methodology and data collection methods. Epistemologies also tell us how to do the research and present one's findings. Each epistemology has its own assumptions, which need to be clear to a researcher—especially when interpreting and/ or reporting the findings.

Qualitative and quantitative research vary at the level of methods, but not at the levels of epistemology or theoretical perspectives. Each has specific strengths and purposes, which must be considered when deciding on which method/s will suit one's research question/s and inquiry. The two methods are also just different and have no hierarchical standing.

Chapter 2 examines the theoretical paradigms most commonly applied in media and communication research.

Further reading

Adler, E S & Clark, R 2003. *How it's done: An invitation to social research.* 2nd edn. Thomson-Wadsworth, Belmont, CA.

Epstein, R L 2002. *Critical thinking.* Wadsworth-Thomson, Belmont, CA.

Wimmer, R D & Dominick, J R 2006. *Mass media research: An introduction.* 8th edn. Wadsworth-Thomson, Belmont, CA.

Theoretical Paradigms and Concepts

Chapter 1 introduced you to the four elements of the research process: epistemologies, theoretical perspectives, methodologies and methods. It also gave you detailed descriptions of the epistemologies of objectivism, constructionism and subjectivism—three of the commonly used epistemologies in research related to media and communication.

This chapter examines the main theoretical frameworks or **paradigms** that fall under these epistemologies. In addition, it introduces important **concepts**, keywords and technical terms useful to any researcher in media and communication.

Specifically, this chapter examines:

- the goals of research
- the basic paradigms and research traditions
- methods of data collection
- **multi-method research**
- concepts and **constructs**
- **variables** and their **operational definitions**
- deductive and inductive reasoning
- **hypotheses** and **research questions**.

GOALS OF RESEARCH

The goals of research are of four types:

- general
- theoretical
- pragmatic
- political.

The intended goal of the research project will decide the paradigm used. At the same time, the paradigm/s used in a research project will shape what goals it can and will achieve.

GENERAL GOALS OF RESEARCH

If the goal of the research is general, it will seek or discover knowledge and gain understanding for its own sake (pure research).

A study with a general goal

A research study with a general goal might, for example, examine a particular home remedy of an Indigenous tribe where it uses certain local plants for treating a particular disease to see what the chemical components of this remedy are.

EXAMPLE 2.1

THEORETICAL GOALS OF RESEARCH

If the research goal is a theoretical, it will seek to check, verify, falsify, modify or discover a theory (pure research).

A study with a theoretical goal

The same research study with a theoretical goal could examine how the Indigenous home remedy works and other scientific factors. Then it will test them against established scientific theories and treatments of the disease/s the remedy is used for, or develop a completely new scientific theory, to explain how this remedy works.

PRAGMATIC GOALS OF RESEARCH

If a research has a pragmatic goal it means the study has a practical purpose (applied research).

A study with a pragmatic goal

A research study with a pragmatic goal could examine how this home remedy can be developed as a commercial product.

POLITICAL GOALS OF RESEARCH

If the goal of a research project is political, it will use its findings to develop social policy, evaluate a program related to it, and provide social criticism. This goal may relate to both pure and applied research.

A study with political goals

A study related to the Indigenous home remedy with political goals will:

o   help develop social policy—for example, about patents related to Indigenous knowledge—to guarantee that some of the profits made by the commercial production of this medicine will be shared with the Indigenous tribe in question (action research)
o   evaluate the programs implemented and carried out by the companies in order to share these profits such as setting up schools and hospitals in the Indigenous homelands (evaluation research)
o   provide social criticism of existing social structures or practices of exploiting Indigenous people and their knowledge worldwide, hoping to bring about positive social change and empower the affected Indigenous tribes who are marginalised or oppressed by those structures and practices (**participatory action research** or PAR).

Therefore, the goals of the proposed research will help the researcher to identify the relevant theoretical perspective (research paradigm) to be used in a given study. Note that multiple perspectives can also be used within a single study.

THEORETICAL PERSPECTIVES (RESEARCH PARADIGMS)

Let us examine theoretical perspectives, which are also known as (research) paradigms. We trace their 'research traditions'—by whom, where and when they were first introduced—and where they stand today.

WHAT IS A PARADIGM?

Defined by Thomas Kuhn (1962), paradigms help us to observe an event, issue or phenomenon in an organised manner so that it becomes easier to understand. A paradigm also relates to questions of focus or point of view because any event, issue or phenomenon can be observed or examined in several ways or using different paradigms. For example, we used to believe that the world was flat. This paradigm was later replaced by another when we began to believe that the world was round.

ONE PICTURE—TWO PARADIGMS

Look at each of the classic examples given in Figures 2.1 and 2.2 that indicate the existence of two paradigms in the same picture.

FIGURE 2.1   This could be a picture of a vase or a silhouette of two people facing each other.

FIGURE 2.2   This could be a picture of an old woman wearing a scarf or a young stylish woman with a feather in her hair.

Source: Boring (1930: 444–5).

You will notice that each of the figures carries two views (paradigms), but you may have taken a while to realise it. When looking at each figure, your eyes will get locked into one view (paradigm) at the expense of the other, at least momentarily. This means a given paradigm we are on or 'locked into' will shape and limit our view of, and reactions to, an event, issue or phenomenon in question. By using a different paradigm, we can 'see' or find different aspects of it.

For example, as long as people believed the world as flat, no one would have tried to sail west from Europe to India (in the opposite direction to the usual route). Columbus did so by following a different paradigm or seeing the world as round. In the process, he 'discovered' the Americas.

DIFFERENT PARADIGMS—DIFFERENT EXPLANATIONS

Different paradigms or points of view can also result in different explanations and understandings of the same event, issue or phenomenon.

The different paradigms of food

Food can be examined from different points of view (paradigms), such as nutrition, aesthetics (as art), economics (costs), culture (rituals involved), history (why a group eats what it eats) and sociology (social practices involved with food).

When we look at food under the paradigm of nutrition, we may not look at it as a work of art and vice versa. Therefore, it is important to know under which paradigm a research study is carried out and what other paradigms may be applicable to it when evaluating a research project and its findings.

OPPOSING PARADIGMS ON THE SAME ISSUE

Paradigms on the same event, issue or phenomenon can be complementary, supplementary or opposed to each other. The various paradigms of food discussed in Example 2.1 can be both supplementary and supportive of each other. However, some paradigms on the same issue, subject or topic can be completely opposed to each other.

Case Study 2.1 OPPOSING PARADIGMS ON THE SAME ISSUE: THE EVOLUTION OF SPECIES

Darwin's theory of evolution, which is the dominant scientific paradigm on how the world and its creatures got to be here, and the conservative religious view of intelligent design (linked to creationism) are incompatible with and challenge each other.

At any given time in society, some paradigms dominate over others. A paradigm can change and/or be challenged at any time. For example, Darwin's theory of evolution replaced, but is continuously challenged by, intelligent design and creationism, with the latter gaining ground in the USA in recent times.

HOW PARADIGMS CHANGE

In the natural sciences, paradigms change or are discarded when:

- they are disproved
- their shortcoming and limitations are pointed out
- they are taken over by new paradigms.

Case Study 2.2 CHANGING PARADIGMS: THE SHAPE OF THE EARTH

An example of changing paradigms is when we stopped believing in the world as being flat, replacing this belief with the paradigm of seeing the world as round.

Once the 'flat earth' paradigm changed (due to being disproved), the old one was discarded and the new one accepted as the norm. It is very unlikely that anyone today will try to argue that the world is not round or is flat.

This aspect of changing paradigms in the natural sciences fits well with the epistemology of objectivism, which assumes there is only one absolute truth or reality out there to be discovered. A new paradigm is introduced once this truth or reality is discovered.

MULTIPLE PARADIGMS ON THE SAME ISSUE

In the social sciences, however, a new paradigm does not mean the old one has been discarded. Different and opposing paradigms on the same issue or reality may remain side by side, with some being popular or dominant at a given time but with different people following different paradigms on the same event, issue or phenomenon.

> **Handy Hint**
> In the social sciences, a paradigm is neither true nor false. It is simply a point of view.

This can be explained as due to the social sciences being based on the epistemologies of constructionism and subjectivism, which do not believe in an absolute reality or truth but in reality as socially constructed (see Chapter 1). This allows several paradigms to exist side by side on the same issue or reality, such as creationism, intelligent design and Darwin's theory of evolution.

MULTIPLE PARADIGMS OF MEDIA EFFECTS   Case Study 2.3

A good example the existence of multiple paradigms of the same reality, issue or topic relates to the different views expressed on the effects of mass media messages today.

Different people believe that:

o   mass media messages are all-powerful (strong media effects and powerless audiences)
o   audiences are more powerful than media messages (weak media effects and powerful audiences)

o   media messages and audiences are both powerful and powerless in different contexts, with the relationship maintained in a state of '**dynamic equilibrium**'.

These can exist side by side with different people believing in each or the same people following different paradigms in different situations or contexts; for example, a specific media message can be seen as powerful on young children and those without real-life experiences, but not on others.

RETURNING PARADIGMS

Some paradigms in the social sciences will lose their popularity but will return to favour at a later data when society or social realities change.

RETURNING PARADIGMS: MARSHALL McLUHAN'S VIEWS   Case Study 2.4

Marshall McLuhan's theories on the effects of communication technologies on society were highly popular in the 1960s (McLuhan, 1964) but lost their dominance in the late 1970s and 1980s.

McLuhan argued that it is the communication medium or technology,

rather than the message or content it carries, that causes any related changes in society. He introduced the slogan 'the medium is the message' and the term 'the global village'. He died in 1980 but had predicted 'an electronic grapevine' long before the internet became an

$\dashrightarrow$

Case Study 2.4

everyday phenomenon, the social networks of MySpace and Facebook were developed or 'blogging' entered our vocabulary.

McLuhan's views returned to dominance in the mid 1990s and remain relevant mainly due to the rise of these new communication and information technologies (McLuhan & Zingrone, 1995; Meyrowitz, 2003; see also www.marshallmcluhan.com).

Having discussed the goals of research that guide the selection of research paradigms and considered the characteristics of paradigms, we can now examine the different theoretical frameworks, paradigms or research traditions most commonly used in media and communication.

THE BASIC PARADIGMS

Five main theoretical frameworks (or paradigms or research traditions) are examined in this chapter:

- positivist
- systems
- interpretivist
- critical theory
- functionalist.

THE POSITIVIST PARADIGM

The positivist paradigm seeks to obtain knowledge by discovery. Therefore, it is linked to pure research and the epistemology of objectivism. Introduced by Auguste Comte (1798–1857), this paradigm suggests that:

- the objective scientific methods used in studying nature (in the physical sciences) should be used when studying society (in the social sciences) as well
- knowledge should be based on what is observed directly through our five senses using scientific methods or empirical observation (that is, all knowledge comes from sense experience)
- other sources of knowledge are unreliable.

The positivist perspective is opposed to the religious or other views that believe that things happen due to God's will, fate, karma, chance, luck and so on.

Assumptions of positivism

Researchers using the positivist paradigm:

- believe in objectivism (see Chapter 1), which sees the existence of an objective reality that is independent of the researcher; this means that no matter who does the research, the results should be the same as there is just one objective reality out there to be discovered
- assume that the only way to learn about this objective reality as through empirical observation (using our senses)
- study variables and develop theories that allow a researcher to describe, explain, predict and control an event, issue or phenomenon under study
- collect data using **measurement** or observation (see Chapter 7)

- use quantitative research methods backed by systematic **sampling** and operational definitions (see Chapter 6), in an attempt to control researcher subjectivity during the research process
- gather evidence based on facts, arguing that facts should be kept separate from the values of the researcher.

The most often used research methods under the positivist paradigm are:
- surveys (see Chapter 8)
- experiments
- content analysis (see Chapter 9).

Types of explanations used in positivism   Positivism uses generalised laws, which can be divided into two types of explanations related to causal reasoning:

- **nomothetic** explanations
- ideographic explanations.

Nomothetic explanations   A nomothetic explanation is based on universal and general causal laws (laws about why something happens in more than one similar situation) that shape and influence social events and relationships. Nomothetic explanations (often used in quantitative research) will identify a few causal factors that affect a collection of situations or events, instead of just one in a simple and parsimonious way. In other words, it provides a more generalised explanation, rather than a unique or idiosyncratic one. Quantitative research often provides nomothetic explanations.

A nomothetic explanation

EXAMPLE 2.6

When University X in Australia experienced a fall in student enrolments for Information Technology (IT) courses after 2002, positivist researchers studying the phenomenon observed a similar trend at many other Australian universities.

The researchers explained this phenomenon as due to the job market slump for IT workers after the DotCom crash in the new millennium.

Ideographic explanations   An ideographic explanation is based on observations of an event, issue or phenomenon, and looks at the idiosyncratic, unusual or peculiar causes for it. As a result, the explanation provided will only be valid for that specific situation or 'case' and will not be generalisable to other situations or cases. This means the research findings are limited in scope. Most qualitative research is ideographic.

An ideographic explanation

EXAMPLE 2.7

Research findings into decreased student enrolments for IT courses at University X explained why IT students at that university did enrol in their courses in 2002, in spite of the slump in the job market for the profession at the time.

In other words, the researchers had examined the issue by analysing what individual students told them during interviews or focus groups, which are qualitative methods.

As positivists look for nomothetic or generalised explanations rather than ideographic or idiosyncratic ones, they also need to use 'laws' or rules that will be generalisable or applicable to a larger group of events, issues or phenomena than to a single one. This is referred to as the '**covering law** approach'.

The covering law approach   Covering laws or theories are the ones used or expected to 'cover' (include the broadest possible number of) similar issues, events or phenomena under study. This generalisability is also called '**external validity**' and is achieved by using **probability sampling** and a large enough sample (see Chapter 6).

EXAMPLE 2.8

Developing a covering law

To examine the phenomenon of decreased IT enrolments and to develop a covering law that would explain the phenomenon, a large enough random sample of students from several (if not all) universities in Australia with IT courses is studied.

This sample represents all states and territories as well as the large, medium and small universities in metropolitan, regional and rural areas. Their enrolment figures for IT courses are examined for several years before the DotCom crash and afterwards. These figures are compared and examined for any observable patterns in the data to conclude if numbers had actually reduced drastically after the DotCom crash across the sample.

At the same time, the study examines if other factors such as increased tuition fees; competition from new courses introduced at the same university or at neighbouring universities are responsible for the situation.

Thereafter, the researcher develops a theory (a covering law) about the decreased enrolments in IT courses using the findings, which is generalised to all Australian universities with IT courses.

THE SYSTEMS PARADIGM

Introduced by Austrian biologist Ludwig von Bertalanffy (1968), the systems paradigm:

- sees an individual, group, organisation, society or any social entity as an 'organism' that is made up of a system of parts
- argues that within this system or dynamic 'whole', organised **interactions** take place continuously, between the various parts that make up the system, to maintain it in a state of equilibrium or balance.

EXAMPLE 2.9

Systems theory: the human body

The human body can be considered a 'system' as it has various organs (lungs, heart etc) and systems (respiratory, vascular etc) that work in coordination with each other to run the body efficiently. In the event of a disruption to a specific part of the body, the system will feel its effects and is designed to react in order to bring it back to a state of equilibrium. For example, in the case of an infection, the human body will react and indicate there is a problem by the person becoming sick or running a temperature. With medication and/or rest, the person will recover and the system regains equilibrium.

Society as a system   A society is also a system—it's similarly designed with many parts working together in synergy to run the system efficiently. Any problems within the system will be indicated by an unusual reaction, which can be seen as the 'symptoms' of the system's problems.

SOCIETY AS A SYSTEM: THE 'SYMPTOMS' OF THE UNDERCLASS   Case Study 2.5

High rates of crimes such as muggings, thefts and burglaries in a successful and affluent society is an indication of economic inequalities within it and the marginalisation (powerlessness and an inability to change their situation) of some of its members.

Such members, known as its 'underclass', are excluded from that society's overall prosperity, and result in disrupting the system's equilibrium.

System synergy: the whole is greater than the sum of its parts   The entire system, or the 'whole', is also greater than the sum of its individual parts—a concept known as synergy. For example, if we make a cake using several ingredients (such as flour, butter, eggs, sugar, baking powder and vanilla essence) that are mixed together and baked in an oven, the resulting cake will taste much better than if we were to consume the raw ingredients separately. This means examining the 'whole system' in a research project will provide a better understanding of the system than when just one or a few parts are examined.

Synergistic team efforts

Generally, the result of a 'team effort' is much greater than the sum of the abilities of its individual members. This is quite marked in sports where having one, two or even several great players in a team does not guarantee that it will win the championship, unless they play well as a team.

On the other hand, having a very weak member could drastically affect the efficiency of a very good team. In other words, just one weak link can break an otherwise strong chain. (Think of a cake made with eggs gone bad, rancid butter or stale baking powder that's no longer effective as a rising agent.)

EXAMPLE 2.10

Researching the system as a 'whole'   According to research grounded or anchored in the systems paradigm, communication for an individual consists of interrelated verbal (linguistic) and nonverbal aspects, which need to work together. A change in one aspect can affect the entire process of communication. For example, when using mediated communication such as email, the nonverbal aspects of pitch and friendly tone of voice or smiles will be absent, which could lead to unexpected interpretations or misunderstandings. This is why the use of emoticons such as smiley faces (:-)) are recommended to indicate when something was intended as a joke or in fun.

Therefore, a researcher needs to study a system as a whole (holistically) instead of its individual parts in isolation.

EXAMPLE 2.11

An holistic inquiry of a system: effects of TV violence on children

Research involving the effects of TV violence on children cannot simply study the TV content (messages) and children's behaviour. It also needs to examine the phenomenon within the context of the children's lives at home and school; aspects about their parents, neighbourhood and community; time spent watching TV; types of TV content viewed; other activities or media available to them; and other sources of violent behaviour observed to understand the **synergies** (factors that work together), interactions (factors influencing each other), **correlations** (interdependence between factors) and **interrelationships** (relationships between factors) within the system.

Systems in dynamic equilibrium   Communication and other systems exist in a dynamic equilibrium where the system stays in a state of balance or equilibrium and the various parts move or are active (dynamic) all the time. The system may get disrupted and lose its balance from time to time due to changes within or outside the system, but the system itself will work to regain its equilibrium.

For example, after an argument between friends, either one or both will apologise and will make their peace or they will stay away from each other thereafter to avoid conflicts. All wars come to an end—eventually.

Types of systems   Systems can be either open or closed, depending on whether the boundary of the system allows the outside environment to interact with the system or not. (For example, our skin serves as the boundary to the system of the human body.)

An **open system** responds to and is affected by external factors or its environment. For example, a friendship can be affected by other people who come into the friends' lives; changes to their lifestyles; the environment, such as the distance between them; and how easy, difficult, necessary or desirable it is for them to remain in contact. All living systems, such as plants, animals, humans and societies, are open systems as they require air, food, water etc from the environment.

A **closed system** is unaffected by external factors or the environment because it can not be influenced by or interact with the environment. An example of a closed system is a research experiment conducted with all outside factors controlled by the researcher. For example, the *Big brother* house in the reality TV show comes close to it.

Systems research   Research grounded or based in the systems paradigm needs to examine:

- what the system in question is
- its boundaries and components
- how those components function and are interdependent
- its equilibrium
- how the components respond to external factors in order to maintain its dynamic equilibrium.

Positivism vs systems theory   Positivism and systems paradigms share some similarities. They both:

- assume an existence of an objective reality
- assume the social world is similar to the natural world
- use quantitative research methods.
  However, they differ because:
- unlike positivism, systems theory does not look for patterns of relationships based on causes and effects among or between variables
- systems theory examines how the different parts of the system work together to maintain a state of dynamic equilibrium, and uses variables to examine issues of equilibrium, while positivism does not.

For example, the 'system of a marriage' is in equilibrium if the parties are satisfied with it. Dissatisfaction with the marriage can lead to disharmony, unhappiness or break-down, caused by factors within the system such as incompatibility of the partners or their dissatisfaction or outside factors such as in-laws, children, finances or third parties.

THE INTERPRETIVIST PARADIGM

Based on the work of Max Weber (1864–1920), Wilhelm Dilthey (1833–1911) and others, the interpretivist paradigm:

- obtains knowledge through interpretation or understanding of human action by examining how people make meanings of them
- sees the social world or human experience as different from the natural world (in common with the critical paradigm, and as opposed to the positivist and the systems traditions)
- argues that this difference is due to the human capacity for reflection or the ability to look at themselves as in a mirror or through other peoples' eyes (**self-reflexivity**)
- sees human action as an activity aimed at meaning-making or interpretation
- uses qualitative research methods in most cases
- argues that, since most human actions are carried out deliberately or for a purpose, people do things based on what meanings their group, society or culture has attached to those actions and will be able to provide a reason for why they do something (note that this aspect places interpretivism within the epistemology of subjectivism, where the object is passive and the subject carries the meaning on to the object—see Chapter 1).

Interpretivism: human action and group meanings

EXAMPLE 2.12

Many a young male buying his first car would rather buy a larger sized, second-hand car of a particular model and make, instead of a brand-new, smaller model from the same manufacturer that costs about the same.

He does so in order to fit his social group's interpretation or the stereotype of the larger model being 'masculine' and for 'guys', and the smaller ones being 'feminine' and meant for 'chicks'. Therefore the interpretations he makes are not just his, but are also shaped by his group's views about 'what a car means'.

Making meanings   Interpretivists assume that meanings are not just 'discovered' but are the result of an active, inventive process. Interpretivists see human action as an activity aimed at meaning-making. A given action has more than one meaning (a web of meanings) for the same person at different times or different people at the same time, based on their culture and group memberships.

Interpretivist researchers use qualitative research methods to understand human action or experiences within the context of people of a specific culture or social group, from the point of view of its members. They generally use anthropological research or field studies for the purpose (see Chapter 12).

EXAMPLE 2.13

Seeing the world through others' eyes: anthropological research

Anthropological research of participant observation involves the researcher:

o   becoming a member of the group being researched
o   experiencing their lifestyle to gain insights
o   understanding why the research subjects do certain things a certain way in a given situation or context
o   what certain actions and phenomena mean to them.

Multiple realities and interpretivist research   Interpretivists researchers:

• do not believe in a single reality, as different meanings are made by different individuals or groups of the same event, issue or phenomenon
• do not see these different interpretations as either right or wrong—just different
• assume different meanings make people carry out different actions in the same situation.

EXAMPLE 2.14

Multiple meanings of not driving to work

Many people living in large cities such as New York or Tokyo deliberately avoid driving to work, choosing to use public transport even if they can easily afford to use a car. They see using a car as less efficient and inconvenient.

Some avoid driving to work to reduce environmental pollution and the use of natural resources. Some ride a bicycle to work for the exercise.

Others drive a car to work irrespective of what they think about the issue, simply because it is essential for their work or family responsibilities and realities.

Forms of interpretivist thought

There are three main lines of thought related to interpretivism:

1   **hermeneutics**—the study of understanding human action and text, credited to Wilhelm Dilthey (1833–1911), Hans-Georg Gadamer (1976) and others
2   **phenomenology**—the study of how people experience the world, credited to Maurice Merleau-Ponty (1908–1961) and others

3 **symbolic interactionism**—the study of structure, functions and meanings of symbol systems (as social life is expressed using symbols such as language), developed by George Herbert Mead of the Chicago School and published by Herbert Blumer (1969); the research methodologies most used in symbolic interactionism are ethnography (see Chapter 12) and grounded theory (see Chapter 15).

The study of meanings and rules   In the interpretivist paradigm, the study of meaning is related to the study of rules because rules specify what can be said, done, encouraged, allowed or banned within a given social group or culture. A rule is shared and believed as to which actions are appropriate or not within a group, subculture or culture (see 'Discourses and power' in Chapter 14).

Rules and meanings

EXAMPLE 2.15

Rules related to grammar, spelling and style exist for written language, and are accepted and followed as 'the standard' by its users. Users know when and which of its forms should be used and by whom and where, and what happens if you do or do not follow these rules in a given context.

In other words, we know how we should or should not address different people when speaking or writing to them—for example, members of the clergy or those of higher status or greater age—and what or what not to wear in different situations, contexts, cultures, subcultures and groups, as well as what happens if we violate or fail to observe them within a given context.

Interpretivist research   Interpretivist research is generally qualitative in nature and examines the communicative actions of a group or setting to understand the rules applicable to them. For example, one could examine the rules applicable to marriage, courtship and their corresponding rituals and practices in a given culture by closely studying them using participant observation (see Chapter 12).

THE CRITICAL THEORY PARADIGM

The theoretical framework of critical theory:

- involves 'knowledge by criticism' or critical reflection
- uses either qualitative or quantitative data
- examines observations or data collected by a researcher to identify the ideological biases in them
- assesses how these biases affect the power relations in society and whose interests are served in the process.

Handy Hint

In simple terms, research based in critical theory examines the ideologies and power relations in society or in a given situation, pointing out what is wrong or unfair with them, and who benefits from the current situation, and tries to make positive changes in society to benefit everyone, especially those who are powerless, marginalised and negatively affected.

Research related to race, ethnicity, class, gender, language use, refugees, human rights violations, environmental issues, anti-globalisation and feminist criticism fall under the critical perspective. As a result, critical research generally takes an advocacy role and carries a political agenda. It challenges actions and decisions seen as inappropriate or unfair and is concerned with abuses of power.

Characteristics of critical theory   Critical theory emerged in the Victorian era due to the power of a small group of people (wealthy, isolated, authoritarian business owners) over their exploited, powerless workers who routinely faced discrimination and experienced terrible living and working conditions (Eisenberg & Goodall, 2004: 148).

In critical theory, social behaviour is seen as a process of conflict where people attempt to dominate others or avoid being dominated by others, which was originally based on the class struggle. It also challenges the assumption (of the positivist and systems traditions) that sees empirical observation as the only way to obtain knowledge of the social world. It often uses the research methodologies of ethnography (Chapter 12), action research (Chapter 2), content analysis (Chapter 9) and textual analysis (Chapter 14), and the epistemologies of constructionism and objectivism (Chapter 1) with respect to media and communication research.

Critical theory and the Frankfurt School   Critical theory is based on the theories of Karl Marx (1818–83), whose work was used by scholars in communication studies at the **Frankfurt School** in Germany (Horkheimer & Adorno, 1994). It became popular in the USA in the 1980s (Grossberg, 1991). Juergen Habermas (1981), Max Horkheimer (1972), Theodore Adorno (1903–1969) and Herbert Marcuse (1898–1979) are some of the leading names in this paradigm.

Ideology and critical research   Critical theory tries to expose the values embedded in a given social structure to help those adversely affected by it. It tries to educate those negatively affected about becoming free or helping them to free themselves from the situation, while explaining why the current situation is unfair and how to change it to benefit everyone.

EXAMPLE **2.16**

Critical theory: negative portrayals of women in media messages

Women are often portrayed negatively in media messages. They can be presented as sex objects or victims of crime; implicitly criticised if they fail to look attractive and thin; or be judged as having sacrificed marriage or family life if they're successful, professional single women. Critical theory shows how the ideological bias of patriarchal (male-dominant) social power is maintained and reinforced by these media messages, which hint that the traditional female role of being sheltered, protected (by males) or being a housewife and stay-at-home mother is best for women.

By pointing out the patriarchal ideological biases in the negative media portrayals of women, feminist or critical researchers show women why such stereotyped portrayals are harmful to them and how they help maintain the status quo in favour of the patriarchy, while pointing out that men are not portrayed negatively in comparable contexts.

In this process, researchers challenge media producers, advertisers and others to portray women more neutrally, realistically and in their diversity of roles.

Case Study 2.6

Critical theory shows that ideologies such as sexism, racism and nepotism can have adverse effects on society at large, not just those directly affected.

In a research study examining sexual harassment or racial or other discrimination in the workplace, critical theorists try to inform and educate those negatively affected that it is illegal, unfair, need not be tolerated and should be changed. Further, they discuss that, while discrimination may help maintain the status quo, benefiting certain groups at the expense of others, it is also detrimental to society because it deprives a workplace from getting the best out of the affected people as it adversely affects their productivity.

If the affected people leave their jobs or are deprived of career advancement due to harassment or discrimination, they may lose their livelihoods or face reduced chances to make a living. Critical theorists will argue that in the long term the world as a whole will miss out on utilising their talents and contributions to the workforce, negatively affecting national and global economic growth and development.

Researcher objectivity and critical research   Researcher **objectivity** requires that a researcher be free of individual views, biases and prejudices during the research process, by overcoming individual subjectivity.

Researcher objectivity and critical theory

EXAMPLE 2.17

Researchers with certain views about media violence must not allow their judgment to influence them when researching the subject. This is achieved through the use of scientific and systematic methods of sampling, coding and data analysis.

Critical theorists also argue that scientific enterprise is part of our social world, not separate from it, and as a result scientific practices used in research should undergo critical reflection just as other social practices.

For example, research needs to acknowledge that social interactions between the researcher and the research subjects are affected by the ideologies and potentially unequal social status and power relations between them within the context of the research setting.

Action research   A form of applied research and a methodology using the critical theory perspective, action research has a problem-solving function in a social situation, and aims to improve the quality of action within it. Based on social justice or the principle of helping the powerless and oppressed, it hopes to empower people and improve their lives. When involving community members in the research process as collaborators and co-participants, action research helps powerless or marginalised people make their own decisions and take action. Therefore it is called participatory action research (PAR).

Like all critical research, action research is activist in nature, performing an advocacy role. It aims for social change to benefit the marginalised and enlighten the powerless (Sarantakos, 2005). Examples of this category of research include most community development research carried out by nongovernmental organisations (NGOs) in developing countries or with communities in crisis (for example, the 2004 Boxing Day tsunami) and the research carried out by Amnesty International into human rights violations worldwide.

Criticisms of critical theory Even though critical theorists may be seen as 'do gooders', critical research is sometimes seen as 'elitist' because, in practice, critical theorists must be willing to argue that certain individuals or groups are oppressed but are unaware of their oppression (Eisenberg & Goodall, 2004: 175).

The final theoretical framework examined in this chapter is functionalism, which is commonly used in media and communication research. (See Chapter 14 for a discussion of the theoretical framework of post-structuralism.)

THE FUNCTIONALIST PARADIGM

Introduced by sociologists Auguste Comte (1896), Herbert Spencer (1896) and Emile Durkheim (1982), and anthropologists A R Radcliffe-Brown (1935), Branislaw Malinowski (1948) and others, the functionalist paradigm assumes that social structures and processes (ways of doing things) have specific 'functions' (actions or uses) and also a mechanism to maintain those structures and processes. Originally used at the systems level of analysis, today it is also applied to levels of the individual, relationships, groups, the mass media, society and culture. Functional analysis, used in ethnographic studies, explains the reasons for particular social behaviours or what causes people to behave in a particular way.

Why do people behave the way they do? Functionalism argues that the reason people behave or act in a specific way is because they know about its consequences (effects). This is the basis of the '**uses and gratifications theory**' about the mass media, which sees people consuming media messages to obtain some uses (functions) as well as pleasures (gratifications) in the process (Blumler & Katz, 1974).

EXAMPLE 2.18

Actions and behaviours

We may consume escapist media content (romance, travel shows, sports etc) because we know they give us pleasure and therefore we keep watching them. Equally, we may do something unfair towards others because we know it hurts them, which is pleasurable to us. Some people may be more willing to hurt others if they knew they would face no negative repercussions.

However, we should not assume that the effects of our actions and behaviours will always be the same and predictable. For example, watching too much escapist TV can make someone depressed instead of happy. Hurting others may result in the perpetrator losing respect and credibility within their group, which is not desirable. In other words, contrary to functionalist arguments, there may be unexpected effects of a person's actions and behaviours.

Later research carried out under the functionalist paradigm was used to suggest how things may be improved by looking at how and why people do things in a given way and how things work. Also known as **administrative research** in media and communication, it has its roots in the **Columbia School**.

The Columbia School In the late 1940s, researchers such as Paul Lazarsfeld, Bernard Berelson and Hazel Gaudet of Columbia University in New York examined the voting behaviours of media audiences. Their results, published in *The People's Choice* (Lazarsfeld et al., 1948), concluded that media messages play a role in reinforcement rather than conversion in voting decisions. This is because people seek messages that reinforce their existing beliefs, rather than those that develop new beliefs. The research provided insights in to how political campaign messages have worked in the past and could be designed in the future to make them more effective.

The applications of persuasion theory in public relations and advertising fits in with the Columbia School perspective (Wilcox & Cameron, 2009: 222–4). Evaluation research (Chapter 8), which is often used in public relations, is also a good example of the application of the functionalist paradigm.

Evaluation research The term evaluation research refers to research with a special purpose rather than a separate research method (Adler & Clark, 2006; Sarantakos, 2005).

Often used in public relations, public policy and advertising, evaluation research seeks to gauge the relevance, suitability and effectiveness of a specific campaign or program (**program evaluation**; see Chapter 8), policy or legal change. They may use exploratory research to identify and design the suitable messages, strategies and tactics for a specific campaign. Variations of evaluation research include:

- outcome evaluation—which examines whether a program, policy or law has accomplished its goal; what the goal is; and how the program was implemented and how it may be improved
- cost–benefit analysis—which explores how to reach the desired goal at the lowest cost or in the most efficient manner
- **needs assessment**—an analysis that identifies potential problem areas, their severity and how they may be addressed
- **process evaluation**—determines whether the program was implemented as designed (Adler & Clark, 2006).

A SUMMARY OF THEORETICAL PARADIGMS

As their research goals, positivists and system theorists look at abstract theories to provide explanations—in the form of 'cause and effect' explanations—and try to make generalised claims on the phenomena under study. Interpretivists seek to develop theories of understanding; critical theorists seek to change things for the better for all concerned; and functionalists aim to examine how things work and how to improve them as desired by those commissioning the research.

Try this …

Examine the research article of your choice selected for analysis in Chapter 1.

1   Identify the research paradigm or paradigms used in this study (that is, positivist, systems, interpretivist and critical theory). Why do you think these were selected?

2   List the assumptions (definitions) of the paradigm or paradigms applied to this study. (These could be the assumptions specifically listed in the article or as specified for the paradigm or paradigms in general.)

3 What other paradigm/s could have been used in the same research project?

4 If these other paradigms had been used, what other research questions could have been examined in the same research project under each paradigm?

5 Which covering law or laws appear to have been used in this study?

6 What type or types of explanations or forms of causal reasoning appear to have been used in this study (that is, nomothetic, ideographic, cause and effect, functional or reason explanations)? Explain why these would have been selected.

MULTI-METHOD RESEARCH

Multi-method research uses more than one methodological tool and data collection method in one study. These tools can be from the same or different paradigms and use a mix of qualitative and quantitative data. In this process, quantitative and qualitative data can supplement each other, while the mix of paradigms provides a more holistic view of the event, issue or phenomenon under study.

Case Study 2.7 MULTI-METHOD RESEARCH: ADOPTION OF DIGITAL TV IN AUSTRALIA

A research project examining the adoption and diffusion of digital TV in Australia uses the critical, interpretivist and positivist perspectives. The qualitative methods used are:

1 depth interviews with consumers who have already adopted digital TV and members of other stakeholder groups, such as dealers of digital TV equipment, policy makers, communication researchers and academics specialising in

the area, members of lobby groups, and executives of media organisations who are in charge of their organisation's digital TV operations

2 focus groups with members of the public who have not yet adopted the technology

3 surveys with members of the public to gather their opinions on digital TV in Australia; these surveys are used to supplement the first two methods.

METHODOLOGICAL TRIANGULATION

The use of several methods of data collection in the same research project is referred to as **methodological triangulation**. The term triangulation is borrowed from navigation and surveying, where a given position of interest or place is located using two other fixed points of location, positioned in a visualised 'triangle'. Methodological triangulation helps increase the validity and reliability of the data collected in a research project. It also allows for better descriptions, explanations, understandings, interpretations, controls and critiques of research findings. This is why most surveys include a few open-ended questions (to obtain qualitative data) seeking respondents' opinions on the topic under examination, in addition to the closed-ended questions (providing quantitative data).

Next we introduce a few useful keywords commonly used in research. They include concepts, constructs, variables, correlations, types of variables, relationships between variables, operational definitions, **systems of logic**, hypotheses and research questions.

CONCEPTS AND CONSTRUCTS

Concepts are considered the building blocks of theory. The term 'concept' is often used interchangeably with the term 'construct' but they do not mean the same thing, because a concept is more general while a construct is more specific.

CONCEPTS

A concept is a name or label given to a specific category of phenomena, which is easily recognisable and distinguishable from other categories. A concept is also the basis for a theory or **hypothesis**. A concept combines particular characteristics of a category of people, events or phenomena, and helps to simplify the research process, in a similar way to technical terms or slang words in everyday conversations.

Concepts: nerds, geeks, cashed-up bogans and mortgage belts

EXAMPLE 2.19

Terms or concepts such as a keen student, nerd (an uninteresting student) and geek (a socially inept teen) are commonly used in school culture. Marketers and advertisers also conceptualise various demographic groups: Dinks (double income, no kids), grey nomads (retirees who roam the country), Cubs (cashed-up bogans—those living in outer suburbs of large cities with high disposable incomes but who lack 'good taste' or 'style') and 'The pink dollar' (gay households with high disposable incomes).

In political advertising and strategising, concepts such as the 'mortgage belt' (newly developed suburbs), Nappy Valley (suburbs full of families with small children) and doctors' wives (used during the 2004 Australian federal election to indicate the Liberal Party's supporters who were socially conscious and disagreed with the party's policies on the Iraq War and refugees) are used to label groups with certain characteristics and priorities. These concepts and their definitions are used as guides when designing specific communication targeted at those groups.

CONSTRUCTS

Concepts are abstract and as a result are unobservable. Therefore, a concept needs to be assigned a construct specifically created for a given research project to carry a specific meaning within that context.

Constructs: a 'keen student'

EXAMPLE 2.20

The concept of a 'keen student' is defined as a construct with a specific set of characteristics for a given research study. Accordingly, it will be someone who meets all the requirements of:

1   having attended 80 per cent of all lectures that semester
2   received a distinction grade or above (over 70 per cent) for each unit taken that semester
3   generally reads at least 75 per cent of the assigned readings each week for every class.

Try this ...

Recall a few labels (concepts) given to people of your age group or those like yourself, by advertisers, marketers, political campaigners and the mass media (for example, Generation X and Y). Write down the assumed specific characteristics (the construct) of those who are considered to fit each of these labels.

See Roy Morgan Research (www.roymorgan.com.au; search for: values segments) for ideas.

VARIABLES AND CORRELATIONS

A variable is the empirical (observable or measurable) counterpart of a construct and describes how the construct is measured by a researcher. A variable has a set of values assigned to it where the values can be either quantitative or qualitative.

Qualitative and quantitative variables: sex and age

The variable of sex has the values of male and female, which are non-numerical or qualitative, while the value of a person's age, such as 40 years, is numerical or quantitative.

By observing variables together, a researcher can see if changes in one variable are accompanied by changes in another. This is called a correlation.

Correlations between newspaper readership and TV viewing

The data collected from research subjects indicated low levels of newspaper reading and high levels of TV viewing. This indicates a correlation between the two.

Correlation vs causality   However, a correlation does not necessarily prove **causality** or that one causes the other to change.

Correlation not necessarily causal

When research subjects indicated low levels of newspaper reading and high levels of TV viewing, it does *not* mean the low reading of newspapers was caused by high levels of TV viewing or vice versa.

Types of variables   Variables are defined based on their relationship to one another. The **independent variable** is one that is systematically changed or manipulated by the researcher, which in turn produces changes in the **dependent variable**, which the researcher seeks to explain.

Independent and dependent variables

EXAMPLE 2.24

In a study examining the relationship between violent media content watched and perceptions of the world as being violent, the 'amount of violent TV content watched' (for example, light, moderate or heavy) is the independent variable, while the subjects' perceptions of the world as being violent (for example, not at all, somewhat violent or very violent) is the dependent variable.

What becomes the independent or dependent variable is shaped by the purpose of each research project. When there is more than one independent variable or several dependent variables, it leads to a **multivariate analysis**.

Relationships between variables   The relationships that exist between corresponding independent and dependent variables are of different types. They are linear, **non-linear** and **curvilinear relationships**.

FIGURE 2.3   Linear relationship: positive

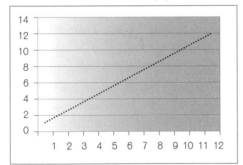

> ### Handy Hint
> Independent variables are either measured or manipulated, while dependent variables are always measured or observed.

FIGURE 2.6   Curvilinear relationship: U shape

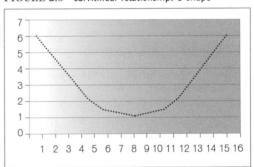

FIGURE 2.4   Linear relationship: negative

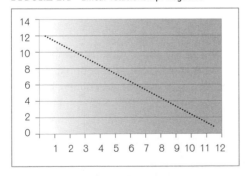

FIGURE 2.7   Curvilinear relationship: inverted U shape

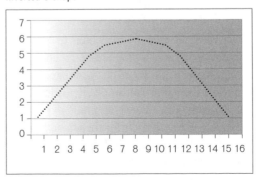

FIGURE 2.5   Non-linear relationship

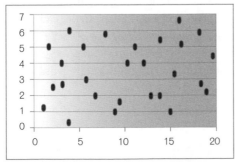

Linear relationships   In a **linear relationship**, when one variable changes so does one or more of the others (see Figure 2.3 and Figure 2.4). This relationship indicates the existence of a dependent and independent variable, with their changes following a predictable pattern. In other words, in a linear relationship, the graph between these two variables will take the form of a straight line.

A linear relationship between the independent and dependent variables can be either positive or negative. It is positive when the values of one variable increase so, too, do the values of the other (see Figure 2.3). In a **negative relationship**, when the values of one increases (goes up), the values of the other decreases (goes down; see Figure 2.4).

Non-linear relationships   In a non-linear relationship no predictable pattern appears to exist between the independent and dependent variable (see Figure 2.5).

Curvilinear relationships   A graph plotted between the values of a dependent and an independent variable can result in a U-shaped curve, which can also be inverted. This is known as a curvilinear relationship (see Figures 2.6 and 2.7).

In a U-shaped relationship, when the values of one variable increase the values of the other decrease up to a point. Thereafter, an increase in one will lead to the increase in the other (see Figure 2.6). In a relationship with an inverted U-shaped curve, as the values of one increase the values of the other also increase up to a point. Thereafter, as one increases the other will decrease (see Figure 2.7).

Operational definitions of variables   The term operational definition refers to the procedure followed in measuring, observing or experiencing a variable or construct. It is the step-by-step explanation of how the researcher observed or measured the variable or construct. Operational definitions are required for both the independent and dependent variables in order to inform others who evaluate the project and its findings, or who need to replicate (repeat) the study.

EXAMPLE 2.25

Operational definitions of variables

In a research project on ethnic minorities and their opinions on a topic under study, the researcher needs to find out who the major ethnic minority groups are in the country, state or city. This information is obtained from the latest census data for population figures by ethnicity. The researcher then selects the ten largest ethnic minority groups from which to draw subjects for interviews.

A list of the most popular films in Australia are identified using official box office figures; the most popular TV programs are identified using AC Nielsen or OZTAM (for Australia) ratings figures; and the major newspapers or magazines can be identified using circulation figures of the Audit Bureau of Circulation (Australia) (www.auditbureau.org.com).

Using the operational definition of a 'keen student' (Example 2.21), a researcher can identify suitable subjects for the research project using attendance records (for 80 per cent attendance), grade reports (for marks over 70 per cent obtained in all units that semester) and self-reports of students who admit to reading more than 75 per cent of readings assigned each week.

THE SYSTEMS OF LOGIC IN SCIENTIFIC REASONING

The research process begins when we are curious about some unknown phenomenon or are faced with a problem that needs a solution. This can be achieved by using one of two systems of logic or methods of scientific reasoning: deductive and inductive methods.

DEDUCTIVE REASONING

The traditional scientific approach to research, **deductive reasoning** is where the researcher predicts a relationship between the independent and dependent variables, stating it as a hypothesis. Thereafter, the hypothesis is tested to see if it is true or false.

> Handy Hint
>
> The theory or hypothesis tells the researcher what variables to observe or measure. Deductive reasoning assumes a causal relationship between the variables and tests it to see if it is true as hypothesised. It is often used in quantitative research.

Deductive reasoning: time spent training vs improvements in athletic performance

EXAMPLE 2.26

A researcher theorises or uses a hypothesis that: 'The amount of time spent training is positively related to the improvements in athletic performance.' The theory or assumption is that higher levels of improvement indicate a better conditioning of the body and that people perform better when they train more.

The variables to be measured will be the 'time or number of hours spent training' (independent variable) and 'improvements to performance' (dependent variable), such as improvements in speed by a runner during a given season. This theory assumes a positive linear relationship, which will be tested if true or false.

INDUCTIVE REASONING

An inductive approach begins with specific observations or data that explains the relationship between the objects examined and ends with generalisations. In this method, every known variable involved or related to the phenomenon under study will be examined to identify any patterns, which helps in the process of generalisation.

> Handy Hint
>
> In **inductive reasoning**, the research will begin with an open mind looking at the full picture to see what's going on and will use research questions.

Inductive reasoning: time spent training and improvements in athletic performance

EXAMPLE 2.27

The researcher collects data from a sample of athletes about the number of hours trained and the improvements to their performance recorded during a given season. The pattern that emerges from the data analysis is that: as the time spent training increases, improvements to their performance (that is, faster times) increase up to a point, but after 25 hours a week of training the performances tend to go down.

The researcher theorises that this is because the person will be too exhausted to benefit from any increased training thereafter. Note that this is a curvilinear relationship with an inverted U shape (see Figure 2.7).

INDUCTIVE VS DEDUCTIVE

Compared with deductive research, inductive research takes much longer to complete due to the large number of interacting variables and factors to be studied. The complexity of the phenomenon under study also makes the patterns between the variables hard to observe.

HYPOTHESES AND RESEARCH QUESTIONS

Once a researcher has identified an area of interest to study and has reviewed the existing literature on the subject to gauge what has already been studied, they will state the problem that needs to be researched in their new project or study. This statement of the problem will be written in the form of a hypothesis (plural: hypotheses) or research question.

A HYPOTHESIS

A hypothesis—which is directly tested by the researcher—is a formal statement about the predicted relationship between variables. A hypothesis is either true or false and is specific about what is being examined or tested. It must be falsifiable (able to be proven wrong) and should only list one possibility. For example, 'It will snow tomorrow' or 'It will not snow tomorrow' but not 'It will or will not snow tomorrow'.

A research hypothesis predicts that changes in the dependent variable will occur in a certain way due to changes in the independent variable. Hypotheses are used in deductive reasoning.

EXAMPLE 2.28

Hypotheses

1 The more positive the attitude of consumers towards digital TV, the more likely they are to have adopted the technology.
2 The adoption of digital TV is positively related to the household incomes of consumers.

A RESEARCH QUESTION

A research question is used when the researcher is not sure what to look for. Research questions indicate the general areas of the phenomenon under study, so that data can be collected to examine the research questions. Research questions are used in inductive reasoning.

EXAMPLE 2.29

Research questions

1 Do consumers' attitudes toward digital TV influence their adoption of the technology?
2 Is there a relationship between consumers' household income and their digital TV adoption?

Summary

The various research paradigms of positivism, systems theory, interpretivism, critical theory and functionalism have different assumptions and take different points of view in a research study. A concept is unobservable, and therefore needs to be defined as a specific construct for a given study. A variable is the observable counterpart of a construct.

Operational definitions are 'recipes' or details of the procedure followed when measuring a construct or variable. Deductive or inductive reasoning is applied when a researcher examines a hypothesis or research question respectively.

A research project and its findings become more comprehensive and reliable when methodological triangulation or multi-method research is adopted in a study where more than one theoretical paradigm and/or data collection method is used. It guards against unreliable or invalid results, as each paradigm or data collection method has strengths and weaknesses that can neutralise each other.

The next chapter examines the steps followed in the research process, beginning with choosing a research topic and ending with the writing of a scholarly research proposal and report.

Try this …

Examine the research article of your choice selected for analysis in Chapter 1.

1 What are the concepts and constructs that have been (or can be) used in this study?

2 Identify the research questions examined and/or the hypotheses tested in this study.

3 Can you identify the independent and dependent variables in this study?

4 Does this study use a multivariate analysis? Why do you think so?

5 What is the relationship (or relationships) between the variables reported in the findings (that is, linear, non-linear, curvilinear, positive or negative)?

6 Identify any operational definitions used in the study and their corresponding variables.

7 Identify the system of logic used in the study (that is, inductive or deductive).

Further reading

Crotty, M 1998. *The foundations of social research: Meaning and perspectives in the research process.* Allen & Unwin, Sydney.

Hall, A & Rist, R C 1999. Integrating multiple qualitative research methods (or avoiding the precariousness of a one-legged stool). *Psychology & Marketing, 16*(2), 291–305.

Kuhn, T 1970. *The structure of scientific revolutions*, University of Chicago Press, Chicago, IL.

3

From Choosing a Topic to Writing Scholarly Reports

Chapter 1 introduced the research process and Chapter 2 discussed the relevant theoretical paradigms. Now it is time learn the steps involved in a research project and how to handle each one successfully. The steps to be followed when conducting a research project in media and communication and reporting the findings are:

1 selecting and narrowing the topic for a research study
2 conducting the **literature review**
3 developing the research design and plan
4 choosing suitable methodologies and data collection methods
5 carrying out the data collection and analysis
6 writing a research report or proposal.

SELECTING AND NARROWING THE TOPIC

> Handy Hint
>
> A research study begins with selecting the topic, issue or problem you want to examine. This sounds straightforward and simple, but it needs careful thinking, selection and examination. Thereafter you need to narrow the focus of the topic to make it clear and doable.

SELECTING A RESEARCH TOPIC OR PROBLEM

Selecting a research topic or problem begins with what you are interested in, curious about or worried about, which might be a phenomenon observed first-hand or an issue dominating the current social, political or media debates. You may also choose a project that: (a) replicates an earlier project to test if the findings of the new one supports, complements or contradicts those of the earlier one; (b) refines the methodology of an earlier project; or (c) adopts a new approach to an existing problem.

You then need to provide a **rationale** for your study. It should explain why it's important, what purpose it serves and what will be its probable outcomes for society or contribution to the discipline.

NARROWING THE TOPIC AREA

Once the topic is identified, you need to narrow it by discarding the less important aspects and choose one idea, problem or factor to be investigated, so that its main issues will be clearer and the project can be completed within the time and resources available.

SELECTING AND NARROWING THE TOPIC: DIGITAL TV ADOPTION IN AUSTRALIA	Case Study 3.1

If you wish to study the adoption and diffusion of digital TV in Australia, and why it appears to be 'slow', you need to examine what the end-users (home viewers) think about it and what reasons they give for not adopting it. You need not worry about the engineering or technical aspects, which are not relevant to the average end-user.

WHAT NEXT?

Once the topic 'Adoption of digital TV in Australia' is selected, consider the:

- main concepts related to the adoption of digital TV—for example, theories of adoption and diffusion of new technologies
- operational definitions used—for example, how you obtain data on adoption figures and identify suitable research subjects.

Next, examine the:

- current situation—for example, the need to adopt digital TV by the deadline of the analogue signal cut off
- major issues—for example, any lack of consumer awareness and/or cost of the new technology
- possible causes and effects of the situation—for example, too few public communication campaigns conducted due to digital services being unavailable nationwide (cause). which results in low consumer awareness of the technology (effect)
- what may be done to remedy the situation—for example, what you plan to find out in your study by asking the end-users for their views and suggestions.

OTHER FACTORS TO CONSIDER

Other factors to consider when choosing and narrowing a topic are the limitations imposed on you by:

- the course of study you are doing the research for—for example, perhaps you are required to choose a specific topic area for a class project
- the areas of research specified and supported by a funding body
- the time frame, financial or other resources available—for example, library resources and costs of travel and/or data collection, such as payments to interviewees, computer facilities and skills
- your access to the data or research subjects—for example, some topic areas have limited information or data available because they are new and/or restricted due to national security or corporate ownership, while some government officials or corporate executives may be unwilling or not permitted to be interviewed.

Once you have a clear idea about what you want to study, you need to search for, read and review the existing literature on the relevant topic area.

THE LITERATURE REVIEW

A comprehensive literature review will indicate if your exact research topic has been studied before, in which case your study will be either redundant or will need to be redesigned, unless you are specifically aiming to replicate an earlier project as a follow-up or update. Research is also about building on existing knowledge. A good literature review will help a researcher and others to achieve this goal more effectively.

Specifically, a good literature review:

- traces the historical development of the research area for a given time period
- comprehensively examines, summarises, describes and analyses the existing literature on the current theorising, methodologies and research studies, and their findings and writings on the topic
- is not just a listing of what X or Y 'said' on the subject but a critical examination of the readings, discussing their strengths, weaknesses and limitations as well as what was done and not done in them
- includes *your opinions* on the existing studies, theorising and findings
- insightfully and analytically indicates what the findings mean to the discipline, and what is missing or needs further study.

EXAMPLE 3.1

Areas for review in the literature

If studying the relationship between digital TV adoption and the gender, age and income level of adopters, the review of literature should include those on the adoption and diffusion of new communication technologies and the effects of gender, age and income of adopters on adoption.

Case Study 3.2   THE SUMMARY OF A LITERATURE REVIEW ON MEDIA EFFECTS RESEARCH

A literature review written on research into the effects of media messages on audiences could trace the history of media effects research from the 1920s to the present day.

Before the First World War, the Magic Bullet or Hypodermic theory of media effects suggested a powerful media. Thereafter, landmark research including the Payne Fund studies (Charters, 1933), Cooper and Johoda's (1947) Mr Biggot study, the two-step model of communication by Katz and Lazarsfeld (1955), Klapper's (1960) study on 'selective processes' used by audiences, and Bauer's (1964) 'obstinate audience' traced how media effects research and findings indicated powerful audiences.

In the 1970s, theories such as 'agenda setting' (McCombs & Shaw, 1972) and 'media consonance' by Noelle-Neumann (1973) returned media effects to that of a powerful media and powerless audience. This was again changed to a powerful audience with British cultural studies in the 1980s (Hall, 1980). It concludes that findings of media effects between the 1920s and 1980s had oscillated between a powerful media and powerful audiences.

The reviewer argues that the theories of the Hypodermic model or powerful media effects existed in an environment of authoritarian state controls of the media as well as political propaganda during the First World War. In the

└┄┄┄┄┄>

1990s, a powerful media was re-introduced with press censorship enforced during the Gulf War of 1991, the War against Terror since 11 September 2001 and the early stages of the Iraq War in 2003 where the media carried the views of those in power. This is attributed to strategies such as the 'national interest' or 'embedded reporting' imposed by the US Government.

At the same time, the 1991 Gulf War gave rise to the CNN Effect (Livingston, 1997); and Iraq War in its early stages to the Fox News Effect (Della Vigna & Kaplan, 2004) as another era of a powerful media.

The literature review also could discuss how the availability of alternative news outlets such as blogs and the internet, and unpopularity of the Iraq War around 2006, moved media effects theorising to a 'dynamic equilibrium' where both the media and audiences can be powerful as well as powerless in a given context.

CRITIQUING THE LITERATURE

The literature review also discusses if the theorising and findings of existing research are limited to a particular context or if they are generalisable to other eras, locations, societies and cultures. That is, can research findings from one country in one decade be applicable to others? It will also critically evaluate the sampling methods, sample sizes, methodologies and units of analysis used; data collection and analysis; theoretical perspectives and epistemologies used; and the research questions posed or hypotheses tested in the existing research in the topic area.

The conclusions, results, theorising, assumptions and arguments made in each of the earlier studies must be compared and contrasted while adding the reviewer's own arguments, conclusions, observations and views about them. The reviewer can also include **alternative explanations** to the findings as to what other reasons may have been responsible for those findings in addition to the ones examined or discussed by the researchers.

PRIMARY AND SECONDARY SOURCES

If the available literature on your selected topic area is very large, it is an indication that your topic needs to be narrowed further. Look for **primary sources**, such as scholarly journal articles and books by authors who report the findings of their own original research. These are the most important sources.

Secondary sources are summaries of existing studies or textbooks written by those who did not carry out the primary research. They will help you to identify the key research studies, theories and scholars in the disciplinary area. A good literature review should include more primary sources than secondary sources. If you're having difficulty locating primary sources, citations in secondary sources can lead you to the relevant primary source material. (Note that the concepts of primary and secondary sources in social research are different from those in journalism, which refer to the individuals interviewed for an article as 'sources'.)

Areas for further research suggested in journal articles provide ideas for further narrowing of your research topic. The **reference list** of articles reviewed provides information on other sources.

NON-SCHOLARLY SOURCES

Newspapers, magazines, trade journals, websites and other internet sources can also be examined for suitable articles or

Handy Hint

How do you know you have read enough? You will know you have reached a saturation point in your literature search when reading more articles does not add any new information or knowledge on your topic.

the latest information and data relevant to a given topic. However, these should not be your main (or only) source of references.

CITING YOUR SOURCES—THE REFERENCE LIST

You must cite all sources of information within the body of the literature review and provide their full citations in the reference list, using the style specified by your organisation or funding body. The American Psychological Association (APA; 2001) or Harvard referencing styles (*Citing your sources, Harvard style*, 2006) are most commonly used in media and communication.

It is essential to provide your sources of information both as a courtesy to the original authors and to abide by rules of copyright while avoiding accusations of plagiarism. 'Endnote' is a popular computer software program that helps make the process of citing your sources and preparing the reference list much easier. Some university libraries provide online tutorials that help you learn to use this software.

Once the literature review has been completed and the topic has been sufficiently narrowed, the research design stage can begin.

THE RESEARCH PLAN AND DESIGN

The following discussion examines a number of areas relevant to the research design of a project or the evaluation of others' research. These involve issues related to the:

- purpose of research
- **unit of analysis**
- **fallacies** and **aggregate data**
- orientations in time and space

When designing a research study, one needs to be clear as to its purpose and indicate whether it is exploratory, descriptive, explanatory (causal/functional) or understanding (reason-based).

TYPES OF RESEARCH STUDIES

Some research studies are designed to serve more than one purpose. When evaluating someone else's study, such as in a literature review, one must identify the purpose of that research as it was intended by the original researcher and judge its merits within that context (Adler & Clark, 2008).

Exploratory studies   **Exploratory studies** are preliminary research that 'explores' a relatively new or unknown topic area to gain a basic understanding of it, but not to provide satisfactory answers to the research questions posed. If the study is inductive, it will begin with a 'blank slate' to examine what is going on, while a deductive study will have the key issues or phenomena under study already known to the researcher.

An exploratory study on digital TV adoption

EXAMPLE 3.2

When examining why digital TV adoption is 'slow' in Australia, an inductive study will begin with no assumptions or plans about what to test for. So it will ask people why they have or have not adopted and/or what did or what will induce them to adopt.

In a deductive study, the researcher may examine if those with higher income and education, and within a particular age group, are more likely to adopt digital TV than others and the relationship between those factors and digital TV adoption.

Descriptive studies   In a **descriptive study**, the researcher describes their observations, findings, results of data analyses, what people said during interviews and so forth.

A descriptive study: ratifying the Kyoto Protocol

EXAMPLE 3.3

Quantitative research involving surveys, polls and content analyses (of media messages) will simply describe what they found, such as what percentage of people surveyed answered 'yes' to a statement such as 'Do you think Australia should ratify the Kyoto Protocol on the environment?' and how they differed based on age, gender, political party affiliation and so on.

Most qualitative research, such as field studies (see Chapter 12) and focus groups (see Chapter 11), are descriptive, describing, for example, what subjects said about the Kyoto protocol during interviews or focus groups. However, the researcher may make interpretations of their findings and observations from a descriptive study, explaining these views.

Explanatory studies   **Explanatory studies** 'explain' and are of two types. If it is a causal explanation, it will answer the question: 'Why is it so?' If is a functional explanation, it will address the question: 'How is it so?'

An explanatory study: negative political campaigns

EXAMPLE 3.4

When researching the effectiveness of political campaign advertisements, a causal explanatory study might ask the question: 'Why do voters remember negative advertisements better than positive ones?' By contrast, a functional explanatory study could examine: 'How can one create a campaign advertisement that will be remembered?'

Studies of understanding   Research that provides a reason-based understanding gives explanations as to why a certain phenomenon under study occurs the way it does. In other words, it will explain what a certain communicative act means and the rules that guide that act in a given society.

Case Study 3.3   A STUDY FOR UNDERSTANDING: WHY DON'T THEY SPEAK TO SOME MEN?

In a certain culture, females will speak with males outside their group only if the stranger has been introduced to them by a male member of their own family. The researcher's understanding of this phenomenon after a field study was that a male member will introduce a strange male to his female family members only if he considers the stranger to be trustworthy and acceptable to their group.

Try this ...

Think of a research topic, problem or question you would like to examine, making sure it is sufficiently narrow to be doable within one semester. The resources needed either should be available free of charge from your organisation or be those you personally own or have access to.

How would you carry out research on this topic under each of the research purposes such as exploratory, descriptive, explanatory (causal and functional) and understanding? In other words, what research questions/hypotheses will be used when carrying out the research for each of the purposes?

Carry out a literature search to identify five primary sources (full text journal articles or books) and five secondary sources (articles, books, book chapters etc) that could be used in the literature review of this study.

THE UNIT OF ANALYSIS

In addition to the purposes of a research study discussed above, a research design also needs to consider a suitable unit of analysis to be examined in the research project.

Handy Hint

A unit of analysis or unit of observation has no limit. It can be an object, event, individual, group, organisation or society, and is the 'who' or 'what' the researcher wants to explore, describe, explain or understand.

The unit of analysis could even be an inanimate object such as a building or city; a phenomenon such as a social role, social position or social relationship; or a social artifact such as a book, magazine or document. It can also be called an entity, element or case.

The focus of the study is generally decided by the unit of analysis (Singleton et al., 1993).

TYPES OF UNITS OF ANALYSIS

There are four types of units of analysis: individuals, groups, organisations and **social artifacts**.

The individual as the unit of analysis   The individual is the commonest unit of analysis in communication research. By aggregating (that is, combining information about individuals to describe the social unit or group to which they belong) the individuals studied—such as students, parents, single mothers, consumers or TV viewers—a researcher can describe, explain and understand the various social groups (including their social roles and relationships). The sample of individuals who are thus selected for a study will have the specific characteristics required for the study.

Units of analysis

EXAMPLE 3.5

Examples of various units of analysis for different studies could be:

o digital TV adopters—individuals with a digital set-top box or a built in digital converter in their TV set at home
o people with mortgages
o undecided voters.

Each study will allow a researcher to examine the differences between those who possess this characteristic and those who do not; for example:

o those with digital TV and those without
o those with mortgages and those without
o those who are undecided about who to vote for and those who are decided.

However, the individual will still be the unit of analysis as it will be the individual who will fill the survey or be interviewed or observed by the researcher.

The group as the unit of analysis   A social group also can be a unit of analysis; for example, management teams in organisations, families without internet connections at home, book clubs, internet chat room contributors or users of a blog. These groups can be compared for a given characteristic, such as how often children in families without an internet connection at home access the internet, compared with those children who do have internet access at home. Ethnographers in qualitative research may study a particular social or cultural group such as an Aboriginal community in a given location. However, in each example it will be the individuals within the group or groups who will be surveyed or interviewed to collect the research data.

An organisation as the unit of analysis   A formal organisation can also be a unit of analysis; for example, University X or Mercy Hospital. The characteristics of an organisation are made up by the characteristics of its individual members. Once again, it will still be the individuals within the organisation who will complete the surveys, be interviewed or be observed.

Social artifacts as the unit of analysis   Social artifacts are another unit of analysis. A social artifact is a product of people and their activities or behaviours. The use of such units of analysis is called unobtrusive or non-reactive research, because the research subjects will be unaware of being observed.

Three types of social artifacts are examined in this chapter:

• **physical traces** (erosion or **accretion traces**)
• **archival records**
• messages (Baxter & Babbie, 2004).

Physical traces   Some social artifacts are physical traces which can be erosion (reduced) or accretion (collected) traces.

Erosion traces involve wear and tear or some form of reduction. For example, clothes worn the most regularly by an individual may look older and more faded than the clothes worn less frequently, and the most walked-over or marked routes on lawns will indicate a short cut taken by people to move between two locations.

In contrast, accretion traces refer to accumulation. For example, uncollected mail in someone's mail box at work indicates them being on leave. Other examples of accretion traces are university courses that are not required to complete a major but nevertheless have high enrolments, indicating they are popular, and the channel settings of a car radio, which indicate the stations the driver listens to the most. Similarly, the most popular novels can be identified by checking the borrowing records of a library, instead of surveying library patrons, and TV program ratings or newspaper circulation figures can help identify the most popular ones.

Archival records Archival records can be both public and private. Public records indicate various social phenomena; for example, court documents or police records indicate the most common forms of crime committed in a given city or suburb in a given time period. Equally, examining the Hansard (parliamentary proceedings) across time can indicate the issues raised by female parliamentarians in the past 50 years, and if they have changed across time and were different from those raised by their male counterparts.

Private records such as diaries, letters and other documents can indicate what life was like in the days they were created and what was important to the person/s who recorded them. For example, *The Diary of Anne Frank* was written by a young Jewish girl while hiding from the Nazis in Amsterdam with her family. It indicates her feelings and how life was for them at the time.

Messages Messages as units of analysis can be those of the media such as newspapers, films, TV programs, advertisements, novels, books, websites, blogs, social networking sites and others that tell us about life and society at a given time because media messages 'reflect' as well as 'shape' society.

Examining conversations between people or public speeches of leaders made at various times in history will tell us how things may have changed over the years and, most importantly, how some things have remained the same.

Social interactions and rituals such as weddings and courtship rituals are also social artifacts that help researchers examine how different social groups conduct such rituals and what they mean to them. Changes in social interactions across time indicate the corresponding changes in society.

Fallacies and aggregate data The above discussion on units of analysis explained how aggregate data are obtained by studying individuals, their demographic or other features and then combining that information to design a composite picture of the group to which the individuals belong. In other words, a researcher makes knowledge claims (or conclusions) about a larger group or an aggregate, based on information obtained from observing individual units of analysis. This however, can sometimes lead to wrong assumptions or fallacies.

There are three types of fallacies:

- ecological
- logical
- individualistic.

A researcher needs to keep this in mind when interpreting their own research findings or when evaluating those of others in a literature review.

Ecological fallacy   The term 'ecological' refers to groups, or systems that are larger than individuals. In committing an **ecological fallacy**, the aggregate data of a unit are used to make inferences about the individual behaviour of people who belong to that group. (This is similar to believing in a stereotype.)

Ecological fallacy: profiling

Commonly held stereotypes and profiling of ethnic, religious or racial groups by law enforcement authorities are examples of ecological fallacies. Here inferences made about the group are applied to all individuals that belong to that group, irrespective of individual differences between members.

Since the events of 11 September 2001, young males of South Asian, Muslim or Arab appearance are suspected of being terrorists and routinely subjected to harassment at airports. This is a result of stereotyping or profiling, because the attacks on New York City were committed by young men of such appearance. (In research, such a generalisation leads to an ecological fallacy.)

EXAMPLE 3.6

Logical fallacy   The problem of a logical fallacy arises when the researcher fails to correctly identify the relevant unit of analysis. This creates confusion and leads to inaccurate or wrong conclusions of research findings.

Logical fallacy: household income of digital TV end-users

When researching digital TV adoption, the household should be the unit of analysis (even if only one member is surveyed) with the total household income considered as affecting the likelihood of adoption. If a researcher surveys an individual and takes that individual as the unit of analysis (instead of the household) and only collects data on that respondent's income, rather than of the household, this will lead to inaccurate data and findings and a **logical fallacy**.

EXAMPLE 3.7

Individual fallacy   An individual fallacy occurs when an exception to a general rule is taken as cancelling the rule. In other words, research data from one or a few cases that do not agree with the general rule do not cancel the rule and should not be interpreted as such.

Individual fallacy: the 'short' basketball player

A male who is less than 174 cm (5 ft 8 in) in height and is a successful professional basketball player is an exception to the rule because most successful basketball players are over 184 cm (6 ft) tall. However, this unusual player does not cancel the general rule of the need for exceptional height to be a successful professional basketball player. If it does, it leads to an **individual fallacy**.

EXAMPLE 3.8

Try this...

1   Return to the research problem, issue or topic of your choice used in the earlier exercise in this chapter.
   a   What would be the unit of analysis to be observed in your study?
   b   What type/s of fallacy can you expect to occur in the study and how and what would the wrong conclusion/s be?

2   Develop another research problem, issue or topic related to your original one (or adapt the original one) to involve a social artifact as the unit of analysis.

ORIENTATION IN TIME AND SPACE

When designing a project or reviewing the literature, one must understand and be familiar with the various research studies that involve an orientation about time and space. This factor applies to qualitative, quantitative and multi-method studies.

THE TIME DIMENSION

The **time dimension** is acknowledged and indicated in **cross-sectional** and **longitudinal** (trend, cohort or **panel**) **studies**. These distinguish between studies that are one-off (cross-sectional) or repeated at pre-determined intervals (longitudinal) with specified samples of the population.

The time dimension is important because it can help determine the causality of effects, such as if they are related to the period in which the research is conducted or if findings change from one era to another.

The time dimension also affects the generalisability of findings from one era to another, if they have been repeated instead of being one-off. Therefore, a research design has to be sensitive to how the study is conducted—as a one-off study or not—as findings can be affected by the time dimension.

CROSS-SECTIONAL STUDIES

A cross-sectional study collects data from a representative sample of the population being studied, but at a single point in time.

A cross-sectional study: poll of voting intentions

A national poll on voter intentions taken one week before an election is a cross-sectional study.

LONGITUDINAL STUDIES

In contrast to a cross-sectional study, a longitudinal study collects data from the same population (but not necessarily the same sample of respondents) at different points in time.

A longitudinal study: digital TV adoption

EXAMPLE 3.10

An example of a longitudinal study would be a survey the population of Australia about the adoption of digital TV every year (beginning this year) until the analogue cut-off date in 2010 (for metropolitan areas) and 2012 (for other areas) to examine how public opinion about the technology has changed during that period.

In quantitative research such as those using surveys, longitudinal studies can be conducted as **trend studies**, **cohort studies** or panel studies.

A TREND STUDY

In a trend study, a topic is re-examined or re-studied at different points in time using different samples of the same population to see if any trends appear in the findings.

A trend study: gauging changes in public opinion

EXAMPLE 3.11

The following are trend studies.
1   Surveys carried out every three years to gauge changes to public opinion on a topic such as gay marriages
2   A content analysis of an established newspaper carried out every 10 years between 1894 and 2004 to see how the newspaper and its content have changed.

A COHORT STUDY

A cohort is a homogeneous group of people who have had the same life experiences or significant life events during a given time period and geographic region. It is based on the concept of 'a generation'.

A cohort study examines different samples of a specific sub-population or cohort across time to examine how they may have changed during that period.

A cohort study: life of Vietnam veterans

EXAMPLE 3.12

A cohort study can survey or interview a sample of Vietnam veterans in Australia every five years to examine their views and life conditions and how they may have changed.

A panel study   A panel study is similar to a trend or cohort study, but examines the same sample of individuals or panel each time across a given time period.

A panel study: issue changes during an election campaign

EXAMPLE 3.13

The same group of people are surveyed or interviewed every week during a six-week election campaign to ask what the most important issue is to them at each stage. A panel study could examine and find exactly who changed their views during that period to what and why.

TABLE 3.1: The time dimension—a comparison between cross-sectional and longitudinal (trend, cohort and panel) studies

Characteristics of method	Cross-sectional studies	Type of method		
		Longitudinal studies		
		Trend studies	Cohort studies	Panel studies
Frequency of data collection	One-off study	Repeated at regular intervals	Repeated at regular intervals	Repeated at regular intervals
Sample	Representative sample from relevant population	Different samples from same population across time	Different samples from same sub-population or cohort across time	Same sample or same subjects each time across time
What do they look for?	A snapshot of the present	Trends in findings over time	Changes between cohorts over time	Changes within same sample and subjects over time
Shortcomings/ problems faced	Findings limited in scope	Costly and time consuming	Costly and time consuming	Costly and time consuming; **panel attrition** Dropouts can be atypical and distort findings

Handy Hint

Longitudinal studies are more useful for a research project than cross-sectional studies as they provide information about the changes over time, but are more expensive and time consuming to conduct.

Panel studies face the problem of panel attrition or losing members of the panel, when subjects drop out or cannot be located for a follow-up study. The ones who drop out may be atypical or different from the rest of the panel, which could distort the findings and lead to inaccurate conclusions.

THE SPACE DIMENSION

The **space dimension** of a research design is related to the location (or physical setting or field) where the research is conducted. It can affect the study and its observations, data collection and interpretation. Research is either field dependent or field independent.

Field-dependent studies   **Field-dependent studies** use participant observation or field studies (see Chapter 12) that require observing the subjects in their natural setting while they go about their everyday lives.

EXAMPLE 3.14

A field-dependent study: participant observation

A study in media anthropology on the TV viewing habits of families requires the researcher to observe them watching TV in their own homes in everyday, natural situations.

Field-independent studies   **Field-independent studies**, such as those using surveys (see Chapter 8), depth interviews (Chapter 10) or focus groups (Chapter 11), are not affected by the setting or location in which the study is conducted or the data collected. But they may be affected by other factors (discussed in later chapters). For example, if interviews with employees were held near their boss's office, some interviewees may not feel as comfortable as they would if they were conducted elsewhere.

Try this …

Return to your research question, issue or problem developed for the earlier exercises in this chapter.

1   Examine how the research can be designed to include each aspect of the time and space dimensions. That is, design the project as a cross-sectional study and then a longitudinal study; that is, a trend, cohort and panel study.

2   Design it as a field-dependent and field-independent study.

CHOOSING SUITABLE METHODOLOGIES AND DATA COLLECTION METHODS

Once the literature review for the proposed study is completed and the research design is drafted, a researcher needs to select the suitable:

- methodologies (qualitative or quantitative or both)
- data collection methods (surveys, content analyses, field studies, interviews, focus groups, case studies etc).

This includes deciding on the:

- population to be studied
- sampling procedures to be used (random or non-random)
- instrumentation and its design (the survey questionnaire or coding manual for content analysis; interview questions for depth and focus groups; setting for a field study; and suitable stimulus materials for focus groups)
- ethical issues involved (see Chapter 5).

The data collection using the relevant research methods is the next stage of a research project.

DATA COLLECTION AND ANALYSIS

The researcher needs to be clear as to what data collection methods should be used and why; how to ensure the **validity** and **reliability** of the data collected; and if any pre-tests or pilot studies are to be conducted and what their findings are. Once the data have been collected, data analysis (qualitative or quantitative/statistical) and interpretation of results (testing of hypotheses or examining the research questions) is the next stage of the research project.

The data collection aspects of a research project are discussed in detail under each research method in later chapters, including surveys (Chapter 8), content analysis (Chapter 9), depth interviews (Chapter 10); focus groups (Chapter 11); field studies (Chapter 12) and textual analysis (Chapter 14). Data analysis is discussed in Chapter 15.

Research findings follow the data collection and analysis. Thereafter, the research needs to be reported. We next examine how to write a scholarly research proposal and research report.

WRITING A SCHOLARLY RESEARCH PROPOSAL AND REPORT

Scholarly research reports differ based on the methodologies (qualitative and quantitative) used in a study.

A QUANTITATIVE RESEARCH REPORT

The report of a quantitative research project should include the following:

Title   The title of the report should be clear, concise and explain what the project is about in 10 to 25 words. A specific word limit within this range is set by each journal, conference or funding body and should be strictly followed. Use the main keywords applicable to your study (for example, violence) and paradigms (for example, effects) in the title to make sure it will be sent to the correct people in the area for reviewing and, once published, will be properly indexed in databases for easy access by subsequent researchers.

Byline   The byline includes the full name and institutional affiliations of all authors, plus telephone, fax and email contact details of the first author.

The abstract   The abstract is the summary of the project, which is generally given in 100 to 250 words, again based on the strict specifications of the entity the report or proposal is submitted to. The abstract describes what is in the report and creates an interest in the reader to read the full report. It indicates the research problem (for example, 'Why are Australians slow to adopt digital TV?'), characteristics of the population and sample of participants (for example, Australian households with and without digital TV), methods of data collection (for example, surveys and interviews), and major findings, conclusions and implications of the study or its contribution to the discipline.

The introduction   This section explains the research problem and its significance, along with the rationale and purpose of the study (what it plans to do) and how the problem will be examined. Include background information about the study (for example, what digital TV is about and its history of adoption in Australia) and the theoretical perspectives used. The literature review informs the reader about prior research in the area and where it stands today. This section ends with the research questions or hypotheses examined in the study and what the expected outcomes of this research project are.

Method   The methods section of a research report explains how the study was conducted and how data was collected and analysed, while explaining who the participants of the study were and how they were identified and sampled. It explains how the participants were recruited, their demographic profiles (age, sex, educational level etc) and the ethics guidelines followed for informed consent, anonymity and confidentiality.

Details of the data collection instruments used and the procedures followed (operational definitions) in collecting, storing and analysing the data are explained. This helps to check the validity of the study and enables replication. This section also discusses the problems faced during the research process. The data collection and analysis instruments, such as the surveys or the coding manuals, are briefly described but the complete documents are provided as appendices.

Results   The results section provides answers to the research questions or hypotheses examined in the study and is the largest section of the research report. The description of variables and the relationships between them, and any trends observed, are explained as statements supplemented by graphs, tables, charts, figures and other methods of visual presentation. This section also reports on tests conducted for validity and reliability of the data and their results.

Discussion   The discussion section summarises, explains and interprets the findings. It should not include any new information not addressed in earlier sections. It also explains the significance of the findings and compares them with those of earlier research and how the new study adds to existing knowledge. Any limitations and shortcomings of the current study, and how they may be improved or avoided in the future, are also discussed in this section.

Conclusion and recommendations   This section describes the implications of this study's findings to theorising and research in the discipline, and its contribution to society. It will examine if the study has answered the research questions fully and convincingly or whether the hypotheses have been supported or not. It will highlight the gaps in knowledge that still exist in the field and what may be examined in any future studies. It will also recommend measures to be taken to improve the conditions and situations related to the research area (for example, what the government may do to improve digital TV adoption.)

References   This section lists all sources of information cited in the report in alphabetical order by the first author's last name, using a style such as Harvard (*Citing your sources, Harvard style,* 2006) or APA (American Psychological Association, 2001) specified by the journal or entity to which the report is submitted. Note that a **bibliography** includes all sources of information consulted but not necessarily cited in the report.

Optional elements   Acknowledgments (of those who supported the study financially or otherwise) and appendices may be included if necessary at the end of the report. Appendices generally include information that provide additional evidence, clarifications or support to the arguments made within the body of the report, survey questionnaires or content analysis instruments, interview questions and the profile of research subjects.

Qualitative research reports are somewhat different from quantitative ones and are examined next.

A QUALITATIVE RESEARCH REPORT

The structure of both quantitative and qualitative research reports is similar with respect to the title, byline, abstract, introduction, literature review, methods, results and discussion sections. However, in a qualitative report, the data collection, analysis and interpretation sections are combined. In a qualitative study, the researcher is also the primary 'research instrument', unlike in quantitative studies where specific instruments—for example, survey questionnaires or coding manuals—are prepared by the researcher.

A qualitative research report includes explanations and interpretations of data collected by the researcher and therefore the reports can be very diverse. John van Maanen (1988) describes three styles of '**narrative tales**' for writing qualitative research reports:

- **realist tales**
- **confessional tales**
- **impressionist tales**.

THE REALIST TALE

A realist tale is written in the third person where the researcher remains an 'objective and uninvolved observer' in the background and presents an accurate representation of what was observed. (This style of report is the most common in qualitative research and journalism.) The researcher's observations or findings are grouped together and organised as emerging themes in the write-up, taking the research subjects' points of view and supported by direct quotations from them.

EXAMPLE 3.15

A realist tale: why haven't they adopted digital TV?

After researching the reasons for the slow adoption of digital TV in Australia, the views presented by interview subjects can be discussed under the themes of 'Costs of the technology', 'Why I haven't adopted' and 'What would induce me to adopt', supported by subjects' quotes such as, 'I am quite happy with my current service.'

Note that a critical theorist will point out that even though realist tales are defined as objective reports presented from the point of view of the research subjects, it is still the researcher who decides what is included or left out in the report and how the data are to be interpreted. Standard qualitative research articles, journalistic writing and intelligence reports are often written in the style of a realist tale.

THE CONFESSIONAL TALE

A qualitative research report written in the style of a confessional tale is less formal and is presented in the first person, taking the researcher's own point of view. It is a self-confession by the researcher who was completely involved as one of the 'natives' (members of the group or population under study) or a full participant in what went on in the setting and what was observed.

The report tells the reader how the researcher's point of view developed and changed over time during the study, and how the researcher gained entry or access to the research setting and was accepted by the other participants. It will also include the researcher's feelings about the experiences and their unexpected aspects—both positive and negative. Most anthropological or ethnographic studies and many travel stories by journalists and other writers are reported in this style. They could also be investigative journalistic reports.

EXAMPLE 3.16

A confessional tale: going undercover

A journalist who goes undercover to investigate the working conditions at a factory will enter the setting as a factory worker actually hired by the management. He or she will work as a regular employee for a while and later write an article in the newspaper or even a book about their experiences to highlight the plight and work conditions of the factory's actual workers.

'Mystery shoppers' hired by retail companies to gauge the levels of customer service of their branches will visit branch outlets as regular shoppers and report on their experiences—both good and bad—to the parent company. These reports will be used by the relevant outlets to improve their services in the future.

Since these reports present the researcher's views and versions of events, confessional tales can be shaped by the writers' personal views, subjectivities, biases and prejudices; for example, **New** or **Gonzo Journalism**.

THE IMPRESSIONIST TALE

The term 'impressionist tale' is derived from Impressionist art. Impressionist writing seeks to describe a feeling or an experience rather than provide an accurate depiction of an event. This style of qualitative research report uses the dramatic format of telling a story in chronological order (in the sequence they happened) with a beginning, middle and end (as a narrative). It provides as much detail as possible of the setting and what happened there, with a storyline and a 'cast of characters'. These characters can be given names, lives and feelings while the story may be told in the first person, with all the aspects of a drama.

AN IMPRESSIONIST TALE: 'LEFT OUT OF THE LOOP' Case Study 3.4

Examples of qualitative research reports written as impressionist tales include the case studies published in the *Harvard Business Review* that discuss timely issues for academic or other discussions and analyses.

A case study by Weerakkody (2006b) titled 'Left out of the Loop' is presented as an impressionist tale and is based on a multi-method research study that examined the limited adoption of an intranet at a rural organisation, which resulted in the marginalisation of the staff who were not given access to it. It is presented as a story with several characters (actually those interviewed by the researcher for the study) telling the story, with the central character (the organisation's new head—also an interviewee) trying to learn about the situation and planning on how to remedy it. The same study—but in complete form, is reported as a realist tale in Weerakkody (2004b).

Media adaptations of impressionist tales   Most docu-dramas and film versions of biographies are impressionist tales based on qualitative research. Even though drawing on facts and real events, these often include fictionalised aspects such as a romance or 'a love interest' for the hero or heroine, or additional characters created for audience appeal. Casting popular and attractive actors to play the leads and other roles is also commonly practiced.

THE DOCU-DRAMA AS AN IMPRESSIONIST TALE: *ANSWERED BY FIRE* Case Study 3.5

The Australian Broadcasting Corporation's docu-drama *Answered by fire* (Australian Broadcasting Corporation, 2006; Samuels et al., 2006), produced with Canadian collaboration and filmed in Queensland, was based on events surrounding the 1999 referendum in East Timor. It acknowledged having used as source material the book *Dancing with the devil* (Savage, 2002), based on the experiences of the Australian Federal Police (AFP) officer Sergeant David Savage as a United Nations Assistance Mission in East Timor (UNAMET) observer in East Timor in 1999. The book is written as a confessional tale.

However, the TV drama is an impressionist tale as it includes a storyline of Julie Fortin (played by Canadian actor Isabelle Blais)—

⌐·····⟩

Case Study 3.7

a young, attractive, female UNAMET observer from the Royal Canadian Mounted Police—falling in love with Ismenio Soares (played by Alex Tilman), an East Timorese university student who works with the UN staff as a translator. The male lead, Mark Waldman (loosely based on David Savage and his experiences), is an AFP officer played by Australian actor David Wenham.

The writers of the drama, Barbara Samuels and Katherine Thompson, had spent two weeks in East Timor speaking to the people about their experiences. In casting nine supporting roles and most of the extras, the producers had used members of the East Timorese community living in Australia, many of whom had actually experienced situations similar to those portrayed in the drama (Enker, 2006).

Research using methodological triangulation may involve a mix of qualitative and quantitative research methods. We now examine how such reports are written.

WRITING A MIXED METHOD REPORT

In a research study that uses methodological triangulation, or more than one method of data collection, the report is written as a hybrid of a quantitative and a qualitative study.

The qualitative part is written as a realist tale (Baxter & Babbie, 2004). If more than one theoretical paradigm (positivist, interpretivist, systems, critical or functionalist) or methodology (qualitative or quantitative) is used in a research study, the more dominant one takes precedence. Quotes from subjects obtained as qualitative data (such as interviews) are used to supplement and support the findings from the quantitative data (such as surveys and content analyses) (Sarantakos, 2005).

Before we can conduct a research study, we often need to submit a proposal if applying for funding, ethics clearance or seeking admission to a higher degree program involving a thesis such as at honours, masters and doctoral levels. Let's see how such a proposal is prepared.

WRITING A RESEARCH PROPOSAL

A research proposal explains the design and plan for a research project and includes the title, byline, abstract (without the findings and conclusions), the introduction with the rationale for the study, theoretical framework, literature review, statement of the problem (research questions or hypotheses) and methods sections. These make up the first stages of a research report. A research proposal also includes a list of references.

A research proposal includes:

- a focused topic
- an introduction stating the research problem, rationale, background and purpose; a brief theoretical framework; and a literature review
- a method section detailing the research design and plan, research questions or hypotheses, expected outcome/s, methodologies and data collection methods to be used, a budget of estimated costs and a proposed schedule.

It does not include the actual data (observations), data analysis, results (findings), discussion or conclusions as these stages are yet to be completed.

Budgeting   The budget for a research project should include:

- salaries for staff (researchers and research assistants to carry out the data entry, data collection and coding, transcribe/translate interview tapes and search for the literature, if applicable) and professional moderators for focus groups
- payments or honoraria for research subjects such as interviewees
- stationery, photocopying, postage, telephone, fax and internet charges
- equipment such as audio or video recorders and cameras; consumables and maintenance costs such as for audio/video cassettes, batteries, computer disks, and software
- travel, accommodation and related costs, if applicable
- room hire for premises to conduct interviews or focus groups
- refreshments for focus groups and so on.

Most funding agencies specify the standard rates of payments for staff and the budget items allowed. So some items may not be included in your actual proposal. But as a researcher, it is useful to examine and cost all items required for your project to avoid unexpected expenses and problems.

> **Handy Hint**
> Research proposals are shortened research reports. In a research proposal, the methods section also includes a proposed schedule indicating when each part of the research project such as data collection will be carried out, so that the project can be kept on track. The schedule also indicates that the project can be completed during the period for which the funding will be approved or the specified number of years of your degree program. A budget of estimated costs is also included in a research proposal.

Summary

This chapter examined the various stages of a research project, such as selecting and narrowing the topic for a study, conducting the literature review, developing the research design and plan, choosing suitable methodologies and data collection methods, carrying out the data collection and analysis, and how to write a quantitative, qualitative or mixed-method research report or a research proposal.

It also discussed the various purposes of research, the types of units of analysis and the fallacies of aggregate data related to units of analysis, and the orientations of time and space with reference to research studies.

In the next chapter, we examine how to write a research report for non-academic settings.

Further reading

Bouma, G D & Ling, R 2004. *The research process*, 5th edn. Oxford University Press, North Melbourne.

Grellier, J & Grerhe, V 2006. *Communication skills toolkit: Unlocking the secret of tertiary success*. Thomson Social Science Press, South Melbourne (pp. 58–80).

Rubin, R B, Rubin, A M & Piele, L J 2005. *Communication research: Strategies and sources*. 6th edn. Wadsworth, Belmont, CA.

Writing Research Reports for Non-Academic Settings

In Chapter 3, we discussed how to write a scholarly research report. In this chapter, we examine how a research study and its findings may be:

o reported in a non-academic setting or

o targeted at non-scholarly audiences; for example, the general public, government policy makers, business or corporate entities, and grant funding bodies, employers or clients who commission projects.

CHARACTERISTICS OF EFFECTIVE REPORTS

Most employees find themselves called on to write reports in their everyday working life. These business reports provide the relevant facts (obtained from existing documents and other reports), experiences (of the writer and the organisation) and observations (obtained via collecting data from interviews, focus groups and surveys) to help the reader make important decisions with respect an issue under examination. A report can also be the result of an examination of the implementation of a decision already made, to see how it has fared so far.

Reports aim to persuade or influence the decisions or actions of others. This means you need to write them effectively, presenting all relevant facts and your findings in a clear and concise manner to provide the information required by those commissioning the study and help them in their decisions and policy making. At the same time, the researcher must maintain high standards of professionalism and ethical practices related to conducting and reporting on research.

Handy Hint
Research reports written in non-academic settings follow the standard format and styles of business reports.

This is achieved by maintaining:

- clarity (avoid ambiguity)
- conciseness (be brief but comprehensive)
- consistency (in writing style)
- simplicity (of language used to fit the targeted audience).

Just as when writing a scholarly research report, reports written for non-academic settings need to maintain high standards of:

- accuracy (of facts and information included)
- empathy (with the reader's needs and feelings and to make the reading easier)
- ethical practice (maintaining objectivity, integrity and truthfulness; not misleading the reader or misinterpreting findings; not excluding unpleasant realities or hiding or de-emphasising them with a 'fine print'; not using euphemisms or dysphemisms

to make things sound better or worse than they really are; and acknowledging those who helped with the project and its collaborators).

WRITING A RESEARCH REPORT

A non-academic research report will not include the theoretical frameworks used or the literature review required of a scholarly report. However, the elements of a scholarly research report—the rationale for the study, the background as to how the area currently stands, the research questions examined, the methodology used, findings, conclusions, discussions, limitations of the study, recommendations based on findings and suggestions for areas of further study—are also part of a non-scholarly report, even though discussed under different titles or headings.

> **Handy Hint**
> When reporting the findings of a scholarly research project for a non-scholarly or non-academic audience, remember the basic difference between a non-scholarly and a scholarly research report relates to 'how' the findings are reported rather than 'what' is reported.

PLANNING TO WRITE THE REPORT

Before we begin to write the research report on a completed study, we need to examine the following questions. These questions and their explanations (based on Kuiper, 2007) are provided in Table 4.1.

TABLE 4.1   Preliminary questions to be asked when planning and writing a research report

The Question	Explanation
Why? (purpose)	Why do this study? What is its purpose?
Who? (audience)	Who is the audience for this report?
Where? (context)	What is the context in which the study is reported? What is the environment it will be released in and what is the best time to release?
What? (content)	What information should be included? What do readers need to know before making relevant decisions? Does the information included in the report match the author's conclusions and recommendations?
How? (medium used)	How or in what medium will the author present this report? For example, an oral presentation, memo, letter, audio-visual report such as a DVD, or written report, based on the targeted audience and their needs.
What relationships? (structure)	How should the report be structured? This is shaped by the why (purpose), who (audience), where (context), what (content) and how (the medium used) of the report listed above, and involves the areas of style; page layout; use of headings; inclusion of visual aids such as photographs, diagrams, figures and tables; and other aspects such as editing that will improve the effectiveness of the report.

THE REPORT AND ITS PARTS

A formal research report presented to a non-academic audience consists of three sections:

- preliminaries
- body of the report
- supplements (Kuiper, 2007: 346).

PRELIMINARY DETAILS

The preliminary section of a research report provides a context to help the reader understand the report and summarise its contents. These include the title page, table of contents, lists of tables and figures, foreword or preface, acknowledgments and the executive summary or synopsis.

However, this section is generally written once the body of the report has been completed, as some information that goes into the preliminary section such as the table of contents or the list of tables and figures cannot be finalised until then.

EXAMPLE 4.1

Sections and headings

1 The preliminaries or the front section
   1.1 Title page
   1.2 Table of contents (of the report)
   1.3 List of tables and figures included
   1.4 Foreword or preface
   1.5 Acknowledgments (of those who helped with the project)
   1.6 Executive summary (of the project and its findings, conclusions and recommendations)
2 Body of report
   2.1 Introduction (background and objectives)
   2.2 Methodology
   2.3 Findings and discussion
   2.4 Conclusions and recommendations
3 Supplements
   3.1 Notes (or details about specific matters discussed in the body of report)
   3.2 List of references or bibliography
   3.3 **Glossary** (of technical terms used)
   3.4 **Appendices** (includes lengthy but relevant information that could be distracting if included in the body of report but provide greater detail and better understanding of the project to the reader) such as:
      3.41 Survey questionnaires used
      3.42 List of interview questions
      3.43 **Index** (of technical terms)

The title page   The title page includes the:

- full title of the report
- full names, addresses, contact phone/fax numbers and email addresses of the authors
- full name of the agency for which the report was prepared
- date of publication.

Note that some research reports, such as projects conducted in-house, may not carry the names or details of authors at all (for example, Australian Communications and Media Authority, 2007) while author contact details of projects commissioned by a specific agency may appear on the page carrying copyright information of the report rather than on the title page (for example, Da Rin & Groves, 1996.)

The agency's logo is included on the title page. The title or name given to the report should be succinct and include the why, who, what when and where details of the research project, listed in Table 4.1.

The title is typed using a larger font than the rest of the page and placed about 4cm from the top of the page and centred. Author details appear about three double spaces below (sometimes as 'prepared by'). Details of the commissioning agency or organisation are listed (under 'prepared for'), below the author details after a double or treble space.

The date of publication of the report appears below the agency details after a double spacing, either with the exact date the report was released or as the month and year of release.

The title page of a research report

EXAMPLE 4.2

**What's on the
Web Now for
Australian Farmers**

A Content Analysis of 206 World Wide Web
Sites for Australian Farm Businesses

A study by Jenny Da Rin and Jim Groves for the
Rural Industries Research and Development Corporation

December 1996

Source: Da Rin & Groves (1996).

Table of contents   The table of contents indicates how the report has been organised or structured, allowing the reader to search for specific topics or sections more easily. It is prepared using the different headings and subheadings of the report, and their corresponding page numbers.

Note that the Table of Contents includes the preliminary sections of the report, such as the pages of the executive summary and the lists of tables and figures, which are numbered using Roman numerals (i, ii, iii etc). The pages of the report proper are numbered using Arabic numerals (1, 2, 3 etc).

List of tables and figures   If the report includes tables, photographs, charts, diagrams or other visual aids, they should be listed to help the reader locate them easily. They will be numbered Figure 1.2 or Table 1.2 and each label will carry a description of what they refer to, such as 'Table 1.5: Profile of Interviewees'.

If only a small number of visual aids is used, all visual aids included in the report can be grouped together as a List of illustrations.

Foreword or preface   The preface explains what led to the study, and its significance, to create an interest in the reader. It may be written by the person who authorised the study.

EXAMPLE 4.3

Foreword (or preface) to the website content analysis report

In Da Rin and Groves (1996: 3), the preface was written by the Managing Director of the Rural Industries Research and Development Corporation, which commissioned the study. It indicated that the researchers had analysed over 200 websites that provided information to isolated farming businesses and communities around Australia, and that the research examined how accessible these sites were, how well the information was presented, the depth of the content and the future of interactive services—which were also the research questions posed in the study.

He mentioned that the research found that 'while there are large gaps in the type and substance of information, there is a large amount available on the web now for farm business use' indicating the study's main findings. The preface also indicated that the authors 'have listed many of the sites' hinting the report as a useful source of information for readers.

He further stated that the report was part of the organisation's Education, Extension and Information Systems Program, which 'facilitates innovation in rural and allied industries through improving the use of communication and education processes'. This indicates the aims and outcomes of the study and report.

Acknowledgments Written in the first person (as 'I' or 'We'), the acknowledgments page written by the authors recognises those who supported or assisted in the conduct of the research study or preparation of the report. It is a 'Thank you note' specifying and acknowledging their contribution.

EXAMPLE 4.4

Acknowledgment of research assistance

A research report also acknowledges the contribution of any research assistants; for example, 'We wish to thank Ms Jane Smith for the valuable research assistance provided in analysing the data.'

Executive summary or synopsis The executive summary or synopsis of the study is analogous to the abstract of a scholarly research report. It summarises the report and provides the background of the project, such as who authorised it and for what purposes, and the aims of the study. It indicates the sources of information used in preparing the report and the research methodology and data collection methods used, then lists the major findings and the author's recommendations to guide the anticipated decision making process of the organisation or agency that commissioned the study. The executive summary, which is one to two pages in length, may include dot points, numbered sections or both to make it more readable and attractive.

After the preliminaries, the body of the report appears.

THE BODY OF THE REPORT

The body of the report details all aspects of the study and how it was conducted. It provides an introduction to the study, describes its methodology, limitations and delimitations, findings, discussion, conclusions, and recommendations. The writer may use creative and descriptive headings instead of the above standard ones to make the report more readable and easier to follow.

Introduction   The introduction provides the background to the study and indicates its aims or objectives, while explaining the current status of the phenomenon being examined and the existing knowledge base related to the topic area. A few sources of information from published reports and books may be cited within this section.

This section is analogous to the rationale for the study, statement of the problem and/or the research questions in a scholarly report. These provide a context to the study and help the reader to understand and interpret the study's findings and conclusions.

Method   The method section of the report briefly explains the sources of information gathered. These include other reports of related studies or official documentation such as census figures. It describes how data were collected—using methods such as surveys, interviews and focus groups—and explains the operational definitions used. It also includes the frames of reference or the scope (delimitations and limitations) of the study—that is, the extent of the topic covered by the research project and what areas were excluded from the study.

Scope of the research or its delimitations and limitations

In a study of digital TV adoption in Australia (Weerakkody, 2007b), the delimitations were that the focus group interviews with non-adopters were drawn from those in households with two or more working colour TV sets. This was due to the assumption that such households can afford to buy a low- or middle-end set-top box or digital converter, which costs less than a colour TV set, but have chosen not to.

The other delimitation was that all interviews were carried out within a one-month period where not many changes to digital TV policy and environment would take place to skew the data collected.

The limitations of this study were that the data was collected from digital TV adopters and non-adopters living in just one regional city. The realities for this phenomenon may be different in metropolitan and rural areas or in other similar regional cities.

EXAMPLE 4.5

Sometimes, the methods of data collection are discussed under the introduction, without being presented as a separate section.

Once the research methods used in the study have been explained, the report turns to discussing its findings.

Findings and discussion   The body of the report also includes the findings of the study and a discussion about them—making it the longest section of the report. Instead of using the headings 'Findings' or 'Discussions', more descriptive ones specific to the study and the data analysis can be used to label different segments of this section of the report. A comprehensive analysis of data must be presented under suitable subheadings and sub-subheadings, which can be the various **themes** and **categories** of content identified. See Examples 4.6 and 4.7 (also refer to Chapter 9 and Chapter 15).

EXAMPLE 4.6

Headings used in a research report

In a content analysis of websites meant for Australian farmers (Da Rin & Groves, 1996: 5), the data analysis was presented in the report under the self-explanatory headings of: 'Accessibility of sites', 'Site Presentation', 'Depth of Content', 'Range of Content' and 'Interactivity'. Note how these themes are linked to the research questions of the study (see Example 4.3).

The heading (or theme) 'Range of content' was described under the subheadings of: 'Technical information', 'News', 'Weather information', 'Marketing information', 'Financial information', 'Environmental information', 'Communications information', 'Education information' and 'Government information', indicating the different **genres** or types of content available on the websites analysed.

Under the theme or heading of 'Accessibility of access' (to the websites), the data analysis was reported under the subheading of: 'Ease of access' and the sub-subheadings of 'Speed of downloading', 'Size of initial homepage', 'Essential graphics', 'Multiple layers of pages', 'Length of pages' and 'Software requirements', which refer to different aspects of a website and its design that affect the ease of accessing a website.

Using the data analysis, the report provides a discussion of the findings by summarising what was observed in the data and make interpretations of them, in the form of recommendations, based on the research questions examined.

Conclusions and recommendations   In shorter reports, these two sections may be combined but larger reports may discuss them under separate headings. Conclusions are a brief summary of the major findings. Recommendations are a list of suggestions about the most suitable courses of action, based on the findings of the study and the realities of the phenomenon or issue under investigation. The study's conclusions and recommendations may be listed as dot points or numbered sections.

Recommendations should include alternative courses of action that may be followed, comparing their strengths and weaknesses of each. For example, the report may point out that the most expensive course of action is also the quickest and the one most likely to succeed.

The report's conclusions should correspond to the findings already discussed. Recommendations should relate to the purposes of the study identified in the introduction and backed by the findings and conclusions. In other words, no new concepts, data, data analyses or information should be introduced in this section. In short, the report should be written in such a way that a reader may reach the same conclusions and recommendations as the author/s, by examining the findings. Recommendations also include suggestions for further research—which is common with a scholarly research report.

Even though the body of the report should provide sufficient information about the research project, some information may be included as supplements for better effect.

Supplements   Information that is useful but not essential to the report is provided as supplements. These include notes, reference lists or bibliographies, glossaries and appendices.

Notes   Notes or endnotes (not to be confused with the Endnote computer software used in referencing) are detailed explanations of topics or phenomena mentioned in the body of the report that may affect the flow of the report or distract the reader if included where they were mentioned. For example, when discussing the adoption of digital TV in Australia, the body of the report may refer to the 'postponement of the cut-off date for the analogue TV signal'[1] where the superscript '1' serves as a note. In the supplement, under the heading of 'Notes' a short but comprehensive explanation of the history and current situation of the analogue TV signal and its cut-off date will be provided under the entry numbered '1'.

List of references and bibliography   References are sources of information used in preparing the report and cited within the body of the report. These need to be listed in alphabetical order by the first author's last name within the reference list.

A bibliography, on the other hand, is a list of sources consulted for the study and its report but all may not be cited within its body.

The citations and references should follow a standard system of referencing such as the American Psychological Association (2003) style or the Harvard (*Citing your sources, Harvard style*, 2006) style—depending on the one used by the commissioning organisation or the researcher's disciplinary area or organisation.

Glossary of terms   In a long report where a large number of technical terms has been used or where the targeted audience is diverse and includes non-specialists in the area of study, a glossary of terms is listed in alphabetical order along with their definitions. In the example of the adoption of digital TV in Australia, a glossary can explain the terms digital TV, HDTV (High Definition TV), SDTV (Standard Definition TV), analogue TV etc. If the number of technical terms used in the report is small, the terms can be briefly explained in the introduction. If the report is aimed at a specialist audience, the glossary may be optional, as the readers are familiar with the terms.

Appendices   An appendix relates to an item referred to within the body of the report (for example, 'See Appendix A') that covers detailed materials that are relevant but not essential to the study and therefore not included in the report proper. These could include lists of interview questions posed to depth and focus groups, survey questionnaires, coding manuals of content analyses, additional tables and figures, and statistical formulas that help others to check the reliability and validity of the research project and its findings, or to replicate the study.

Index   An index of terms helps a reader locate a specific topic or keyword within the body of a long report with ease. However, a short report may do without an index by using descriptive headings that are then listed in the table of contents, making it easy for the reader to locate them.

EXAMPLE 4.7

The table of contents of a research report:
Telecommunications availability in Australia 2004–2005

A REPORT ON THE AVAILABILITY OF FIXED VOICE, MOBILE AND DATA SERVICES IN AUSTRALIA.

Australian Communication and Media Authority, Melbourne, Victoria, November 2005

Contents

We have so far examined the various aspects related to the structuring of a research report. We now examine the stylistic aspects of report writing.

MATTERS OF FORMAT AND STYLE IN WRITING RESEARCH REPORTS

When preparing any type of manuscript, an author needs to follow set guidelines related to its format and style. These refer to section numbering, headings, margins, spacing, typefaces, font sizes and page numbering. Most publishers and organisations will indicate which style they would like authors to use, such as the American Psychological Association (2003).

SECTION NUMBERING

In reports, individual sections are numbered as 1, 2, 3 etc; subsections as 1.1, 1.2, 1.3 etc and sub-subsections as 1.10, 1.11, 1.12 etc (see Example 4.1). In the body of the report, instead of using titles such as Introduction, Findings or Discussion, one may use specific titles or headings that describe the content included under that heading, as shown in Example 4.7.

HEADINGS

The report cited in Example 4.7, *Telecommunications availability in Australia 2004–2005* (Commonwealth of Australia, 2005), does not use the standard numbering system but uses headings instead. But if it did, its Introduction (page 1) would have been section 1; About this report on page 1 would be subsection 1.1; and Key themes on page 1 would be subsection 1.2. Its headings and subheadings are quite descriptive and self-explanatory as to what each chapter (section) and sub-theme (topic) is about. This report is available to the general public for downloading from the organisation's website (www.acma.gov.au; search: telecommunications services availability).

Even though we assume that the format of standard business reports is the one used in research reports aimed at non-academic audiences, the section numbering style used may vary from one report to another. However, the structure of the report in terms of the introduction, body of report and supplements, and the order of the sub-themes, remains consistent.

MARGINS

Margins should be 2.5 cm on all sides if the report is going to be stapled at the top left-hand corner. If the report is to be bound or side-stapled, a 3.75 cm margin on the left is needed.

SPACING

A report may be single spaced. But a double spacing is used when beginning a new heading or between paragraphs.

TYPE FACES

A single report should not use more than two type faces: **Arial** and **Times New Roman** are the most popular. Headings may use **bold** or *italics* as necessary, when emphasis is intended.

FONT SIZES

The font size suggested for an overall report is 12 pt, which makes for easy reading. To make the report pleasant to the eye, use illustrations in sizes and positions that fit the overall layout and setting of a page and the report. Make sure the illustrations complement the text and improve the effectiveness of the report's content rather than be included simply to 'look good'.

PAGE NUMBERING

The pagination or page numbering of the report is also of interest as the preliminaries are assigned Roman numerals starting with the title page, which is page i. However, it is not printed on the title page. The body of the report is assigned Arabic numerals of 1, 2, 3 etc. Again, the number '1' does not appear on the page. Generally the page number is centred at the bottom of the page, but other positions may be used. For a detailed explanation of the stylistic aspects of report writing, see Kuiper (2007).

POLISHING THE FINAL PRODUCT

Once the report has been written, just like any other manuscript it needs to be edited, re-written and re-arranged to improve its effectiveness. Make sure you have used inclusive and non-sexist language and checked for errors in spelling, grammar and punctuation. Make sure there are no repetitions and redundancies in the language used. Check the reference list to see if it is complete and accurate according to the style followed (Campbell, 2001). Most of all make your report short and sweet!

Summary

This chapter examined how a research report in a non-academic setting is written and examined the main characteristics of effective report writing. The stages of the process were identified as planning the report by answering several questions (the why, who, where, what and how of the report), plus what relationships are maintained in terms of its structure, style and format.

It also discussed how a report may sometimes deviate from the standard business reporting style and format and pointed out the similarities and differences between research reports written in academic and non-academic settings.

Try this . . .

1   Select a journal article or book chapter of your choice that is a scholarly report of a formal research project. Assuming you are the original researcher and using the selected scholarly report as a guide, write a research report on the same project aimed at a non-scholarly audience, following the guidelines set out in this chapter.

2   Log on to the websites of the (Australian) Department of Broadband, Communications, and the Digital Economy (DBCDE), the Australian Communications and Media Authority (ACMA), and the US Federal Communications Commission (FCC). (Website addresses and search terms appear below.) Search for any recent research reports publicly and freely available for you to download. Examine a few of these reports to see how they have been written; what sort of research projects have been commissioned by them in recent times; and what policy-making processes they may have informed; for example, media ownership laws; digital TV adoption; children and mobile phones; and broadband services in rural areas.

Further reading

Plotnik, A 1982. *The elements of editing: A modern guide for editors and journalists.* Macmillan, New York.

Strunk, W & White, E B 2004. *The elements of style: A style guide for writers*. KT Publishing, Caboolture, Qld.

Additional resources

Department of Broadband, Communications and the Digital Economy (DBCDE)—www.dbcde.gov.au/communications_for_consumers (accessed 30 January 2008). Click on 'All publications, research and reports'. Free downloads of reports published between 1999 and 2007 are available.

Australian Communications and Media Authority (ACMA)—www.acma.gov.au (accessed 30 January 2008). Click on 'Publications and research'.

US Federal Communications Commission (FCC)—www.fcc.gov (accessed 30 January 2008). Search for 'research reports'.

Research Ethics in Media and Communication

5

Researchers and postgraduate students (working on their theses), often complain about the delays and 'hassles' faced when they apply for ethics clearance. If a research project plans to use human subjects, and you are based in Australia, ethics clearance is required before any data collection begins, even if done overseas.

Ethics clearance guarantees that a formal committee has reviewed your research design and data collection methods and have made sure the proposed research project falls within the current legal and administrative requirements and guidelines. It tries to eliminate any potential harm that may be caused to your research subjects during or after their participation in the project and addresses issues such as of informed consent, privacy, **confidentiality**, no harm to subjects, and **anonymity**. Ethics guidelines also reduce the chances of individual researchers or their employers facing future legal action related to the treatment of research participants or the conduct of the project and helps protect the organisation's reputation.

In this chapter, we discuss the very important aspect of the ethical behaviour involved in the research process.

ETHICAL BEHAVIOUR

Ethical behaviour should be the hallmark of research and covers the following stages:

- design
- data collection
- data analysis
- reporting of findings
- publication.

As a book dedicated to media and communication research, we also examine how the same ethical issues that apply to social science research is relevant to documentary film or video making, public relations and journalism. This is because people in these industries use research methods such as surveys, interviews, field observations, focus groups and archival research in their everyday professional activities. Research in non-academic settings is generally covered by the relevant professional Codes of Ethics or Codes of Professional Behaviour.

WHAT ARE RESEARCH ETHICS?

Ethical research ensures the researcher is 'doing the right thing' by the project, its participants and society at large. However, what is 'right' can be subjective, which means different people will have different ideas and standards about what is right or wrong and acceptable or unacceptable. Therefore, formal ethics guidelines are established by organisations or governments. These ethical standards vary, based on the:

- discipline (for example, in medicine or psychology real physical and psychological harm to subjects can occur)
- political system (democracies vs others)
- legal system (laws in place vs otherwise)
- religious and social systems (within which research is conducted in a given geographic region)
- research context (for example, why and how it is done, involving whom and what the benefits are)
- setting in which it is conducted (such as in an educational one)
- period in history.

The standards of ethical behaviour include:

- guidelines
- administrative procedures
- laws and legislation governing the proper conduct of research.

These take the form of Institutional Review Boards (IRBs) and Human Research Ethics Committees (HRECs), professional Codes of Ethics and Codes of Professional Behaviour, which provide guidelines and assess research proposals to maintain consistency in ethical standards and the quality of the research process. They also safeguard the interests and well-being of all parties concerned.

'GHOSTS' FROM THE PAST

The concern over research ethics—especially in medical and biological sciences—arose due to the extremely inhuman and often fatal experiments conducted on prisoners of war and the predominantly Jewish concentration camp inmates by the Nazis during the Second World War. *The Nuremberg code* (US Government Printing Office, 1949) set down the basic ethical guidelines originally meant for the biomedical sciences. Similar guidelines were later applied to the social sciences.

IT'S NOT JUST THE NAZIS!

However, the Nazis had not been the only unethical researchers—either before or after *The Nuremberg Code* had been established, as the following case studies demonstrate.

Case Study 5.1   THE TUSKAGEE SYPHILIS EXPERIMENT

In 1932, the United States Government conducted an experiment in the state of Alabama to examine the effects of the disease syphilis using 412 poor, infected African-American men as test subjects without seeking their consent. These subjects were given placebos (dummy medication to the control group) or liniments (liquids rubbed on the body to reduce pain) and once a cure was found, were not provided with the proper treatment and were allowed to die.

Decades later, US President Bill Clinton publicly apologised for this unethical act on behalf of the US government.

The telemovie *Miss Evers' boys* (Feldshuh & Bernstein, 1997) is a dramatisation of these events.

THE STANFORD PRISON EXPERIMENT

Case Study 5.2

In August 1971, Professor Philip Zimbardo of the Department of Psychology at California's Stanford University carried out an experiment to test 'people's reactions to power dynamics in social situations' (Alexander, 2001).

In a simulated study of the psychology of imprisonment, he had police pick up 'suspects' (who were actually student volunteers) in their homes, follow the usual procedures of arrest in full public view and drop them off in jail, where they were subjected to strip searches, sprayed for lice and chained at their ankles. Another set of student volunteers were the 'guards' and were given complete and round-the-clock authority over the 'prisoners'.

In a situation similar to the Abu Gharaib prison scandal in Iraq in 2004, where US military guards mistreated and humiliated Iraqi suspects in custody, the 'guards' in this experiment behaved like monsters towards the 'prisoners'.

The two-week experiment had to be abandoned after six days as some of the 'prisoners' had nervous breakdowns, indicating real harms caused to participants. However, this study showed that the personalities of both the 'prisoners' and 'guards' were 'warped by their given roles' as the subjects began to act as real guards and prisoners (Alexander, 2001).

Fortunately, under current ethics guidelines and rules, such a research experiment is unlikely to be repeated today.

TESTING THE QUADRUPLE ANTIGEN VACCINE IN AUSTRALIA

Case Study 5.3

Between December 1959 and early 1961, babies as young as 3 months old were used as experimental subjects to test a quadruple antigen vaccine. The tests were conducted by Australian Federal Government agencies, using babies from five institutions such as orphanages and children's homes in the state of Victoria.

This vaccine included the polio vaccine possibly contaminated with a monkey virus, which has since been linked to causing cancer.

ETHICAL ISSUES IN THE RESEARCH PROCESS

The ethical issues involved in the research process relate to the stages of:

- the process of conducting research
- analysis (of data)
- reporting of findings
- publication.

Each of these stages has areas that involve ethical issues (Baxter & Babbie, 2004; Wimmer & Dominick, 2006).

TABLE 5.1   List of ethical issues related to research

Ethical issues in the process of conducting research:	Ethical issues arising during the analysis of data and reporting of findings
This stage consists of the areas of:	*This stage includes the issues of:*
• voluntary participation • ensuring no harm comes to participants, including obtaining informed consent • anonymity and confidentiality • **concealment** and **deception** including **debriefing**	• objectivity and **ideology** • protection of study participants • **honesty** and **integrity** • avoiding **plagiarism** • ethics in publication

ETHICAL ISSUES IN THE PROCESS OF CONDUCTING RESEARCH

Here we examine each of the above mentioned issues in detail, supported by relevant case studies.

VOLUNTARY PARTICIPATION

The current assumption about research is that the findings will benefit society, so it is the duty of the public to participate in research when invited. However, participants should not be compelled, coerced or required to take part in a research project.

A research project should not require participation as a requirement for receiving something that is legitimately theirs. Most often, research seeks personal information such as demographic details (for example, age, income, level of education, professional or employment status), which not all participants are willing to divulge. Some information we seek about participants' past or life experiences may be embarrassing or traumatic.

A researcher must remember that research data are not protected by law from being summoned by courts or law enforcement, unlike the 'privileged information' between lawyers and their clients or priests and parishioners in the confessional.

POWER RELATIONS BETWEEN RESEARCHERS AND THEIR PARTICIPANTS

Most research involves researchers and participants who are unequal in their power and social status in society, as well as the research situation. Student participants and teacher researchers is an obvious example where the student may fear repercussions in terms of his or her grade in the teacher's class or feel awkward about refusing participation in a research project he or she sees as a favour sought by the teacher.

Some teachers offer extra credit (marks) in their unit to students taking part in a research project that may be theirs or that of a colleague, which often is not related to the subject matter of the unit the students are enrolled in. This has raised important ethical issues in academia. In such cases, students should be provided with an alternative assignment offering the same level of extra credit if they choose not to participate in the research project.

Similarly, members of powerless and marginalised groups in society—such as the poor, unemployed, refugees, Indigenous people, minorities and the less educated—may feel unable to refuse or compelled to participate in research projects. This is because they see the research as conducted by the 'elites' in mainstream society, who are powerful, rich, higher in status and highly educated.

When research participants feel forced or coerced, they generate bad or unreliable data. A former classmate of mine recalled being required to take part in three research projects conducted at her university each semester of her undergraduate study. She remembered ticking responses for surveys at random, without reading the questions. Such coercion can also leave students or others with bad feelings and an aversion to research participation, which negatively affect research in the long run. Offering a payment, small gift or a gift voucher could help alleviate this situation and encourage voluntary participation (Hindman, 2006).

VOLUNTARY PARTICIPATION

Case Study 5.4

Most universities provide an evaluation form as a survey of students for each unit they offer. This survey seeks feedback for teaching staff about a unit's strengths and weaknesses, which can be used to improve teaching and unit administration in the future. Supervisors of teaching staff use the evaluations to gauge the efficacy of a given staff member's teaching, which the individual staff member may use to support their promotion applications or when seeking recognition such as teaching awards.

At University X, these survey forms traditionally were completed in class during the last week of semester. However, when the forms were provided online on the university's website the response rate for these evaluations became very low. To rectify this situation, one staff member suggested making it compulsory for students to complete this online survey before their final grade in a unit was released. This is clearly a violation of the ethical principle of voluntary participation and an example of coercion. The university rightly refused to even consider it.

NO HARM TO PARTICIPANTS

The Nuremberg code (US Government Printing Office, 1949) specifies that research should avoid the possibility of causing unnecessary physical or psychological suffering, nor should it inflict pain, trauma, injury or harm to subjects. This includes the protection of information or data collected from participants to prevent any potential harm to their self-esteem, reputation or safety, or cause them embarrassment or disadvantage should the information be made public or fall into the wrong hands.

A researcher must avoid asking questions of a personal or embarrassing nature that are not required for the study. A researcher is duty bound to anticipate any negative repercussions for a participant and take precautions to avoid them; for example, when asked to recall traumatic experiences from their past, as required for the research.

In case of any negative effects to the person's self-esteem—such as if the research implies the participants' behaviour is deviant, immoral or socially unacceptable or unfashionable (suggesting they may be racists or 'losers' and so on)—the researcher must debrief the participants and explain that the study was only a simulation that examined a specific hypothetical research question and was in no way judgmental of the participants.

Research must also avoid the possibility of causing death or disabling injuries to participants and researchers must immediately end any experiment or research project if found to be causing harm, stress or trauma to the participants. At the same time, if an experiment is successful, the control group should be offered the experimental treatment at the completion of the experiment. For example, in 2003 an experimental research project examining the effects of hormone replacement therapy (HRT) on menopausal women found that the use of one of the hormones in HRT increased the likelihood of the experimental group developing breast cancer at a higher rate than the control group or the population at large. The experiment was immediately terminated and the finding publicised worldwide so that women on HRT could consult their doctors about future courses of action. Many doctors stopped prescribing it, while some women and their doctors decided to abandon using HRT altogether.

Research should only be conducted by suitably and highly qualified researchers and be in the best interests of society. Accordingly, ethics clearance applications ask for the details, qualifications and experiences of all researchers to be involved in a project and what each person's role in and contribution to the research process will be.

Case Study 5.5 NO HARM TO PARTICIPANTS

In the early 1990s, an instructor at a university in the USA decided to conduct an experiment on the students in his class to examine how people behave and act in an unexpected crisis that was life threatening. He did so without seeking any permission from his superiors or the university's Institutional Review Board (IRB) that provides ethics clearance for research involving human subjects.

He arranged for an acquaintance to suddenly walk into the class brandishing a gun (that was not loaded) and pretend to take the students and the staff member hostage. This dramatic situation caused controversy within academia and trauma to the students involved. It was later revealed that this class usually had a student who carried a gun to class. (In the USA, the right of citizens to bear arms is protected by the constitution and the nation's gun culture is greatly different from those in other democratic countries.)

Fortunately, the student who usually carried a gun was absent that day, which possibly averted a very dangerous situation.

INFORMED CONSENT

In medical research experiments—especially for new cures—participants take part in studies knowing about the possible negative effects. However, they provide informed consent where all possible, anticipated or known negative effects have been explained to them beforehand. This is similar to our being informed of possible side effects of medication at the time they are being prescribed. Many people decide to participate in a potentially risky study due to the payment involved or their desire to get experimental treatment for an incurable disease.

Case Study 5.6 INFORMED CONSENT

In 2006, two young male participants in a medical experiment in the United Kingdom faced near-fatal reactions to the experimental medication. They volunteered for the study due to the attractive payment offered and had provided informed consent. The researchers fully disclosed the situation to the world when the healthy young men were faced with the inexplicable reaction and the hospital managed to save the two lives.

ANONYMITY AND CONFIDENTIALITY

Anonymity and confidentiality have distinct differences.

Anonymity of research participants occurs when no one, including the researchers themselves, will know who provided which responses to a survey or interview questions. This anonymity can be maintained by not seeking any identifiable information, such as the respondent's name in the survey, or by not having a sequence number or records maintained to indicate which respondent was sent which survey. Interview tapes and transcripts can be labelled only with a number instead of the participant's name, with their personal details stored separately and securely. Promises of anonymity will encourage respondents with sensitive information to come forward and provide more accurate or confidential information, such as those expressing opinions against the authorities or those involved in deviant behaviour or illegal activities (for example, drug dealers or users).

ANONYMITY AND CONFIDENTIALITY

Case Study 5.7

An organisation conducting a study about its staff's job satisfaction and morale had contracted the project to an outside research company. The company, with permission from the client organisation, sent a global email to all staff of its client requesting them to click a link that would take them to the confidential and secure survey.

The survey carried a statement claiming full confidentiality and anonymity of respondents as an incentive for them to complete the survey, and to be direct and candid in their comments without fear of repercussions. The research report was made available to all staff and the organisation followed up on its recommendations.

Confidentiality is maintained when a research participant's identity is protected and not made public by the researcher, even though the participant's contribution to the study is identifiable by the researcher. In maintaining confidentiality, research reports and related publications will carry pseudonyms and not provide specific information—such as the respondent's exact job title, city of residence and the name of their organisation— that could allow a reader familiar with the individual, the region or organisation to correctly guess who the participant was.

ANONYMITY

Case Study 5.8

In a study that involved ethnic minority members as participants, I interviewed a person who volunteered in response to a public advertisement. This study had been approved by my university's ethics committee and was funded by a grant, which provided a $50 honorarium to each interviewee as an incentive to participate.

The participant was a recent migrant to the country and was very cordial, enthusiastic and cooperative during the interview. However, a few hours afterwards he called me to say that he just realised I was required by the university to retain the interview tapes for six years for legal

and administrative purposes, and was concerned about the confidentiality of his identity. He was worried that a third party who knew him and who might get to hear the tapes or read the transcripts might be able to guess who he was and where he now lived, because during the interview he referred to his place of birth, unique educational qualifications in a third country, and current and past employment. As a survivor of a brutal regime, he was concerned about his safety.

I promised to take it into account when writing reports for publication and storing the interview tapes and transcripts.

CONCEALMENT AND DECEPTION

Concealment occurs when some information about the project is not provided to research participants. Deception refers to deliberately providing false information to them.

In field studies or participant observation, the identity of the researcher and the purpose and sponsors of the research often need to be hidden from the participants so that the latter will act and behave normally within the setting. When people know they are being observed, it might lead to the 'social desirability effect' where they say and do what they think the researcher wants to see, or hear or act in a manner considered 'proper' by society at large. They could also 'act up', especially if there is a camera present recording the activities.

In contrast, deception of participants is very much discouraged in research unless as a last resort or when there is no other way to study the phenomenon. In such situations, deception has to be justified by weighing the good that is expected against the negatives of deception.

Case Study 5.9 CONCEALMENT

In the mid 1990s, a female journalist from a leading newspaper in the USA went undercover as a factory worker to research for an investigative report on the alleged oppressive and dangerous working conditions at the factory and ill-treatment of its mostly migrant female workers. She did not seek permission from the factory management to carry out this participant observation or divulge her identity or purpose to anyone at the factory. At the end of her undercover operation, she published her findings in the newspaper.

The factory management was enraged about this negative publicity and sued the journalist for lying on her application for the job at the factory on the grounds that she had concealed having a university degree.

One could argue that the management would not have allowed her or any journalist free access to this factory if she had not done so undercover and that her intentions were honourable in highlighting the plight of its powerless workers.

CONFEDERATES

Sometimes, a **confederate** (a person working for the researcher) is used in a research project such as in an interview, where they will act in a certain way or say certain things as designed in the study to examine how participants react.

DEBRIEFING

In situations where concealment or deception is used or the real nature of the project is hidden from the participants, it is necessary to carry out a debriefing. When the true nature of the research is revealed to participants, they can feel like the researcher is effectively saying, 'Smile, you are on *Candid camera*' or 'You have been punked'—as in the reality TV programs that set people up and record their behaviour.

Debriefing explains the real purpose of the research and why the researchers needed to use concealment or deception. Participants who feel they have been deceived often feel resentful and angry with the researchers or embarrassed if they had acted in a negative manner. Therefore, the debriefing needs to be handled very delicately and diplomatically, depending on the level and type of deception involved. In short, the researcher must make sure there will be no further doubts, trauma or hard feelings for the participants after the debriefing.

DECEPTION

Case Study 5.10

In a study of racial prejudice, a focus group is gathered to discuss the issues of immigration. Unknown to the participants and the moderator, the group includes a confederate. The group begins to discuss the issue of refugees and most participants express neutral views on the subject. After a while, the confederate makes a few strong racist remarks encouraging some others to join him resulting in an extremely prejudiced discussion about refugees of colour and from particular geographic regions. This upsets some participants.

Once the focus group was completed, the researcher came in to explain to the group that the confederate was deliberately used to examine how people feel encouraged to express racist or prejudiced views about others when they find someone sympathetic to their views within the group—and that others become fearful to argue against the perceived dominant views.

Some participants felt angry and embarrassed for being deceived into expressing racist views and others were upset that the researcher had instigated such prejudiced behaviour.

ETHICAL ISSUES ARISING DURING THE ANALYSIS OF DATA AND REPORTING OF FINDINGS

Ethical behaviour does not end with the collection of data. There are several areas involved with the data analysis and reporting of findings that require ethical behaviour from researchers. Once again, we examine each of these areas in detail, supported by relevant case studies.

OBJECTIVITY AND IDEOLOGY

A research project should be conducted in an objective manner free of the researcher's personal biases or prejudices. However, we also know that it is impossible for humans to practice 'absolute objectivity' because we carry a certain level of subjectivity in whatever we do. This subjectivity is shaped by our upbringing, life experiences, values, gender, ethnicity, culture, social status, education, professional field, income level, individuality and other factors.

Researchers maintain some level of objectivity via inter-subjectivity or shared reality, due to training in the same methodologies and theoretical frameworks as well as following the same ethical standards that allow different researchers to achieve uniformity in how they conduct the research. This is similar to a sport played worldwide by different nationalities following a uniform set of rules.

During the research process, researchers must set aside their personal views and values so that they can see facts as value free or free of personal politics and ideologies. However, we also know that the 'personal is political' and that nothing is value free or value neutral.

DOMINANT PARADIGMS

At different times in history (and in different locations, contexts, disciplines and so on), different research paradigms, theoretical approaches, methodologies and research areas have become dominant, or fashionable, and they then become privileged over others. The 'others' then become marginalised or even excluded from gaining prominence or recognition. Even in the publication of research, the favourite paradigms, research methodologies or the topic areas of the editor of a journal and its reviewers can become privileged and may enjoy a higher chance of publication.

Case Study 5.11 THE DOMINANT PARADIGMS

The Australian Research Council (ARC) Discovery Grants Scheme for 2007 listed four research priority areas: They are:

o an environmentally sustainable Australia
o promoting and maintaining good health
o frontier technologies for building and transforming Australian industries
o safeguarding Australia.

When awarding funding, preference is given to projects within these areas. However, this may be a legitimate practice due to national interest and that public money is being used. At the same time, Murphy (2008) reports on a recent situation where nine ARC grants approved by expert selection panels were vetoed by the then Federal Minister of Education, Science and Training, Dr Brendan Nelson (November 2001–January 2006), without explanation, due to pressure from sections within the ruling Liberal and National parties.

Any grant or funding body—including internal grants at universities or research institutions—establishes areas of priority and guidelines. These are set by those with the power to do so, such as selection panels, based on their own subjectivity. However, many projects falling outside these research priority areas or those that challenge the dominant ideology and the status quo in society at the time have often won these grants.

PROTECTION OF STUDY PARTICIPANTS

Research participants need to be protected both at the individual and collective levels (such as an organisation or town which will be the unit of analysis). When reporting results, researchers must make sure the individual or collective identity of participants or the units of analysis cannot be identified by the details provided about them and their responses.

Research reports should not present any participants or collectives in a negative light as it may cause them harm, embarrassment or pain. For example, any racist, sexist or other offensive opinions expressed by participants, as well as their antisocial and deviant behaviour or addictions, should not be reported in a manner deemed judgmental. Presenting both the positives and negatives of the participants in a balanced manner or describing them as a group (for example, a group of female senior citizens, recovering substance users and so on) instead of as individuals, would help alleviate the situation.

PROTECTION OF RESEARCH PARTICIPANTS — Case Study 5.12

In 2004, the Australian media reported an ethics violation related to a database containing two million entries maintained in Melbourne, Australia since 1965. These contained blood samples collected from newborn babies. These samples are retained for two years in order to test for congenital diseases. Thereafter, parents can ask for the card containing the blood sample. However, few parents know about this right or how to obtain the cards.

The organisation that held the database had changed ownership several times and at one time was owned by a commercial entity that did not fall under the purview of the State Parliament. This company had released 1000 of these cards to researchers without seeking consent from the parents or the owners of the blood samples— many of whom were adults at the time. These blood samples can be stored indefinitely and be given to police with a court order, which can violate the privacy of the owners of the samples, potentially causing harm and violating confidentiality and anonymity of the data collected (Noble, 2004).

HONESTY AND INTEGRITY

Just as in any other sphere of professional activity, research also requires integrity and honesty from its practitioners. Ethical responsibilities of researchers extend beyond research subjects to one's colleagues, academic discipline and the general public. A researcher must be honest with and true to his or her data in both collection and analysis, and under no circumstances falsify, selectively discard or change them.

To maintain the integrity of their research projects, researchers should:

- list the shortcomings and limitations of their study at the end of their reports, along with any mistakes made
- report any unexpected findings or those that do not fit their original hypotheses, which could still make a contribution to knowledge
- not attempt to fit those findings to a new research question or hypothesis
- make sure the conclusions of research findings are supported by one's data analyses and findings.

In addition, the researcher should:

- describe the methodology followed in sufficient detail
- provide the data analysis protocols, surveys or list of interview questions as appendices (or offer to make them available to interested readers).

Any changes made to the standard data collection methods should be reported and explained why they were made.

HONESTY AND INTEGRITY — Case Study 5.13

In September 2001, Professor Bruce Hall— an eminent organ transplant immunologist at the University of New South Wales (UNSW), Australia—was accused by two of his fellow researchers and a doctoral student of fabricating data on experiments not carried out and applying for a grant claiming they were.

UNSW was accused of not taking action on this accusation but instead choosing to punish the whistle-blowers (the complainants). In early

Case Study 5.13

2003 the Vice Chancellor of UNSW, Professor Rory Hume, overturned the findings of an external inquiry chaired by former Chief Justice Gerard Brenan and declared Professor Hall not guilty of 'scientific misconduct' but guilty of the lesser offence of 'academic misconduct', which does not carry the punishment of dismissal or demotion. Vice Chancellor Hume resigned as a result of this controversy in April 2004. Such misconduct by academic researchers is explained as due to the pressure to continue winning grants that will support their research, and to get articles, chapters and books published, in order to demonstrate to their employers that they are being productive (Gerard & Dayton, 2003; Cooper, 2004).

NEGATIVE REPERCUSSIONS OF MISCONDUCT

Case Study 5.13 indicates that the spill-over effects of such unethical behaviour extend beyond the person accused of it. As a result of this incident, the organisation had its reputation and credibility damaged, the Vice Chancellor had to resign and a perception of a negative organisational culture was created for UNSW. The general public could also lose their respect for and trust of academic institutions and their research.

AVOIDING PLAGIARISM

Plagiarism in research publication can be of two types:

- the use of others' work or ideas without acknowledging their original source
- authorship of publications.

USING OTHERS' WORK

When more than a few words are taken directly from another source, the page number and reference details of the original source must be provided.

A few years ago, the Vice Chancellor of Monash University in Australia had to resign from his job when it was revealed that he had failed to cite some sources of information in his early publications. But Caterson (2004: 8) argues that 'the line between stealing someone else's work and alluding to (refer or mention) it is not always a clear one'. However, some ideas and information are regarded as very much in the public domain and are commonly used, giving the impression of not belonging to anyone in particular; for example, the list of ethical issues related to research or definitions of common terms.

AUTHORSHIP ISSUES

When those other than the chief investigator have contributed to a research project, the resulting publications should give them credit in the form of co-authorship and acknowledge the contribution made by research assistants and others at the end of the paper. Some postgraduate students claim that their supervisors expect to be cited as co-authors in publications arising from their thesis projects. Many postgraduate students working as (paid) research assistants complain about neither being given co-authorship nor acknowledgment of their contribution in the resulting publications.

The common standard for giving someone co-authorship is based on the principle of 'significant contribution' to the project during the:

- conceptualisation or research design
- data collection and analysis
- write-up for publication.

The person making the highest contribution gets first billing. The order of authorship needs to be discussed early in the project, but the order may be adjusted if changes occurred to their level of contribution. It is unethical to give authorship to those who did not make a significant or any contribution to a project. Sometimes researchers give co-authorship to spouses or friends not entitled to it, in an attempt to increase the latter's standing in the discipline or to help their career advancement.

ETHICS IN PUBLICATION

Ethics also extend to the final stage of a research project, which is the publication of findings. They apply to:

- authors
- editors of journals
- reviewers of manuscripts.

Authors   It is unethical to submit the same manuscript to more than one journal or outlet at the same time, as it is a misuse of editors' and reviewers' time and efforts. It is also unethical to publish the same manuscript or almost similar ones in more than one outlet. One must also avoid using the same data set in more than one publication if they address the same issues, research questions or hypotheses—even if the manuscripts are written differently.

Journal editors and reviewers of manuscripts   Reviewers of manuscripts for conferences or journals and editors of journals or books have ethical responsibilities to provide:

- fair and timely reviews
- constructive criticism and feedback to authors who can use them to improve the manuscript.

They should not:

- review manuscripts in areas they are not expert in
- reject or unfairly criticise those that disagree with the manuscript reader's point of view
- have included unflattering critiques of the editor's or reviewer's own work.

Try this ...

Carry out the following exercises to test and expand your knowledge of research ethics learned so far in this chapter.

1   Look up the website www.prisonexp.org and make notes on each of the ethical issues involved in the Stanford Prison experiment of 1971.

2   Collect any newspaper articles or items that deal with violations of research ethics both locally and overseas. List the ethical issues involved in each, with reference to the research data collection process, analysis of data, reporting of findings and publication.

3   Think of a small research project you would like to carry out. What ethical issues (for example, informed consent, voluntary participation, confidentiality and anonymity, and no harm to participants) are likely to arise? What precautions would be necessary to protect the subjects and meet the ethical guidelines of your country or organisation?

4 Examine each of the case studies provided in this chapter. Make notes on the violations of the various ethical standards involved in each case. Write notes on how they could have been avoided.

Ethical behaviour is not limited to scholarly research. The professional practices of media production, journalism and public relations—which use the same social science research methods such as surveys, content analysis, archival research, interviews, focus groups, participant observation and case studies—are required to follow the same ethical standards. These are generally covered in their respective Codes of Ethics or Codes of Professional Behaviour.

ETHICS IN RESEARCH RELATED TO JOURNALISM, PUBLIC RELATIONS AND MEDIA CONTENT PRODUCTION

Journalists, documentary video/film makers and script writers often use the data collection or research methods from the social sciences. However, their standards of ethical behaviour towards participants or sources are less stringent in comparison with academic research, due to the realities of their professions being different from those of scholarly research.

Journalists present the argument of 'freedom of the press' and film makers and script writers mention 'artistic freedom' as absolving them of the ethical responsibilities and guidelines binding social research. However, some journalism scholars disagree arguing that if the same research methods are used, the same ethical standards should apply (Awad, 2006).

ETHICS OF DOCUMENTARY FILM/VIDEO PRODUCTION

Even though documentary film makers have the right to artistic expression, the rights of participants interviewed or featured on screen must be protected in the same way as research participants—the right to privacy and freedom from slander, and the need for informed consent and protection from harm—so that they would not become 'victims' of the process (Butchart, 2006: 428).

Film makers must be socially responsible when making representations of people and make the portrayals balanced, in good taste and recognise that a power imbalance exists between the documentary makers and those individuals or groups featured, just as between researchers and their participants.

Documentary makers should avoid concealment or deception of participants and have an obligation to present unbiased representations (or tell the truth) in their portrayals respecting the rights of their participants, just as in research.

Case Study 5.14 ETHICS IN FILM-MAKING: *BORAT*

The 2006 comedy–drama *Borat: Cultural learnings of America for make benefit glorious nation of Kazakhstan* (Cohen, Hines & Charles, 2006) features many members of the American public being interviewed by the lead character Borat, who plays the title role of a journalist from Kazakhstan, visiting the USA.

⌐·············>

Once the film was released, the interviewees complained that they were not informed about the nature of the film (which the Kazakhstan Government also considered demeaning and insulting to their country and its people) or what their role was when providing answers and comments to Borat's questions. In other words, they had not provided informed consent to their participation and the real purpose of the interviews had been concealed from them.

ETHICS IN JOURNALISM IN THE TREATMENT OF NEWS SOURCES

In their everyday news gathering and reporting, journalists follow the same research methods of interviewing their sources (similar to research participants) and carry out field studies or participant observation in natural settings the same way as anthropologists. However, journalism is not bound by the strict ethics guidelines of research that would protect journalists' sources (similar to protecting of research participants or subjects in anthropology) (Awad, 2006).

Mistreatment and manipulation of sources by unscrupulous individuals may occur in journalism due to sensationalism. The strategies used include 'empathic listening' and 'flattering' to encourage sources to tell more than they otherwise would—which amounts to deception. The power relationship between journalists and their sources among the general public is also unequal, just as it is between researchers and participants—especially in terms of 'what' and 'how' things are reported. At the same time, news sources too may manipulate and 'use' journalists for their own ends.

Journalists need to consider the issues of privacy and harm to participants, and maintain confidentiality and anonymity of sources, even though the sources' identity may need to be disclosed for credibility of the information reported. Journalism justifies intrusion into a person's privacy and undercover reporting (sometimes involving concealment or deception) in the name of the 'public's right to know'. Ethical quality in journalism appears to be about 'getting it right' rather than 'treating the sources right' (Awad, 2006: 935). Unfortunately, perceived unethical behaviour of journalists leads to misinformation and the loss of credibility and respectability of the profession.

The Australian Journalists' Association's Code of Ethics lists honesty, fairness, independence and respect for the rights of others as the main ethical commitments. Its 'guidance clause' states that 'basic values often needs interpretation and sometimes come into conflict. Ethical journalism requires conscientious decision-making in context. Only substantial harm to people allows any standard to be overridden' (Australian News Commentary, 2008).

From time to time, we hear of fabrication of information or plagiarism by unscrupulous journalists that are detected and made public. The Jayson Blair incident at the *New York Times* is a prime example of this (Christians et al., 2005) and relates to issues of honesty and integrity that hurt the journalistic community and their organisations' reputations (Quinn, 2004: 167).

ETHICS RELATED TO RESEARCH IN PUBLIC RELATIONS

The most common research methods used by public relations practitioners are surveys (for public opinion and program evaluation), focus groups, content analysis (for media monitoring) and case studies.

In principle, the Public Relations Institute of Australia (PRIA) has a Code of Ethics (www.pria.com.au; see Code of Ethics) that must be followed when research is conducted within the profession by PRIA members themselves or commissioned to outside consultants. The Australian Market and Social Research Society's Code of Behaviour (mrsa.com.au; see Code of Ethics) guides research conducted in marketing and public relations. In short, research conducted by and for the public relations or marketing professions is expected to follow the same ethical guidelines as standard social research covering issues of privacy, no harm to participants, voluntary participation (opt in–opt out) and informed consent.

At the same time, when publicising and utilising research findings in their everyday functions, public relations practitioners must maintain high ethical standards and not downplay the negative findings or selectively report results. The public relations profession in the USA lost credibility after the Enron and Arthur Anderson fiascos, where the companies were involved in unethical accounting practices and their public relations practitioners were perceived as having helped the managements to hide the reality from shareholders and the public, all of which relate directly to honesty and integrity.

Try this …

Look up the websites that set out the Codes of Ethics or Codes of Professional Behaviour of your own professional field—such as journalism, public relations, advertising, market research or media production—within your geographic region. Examine the ethics guidelines that apply to conducting research or working with members of the public in the everyday functions of that profession.

It is useful to know the official procedures and structures set up for maintaining ethical standards in research in Australia, which is addressed in the next section.

NATIONAL GUIDELINES FOR RESEARCH ETHICS IN AUSTRALIA

In Australia, research ethics are guided by the *National statement on ethical conduct in research involving humans* (Commonwealth of Australia, 1999). The main ethical principles addressed in this statement relate to:

- integrity
- respect for people
- consent
- research merit and safety
- ethical review and conduct
- research involving people in dependent or unequal relationships
- research involving collectivities (such as cultural, ethnic or Indigenous communities)
- research with Aboriginal and Torres Strait Islander people
- research involving deception of participants, concealment or covert observation
- privacy of information and storage
- security of personal information.

This statement issued by the National Health and Medical Research Council (NHMRC) in Australia is endorsed by the Australian Vice Chancellors' Committee (AVCC), Australian Research Council (ARC), Australian Academy of Humanities, Australian Academy of Science, Academy of the Social Sciences in Australia and the Academy of Technological Sciences and Engineering.

HUMAN RESEARCH ETHICS COMMITTEES

Australian universities have established Human Research Ethics Committees (HRECs) to examine and review all research proposals of their staff and students. Researchers are not allowed to begin data collection without ethics clearance.

THE NATIONAL ETHICS APPLICATION FORM (NEAF)

The standardised ethics application to be used nationwide in Australia can be lodged online via NEAF by logging on to its website at www.neaf.gov.au. The NEAF requires the following information at regular intervals during and at the conclusion of the project:

- its duration and location
- the research plan
- significance
- peer review
- information about participants and how that information will be used
- storage of information
- ownership of information collected
- disposal of information
- reporting individual results to participants and others
- dissemination of final results
- benefits and risks
- monitoring (where researchers are periodically required to file reports on the ethical issues involved in their projects to their ethics committees.).

NEAF AND RESEARCHERS

The NEAF seeks information about the researchers and their certification and training to guarantee the project will be carried out by highly qualified and trained researchers. It also examines any project-specific details related to deception, concealment and/or covert observation; research involving Aboriginal and Torres Strait Islander peoples; research on workplace practices or possibly impacting on workplace relationships; and research conducted overseas.

NEAF AND PARTICIPANTS

With regards to participants, NEAF seeks information on:

- participant description
- experience of the researcher
- the relationship of researchers to participants (that would address issues of power imbalances)
- the recruitment and the consent processes.

It also deals with research conducted with specific groups of participants in Australia, such as:

- people whose primary language is other than English (LOTE)
- children and/or young people with an intellectual or mental impairment
- concealment, deception or covert behaviour
- people in dependent relationships
- collectivities.

OBTAINING INFORMED CONSENT FROM PARTICIPANTS

Ethics applications also require the researchers to provide Plain Language Statements (PLSs), which are given to prospective participants and explain the project, its possible risks, their rights and the purposes of the research, written in simple language that would help participants to provide informed consent. For example, participants are free to withdraw their consent and participation in a project at any time—even after data have been collected. In such cases, the researcher is required to exclude that data from the analysis and reporting of results.

Consent forms for adults as well as minors and any advertisements that will be used in the recruitment of participants also need to be submitted for approval by the ethics committee.

SUPPLEMENTARY MATERIALS

Surveys, interview questions and other protocols to be used with research participants also need to be submitted for ethics clearance. This process aims to protect participants from harm and to guarantee the project adheres to all ethics requirements.

Try this …

Think of a simple research project you would like to carry out. Look up the National Ethics Application Form (NEAF) on its website (www.neaf.gov.au). Examine how the various questions posed attempt to address each of the ethical issues such as informed consent, confidentiality, harm to participants and so on that may be relevant to your project.

Examine such other research ethics review processes and guidelines in place in your country of origin or current residence, if you are not an Australian citizen or permanent resident presently living in Australia. For example, in the USA, there are Institutional Review Boards (IRBs).

Summary

This chapter explained why following the standard ethical guidelines is necessary and useful for any researcher as well as journalists, public relations professionals, film or documentary writers and producers. The chapter addressed in detail the various ethical issues related to the research process including data collection, analysis of data and reporting of results, and the ethics of publishing. These were explained via several case studies.

Further reading

Baker, L W 1993. *The credibility factor: Putting ethics to work in public relations*. Business One Irwin, Homewood, IL.

Ettema, J S & Glasser, T L 1998. *Custodians of conscience: Investigative reporting and public virtue*. Columbia University Press, New York.

Gross, L, Katz, J, & Ruby, J 2000. *Image ethics: The moral rights of subjects in photographs, films and TV*. Oxford University Press, New York.

Mauthner, M, Birch, M, Jessop J & Miller, J (eds) 2002. *Ethics in qualitative research*. Sage, London.

Sanders, K 2003. *Ethics in journalism*. Sage, Thousand Oaks, CA.

Additional resources

Australian Journalists Association (AJA). *Code of ethics*. Retrieved 17 March 2008 from www.australian-news.com.au/codethics.htm.

Australian Market and Social Research Society. *Code of professional behaviour*. Retrieved 17 March 2008 from www.mrsa.com.au/files/code%20of20Professional%Behaviour%20Jan08.pdf.

Council of Better Business Bureaus (USA). Retrieved 17 March 2008 from www.bbb.org.

Journal of Mass Media Ethics. www.jmme.org.

Public Relations Institute of Australia (PRIA). *Code of ethics*. Retrieved 17 March 2008 from www.pria.com.au.

St James Ethics Centre. www.ethics.org.au.

The Office of the Federal Privacy Commissioner, Australia. www.privacy.gov.au.

Public Relations Society of America 2000. *Member code of ethics*. Retrieved 17 March 2008 from www.prsa.org/aboutUs/ethics/preamble_en.html.

Zimbardo, P G 1999–2007. *Stanford Prison experiment—Slide show*. Retrieved 23 February 2007 from www.prisonexp.org.

Zimbardo, P G (director/producer) n.d. *Quiet rage: The Stanford prison experiment*. DVD/video documentary (50 min). Stanford, CA.

6 Sampling

In the previous chapters, we examined how a research study is conducted within the context of the theoretical perspectives applicable (Chapter 1) and epistemologies used (Chapter 2), and explained how to carry out a literature review and write research reports or proposals for scholarly and non-scholarly settings (Chapters 3 and 4). Chapter 5 discussed the ethical issues involved in communication and mass media research that use human subjects.

The next stage of a research project is to design the study and decide how to collect the data and from whom, where and how. This involves examining the **population** targeted by the study and the methods of **sampling** to be used.

This chapter introduces the following:

o   what sampling is and why we need it

o   probability and non-probability sampling

o   sampling in qualitative research

o   different types of sampling and their characteristics, advantages and disadvantages

o   issues related to **sample** sizes

o   **sampling error**.

TAKING A CENSUS OF THE TARGETED POPULATION

It would be great if researchers could collect data from every unit of analysis or every member of the **targeted population** in a given study (as in a **census**), so that we could have 'accurate results'. For example, since we have compulsory voting in Australia, asking every registered voter (the target population) who he or she plans to vote for should allow any pollster to predict the correct outcome using 'almost perfect' figures before an election—at least in theory. (In practice, some voters may not tell the pollsters what they really think or change their minds after the research data have been collected. The answers voters give the researchers also depend on the questions asked.)

Handy Hint
It is not always practical, affordable or even necessary to study every member of the targeted population (that is, conduct a census) or study a very large number of units of analyses or research subjects to examine a specific aspect about them. Therefore, researchers make 'estimations and predictions' about a targeted population of a study based on findings obtained by using a sample of that population.

SAMPLES AND POPULATIONS

A sample is a selected number of individual cases or research subjects drawn from a larger population for a specific study; for example, 100 students selected from all those enrolled at a given university (the targeted population).

A population in a given research study refers to all members of a group, case or class of subjects, variables or phenomena under study; for example, all programs aired on the six Australian free-to-air TV channels in a given week or all students enrolled at a given university.

A census includes every member of the target population in a research study. For example, every five years the Australian Bureau of Statistics (ABS) carries out a census, collecting information about all residents of Australia, overseas visitors and the homeless. For example, a survey of all enrolled students at a given university is a census.

REPRESENTATIVE AND NON-REPRESENTATIVE SAMPLES

A sample is a subset of the population and may be representative of the population. For example, the 100 students selected for the survey sample should come from all year levels and all faculties and majors offered at the university if it is to be a **representative sample** and if the findings are to be generalised to the population.

Research findings obtained from a **non-representative sample** cannot be generalised to the population. This can lead to wrong results or predictions if generalised to the population, as shown by the *Literary Digest* survey with their 1936 poll (see Case Study 6.1). In other words, if the sample of 100 students from a university only included students from one faculty, the findings could not be generalised to other faculties or the entire university.

> Handy Hint
>
> A representative sample includes cases or individuals from all sub-groups of the target population, while a non-representative sample does not.

'GETTING IT WRONG' WITH A NON-REPRESENTATIVE SAMPLE   Case Study 6.1

You might remember how several American and Australian pollsters predicted 'close contests' at the 2004 US presidential election and the 2004 Australian federal election, which actually turned out to be landslide victories for incumbents George W Bush and John Howard respectively. The predictions also varied in terms of the estimated figures quoted in different research findings.

During the US presidential primaries in early 2008, Senators Hillary Clinton (of the Democratic Party) and John McCain (the Republican Party) disproved the predictions of most pollsters by winning in the State of New Hampshire.

Pollsters (even the experienced ones) getting their predictions wrong is nothing new. In

1936, the *Literary Digest* magazine in the USA surveyed two million of its almost ten million readers about the outcome of that year's US presidential election. It predicted the wrong outcome. In contrast, the Gallup Poll used only 4000 respondents as a **purposive sample** and correctly predicted the winner. However, their estimated figure was 54% of the vote for incumbent President Roosevelt when his actual figure turned out to be 61%.

This is because the *Literary Digest* and Gallup polls had each used different samples of voters in their polling. In the *Literary Digest* sample, differences existed between the individuals that made up the sample and the general voting population, as well as between those who had the opportunity to respond to the poll and did so and those who chose not to respond.

For example, the *Literary Digest* was subscribed to and read by mostly the well-to-do who were predominantly Republican voters. They had indicated their vote for their party's nominee Alf London, instead of the incumbent Democratic President Franklin D Roosevelt. In other words, how the samples were selected by the *Literary Digest* and Gallup, the characteristics of the voters (or respondents) that made up each sample and the questions posed to them in each poll were not the same.

This brings us to the issue of errors in sampling during research, which can also explain why the Gallup poll could not predict a more accurate figure either.

ERRORS IN THE RESEARCH PROCESS

Shortcomings in the sampling, measurement (see Chapter 7) or the research process lead to errors in findings. There are three types of errors in the research process that lead to and result in inaccurate research findings:

- **measurement error**
- sampling error
- **random error**.

MEASUREMENT ERROR

Measurement error is caused by errors in the research instrument such as with a survey questionnaire or shortcomings of the coding instrument in a content analysis. In a census, only measurement and random errors can occur as there is no sampling involved.

SAMPLING ERROR

Sampling error is based on the degree to which the sample differs from the population under study. This could occur due to using the wrong sample or an unrepresentative sample. For example, when using a sample of internet users, selecting only those who have an internet connection at home excludes those who do not have a connection at home but access it at school, work, friend or relative's house, library or internet cafe, creating a sampling error.

RANDOM ERROR

Random error occurs due to unexpected, uncontrolled or unknown factors. The sum or the combined effects of the three types of error in a study is the **standard error** of the research findings. The standard error indicates with a certain amount of confidence the estimated difference between a study sample and its target population.

Case Study 6.2   THE NEW UNDERGRADUATE MAJOR: HOW THE SURVEY GOT IT WRONG

A few years ago, a university was interested in introducing a new major within one of its faculties. As the major was from a disciplinary area related to the study of popular culture, they expected it to generate a lot of interest from younger undergraduate students and be successful.

The university commissioned a private research company to carry out a survey of current first-year students of the university

⌐⋯⋯⋯⋯>

who were enrolled in units offered by the same faculty that was planning to introduce the new major. The survey findings indicated a high level of interest from students who answered the question 'Would you like to take this major, if introduced at the university?' on a scale of 1 (not at all) to 5 (very much). The major was duly introduced but failed to attract sufficient student numbers and was discontinued at the end of its third year of existence.

This study had encountered all three types of errors—measurement, sampling and random—which explains its failure to correctly predict the outcome.

An error in sampling was caused when the survey was given to first-year students already enrolled in the university, rather than to high school students in Year 12 who would be entering university the following year. Most current students in the faculty were already committed to a major, often with specific professional goals, and were not necessarily

going to enrol in a new one, even if they thought the new disciplinary area was interesting.

An error in measurement existed in the survey questionnaire because there was no indication that students were expected to change their current major to take the new one, in the case where they already had committed to one. The survey only explained the type of topics included in the units offered in the major, which sounded quite interesting.

A random error occurred when the students who enrolled in the first-year unit of this new major in the very first semester it was offered— taking it either as required for the major or as an interesting elective unit—dropped out of the unit in large numbers during the first few weeks of class as they found the instructor difficult to follow.

As only a small number of students actually ended up enrolled in the major, its second- and third-year units had too few students enrolling in them, making the major unsustainable.

The combination of these three types of errors (the standard error) is used to indicate the **margin of error**.

MARGIN OF ERROR

You may have noticed that poll results reported in newspapers will include a margin of error, such as '+ or –3%'. This indicates that the actual result may vary from the figures cited by –3% to +3%. In other words, if we take the margin of error as +3 or –3%, since the distance between +3% and –3% is 6%, the actual result can vary from the cited one by 3% either way.

Calculating the margin of error: poll results

EXAMPLE 6.1

If a poll about voters' party preference at an upcoming election indicates Party A as polling 53% of respondents and Party B as 47% (the gap between them being 6%), and the margin of error is '+ or –3%' (the distance between them being 6% as well), the results can be interpreted as 'too close to call' or 'neck and neck'.

So when we decide if the poll actually means Party A is 'leading' and likely to win, we need to see if the gap between the two findings (53% and 47% = 6%) is larger than the margin of error (gap between +3% and –3% = 6%).

Now that we have examined the issue of sampling error, we can explore the different types of sampling methods most often used in media and communication research.

TYPES OF SAMPLING

The various sampling methods used in research can be of two types:

1 probability sampling   **2 non-probability sampling**

Probability sampling is most often used in quantitative research while non-probability sampling is used in qualitative research.

PROBABILITY SAMPLING

Probability samples are selected according to standard mathematical guidelines so that each member or unit in the study population will have a known chance (probability) of being selected for inclusion in the sample. This chance has to be more than zero.

EXAMPLE 6.2

Probability samples: tossing a coin

o If a researcher selects 10% of all students enrolled in a class for a research study, each student will have a 10 in 100 (or 1 in 10) chance of being included.

o Tossing a coin gives a 50% chance of either 'heads' or 'tails' to win.

o Throwing a dice (a cube used in gambling with six sides numbered 1 to 6 with dots), a gambler has a one in six chance of getting each of the numbers 1, 2, 3, 4, 5 or 6.

NON-PROBABILITY SAMPLING

In non-probability sampling, a sample is chosen from the population under study without following any mathematical guidelines related to probability. In other words, each member of the population will not have an equal or known chance or even any chance at all of being included in the sample.

EXAMPLE 6.3

Non-probability samples: the *Literary Digest*

When the *Literary Digest* asked its 10 million readers to respond to their survey, only its readers had the chance to be part of the study or sample. Non-readers of the magazine—even if they were registered voters and therefore part of the target population—had no chance of being included in the two million sample.

Since this was a non-representative sample the magazine should not have generalised the findings to all voters in the country.

DECIDING ON THE TYPE OF SAMPLING TO USE IN A RESEARCH STUDY

Even though studies using probability sampling are able to provide more valid and generalisable results than those using non-probability sampling, the decision to use one or the other depends on several factors. They are the:

- purpose of the study
- balancing the cost of the process with the value of the data collected
- time constraints
- level of acceptable error.

PURPOSE OF THE STUDY

If a study aims to generalise its findings to the population, it must use probability sampling. This means non-probability sampling is more than adequate if the study is: only exploratory in nature; a trial or a pilot study; looking for data that would help a researcher design a research instrument; or testing a draft measurement instrument such as a questionnaire or coding manual for a content analysis.

COSTS VS VALUE OF DATA COLLECTED

It is cheaper to use non-probability sampling than probability sampling. So a researcher needs to balance the cost of the resources required with the importance of the study and the value or usefulness (utility) of the data collected when deciding on which sampling method to use.

TIME CONSTRAINTS

Studies using probability sampling are more time consuming than those using non-probability sampling. If a study is preliminary in nature and the researcher is pressed for time, non-probability sampling may be used.

LEVEL OF ACCEPTABLE ERROR

For preliminary and pilot studies, controlling the sampling error is not very important. Under such situations, using non-probability sampling will be acceptable.

NO GUARANTEES OF REPRESENTATIVENESS

Even if a probability sample is selected with the utmost care and systematically following the standard procedures to the letter, there is no guarantee that a truly representative sample will be obtained, and thereby the findings will be free of sampling error. For example, in a study using a probability sample of 100 students from a university to examine 'undergraduates' drinking habits' a researcher could end up with a sample of 100 people who are non-drinkers.

Let us examine the methods of non-probability sampling.

> ### Handy Hints
> The rule of thumb is to use probability sampling when the study is:
> - aiming to support or refute a significant research hypothesis
> - examining an important research question
> - needs to generalise its findings.

TYPES OF NON-PROBABILITY SAMPLES

Six types of the non-probability samples are examined in this chapter:

- convenience or **availability samples**
- **volunteer samples**
- purposive samples
- **typical case sampling**
- **quota sampling**
- **snowball samples**.

CONVENIENCE OR AVAILABILITY SAMPLES

A convenience or availability (or opportunity) sample is one that uses readily available subjects for a research study.

EXAMPLE 6.4

Convenience samples

1   A university teacher carrying out a research project gives out its survey to her students in a class she teaches.
2   A research company will approach shoppers in a mall on a given day to be subjects of a research study it is conducting.

Sample bias in convenient samples   In a **convenience sample**, subjects may be selected haphazardly based on the appearance of subjects who fit the characteristics the researcher is looking for or based on who's available to be part of the study. Thus the researcher doesn't have to make too much of an effort to find subjects.

For example, when testing an advertising campaign for eye glasses, a researcher may approach and recruit shoppers at the mall who are wearing glasses, or media workers may stop people on the street to seek their opinion on an issue (vox populi or vox pop).

Researcher subjectivity in convenience samples   Selecting subjects for a convenience sample involves high researcher **subjectivity** and sampling bias as the researcher may approach those who are better looking or appear friendly and less likely to refuse when asked to participate. This means subjects of a convenience sample tend to be very much alike, in addition to being highly non-representative of the population. For example, students in a class tend to be of the same age group and level of education, have similar levels of intelligence and so on.

Limitations of convenience samples   As the sampling error of a convenience sample cannot be calculated, research findings obtained with them lack generalisability or external validity. Therefore, convenience samples are more suitable for exploratory studies, and when checking a data collection instrument such as a draft questionnaire or a new methodology or procedure.

Sometimes, in an effort to include some aspect of randomness to a convenience sample, and thereby some representation of the population, the researcher may select, say, every tenth person who passes her in the mall or choose a large number of subjects to invoke the '**law of large numbers**'. This may give an appearance of a probability or random sample, but since not everyone in the mall has the same chance of passing the researcher at the time of the study—and not every one of that town or the population is going to be at the mall that day—such a sample will still remain a convenience or availability one.

VOLUNTEER SAMPLES

Volunteer subjects are those who respond to a researcher's call for participation in a research study—be they remunerated or otherwise. They are therefore not selected based on mathematical principles. This means those who volunteer will also be very different from those who do not. A volunteer sample will be highly unrepresentative of the target population, thereby creating sampling error and skewed results.

Who volunteers?   Subjects who volunteer are found to be younger, higher educated, of higher occupational status and intelligence, more altruistic (concerned about others), seekers of arousal and approval of others, possessing lower levels of authoritarianism (less domineering), more sociable and unconventional. Research findings involving volunteer samples therefore can lead to inaccurate estimates of population characteristics or parameters and often support the researcher's hypothesis.

A volunteer sample: student evaluations

EXAMPLE 6.5

A university seeks its students' feedback on their classes taken each semester by filling in an online student evaluation. In the past, the evaluation surveys were distributed and collected after completion in person by university administration staff during the last week of classes.

After the online evaluation was introduced, the response rate for student evaluations became very low. The few students who responded generally provided very good evaluations and comments or very bad ones, suggesting that those who took the trouble to log on to the university's website to respond were the ones angry about something or very diligent students who wanted to show their appreciation of the teacher.

However, as the ethics guidelines of social research today require voluntary participation of all subjects, some argue that all research subjects today are volunteers and all samples voluntary ones. However, in a volunteer sample subjects approach the researcher responding to an open invitation, while in a convenience sample the researcher decides to invite specific individual subjects or groups accessible to them, who may accept or refuse to participate.

PURPOSIVE SAMPLES

A purposive sample is often used in qualitative research. Here, the researcher selects subjects or elements that possess the specific characteristics or qualities required for the study. In other words, the subjects serve the 'purpose' of the study. As with all non-probability samples, results obtained with purposive samples are not generalisable and the sample is not representative of the population under study. But they may provide very specific and valuable insights into a research question or hypothesis under examination.

Purposive samples

EXAMPLE 6.6

1   In a study about the experiences of Temporary Protection Visa (TPV) holders in Australia, a researcher will select a purposive sample of those currently holding that category of visa.
2   When testing an advertising campaign for a new brand of toothpaste for those with sensitive teeth, a purposive sample of individuals with sensitive teeth and currently using special toothpastes for the condition will be selected for a focus group.
3   In an exploratory study that examined the measures to improve digital TV adoption in Australia, its purposive sample included subjects from the various stakeholder groups of digital TV for interviews: householders who had adopted the technology and who had not; journalists who had written about the subject; academics who had carried out research on the topic; executives from the industry group Digital Broadcasting Australia; staff at TV broadcasting organisations overseeing the broadcasters' digital TV operations; and officers from the Department of Broadband, Communications and the Digital Economy (DBCDE).

4 In a study examining those who contribute audio-visual content to the internet site YouTube, a purposive sample of those who have done so in the past six months will be selected.

Purposive samples are commonly used in qualitative research such as depth interviews or focus groups, where individuals are selected based on who can shed light on, or are experts on, the subject or issue under study. This method of sampling is commonly used by journalists and biographers.

TYPICAL CASE SAMPLES

Typical case sampling is a variation of purposive sampling, where a single instance of a standard example or 'case' is selected from the target population for an exploratory study.

A typical case sample: sports fans and digital TV

A typical case sample will choose a householder who purchased a digital TV set-up to watch sports broadcasts, just before the football season begins, to examine the main characteristics and opinions of a typical 'sports fan' adopting the technology.

QUOTA SAMPLES

Quota sampling is a form of purposive sampling, but it selects subjects to include known or predetermined percentages (or quotas) of people from various groups in the population, based on their actual distribution in the population.

Quota samples

1 A quota sample from a target population will include 50% each of males and females, if it is the distribution of the sexes in that population.

2 A quota sample used in a study examining patterns of internet usage at home will select 40% of subjects with an internet connection at home and 60% from those without, as that is the actual distribution of internet users in the population.

Advantages and disadvantages of quota samples   Quota samples are more representative than convenience samples and less expensive to use than probability samples.

Quota sampling depends on the researcher having access to accurate and up-to-date census figures for the relevant target population characteristics on which the quotas are set.

For example, figures for the rates of penetration of new communication technologies such as digital TV or broadband mobile phone ownership may changes so rapidly that up-to-date figures will be hard to find. At the same time, just as with any sample, the selected individuals could end up unrepresentative of the target population.

SNOWBALL SAMPLES

Often used in academic media and communication research and sometimes known as 'referrals', snowball sampling uses the strategy of choosing one or a few qualified respondents for a study and seeking their help in identifying other suitable subjects.

Snowball samples

EXAMPLE 6.9

1 A doctoral student working on his thesis research (on African-American screenwriters of TV dramas in Hollywood and their experiences) contacts the brother-in-law of one of his friends who fits the description. After interviewing this writer, the student asks the subject to suggest some other writers of his acquaintance who meet the criteria of the target population and interviews them. This process is repeated a few times and the student is able to find a large enough sample of subjects to interview for his project.

2 A researcher carrying out a preliminary study on people's opinions on the use of biometric devices in the workplace for keeping track of employee work hours (even for permanent, full-time employees) gives her survey to many of her colleagues, family members and friends asking them to respond to it. She also gives ten more copies of the same survey to each of these respondents asking them to distribute them to their friends, family members and acquaintances who are in permanent, full-time employment. She manages to collect 100 completed surveys that give her sufficient information to test the survey instrument and explore further areas of research on the subject.

Advantages and disadvantages of snowball samples When snowball samples depend on referrals from the subjects to identify other suitable units or individuals, the resulting sample can consist of individuals and units that are similar to each other, creating **sample bias**. People may recommend others who are members of the same social group or professional association, or who went to the same university, because they are the only other suitable subjects they know.

They may also recommend individuals personally close to them in an effort to improve the profiles of friends and acquaintances, and deliberately not recommend others, in a manner similar to the 'old boy network'. This could reduce the diversity or representativeness of the sample and fail to identify the best possible group of subjects for the study.

However, often this method is the best and only one available to identify suitable individuals with very specific and less common characteristics, such as female stand-up comics from a particular minority ethnic group. Therefore, it is useful if the aim of the research is to examine, explore or understand a lesser known, less common or hidden phenomenon, topic or issue.

TYPES OF PROBABILITY SAMPLES

Six types of probability sampling methods are examined in this chapter:

- simple random samples, with and without replacement
- **random digit dialling**
- systematic random samples
- **stratified (strata** or **segment) samples**
- **proportionate samples**
- **disproportionate samples**.

SIMPLE RANDOM SAMPLES

In **simple random sampling**, each subject or unit in the population has an equal chance of being selected, thereby reducing sampling error and allowing for the generalisability of findings. However, this method requires a complete list of all members (sampling units or elements) of the target population—referred to as the '**sampling frame**'—if the process of sampling is to be accurate.

EXAMPLE 6.10

A sampling frame: the students of a university

A complete and up-to-date database of all students registered at a university is an accurate sampling frame, but a telephone directory is not because it does not include 'silent' or unlisted numbers, nor all those people living in a household with a listed phone. The telephone directory also excludes the homes or individuals with no landline phones.

When using a list, the members of the sampling frame or each member of the target population are given an identification number and then, using the lottery system, the required number of subjects or units will be randomly selected from the list.

Random samples without replacement The most commonly used method of random sampling is random sampling **without replacement**. Here, each selected number is removed from the sampling frame before the next number is drawn. This, however, gradually reduces the probability of each item being selected; that is, if the sampling frame has 1000 names, we begin selecting the sample with the probability of each number or name being drawn at one in 1000, and it will gradually go down to one in 999, one in 998, one in 997 etc as each number or name is drawn.

Random samples with replacement In **random sampling with replacement** method, the selected number is returned to the sampling frame to keep the probability the same throughout the selection process of the sample. If the same number is drawn twice, it will be disregarded and another number drawn. This meticulous method is used for more complicated, large and nationwide studies that require high levels of precision.

Using random number tables A random number table can be used instead of the lottery system when selecting a sample from the sampling frame. After randomly choosing the first number from this table, each corresponding number in the sampling frame will be selected using the order in which the identification numbers of the elements in the sampling frame appear in the random numbers table (for **random number tables** go to www.randomizer.org). Based on the size of the sample, indicate how many random numbers are needed and the size of the population listed in the sampling frame when asking the computer to generate a random numbers table. For example, if you have a population of 1000 and need a sample of 50 elements, ask the randomiser to list 50 random numbers between 1 and 1000.

When contacting research subjects over the phone for surveys or interviews, the most often used sampling method is random digit dialling. We examine it next.

RANDOM DIGIT DIALLING

Random digit dialling is a better method than using a telephone directory and random sampling when contacting prospective research subjects. This is because random digit dialling can include silent or unlisted numbers missing from the telephone directory. Households with silent numbers may resent unsolicited calls, so a researcher needs to set a policy and mechanism for including or excluding them.

Random digit dialling

EXAMPLE 6.11

Let's assume your study is carried out in Australia and we are using the Australian phone numbering system of ten digits. They comprise state (two digits), city (two digits), suburb (three digits) and home (three digits).

The numbers to be called are generated by random digit dialling as follows. Generate a randomly selected list of numbers made up of a three-digit set (between 000 and 999) to represent the last three numbers (that is, the home) for phone numbers, to which any number of the three-digit suburb codes can be added.

For example, the suburb codes selected are 271 and 272 (for Waurn Ponds). To this the two-digit city code (52 for Geelong) and the two-digit state code (03 for Victoria) can be added. Thus, the numbers called will be (03) 52 271 xxx, (03) 52 272 xxx etc.

When using random digit dialling, it may be necessary to generate and call up to three times the required number of phone numbers to compensate for invalid, non-existent or discontinued numbers and missed calls, as well as those who 'slam the phone' on the researcher.

SYSTEMATIC RANDOM SAMPLES

In media and communication research, **systematic random sampling** is often used as a means of saving time, resources and effort. This involves a sampling interval.

Sampling interval   If the sampling frame has a population of N and the researcher needs a sample the size of S, the sampling interval K will be population size ÷ sample size = sampling interval or $N \div S = K$. The researcher randomly chooses a starting point on the sampling frame and picks every 'Kth' element or unit in the sampling frame until a sample the size of S is selected.

A systematic random sample

EXAMPLE 6.12

If the population size (N) = 100 and **sample size** (S) = 25, the **sampling interval** (K) is $N \div S = 100 \div 25 = 4$.

If we randomly select the starting point as 8, the selected elements will be 8, 8 + 4 = 12, 12 + 4 = 16, 16 + 4 = 20 … and so on till the 25 elements have been selected.

Cyclicity   However, systematic random sampling can result in a biased sample if the sampling frame indicates a 'cycle', such as days of the week or months of the year.

Cyclicity

If we were to carry out a content analysis of newspapers for a period of six months and the sampling interval was 7, we may end up with the same day of the week of the newspaper to be analysed for the entire six-month period, creating a sample bias.

Therefore, we need to check for **cyclicity** of the sampling frame before calculating the sampling interval. Sometimes, researchers use a '**composite week**' (Monday from week one, Tuesday from week two, Wednesday from week three etc until the entire six-month period is exhausted) to avoid a sample bias. They will also randomly select a day of the week to begin when selecting the sample; for example, if Thursday were the randomly selected day, Thursday is selected from week 1, Friday from week 2 etc.

Periodicity   Similar to cyclicity, **periodicity** refers to sampling bias caused due to the order in which sampling units or elements are listed in the sampling frame. Periodicity often occurs by chance and results in unrepresentative samples, which negatively affect the generalisability of the findings and skew the results, even if probability sampling has been used.

Periodicity

1   Using the sampling frame or list of all films released in 2008 to select a systematic random sample, a researcher ends up with a sample consisting entirely of either action films or films from the same studio, such as Miramax.

2   When using a telephone directory to obtain a systematic random sample, a researcher found that she had no ethnic last names included in her sample. This occurred because most ethnic names are few in number and placed far apart in the sampling frame, so they had been missed due to the sampling interval 'jumping over' those names. This also meant that the more common last names had a higher chance of being included in the sample as they occurred in higher numbers in the sampling frame.

STRATIFIED (STRATA OR SEGMENT) SAMPLES

Stratified sampling is useful when the target population is made of diverse groups and has the advantage of making sure that each specific subgroup or sub-sample of the population is represented in the sample, which is not always possible with simple random sampling. Demographic characteristics or variables such as sex, age, religion, income and choice of TV channel are often used as each stratum or segment (group sharing a particular characteristic). Thereafter, the units from each stratum are selected randomly. However, with each variable added, it will become harder to find suitable subjects that fit the criteria; for example, females within a particular age group and income bracket and belonging to a specific minority ethnic group.

Stratified sampling is used to increase the representativeness of the sample with the target population, which reduces sampling error and bias.

A stratified sample

EXAMPLE 6.15

A researcher examining the relationship between household income and the adoption of digital TV (via pay TV subscription) divided the sample into different strata based on annual household income as:

o   below $35,000 per year
o $36,000–$60,000
o $61,000–$80,000
o $81,000–$100,000
o $101,000 and over.

This is to examine the hypothesis that households with higher income are more likely to subscribe to digital pay TV services.

The sample is also stratified according to the age group of the oldest male in the household:

o   below 25 years
o   26–35
o   36–45
o   46–55
o   56–65
o   66 and above.

This is to examine the relationship between the age of oldest male in a household and adoption of digital TV via pay TV.

Stratified sampling can be further refined to include various proportions of the subgroups in the sample to make it more representative of the target population, known as **proportionate stratified sampling**.

PROPORTIONATE STRATIFIED SAMPLES

In a proportionate **stratified sample**, the units or elements from the various groups or strata are selected based on their proportion in the population, either using the exact population figures or as required for the study.

A proportionate stratified sample

EXAMPLE 6.16

If households earning over $100,000 a year are 20% of the population, the sample will consist of 20% of households earning over $100,000.

DISPROPORTIONATE STRATIFIED SAMPLES

If a specific stratum in a stratified sample is important or useful to the research project, that stratum will be over-sampled to over-represent it above its actual percentage of occurrence in the target population.

A disproportionate stratified sample

EXAMPLE 6.17

A research project on the efficacy of an advertising campaign for a luxury car over-samples households with incomes over $100,000 a year as they are the targeted audience of the advertising campaign and the ones who can afford to purchase the advertised car.

Probability sampling is mostly used in quantitative research, while qualitative research uses non-probability sampling. Let us examine the latter in detail.

SAMPLING IN QUALITATIVE RESEARCH

Unlike with quantitative research, findings from qualitative research are not generalisable to the population as they do not use probability sampling. There are three regularly used sampling methods in qualitative research:

- purposive
- snowball
- convenience.

Qualitative research often selects typical cases or suitable subjects, rather than large numbers of units or elements as the sample. Qualitative research is also less rigid about the sample size and the type of subject used. In qualitative research, it is quite common to decide on the sample after the study and its data collection has begun. This allows researchers to have an idea about the research setting and the population so that they can identify the most suitable research subjects. In contrast, quantitative research selects the sample before the data collection begins.

Handy Hint

In qualitative research, the data collection ends when the **saturation point** is reached—which means that after a certain point, no new data or knowledge is obtained with new subjects studied or interviewed. This is similar to the saturation in a literature search, where after a particular point no new information is gained with further additional readings of past research.

CHOOSING A SUITABLE SAMPLE SIZE

In both qualitative and quantitative research, the **optimal sample size** (the best under the circumstances) is considered to be one that is both the smallest one possible and the largest one necessary. There is no standard size of sample recommended for a given research method or specific area of study.

SAMPLE SIZE AND TYPE OF PROJECT

Sample size also depends on the following:

- type of project (qualitative vs quantitative and data collection method used)
- purpose (if exploratory or testing important hypotheses)
- complexity (the number of variables involved in a multivariate analysis requires a large sample)
- amount of error tolerated (such as with medical and pharmaceutical research where the error has to be extremely low)
- time and financial constraints
- guidelines and precedents (set by previous research)
- size of budget.

SAMPLE SIZE AND TYPE OF PROJECT

Handy Hint

Smaller samples are sufficient for preliminary research, while larger samples are needed for studies that require high levels of precision and will be the basis of important decisions. In a pilot study or a pre-test using a survey, a sample size of 10–50 elements or units will be sufficient.

Qualitative research uses smaller samples because it is more in-depth, while quantitative research aimed at generalising its findings needs a large enough probability sample to allow this. Surveys (see Chapter 8) generally require larger samples while case studies (Chapter 13) may need just one element or case to be studied in depth.

Recommended sample sizes Slonim (1960) recommends suitable sample sizes for corresponding populations (see Table 6.1) when using simple random sampling to reach a rate of 98% precision or better for 99 samples in 100. However, these samples need to be representative, if the findings are to be generalisable. (Note that sometimes the sample size is denoted as 'N'.)

TABLE 6.1 Suggested sample sizes (for 98% precision or better for 99 samples in 100)

N (S)	%
200 (105)	52.5
500 (152)	30.4
1000 (179)	17.9
2000 (197)	9.8
5000 (209)	4.2
10,000 (213)	2.1
20,000 (216)	1.1
50,000 (217)	0.4
100,000 (217)	0.2

N = population; S = sample size; % = sample size as the percentage of population.

Source: Slonim (1960: 74).

Sample size and margins for sampling error   Table 6.2 indicates how increases in sample size do not result in corresponding or matching decreases in sampling error. This is because the sampling error will reduce with larger sample sizes only up to a point, and thereafter it will not be significantly reduced with an increased sample size.

TABLE 6.2 Relationship between sample size and margin for sampling error

Sample size (S)	Margin for sampling error + or − (%)
10	0.316
100	0.100
400	0.050
1000	0.032
1600	0.025
2500	0.020
4000	0.016
10,000	0.010

Source: Smith (1988: 343).

As shown in Table 6.2, to obtain a significant reduction in sampling error beyond a sample size of 1000, a substantial increase in sample size is required. Modern political pollsters use a sample between 1500 and 4000, which gives a sampling error of around + or −3% to + or −1.5%.

This explains why TV ratings research in the USA is carried out with only a 3000-strong sample of households. The population of the USA at its last census in 2000 was 281.4 million with an estimated figure of 301.6 million by 13 April 2007 (United States Census Bureau, 2007).

Summary

This chapter discussed the main probability and non-probability sampling methods used in media and communication research within the context of their advantages and disadvantages. Optimum and recommended sample sizes—as mainly applied to quantitative research—were discussed with reference to their link to reducing sampling error.

The next chapter examines the issues of measurement related to the data collected.

Further reading

Adler, E S & Clark, R 2003. *How it's done: An invitation to social research*, 2nd edn. Wadsworth-Thomson, Belmont, CA (pp. 103–66).

Clegg, F 1982. *Simple statistics: A course book for the social sciences*, Cambridge University Press, New York (pp. 113–23).

Kalton, G 1983. *Introduction to survey sampling*. Sage, Newbury Park, CA.

Sarantakos, S 2005. *Social research*, 3rd edn. Pelgrave Macmillan, New York (pp. 72–100).

Wimmer, R D & Dominick, J R 2006. *Mass media research: An introduction*, 8th edn. Wadsworth-Thomson, Belmont, CA (pp. 87–111).

Additional resources

Gary Morgan's analysis of polls leading up to the 2004 Australian federal elections—www.roymorgan.com/news/polls/2004/3796 (retrieved 20 January 2008).

Measurement

In Chapter 6, we examined the different methods of probability and non-probability methods of sampling a target population for a research study. In this chapter, we examine the next stage of a research study—how the data are collected or observations measured. This chapter introduces the following:

o   measurement of variables and concepts

o   **levels of measurement**

o   Likert and **semantic differential scales**

o   **measures of central tendency: mean, median, mode** and **range.**

MEASUREMENT OF VARIABLES AND CONCEPTS

In Chapter 2, we learned about concepts and constructs, operational definitions and the units of analysis we need to identify in order to observe the variables in a given research study. Even though some variables such as age, sex, height, income and so on can be directly measured or observed, others based on various concepts such as 'job satisfaction' or a 'keen student' cannot. Therefore, in such situations, we need to follow some special procedures to do it indirectly. This is the role of 'measurement' in research.

Do 'keen students' get better grades than others?

EXAMPLE 7.1

Let's say you are interested in examining if 'keen students' always get better grades in their school work than others. This means you need to find what the concepts of 'a keen student', 'grades' and 'school work' really mean in your study. You will then need to define these concepts to describe how you will collect data on them to compare different students, their study habits or 'keenness' and grades with each other.

You can measure each of these concepts for each respondent in your study by asking them:

o   how many hours they study each week (for example, mention an average figure)
o   how they study (for example, by taking good notes in class or participating in group study)
o   if they do all assigned readings (always, sometimes, never)
o   if they do additional readings from the library (yes or no)
o   how often they attend classes (all the time, sometimes, rarely, never)
o   if they seek help from the teacher (yes or no)
o   what classes they have taken (for example, list the names of the units taken last semester for which they have received results)
o   the grades or marks they have received for each (Fail or 49% or below, Pass or 50–59%, Credit or 60–69%, Distinction or 70–79% or High Distinction 80% or above).

EXAMPLE 7.2

Do students do better in class if they like their teacher?

You may also want to know if students do better in class if they like their teacher. So you can ask them to indicate how much they like the teacher of each class on a scale of 1 to 5, with 1 being 'dislike very much' and 5 being 'like very much'.

You can request students to describe how they see their teacher on a 1–5 scale where 1 indicates the teacher is very unlikable and 5 as very likeable.

You can also ask them to explain in their own words how they like each class and its teacher or what makes them do better in some classes than others, even when they study about the same for all classes. These will be posed as 'open-ended questions', which will generate qualitative data.

In any research study, the most important factor in collecting data is to know exactly what information you will need to answer your research question or hypothesis, and how you will go about collecting it. Examples 7.1 and 7.2 indicate the different ways of collecting data from subjects. This brings us to the topic of measurement.

MEASUREMENT

Once you have decided on your unit of analysis (see Chapter 2)—which is 'an individual student' in the above examples—you need to classify these individuals or 'cases' into categories or groups.

EXAMPLE 7.3

Example 7.3 Different categories of variables

You can classify the variable of sex into 'male' and 'female' categories (**nominal**) and the grades or marks they receive in a class as Fail (49% or below), Pass (50–59%), Credit (60–69%), Distinction (70–79%) and High Distinction (80% or above) (**ordinal**).

The number of hours studied per week can be sought as a number (from zero to x number of hours per week, including decimals) (**ratio**) and how much they like their teacher on a scale of 1 to 5 or 1 as 'dislike very much', 2 as 'dislike somewhat', 3 as 'neither like nor dislike', 4 as 'like somewhat' and 5 as 'like very much' (**interval**). Note how these illustrate different types of measurement.

CATEGORIES OF VARIABLES

You will notice that the above levels or categorisations of the variables of sex, grades or marks, number of hours studied per week and how much they like their teacher are not measured the same way. Some have names and some have numbers. This is due to the different levels of measurement used in the categorisation of the variables.

LEVELS OF MEASUREMENT

Four levels of measurement or types of categorisation are used when classifying variables:

- nominal
- ordinal
- interval
- ratio.

These four different ways of measuring or categorising variables—by assigning them different values or scales—are based on a set of established rules, which we now examine in detail.

NOMINAL LEVEL VARIABLES

At the nominal level of measurement, variable categories are simply assigned names or labels. For example, the variable of the sex of each student is measured by categorising the peerson as either male or female. The different categories of a nominal variable are equal in importance or rank.

A nominal variable: flavours of ice cream

EXAMPLE 7.4

Another example of a nominal variable is the flavours of ice cream sold in an ice cream shop. They can be categorised as chocolate, vanilla, strawberry etc.

The categories of a nominal variable must be **mutually exclusive** (that is, they must not overlap where one case or observation should only belong to one category).

Mutually exclusive nominal categories: Neapolitan ice cream

EXAMPLE 7.5

When creating **categories of variables** for 'flavours of ice cream', the researcher must create a separate one for Neapolitan ice cream (which is made up of vanilla, chocolate and strawberry flavours) to avoid confusion as to where it should belong.

Nominal categories of a variable should also be **exhaustive** (that is, the researcher must create a sufficient number of categories to include all cases or observed values for that variable).

Exhaustive nominal categories: rocky road, rum and raisin, and others

EXAMPLE 7.6

The variable 'flavours of ice creams' should have categories for other flavours of ice cream, such as rocky road, rum and raisin, melon and raspberry, if they or any other flavours are included in the data collected for a study or sold in the shop being studied.

Nominal is the simplest level of measurement as nominal categories are just names and can only be counted, and are unable to be used in sophisticated statistical tests.

ORDINAL LEVEL VARIABLES

The categories assigned to a variable with the ordinal level of measurement are also names or labels, but these names have a distinguishable ranking order or hierarchy. Just like nominals, ordinals can only be counted and not used in sophisticated statistical tests.

Ordinal level variables: year level at university and grades

The variable 'a student's year level at university' can be 1st, 2nd or 3rd year. These are names (nominal) but also have a hierarchy (ordinal) with 1st year being the lowest and 3rd year the highest, with 2nd year placed in the middle.

It could also be an ordinal level measurement if we categorised the variable of person's 'level of job satisfaction' as low, moderate or high, or a student's grade in a class as Fail, Pass, Credit, Distinction or High Distinction.

However, the difference between adjacent (adjoining) categories of an ordinal variable is not necessarily equal. For example, we can categorise the variable of the 'placing at the 100 metre freestyle swim' at the Olympics as Gold (1st), Silver (2nd) and Bronze (3rd) medallists. But it only means that the three athletes achieved these placing in this order and not how close or far apart their times were. In other words, the time or distance that separated the winners from each other may not be equal, and the placing does not indicate what their times were or the distances between them at the finish line.

Converting ordinal categories to nominal   Ordinal level variables can be treated as nominal ones if necessary, but nominal categories cannot be treated as or converted into ordinals.

Converting ordinal categories to nominal

Take the placings of a race at the Olympics as Gold, Silver and Bronze medals. Even though these are ordinals, they can be used also as nominals because they are names or labels, while 1st, 2nd and 3rd placings are ordinals. But the flavours of ice cream, which are nominal categories, cannot be used as ordinals as they are simply names with no hierarchy among them.

INTERVAL LEVEL VARIABLES

Interval level variables:

- can be names or labels (like nominals) or numbers
- can have a ranking for their categories (like ordinals)
- have an equal difference between adjacent categories (unlike ordinals)
- have no true zero.

Interval level variables: property of equal difference

In the interval variable 'how much a student likes their teacher' can be categorised on a scale of 1 to 5, with 1 as 'not at all' and 5 as 'a lot'. The gap between 1 and 2, 2 and 3, 3 and 4 and 4 and 5 are mathematically the same, indicating the property of equal difference. This allows for the numbers in interval level categories to be counted, added or subtracted.

Interval categories have no true zero   However, in interval level scales there is no true zero, where the value zero (0) means the variable or phenomenon does not exist.

Interval variables have no true zero

EXAMPLE 7.10

In the variable of temperature, the value of '0' (zero degrees) in the Celsius scale is an interval level measurement, but this does not mean there is no heat or temperature whatsoever at 0°C. This is because the 'zero' of an interval level measurement is only an 'arbitrary zero'.

This absence of a true zero makes it hard to compare different interval values as proportions of each other, nor to multiply or divide them; for example, Celsius and Fahrenheit degrees for temperature.

Converting interval variables to nominals and ordinals   Interval level variables and categories can be converted into and treated as ordinals and nominals.

Converting interval variables to nominals and ordinals

EXAMPLE 7.11

The interval variable 'How much do you like your teacher', given as 1 (dislike a lot) to 5 (like a lot), can be converted into ordinals and nominals as 1 (dislike a lot), 2 (dislike somewhat), 3 (neither like nor dislike), 4 (like somewhat) and 5 (like a lot).

But ordinal or nominal categories cannot be treated as or converted into intervals because adjacent ordinal categories do not equally vary from each other or indicate the 'property of equal difference', while nominal categories are simply names that are equal in rank with each other (see Example 7.8).

Measuring attitudes with interval scales   Interval scales are often used to measure attitudes, IQ (intelligence quotient) or other scales and opinions. This is because these concepts have no true zeros. For example, there is no such thing as 'no attitude' or 'no intelligence'—having 'no opinion' on an issue is also an opinion or attitude towards it and a person cannot be without any intelligence (it may be simply considered low in comparison with other people.)

RATIO LEVEL VARIABLES

Categories of ratio level variables:

- can be names (of the number one etc as nominal) or numbers including decimals (2.1, 2.2, 2.3 etc) and fractions (¼, ½, ¾ etc)
- can be rank ordered (as in ordinal)
- indicate the property of equal difference between adjacent categories (as in interval), but unlike at the interval level
- have a true zero, where the variable or phenomenon under observation does not exist.

Ratio variables and a true zero   Having a true zero allows a researcher to calculate proportions (divide) and calculate ratios for a variable when using ratio levels of measurement. For example, a car that runs at a speed of 100 km per hour is twice as fast as one running at 50 km per hour (that is, the proportion is $100 \div 50 = 2$) and their ratio is 100:50 or 2:1).

Ratio variables are mostly used to measure demographic variables such as height, age and income.

SUMMARY OF VARIABLE CHARACTERISTICS

Table 7.1 lists a summary of characteristics for nominal, ordinal, interval and ratio variables and their respective categories for easy reference.

TABLE 7.1   Types of variables: summary of characteristics

Type of variable	Characteristics of variable categories
Nominal level	• comprises names or labels with no hierarchy between categories • categories must be mutually exclusive and exhaustive • simplest form of variable • can only be counted
Ordinal level	• comprises names or labels with hierarchical order • may be converted to (or used as) nominals • difference between adjacent categories is *not* equal (no property of equal difference)
Interval level	• comprises names (like nominals) or numbers, with hierarchical order (like ordinals) • may be converted to (or used as) nominals and ordinals • difference between adjacent categories is equal (property of equal difference exists) • no true zero exists (has an arbitrary zero, so variable still exists at '0')
Ratio level	• comprises numbers or names with hierarchical order • includes decimals and fractions of numbers • may be converted to (or used as) nominal, ordinal and interval • difference between adjacent categories is equal (property of equal difference exists) • has a true zero, where '0' means the variable does not exist

MEASURING AN OBSERVABLE VARIABLE

Measurement allows a researcher to classify the various characteristics of a unit of analysis (for example, an individual) into different observable variables (for example, sex, age, height and income) and then into their corresponding categories (for example, the variable of 'sex' is divided into the nominal categories of male and female; 'age' is measured in years (ratio) or under age brackets (such as under 18 years of age, 19–30 years or 31–50 years) (ordinal); height is measured in centimetres (ratio); and income is measured in dollars (ratio)).

MEASURING AN UNOBSERVABLE VARIABLE

A directly unobservable variable construct (see Chapter 2) such as 'job satisfaction' or 'a keen student' will be designed in a special way so that it can be measured such as 'high, moderate or low' for a given research subject. It will be calculated using several other measurements that are observable, such as by asking students if they like their boss, work environment, colleagues, pay etc and developing a composite measurement for 'job satisfaction'. This leads us to think about measurement scales.

MEASUREMENT SCALES

Some concepts such as 'job satisfaction' or 'attitude towards body image' cannot be measured directly, and they also cannot be measured with a single item or survey question. When faced with such complex or complicated variables, a scale that has more than one item or question is used as a composite measure of that variable, and its value is calculated using this scale (explained in Example 7.13). (See concepts and constructs discussed in Chapter 2.)

A **Likert scale** is a commonly used such measure. It is also known as the '**summated ratings**' **approach**.

Likert scales   In a Likert scale, several statements that address the concept under examination are prepared by the researcher. Respondents are asked to choose their answers to these questions on a 1–5, 1–7, 1–9 or even a 1–100 scale. The scale addresses the two opposing positions at each end such as 1 as 'strongly disagree' and 5/7/9/100 as 'strongly agree'.

A single, composite score is then obtained by adding the numbers assigned to each item by the respondent. The higher the composite score, the stronger the respondent's attitude is towards the concept (if the statements are positively worded). It may be negatively worded, too, by assigning 1 to 'strongly agree' and 5/7/9/100 to 'strongly disagree'.

A Likert scale: support for biometric devices

EXAMPLE 7.12

The following is an example of a Likert scale. It measures respondents' support for the use of biometric devices in everyday situations.

Biometric devices are electronic devices that measure some aspect of your physical uniqueness and are used to verify your identification instead of using passwords or personal identification numbers (PINs). The most popular biometrics are fingerprint scans, hand geometry, retina scans, iris scans, facial recognition, voice recognition and handwriting recognition. Use the following scale to indicate your agreement on each of the following five items.

1	2	3	4	5
Strongly disagree	Somewhat disagree	Neither agree nor disagree	Somewhat agree	Strongly agree

o   Item 1: Biometric devices provide more security at an ATM (Automatic Teller Machine for banking) than passwords and PINs.
o   Item 2: I am willing to use a biometric log on when purchasing items on line or via e-commerce (electronic commerce).
o   Item 3: Biometric devices are a good way to keep track of employee work hours.
o   Item 4: Biometrics should be used for air-travel security purposes.
o   Item 5: Biometric devices make computer log on faster and are more convenient.

Note that the statements are positively worded as the positive end is assigned the higher number. This means the higher the composite score, the higher the respondent's support for the devices will be.

Assume that the selected responses to the five items by an individual survey respondent were 4, 5, 2, 5 and 3. The composite score for this respondent for this concept or variable is 4 + 5 + 2 + 5 + 3 = 19. If another respondent indicates a composite score of 22, it means the second respondent has a more positive attitude towards biometrics.

Source: Moody (2003); Weerakkody (2004a).

Semantic differential scales   Semantic differential scales, or the bipolar rating system, is another measure used in examining respondents' attitudes towards a given issue or topic. A semantic differential scale measures the meaning a respondent has for a given item and is often used to evaluate respondents' attitudes towards individuals (for example, politicians or teachers). The researcher selects a concept to be examined and places it in positive terms at the high end of the scale and the negative one at the low end (see Example 7.13).

Different attitudes of respondents towards this individual on different dimensions are examined by listing the various opinions about the person under evaluation (for example, as good/bad or organised/disorganised) at the two ends of a 1–7 point scale. The individual scores assigned to each item are then added to obtain a single composite score for the concept for each individual respondent. If the two ends of the continuum are set with negative as 1 (for example, bad) and positive as 7 (for example, good), then the higher the composite score, more positive the evaluation of the person will be.

These scales are useful when carrying out statistical tests such as factor analyses.

EXAMPLE 7.13

A semantic differential scale

Item: I think the politician Mr A is:

Dishonest	1	2	3	4	5	6	7	Honest
Untrustworthy	1	2	3	4	5	6	7	Trustworthy
Arrogant	1	2	3	4	5	6	7	Modest
Self-centred	1	2	3	4	5	6	7	Altruistic
Unlikeable	1	2	3	4	5	6	7	Likeable
Conservative	1	2	3	4	5	6	7	Liberal
Bad for the economy	1	2	3	4	5	6	7	Good for the economy
Bad for national security	1	2	3	4	5	6	7	Good for national security
Bad for the country	1	2	3	4	5	6	7	Good for the country

If the nine responses selected from the 7-point scale by a respondent are: 1, 2, 1, 3, 2, 1, 6, 5, 5, the composite score for the respondent is 26 from a highest possible score of $7 \times 9 = 63$. The lower the composite score the more negative a respondent's attitude towards the politician being evaluated.

THE SIGNIFICANCE OF THE LEVELS OF MEASUREMENT

Most variables can be measured at more than one level—nominal, ordinal, interval and ratio—and sometimes at all four levels.

EXAMPLE 7.14

Measuring the same variable at all four levels

The age of a person can be measured at the nominal and ordinal levels when we categorise it as infant, child, adolescent, adult, middle-aged or senior citizen.

It can be measured at the interval level when ages are grouped as under 10 years, 11–20 years, 21–30, 31–40, 41–50, 51–60, 61–70, 71–80 years etc. This is because the differences between adjacent categories (for example, 60 and 61, and 70 and 71) are equal (that is, 1).

It can be measured at the ratio level when we measure as their actual age, such as 43 years old (age has a true zero as a person cannot be younger than age 0).

We now examine the relevance of choosing a specific level of measurement (nominal, ordinal, interval and ratio) for a given variable.

MEASURES OF CENTRAL TENDENCY

As researchers, we need to be aware that most statistical tests are designed for specific levels of measurement. Therefore, we need to use a suitable measurement to a variable, based on the statistical tests we need to use in a given study. For example, the 'central tendency of a variable' (or the summary statistics of the mean, median, mode and range) can only be applied to some levels of measurement. The central tendency statistics tell us what a typical score for the distribution is.

THE MEAN

The mean is the average or the arithmetic mean of a group of values. It is easy to calculate, as one simply needs to add up all the available values of a variable and divide it by the total number of values or cases.

Calculating the mean

EXAMPLE 7.15

A list of 'N' number of observed values (for example, nine) for the 'number of hours per week studied' (by each students in a project) consists of the following numbers (arranged in ascending order).

| 5 | 6 | 6 | 7 | 7 | 10 | 10 | 10 | 12 |

The sum of these nine numbers is: 5 + 6 + 6 + 7 + 7 + 10 + 10 + 10 + 12 = 73

Mean = sum ÷ number of observed values (N) = 73 ÷ 9 = 8.11 hours per week.

Note that the 'number of hours studied' is measured as a ratio variable. This is because the mean value for a distribution of values can be calculated only for ratio and interval variables, as they are the only ones that possess the property of equal difference that allows the values to be added and subtracted.

The matter of extreme values or outliers   Since the calculation of the mean value requires adding up all the values in the distribution, it can be easily influenced by **extreme values** known as '**outliers**'. For example, a tenth person in the group who does not study at all (0 hours per week) will make the average go down considerably (73 ÷ 10 = 7.3 hours per week), just as someone who studies 20 hours a week will take it up (93 ÷ 10 = 9.3 hours per week).

The mean can only be calculated for interval and ratio data, such as the average age of subjects or the average marks scored by students in a given class (ratio) or the students' average value for liking their teacher of a class (interval). We cannot calculate the average for the differently named classes taken by students (nominal) or the average year level of students (ordinal) because they are simply names or labels.

MEDIAN

The median is the midpoint of a set of values when they are arranged in ascending or descending order, with half the number of values lying above it and the other half below it. For an everyday example, consider the 'median strip' of a highway that divides the road into equal halves as an analogy of the arithmetic median.

The median can be calculated for ordinal, interval and ratio levels of measurement and variables. The median is less influenced by outliers than the mean is.

Calculating the median: ratio or interval variables

FOR AN ODD NUMBER OF VALUES

A list of an **odd number** of observed values (for example, nine) for the 'number of hours per week studied' (by the students in our project) consists of the following numbers (arranged in ascending order).

5	6	6	7	**7**	10	10	10	12

The median lies at the point where four of the values are above it and four below. The median value is 7.

FOR AN EVEN NUMBER OF VALUES

For a list of an **even number** of observed values (for example, 10) for the same variable, the median can be calculated as follows. (Note that the 'outliers' have been included in examples A and B.)

EXAMPLE A (when a low extreme value is included)

0	5	6	6	**7**	**7**	10	10	10	12

The midpoint of this distribution is the average of the two middle scores.
Median = 7 + 7 = 14 ÷ 2 = 7

EXAMPLE B (when a high extreme value is included)

5	6	6	7	**7**	**10**	10	10	12	20

Median = 7 + 10 = 17 ÷ 2 = 8.5

Notice how the changes to the median caused by the outliers is much less than those for the mean (see 'The matter of extreme values or outliers' section earlier).

Calculating the median: ordinal variables

The distribution of grades for nine students in a group when they are graded as HD (High Distinction), D (Distinction, C (Credit), P (Pass) and F (Fail) showed that there were two HDs, one D, three Cs, two Ps and one F. When arranged in descending order they appear as:

HD	HD	D	C	**C**	C	P	P	F

The median value or the midpoint of the distribution is a C.

MODE

The mode is the value that occurs 'most often' in a distribution of values for a given variable. The mode can be calculated for all four levels of measurement—nominal, ordinal, interval and ratio. For example, we can calculate the flavour of ice cream that was requested by the highest number of customers of the ice cream shop on a given day was chocolate (nominal), the year level of the largest number of students in a class as second year (ordinal), the most often cited answer on a scale of 1–5 as 3 (with no true zero; interval) and the most often cited figure for pocket money received by children between the ages of 10 and 12 as $10 per week (ratio). As some children do not receive any pocket money, this variable has a true zero.

Calculating the mode

EXAMPLE 7.18

A list of observed values (for example, eleven) for the 'number of hours per week studied' (by the students in our project) consists of the following numbers (arranged in ascending order).

For a ratio level variable:

| 5 | 6 | 6 | 7 | 7 | **10** | **10** | **10** | 12 | 20 |

As the number that occurs the most number of times (it appears three times) is 10, the mode of this distribution is 10.

For an interval level variable (for example, 'How well do you like your teacher?') on a 1–5 scale with 1 as 'not at all' and 5 as 'very much', the distribution of values is:

| 1 | 2 | 2 | 3 | 3 | 3 | **4** | **4** | **4** | **4** | **4** | 5 |

As the number '4' occurs five times in the distribution, the mode is 4.

For an ordinal level variable (for example, the year level of students surveyed):

1st year = 115 students; 2nd year = 112 students; 3rd year = 100 students

The mode is '1st year students' as they are the largest category in the distribution of the variable.

For a nominal level variable (for example, the sex of the students surveyed):

males = 200 students; females = 127

The mode is male as they record the higher number between males and females.

THE RANGE

The range is the distance (difference) between the lowest (**minimum**) and the highest (**maximum**) values in a distribution for a variable. It can be calculated for ordinal, interval and ratio level variables, because each of their categories may be placed in a hierarchy.

The range helps a researcher to spot the differences in the scores or values between two groups of respondents or subjects. For example, let's calculate the differences between the ranges for the marks scored in a class by two groups of students taught by two different instructors. If the marks for the first instructor's group fell between 40% and 78%, then the range is 38 marks (78 − 40= 38). If the second instructor's group had marks between 50% and 86%, the range is 36 (86 − 50= 36). So we can say that the range of distribution of the marks among the two student groups is similar (38 and 36), but that the second instructor's group has scored higher than the first instructor's group.

EXAMPLE 7.19

Calculating the range

For ordinal and interval level variables:

How well do you like your teacher can be measured on a 1–5 scale: 1 (not at all), 2 (dislike somewhat) 3 (neither like nor dislike) 4 (like somewhat) and 5 (like very much). If no one had picked 1 (not at all) as their response, the range is between 2 and 5 = 3 (5 – 2 = 3) (for interval) or between dislike somewhat' to 'like very much' for (ordinal).

For a ratio variable (for example, the number of hours studied per week by each of the 11 students):

0	5	6	6	7	**7**	**10**	10	10	12	20

The range is (20 – 0) = 20 hours per week.

However, the range of a data distribution is not the best way to describe variability in a set of data or values for a variable because it only considers the highest (maximum) and lowest (minimum) values of the data set and not how the data within this range are distributed (**variance**). But for ordinal variables, the range is the best statistic available. For interval and ratio variables, better statistics than range (for example, the **Standard Deviation**—SD) are available to measure the variance in the data distribution. These aspects are beyond the scope of this book, but see Field (2000) and Smith (1988) for a detailed discussion.

Handy Hints

- In order of 'power'—or the sophistication of the statistical tests that can be performed on them—the hierarchy of the levels of measurement in ascending order is nominal, ordinal, interval and ratio.
- The higher the level of measurement used (that is, interval and ratio), the wider the choice of statistical procedures available to a researcher in a given study.

- Nominal and ordinal data can only use the less powerful statistics, such as cross-tabulations (see Chapter 15), which can be used with interval and ratio data as well.
- Ratio and interval data can be easily converted into ordinals and subjected to statistical tests applicable to ordinals.
- These factors need to be kept in mind when selecting the level of measurement for variables in a proposed research project.

Try this ...

1 Using an ice cream shop and its sales as a starting point, think of one or two research questions or hypotheses you would like to examine about them. Using these research questions or hypotheses, prepare a list of variables you will need to observe and measure for the purpose. Make sure that you have at least one variable each that will fall under the nominal, ordinal, interval and ratio levels of measurement.

2 Take the latest ARIA (Australian Recording Industry Association) Top 40 list or the *New York Times* best sellers list (for books) for the current week and examine how you can use those data to create variables under each level of measurement of nominal, ordinal, interval and ratio. Hint: you can use the name of the song or book, artist/group or author, music or book genres represented in the list, the top 10 items on the list, number of weeks each song or book has been on the list and the number of records or /books sold or revenue earned during the week immediately afterwards.

3 Design Likert scales with five items on a 1–7 scale to measure the attitudes of the general public towards funding higher education by the government of your country. Hint: you may include a few questions on the value of higher education, the use of taxes to fund universities, whether public funds should be spent on education etc.

4 Design two semantic differential scales with five items each:
   a A scale to be included in the official unit evaluation at your tertiary educational institution to measure students' attitudes towards their teachers. Hint: you may include how well teachers are organised, how well they appear to know the subject matter, how approachable they are etc.
   b A scale to examine how people feel about using different biometric devices in various everyday functions. Hint: biometric devices include fingerprints, retina and eye scans, and face and voice recognition, which are collected and stored as large centralised databases. They can offer convenience and efficiency and higher levels of security when accessing computers, databases, buildings and other facilities. On the other hand, they can lead to invasions of privacy, authoritarian control and violation of civil liberties if misused or abused, or they fall into the wrong hands.

5 Examine the variables listed in Example 7.1 related to the concept of a 'keen student'. Identify the level of measurement involved in each; for example, how many hours they study.

Summary

This chapter examined the issues related to measurement and the various levels of measurement such as nominal, ordinal, interval and ratio. The measures of central tendency of a distribution of data such as the mean, median and mode and range were discussed briefly. The next chapter examines the quantitative research method of surveys.

Further reading

Adler, E S & Clark, R 2008. *How it's done: An invitation to social research*, 3rd edn. Wadsworth-Thomson, Belmont, CA (pp. 103–66).

Clegg, F 1982. *Simple statistics: A course book for the social sciences,* Cambridge University Press, New York.

Field, A 2000. *Discovering statistics: Using SPSS for Windows*. Sage, London.

Mazzocchi, M 2008. *Statistics for marketing and consumer research,* Sage, Newbury Park, CA.

Sarantakos, S 2005. *Social research*, 3rd edn. Pelgrave Macmillan, New York (pp. 72–100).

Smith, G 1988. *Statistical reasoning*, 2nd edn. Allyn & Bacon, Boston, MA.

Wimmer, R D & Dominick, J R 2006. *Mass media research: An introduction*, 8th edn. Wadsworth-Thomson, Belmont, CA (pp. 87–111).

Part

2

Research Approaches: Quantitative

8 Survey Research

In the previous two chapters, we discussed the topics of sampling (Chapter 6) and measurement (Chapter 7). They figure prominently in survey research, the most commonly used quantitative data collection method, which is discussed in this chapter. Therefore, it's important that you are familiar with both sampling and measurement before reading about survey research.

This chapter will introduce you to:

o functions of survey research

o survey methodology, including designing the survey instrument or questionnaire

o selecting suitable populations and samples

o administering of face-to-face and telephone interview surveys, and online and mail surveys

o issues or validity and reliability in survey research

o issues of measurement in survey questions

o advantages and disadvantages of survey research

o applications of survey research to journalism, media and communication and public relations.

FUNCTIONS OF SURVEY RESEARCH

Today, it would be very difficult to find an adult who has never participated in some form of a survey. For example, a multiple choice question (MCQ) examination that checks a student's factual knowledge of the subject matter is a form of a survey. The unit evaluation each student in a university course fills in, providing feedback on their opinions about or perceptions of the teacher and the unit, is an application of a survey questionnaire.

Case Study 8.1   IS THIS THE WORLD'S OLDEST SURVEY RESEARCH PROJECT?

Survey research carried out in the form of a census dates back to AD 1085 when William the Conqueror collected information about his English lands and tenants. In addition to individuals, this census also counted the Church, the nobility and merchants. Its aim was to calculate how much tax could be collected and who was going to pay it. The results were published in the *Domesday Book* (Feil, 2006).

Surveys are also used to collect data on consumer characteristics, such as demographic data, each time we return the owner registration card provided with an appliance we purchase. Marketers use surveys to obtain data related to consumer choices, beliefs, attitudes and behaviours when they ask us what we like or dislike about a given product and what changes we would like made to it in the future. Opinion polls are surveys conducted to gauge, for example, respondents' opinions about or preferences for various political candidates, parties or issues, and what they think about a government policy (such as stem cell research). The official census we complete in our households (once every five years in Australia) is provided in the form of a survey questionnaire.

> ## Handy Hint
>
> Surveys collect data or information about respondents' demographic characteristics, opinions, choices, preferences, goals, attitudes, beliefs, perceptions, feelings, practices, motivations, plans, personal backgrounds and behaviours to describe, compare or explain them.
>
> They answer the question 'What do people think, do or feel about a specific issue or topic?' For example, 'Would you support policies allowing for stem cell research to be conducted in Australia?' Or, 'What features will you look for when buying your next car?'

WHAT SURVEYS CAN AND CANNOT DO

Surveys cannot answer the question 'Why do people feel, think and do what they do?' because the survey findings can only indicate correlations between variables and not their cause–effect relationships with each other (see Chapter 2). For example, a correlation cannot explain why a person supports or opposes stem cell research or why respondents like specific features in their next car.

Surveys can describe and compare the relationships between variables such as gender, political party affiliation and support for stem cell research when they indicate that males supporting a specific political party appear more likely to oppose stem cell research than others. But it cannot say that opposition to stem cell research is caused by being male and a supporter of a specific political party.

The examination of cause and effect relationships between variables requires experimental research designs, when variables or factors can be controlled during the experimental situation. The research method of experimental design is not covered in this book, but interested readers can read 'Experimental research' in Wimmer and Dominick (2006: 230–54).

SURVEY METHODOLOGY

The methodology followed in survey research needs to be scientific, accurate and involve the following three steps:

1 developing the survey instrument or questionnaire
2 selecting a suitable population and sample of respondents
3 administering the survey efficiently to obtain valid and reliable data and optimal response rates

DEVELOPING THE SURVEY INSTRUMENT OR QUESTIONNAIRE

Before designing a survey instrument or questionnaire to be administered to respondents, a researcher must be clear about its context. This could be related to:

- what the research study is about—for example, the exact phenomenon to be examined in the study, such as Australians' opinions on stem cell research.
- its purpose—for example, to gauge public opinion on the issue in order to develop suitable government policies and legislation.
- research questions examined—for example, for what purposes and under what circumstances will Australians support stem cell research? Or the hypotheses tested—for example, Australians do not support the use of stem cell research due to its possible applications in human cloning.
- what information or data should be collected to examine the research questions or test hypotheses; for example:
  - demographic data of respondents such as sex, age, education, profession, religion, ethnicity, political party affiliation, income and where they live
  - support or opposition to various uses of stem cell research, such as therapeutic cloning vs human cloning
  - support or opposition to the various sources of obtaining stem cells for research, such as from foetuses or umbilical blood
  - support for the various benefits of stem cell research, such as finding a cure for Parkinson's disease or other conditions
  - what time frame do they suggest for legislation to allow stem cell research to be conducted: 0–10 years or never (zero means they should be allowed immediately).
- type of survey used—descriptive or analytic:
  - descriptive surveys discover aspects about and describe the situation or phenomenon under study—for example, current public opinion in Australia on stem cell research
  - analytic surveys describe and explain the interrelationships among variables and develop explanations or inferences for them such as to how individuals' opinions on stem cell research may determine their voter preferences towards political parties or candidates.
- suitable language to be used in the wording of the survey—for example, can the target population of the survey easily understand the survey questions, instructions and terms used?
- time taken to complete the survey—for example, the length of the survey should fit the time suggested as required to complete it: say, 20 minutes.
- whether both quantitative data (with close-ended questions where a respondent chooses the suitable response from the list provided) and qualitative data (with **open-ended questions** where the respondent's own opinions are freely expressed) are to be collected.
- how the survey is to be administered—for example, is it self-administered (meaning it is provided to respondents to complete by themselves and is in the form of a printed or internet survey) or interviewer-administered (used by an interviewer over the phone or face to face, where responses are ticked and answers to open questions written down by the interviewer)?
- method of dissemination used—for example, is the survey to be presented to respondents by mail, telephone, online (email or internet) or face to face? This factor influences the number of responses that may be provided to a survey question or item. Mailed, printed and internet surveys may have up to about ten responses to a

question, whereas telephone and face-to-face surveys should have no more than four or five, as the telephone and face-to-face respondents cannot 'see' all the responses together as a list before making their selection.

Designing the survey instrument: public opinion on stem cell research

EXAMPLE 8.1

As this survey is related to stem cell research, a general explanation—about what stem cell research is, what it can and cannot do, arguments for and against its uses and the current debates on the subject—is provided in the 'plain language statement' and at the beginning of the survey to make sure respondents are clear about what the relevant issues are. The survey also provides clear instructions on how to complete it.

The research questions posed or hypotheses tested in the project shape how the survey is designed and what questions are included. Each survey question uses a specific type of measurement for its variables, such as nominal, ordinal, interval and ratio (see Chapter 7). The survey contains both closed- and open-ended questions. For example, the survey asks the following **closed-ended questions**:

1 What is your sex?
 a male   **b** female
 Therefore, sex is measured as a nominal variable.

2 What age group do you belong to?
 a 18–30 years
 b 31–40 years
 c 41–50 years
 d 51–60 years
 e 61 years and above
 The age group is measured as an ordinal variable.

3 I believe that the potential benefits of stem cell research to society are:
 Low   1   2   3   4   5   High
 The above is an interval variable that is measured on a scale of 1 to 5.

4 I think we should allow stem cell research to be conducted in Australia in the next _____ years. (Please indicate the number of years from zero (0) to ten (10). You may write 'never' if you think it should never be allowed. Zero (0) years means it should be allowed immediately.)   The above is a ratio variable.

The following is an open-ended question that may be posed to respondents:

5 I think stem cell research is _____
 _____
 _____

How to organise the survey questionnaire   The organisation of the questionnaire or survey instrument influences how respondents answer the questions. This relates to its layout and design, instructions provided, question order and contingency order. Pre-testing the survey with a few respondents from the target population helps to fine-tune the instrument and spot any problems.

Layout and design The layout of the survey should be attractive and be 'uncluttered'. Remember you want the respondents to feel encouraged to complete it, so you need to win them over. People would rather complete a long survey than a 'hard to read' one.

Providing instructions Respondents need some instructions to follow when completing the survey. So provide detailed guidelines as necessary. For example, when providing interval measures to survey questions, you need to indicate that they are expected to choose a number between 1 and 5 to fit their opinion.

Question order Sometimes, the demographic questions that are easy to answer are listed at the beginning of the survey (**reverse funnel format**) while other times they appear at the end (**funnel format**). The decision depends on the population being surveyed and the topic under examination. The higher educated prefer the funnel format while others prefer the reverse funnel format. In the case of sensitive questions or controversial topics, the reverse funnel format is recommended.

When listing questions in the survey, make sure their order makes sense. Group those on the same topic together. Sometimes the order in which the questions are posed influence the responses—especially those of the less educated.

EXAMPLE 8.2

Question order

In a student evaluation survey, there were three questions related to the opinions of the student about the class. They are:

1 The unit was enjoyable.

Strongly disagree	1	2	3	4	5	Strongly agree

2 The mark you received for the latest assignment in this class was:
 a below 50%
 b 51–59%
 c 60–69%
 d 70–79%
 e 80% and above

3 How often did you attend lectures in this class? (The class had 13 lectures.)
 a never
 b rarely (1–3 times)
 c sometimes (4–6 times)
 d most of the time (7–10 times)
 e regularly (11–13 times)

If question 1 was listed last, the response could be somewhat different from if it was listed first, as the student may feel differently about indicating how enjoyable it was when they had indicated not having attended class regularly and/or receiving a lower grade.

Contingency ordering Sometimes, the responses given to a question makes the question (or questions) im-mediately following it not applicable to a respondent. In such a case, the respondent needs to skip them and directed to 'go to' the next relevant question. These are known as '**filter questions**' and require **contingency ordering**.

Contingency ordering

EXAMPLE 8.3

These four questions appeared in a survey about the adoption and diffusion of new communication technologies.

1 Do you use email?
   a yes
   b no (go to question 4)

2 How often do you use email?
   a several times a day
   b once a day
   c several times a week
   d once a week
   e rarely

3 Who is your internet service provider (ISP)?
   a Big Pond
   b iPrimus
   c OzEmail
   d Optus
   e other _____ (please fill in)

4 Do you use a mobile phone?
   a yes
   b no

If the respondent does not use email, questions 2 and 3 will be irrelevant to them and should be skipped. So question 1 as a filter question tells the respondent to skip questions 2 and 3 and go to question 4.

SELECTING A SUITABLE POPULATION AND A SAMPLE

When planning a survey, the target population needs to be identified (for example, registered voters), along with the sampling frame (for example, the list of registered voters). A suitable **sampling method** also needs to be chosen, based on the purpose of the study—such as an **exploratory study** (when a convenience sample may be adequate) or one where the researcher needs to generalise the findings to the population.

If generalisation, explanation and interpretation are the aims of the study, a proportional, stratified, representative, random sample of registered voters will be required. The sample size needs to be large enough to allow for generalisation (see Chapter 6). However, as the following case study indicates, this process may not be perfect (Kagay, 1999).

FINDING 'TYPICAL' RESPONDENTS FOR OPINION POLLS   Case Study 8.2

Opinion polls, which are commonly used to gauge the public's general views on a topic, try to use a representative and stratified sample in order to make sure their findings are valid (accurately measuring or observing what they are supposed to) and reliable (the same results obtained if repeated). They make multiple telephone calls to a household selected using random digit dialling of phone numbers, and try to reach the person they want to interview based on the respondent characteristics required for the sample. They leave messages, make appointments and offer to call back when it is more convenient for the respondent.

However, most samples used in opinion polls include higher proportions of women, retirees, university students and members of the majority ethnic or racial group, in comparison to census figures. This is due to these individuals being home when pollsters call, being willing to talk and having the confidence to discuss political, economic or social issues with a stranger on the phone. Therefore, polls use the strategy of 'weighting'—or increasing the proportion of men, younger people, the less educated and minorities—to bring their proportions to those close to census figures. This procedure results in 'balancing' the sample.

Case Study 8.2

Some pollsters also make adjustments for the size of the households (number of people living in it) and the number of telephone lines in the home to make sure the individuals in these households and households with multiple phones will have an equal chance or probability of being included in the sample.

However, most political polls (in the USA or even Australia) are conducted only in English, which can skew the data collected and their findings as non-English-speaking people are excluded from the sample, even though they vote at elections, buy things marketed and are part of the nation's population (Kagay, 1999).

ADMINISTERING THE SURVEY

A survey can be administered as a face-to-face interview, over the phone, online (email or internet) or by mail (Wimmer & Dominick, 2006; Adler & Clark, 2008; Baxter & Babbie, 2004; Fink, 1995; Amatas, 2003).

Face-to-face survey interviews In face-to-face interviews, a trained interviewer will orally pose the questions to a respondent and record the responses. These have high response rates (80–85%) compared with mail surveys, which have low response rates (50–70%) and are useful when the respondents (such as children, the elderly and those not literate enough to read a survey) may not be able to read and answer the questions themselves. Face-to-face interviews are also useful because they reduce '**missing data**', which is where respondents leave questions blank or choose the 'don't know' response when they do not understand the question. A face-to-face interviewer is able to clarify a question for a respondent and ask for more details when the response given is not sufficiently clear for the research purpose.

In a face-to-face survey interview, interviewers should present themselves positively in grooming and temperament, and be dressed similarly to their target population to appear non-threatening. For example, if the interviews are conducted at a shopping mall during a weekend, an interviewer should be clothed as a casual but well-dressed shopper.

Interviewers should not assume the demographic and other details of respondents, such as their age group, ethnicity or education, during face-to-face interviews but ask the respondent to choose the category they belong to. For example, once at a shopping mall in Philadelphia I was interviewed by a young woman to survey my preferences for eye glasses. (I fit the target population as I wear them.) She tried to write down my race/ethnicity as 'Latina', assuming I was of Spanish origin, which is inaccurate.

Telephone interview surveys Telephone interviewers, too, should be properly trained to ask the questions effectively and gather the necessary data. Telephone surveys are best for short surveys and when a follow-up data collection or clarification is needed. Telephone surveys can be administered to respondents who live outside the local area of the researchers, in remote locations and unsafe neighbourhoods. They are cheaper in terms of staff costs than when hiring face-to-face interviewers because travel and related costs are not involved. However, they will incur costly phone bills if calling people long distance.

Today, however, many respondents refuse to participate in telephone surveys or hang up before the interview is completed. With the popularity of mobile phones, using only landline phone numbers from the directory as the sampling frame biases the sample and excludes those households with unlisted phones or no landline phones. This also excludes those young people who use mobile phones exclusively.

Training of interviewers   Survey interviewers—both face to face and over the phone—need to practise reading the questions with someone as a pre-test, and be familiar with the instrument and the subject matter of the study. They must have good verbal communication and people skills and be advised to write the answers to open-ended questions exactly the way they were provided—including mistakes in pronunciation and grammar. They should note any non-verbal cues that stood out during the interviews. These include tone of voice, pitch and indifference, boredom or impatience expressed.

Use of technologies in survey research   The most common method of sampling used for telephone surveys is random digit dialling (see Chapter 6). Many computer-assisted interviewing methods—both telephone and face to face—use laptop computers. Voice recognition software makes the job faster and more convenient. For a detailed discussion on such technologies see Baxter and Babbie (2004: 166–76, 184–203).

Online (email and internet) surveys   Online surveying is quicker and more cost-effective in comparison to face-to-face and telephone survey interviews and mail surveys. Sending reminders (to those not yet responded), data coding and analysis take place automatically and allow the researcher to reach a large sample worldwide. A researcher may use computer software such as *SurveyMonkey* (www.surveymonkey.com) to create a survey, collect responses and analyse the results.

However, technical failures, incompatible software, sample bias and unrepresentativeness of the sample—because the survey is limited to those with email or internet access—are among the shortcomings of online surveys. But this method could be the best suited to sample populations such as teenagers who are heavy users of websites and internet social networking sites such as Facebook and MySpace, and professionals who regularly use email and the internet at work.

The average time required for completing a survey should not exceed 15 minutes to avoid respondents losing interest and logging off halfway through the survey. For detailed discussions on online or internet surveys, see Sue and Ritter (2007).

Mail surveys   Mail surveys have the lowest response rates as people tend to ignore them or forget to complete and return them. So offering an incentive such as a gift voucher or a valuable prize in a raffle may encourage people to participate. Respondents often leave questions blank—especially open-ended questions—leading to missing data that creates problems during the data analysis. Mail surveys also need reminders sent to respondents by the end of two weeks.

Mail surveys are convenient and cheaper than telephone and face-to-face survey interviews. Both internet and mail surveys are best suited for examining sensitive and controversial topics due to the anonymity and confidentiality they provide.

LIVE AUDIENCE VOTING TECHNOLOGY FOR COLLECTING SURVEY DATA AND THE 'WORM'

Case Study 8.3

Sometimes, when collecting data for a survey from a live audience—say, at a staff-training workshop—computer software such as IML

Question Wizard 7 can be used along with a PowerPoint presentation that provides the survey questions and responses on the screen.

Case Study 8.3

Each participant is given a handset to press the corresponding number for the relevant response for each question posed.

This is similar to what we see on the TV game show *Who wants to be a millionaire?* when a contestant chooses the 'Ask the audience' option. Audience members indicate the response to a question they think is the correct answer by using a handset. The software immediately calculates the frequencies and percentages of the various responses, anonymously entered by the participants, while in a live group setting.

The software can instantly provide graphs and cross-tabulations of the data collected. However, at the moment, the number of responses that can be provided to a survey question is four or less, which is a limitation of this technology (Australian Bureau of Statistics, 2007a).

The 'Worm' used by the studio audience during televised political debates to indicate their interest in what is being said by a speaker is another example of this technology.

ISSUES OF RELIABILITY AND VALIDITY IN SURVEY RESEARCH

The data collected from survey respondents are '**self-reports**', which are not always accurate or reliable—irrespective of whether the survey was self-administered or researcher-administered. Problems with the design of the survey instrument can also lead to contamination of data. Therefore, the following facts must be taken into account.

UNRELIABILITY OF RESPONSES

Most survey questions require respondents to recall past events which they may have forgotten or only partly remember. They may not provide the correct information if they consider it personal or private, such as their real age or income. Sometimes they may misunderstand the question or be affected by their emotional state at the moment. For example, answers given to a question on an opinion or attitude may vary depending on how they feel at the time (for example, happy, sad, tired, hungry, busy, bored or annoyed). Respondents may change their mind about an issue as they learn new information about it while completing the survey. This leads to inconsistent opinions.

THE SOCIAL DESIRABILITY EFFECT

We all want to look and feel good when among others and a respondent may give answers that are 'politically correct' or 'sound good'. This is called the **social desirability effect**. For example, people may not express prejudiced views to a researcher as they know they are not acceptable. What people say and actually do are not always the same. They may also reply assuming that's what the researcher wants to hear.

Respondents also might leave a question blank, leading to non-response and missing data, especially when survey questions relate to:

- sensitive issues—for example, HIV-positive status
- respondents who are marginalised or powerless—for example, victims of domestic violence or rape, and the poor
- stigmatised groups—for example, the unemployed or welfare recipients
- immoral or illegal behaviours—for example, adultery or corruption
- minority views—for example, opposition to a popularly held policy or view.

HOW QUESTIONS ARE WORDED

The same question worded differently can lead to different answers from respondents. For example, the questions 'What is your age?', 'How old are you?' and 'What age group do you belong to?' may lead people to answer the question differently. For example, those who are sensitive about telling people their age may lower their real age in the first two questions but may give the true answer in the third. Giving false answers to one's age can affect the data analysis and findings as well as their interpretations when the researchers calculate the mean, median and mode for age in the sample of respondents.

'**Push polling**' is a strategy of using specific words, phrases or facts in a way that they create a specific impression or perception of what is being discussed in the mind of the respondents. It is an unethical practice that's often used in political campaigning, where a specific question with specific words is used to deliberately create the desired (and generally negative) impression in the respondent's or voter's mind. Often these push polls are not real, and are carried out just before an election. The Australian Social and Market Research Institute Code of Professional Practice does not approve of push polling.

PUSH POLLING THE MAYOR'S 'ACCENT'   Case Study 8.4

A few years ago, just before the election for the City of Melbourne, push polling allegedly was carried out by the main opposition party against the incumbent mayor. It asked voters, 'Do you think (the Hong Kong-born, ethnic-Chinese) Mayor John So's (English) accent is an embarrassment to Melbourne?'

Surveys should also avoid using **negative wording**. For example, use 'Should we do X?' instead of 'Should we not do X?', which is confusing.

Biased wording that gives a positive or negative connotation (implied meaning) in a survey question should be avoided. For example, 'Several medical experts at the Royal Melbourne Hospital say X. Do you agree?' indicates the importance or validity of the fact provided, which biases the question and influences the respondent.

Use of neutral terms can protect a survey question from bias. For example, instead of saying 'working poor' say 'low-income earners'.

LACK OF CLARITY OF TERMS USED

If respondents find the wording in survey questions ambiguous or unclear, they can misinterpret them. Therefore, surveys should avoid words such as 'may' and 'shall', and clearly define what they mean.

For example, instead of asking 'What TV programs do you watch regularly?', ask them to 'Name the TV programs you watched last night'. Be specific with time periods and avoid phrases such as 'a typical day' or measures such as 'a serving of food'.

Survey questions should avoid the use of abbreviations (for example, 'resi' for a university student residence or 'dorm' for dormitory) and acronyms (for example, DBCDE for the Department of Broadband, Communications and the Digital Economy), without explaining them.

RESPONDENTS CHOOSING A RESPONSE SET

Some respondents feeling obliged, bored or too lazy to fill in a survey will do it randomly—often without reading the questions. They may choose the same response—say response number three for all the questions or mark them as 1, 2, 3, 4, 5, 1, 2, 3, etc for consecutive questions. This is called a **response set**.

A well-known application of a response set in Australia is the 'donkey vote'.

Case Study 8.5   CASTING THE 'DONKEY VOTE'

In Australian federal elections, it is compulsory to vote and to indicate preferences for each of the candidates on the ballot paper for the House of Representatives. Political parties generally provide their 'How to vote' cards indicating the party's preferred order of preference for each electorate.

However, some voters cast a 'donkey vote' by giving their first preference to the candidate whose name appears first in the list of candidates, their second to the next one and

so on. This list of candidates is prepared in a random order.

Anecdotal evidence suggests that most candidates wish to be the first name on the list, hoping to get some donkey votes. To avoid the donkey vote benefiting the person lucky enough to be listed first, some propose different versions of the voting card to be printed.

This principle is often applied in setting examinations using multiple choice questions (MCQ) to discourage cheating.

AVOIDING CULTURAL BIAS

In a globalised world, we need to be aware that our survey, especially if it is on the internet, may reach a diversity of respondents—including those from overseas. Therefore, we need to be careful when using slang terms, jargon, acronyms, unconventional spelling and complex grammar and punctuation, and make sure to either avoid them or have them explained in simple English. Any technical terms or policies must be explained to avoid misinterpretations.

The survey should also fit the language competencies of the target population, as the same word can mean different things to different people, based on cultural differences. Some topics such as personal details or issues such as domestic violence or rape may be considered sensitive or even taboo for discussion with a stranger or an outsider in certain cultures. This can cause offence when included in a survey and should be kept in mind when designing it.

EXAMPLE 8.4

The 'Big Brother' of many kinds

The term 'Big Brother' may mean different things to different people based on cultural and individual differences and subjectivity. For example, it can be taken as the Big Brother in George Orwell's *Nineteen eighty-four* (Orwell, 1949), the popular reality TV program of the same name, or one's older brother. Therefore, such terms need to be defined clearly.

RESPONSES OF UNQUALIFIED RESPONDENTS

Sometimes, respondents may answer a question to which they do not know the answer by randomly picking one response or simply guessing the answer. To avoid such situations include additional responses such as 'don't know', 'not sure' or 'not applicable'.

RELIABILITY OF DATA COLLECTION

Reliability of the data collection can be maintained by training the survey interviewers well and uniformly to conduct the interviews the same way. Asking an expert and a few potential respondents to check the instrument will help spot problems.

BORROWING FROM EXISTING RESEARCH

Using categories of variables, survey questions or even entire surveys used in earlier studies—with a few additional questions to fit your specific purposes or questions from the census—can help researchers compare their findings with those of previous studies. This is most useful for demographic variables.

Using the categories of measurement—or the list of responses used for measuring demographic variables in the national census or landmark research projects—is useful because these surveys, variables and categories of responses have been tested and proven valid and reliable.

COUNTRY OF BIRTH OF AUSTRALIANS: CENSUS CATEGORIES   Case Study 8.6

The Australian Census on 8 August 2006 collected data on the country of birth of respondents. Even though the Australian population consists of people who originated from almost every country in the world, the responses provided in the census form were limited to seven countries. They were Australia, England, New Zealand, Italy, Vietnam, Scotland, Greece and Other _____ (where the respondent has to fill in the answer).

This is based on previous census figures that identified these seven countries as the most common ones in which Australian were born (Australian Bureau of Statistics, 2006).

Therefore, in a future research project where data needs to be collected on a person's country of birth, these seven responses can be used, which will make the number of responses manageable and the findings easily comparable with those of the census.

ISSUES OF MEASUREMENT IN SURVEY RESEARCH

Several issues related to measurement (see Chapter 7) apply to the design of survey questionnaires. These include:

- mutually exclusive categories of responses
- matching responses to the survey question
- logical order of responses
- avoiding **double-barrelled (two-edged) questions** (Baxter & Babbie, 2004; Fink, 1995).

MUTUALLY EXCLUSIVE CATEGORIES

Responses provided to survey questions should be mutually exclusive. This means the data collected can fit only one response in a given question.

Mutually exclusive categories of responses: income brackets

Income levels of respondents can be measured as:

a below $25,000 per year   **b** $25,000–$40,000 per year (etc).

However, a respondent earning $25,000 may wonder where his income will fit within the first or second response. Therefore, these categories need to be rephrased as:

a below $25,000 per year   **b** $25,001–$40,000 per year (etc).

MATCHING THE RESPONSES TO THE SURVEY QUESTION

Matching responses to the question relates to the validity of a measurement or the answer to the question, 'Are we measuring what we are supposed to measure?'

Matching responses to the survey question

The question 'How often do you use the internet?' should have the responses:

a less than once a week   and not:
b once a week   **a** not at all
c several times a week   **b** a little
d once a day   **c** somewhat competent
e several times a day   **d** very competent

which fits the question, 'How competent are you in the use of the internet?'

LOGICAL ORDER OF RESPONSES

The responses to a survey question should be listed in a logical order indicating an observable continuum; that is, low to high or high to low. This relates only to ordinal, interval and ratio measurements, which have a ranking order, and not to nominal categories, which are equal as they are simply 'names' (see Chapter 7).

The logical order of responses for a survey question: income brackets

When listing income brackets, they should begin from the lowest and end with the highest:

a below $25,000   **d** $60,001–$80,000
b $25,001–$40,000   **e** $80,0001 and above.
c $40,001–$60,000

AVOIDING DOUBLE-BARRELLED (TWO-EDGED) QUESTIONS

A single survey question should only pose one issue at a time. It should not combine questions or issues as the respondent may have different views on each issue.

A double-barrelled question

EXAMPLE 8.8

The following survey question is a double-barrelled one.

'Pay (subscription) TV regulation must strive for community standards and protect the public interest with anti-siphoning laws.'

Completely disagree	1	2	3	4	5	Completely agree

The correct format should be:

'Pay (subscription) TV regulation must strive for community standards.'

Completely disagree	1	2	3	4	5	Completely agree

'Pay (subscription) TV regulation must strive to protect the public interest with anti-siphoning laws.'

Completely disagree	1	2	3	4	5	Completely agree

ADVANTAGES AND DISADVANTAGES OF SURVEY RESEARCH

Just like any other research method, survey research has its advantages and disadvantages.

ADVANTAGES OF SURVEY RESEARCH

The advantages of the survey research method are:

- Large amounts of data can be collected from large samples and large populations in a cost-effective way.
- Characteristics of large, diverse, populations can be described.
- Information about attitudes, opinions, lifestyles, goals, demographic data, beliefs, perceptions, preferences and behaviours can be collected.
- Flexibility in design allows a large number of questions to be posed to a large number of people in one survey.
- Phenomena can be examined in real settings instead of in experimental settings.
- Data collected from a census or other survey can be used in later studies as **secondary analysis** for other research questions or hypotheses.

DISADVANTAGES OF SURVEY RESEARCH

The disadvantages of the survey research method are:

- Data collection is based on self-reports of respondents, which are not always accurate or reliable.
- An inability to manipulate variables creates an inability to provide cause–effect explanations.
- A survey may be responded to by those outside the target population, resulting in data contamination—especially in online surveys.
- Low response rates lead to unrepresentative samples.
- Sensitive and controversial topics are unsuitable for examination.
- The researcher can only collect data on past, future or hypothetical actions, not present or current actions.

- Missing data or non-responses result when respondents fail to answer all questions, creating problems during the data analysis. (Some data analysis software allow for the substitution of the mean or median value of the variables for missing data, which somewhat manages this problem.)

Case Study 8.7   MISSING DATA: 'FUNNY' OR NON-RESPONSES IN CENSUS DATA

Taking a census is considered the ideal situation in survey research as every single member of the population is included in the sample, avoiding sampling error. The government makes respondents understand the importance of providing their data via public information campaigns. Respondents are assured that the anonymity and confidentiality of their information and census data are protected by specific laws and legislation. Respondents also receive ample time and instructions to complete the census form and can seek help from census staff if necessary. In spite of all these precautions, the census still has some respondents giving 'Jedi Knight' (from *Star wars*) or 'Klingon' (from the TV series *Star trek*) as responses to some of their demographic data.

A census also has some questions left blank by a significant percentage of respondents to whom the question is relevant (applicable), which is called a non-response. For example, in the 8 August 2006 Australian Census, several questions had significant levels of non-responses. The percentage of people who fail to respond to a census question that is applicable to them is referred to as the '**non-response rate**'.

The significant non-response rates given in percentages included the following variables:

o   residential status in a non-private dwelling (15.44%)

o   religious affiliation (11.20%)

o   unpaid domestic work (10.12%)

o   highest year of school completed (9.88%)

o   individual income (8.90%)

o   full-time/part-time student status (7.49%)

o   country of birth (7.01%)

o   number of children ever born (6.87%)

o   age (4.91%) (Australian Bureau of Statistics, 2007b).

These non-response rates affect the findings of the census that are used in policy making for the future. These may include calculating the value of unpaid domestic work for taxation, Centrelink payments (government support) or other financial purposes. The same applies for the figures on non-private housing (residential status), fertility levels (number of children born), level of education of Australians, student numbers in Australia, the mean (average) and median age of Australians, and the average individual income of the population.

APPLICATIONS OF SURVEY RESEARCH IN JOURNALISM, MEDIA AND COMMUNICATION, AND PUBLIC RELATIONS

Survey research is widely applied in journalism, media and communication, and public relations. The following are a few examples from actual research studies.

JOURNALISM

Journalists in small media organisations may carry out phone surveys on various current issues and report on them. Others in larger organisations regularly commission surveys and/or report on polls and survey findings provided by pollsters and researchers in their news reports and analyses. Therefore, a journalist needs to be well versed in how to evaluate poll figures or survey results and be able to check the validity, reliability and generalisability of such research findings.

Surveys are often used to study the profession of journalism, gauging the opinions of journalists, editors and publishers about their work and skills used and required in their everyday tasks. News workers' job satisfaction has regularly been surveyed in order to examine specific trends and relevant factors. Surveys have also been used to examine what the journalism profession believes should be included in the curriculum of journalism degree programs and which qualities and attitudes the journalism profession expects from new and future graduates.

David H Weaver and G Cleveland Wilhoit (1986, 1996, 2006) surveyed US journalists for their project on 'The American Journalist' once every decade for comparison. These have become landmark studies providing useful data to track the evolution of the profession in the USA.

THE GLOBAL JOURNALIST: NEWS PEOPLE ACROSS THE WORLD — Case Study 8.8

Edited by David H Weaver (1998), the book *The global journalist: News people across the world* reports on a survey of journalists in 23 countries from the Far East/Asia, Australia/Pacific, Europe, North Africa, North America, and South and Central America. The researchers taking part in this cross-cultural study used the US surveys of Weaver and Wilhoit (1992) as a guide, which allowed for comparisons between different countries.

The book's chapter on Australia, by John Henningham (1998), reports the findings of a 1992 telephone survey of 1068 news people with a response rate of 90%. Henningham concluded that Australian journalists are similar to those in other Western democracies in many demographic characteristics. They were more likely to disapprove of the use of deceit than US journalists and strongly support protection of confidential sources. Australian journalists' main challenge at the time was to convince the Australian public of the importance of their work in terms of their professional and ethical commitment.

MEDIA AND COMMUNICATIONS

Surveys are often used to gauge media consumption, audience opinions on specific media content and technologies, and the level of adoption and diffusion of new communication technologies. For example, the 8 August 2006 Australian Census examined household internet connections to gauge the adoption and diffusion of the internet in Australian homes.

THE ADOPTION AND DIFFUSION OF INTERNET IN AUSTRALIAN HOMES — Case Study 8.9

The 8 August 2006 Census in Australia included the question:

'Can the internet be accessed in this dwelling?' (Question 59.)

The responses provided were:

1 No internet connection

2 Yes, broadband connection (including ADSL, cable, wireless and satellite connections)

Case Study 8.9

3 Yes, dial-up connection (including analogue modem and ISDN connections)

4 Other (includes internet access through mobile phones).

(Australian Bureau of Statistics, 2006).

Using census data collected for this question and those related to respondents' demographic and other variables for the Australian population, a researcher is able to carry out a secondary analysis describing the profile of those households that had adopted the technology and the type of connections used. They can also compare the differences between adopter and non-adopter households with reference to their demographic and other factors.

Media and communications in Australian families The Media and Society Research Project (Commonwealth of Australia, 2007b) surveyed media and communications in Australian families and concluded that 'Australian families are media rich, with multiple communications devices in the home, value the internet and are striking a comfortable balance in their children's media use' (Australian Communications and Media Authority, 2007).

PUBLIC RELATIONS

Survey research is often used in public relations as **introspective research** when examining itself (Wimmer & Dominick, 2006). (Also see Case Study 8.10.) Surveys are one of the social research methods used in public relations practice to understand the environment they operate in and how to or how well it is communicating with its target publics. Most public relations research is conducted by independent research companies.

EXPLORATORY SURVEYS

Exploratory surveys gauge a target public's attitudes towards and knowledge of an issue; for example, road safety. In conjunction with data collected from other methods, such as focus groups, the findings help develop campaign materials, such as advertising, brochures and booklets, to support the program.

PROGRAM EVALUATION

Program evaluation helps to develop, monitor and evaluate a program or public relations campaign. Surveys are used in 'evaluation research' or 'program evaluation' to examine what communication tactics should be used, and what will appeal best to the target public. An important step is to set a benchmark at the beginning of the program so that any changes can be measured during and after the program has been implemented.

Once the campaign is under way, a 'tracking survey' is conducted to check 'Where the target public is (located)', 'Is there an awareness (of the issue within the target public)?' and 'What are their related attitudes and particular behaviours?'

To gauge if the campaign goals have been achieved, an evaluation will be conducted at the end of the campaign to examine its impact and to see if any changes have taken place to people's knowledge or attitudes on the topic as a result of the campaign.

Surveys have been used to gather opinions of members of the Public Relations Student Society of America and professionals in the Public Relations Society of America about the proper roles of public relations practitioners, public relations education and professional socialisation (Berkowitz & Hristodoulakis, 1999). Other surveys have examined how public relations practitioners have been involved in strategic management in various speciality areas in the UK (Moss, Warnaby & Newman, 2000). Still others have surveyed how women public relations professionals feel about the 'glass ceiling' in their profession (Wrigley, 2002).

Summary

This chapter examined the functions of survey research, and the procedures and guidelines to be followed in designing survey questionnaires and conducting telephone and face-to-face interview surveys, and online and internet surveys. Thereafter, it examined the issues of reliability and validity of surveys, data collection and measurement. The advantages and disadvantages of survey research were discussed and examples examined of the application of the survey research method in journalism, media and communication and public relations.

The next chapter is devoted to the quantitative research method of content analysis.

Try this . . .

An audience survey of a popular TV comedy: *Kath & Kim*

Kath & Kim is a popular Australian TV comedy. The series is about a suburban mother Kath Day-Knight (Jane Turner) and her adult daughter Kim Craig (Gina Riley), their respective spouses Kel and Brett, Kim and Brett's baby daughter Epponnee Rae and Kim's friend and netball-mad single woman Sharon.

In order to examine the audience appeal of this TV comedy, a researcher can use a survey to examine specific research questions, using a suitable sample including both fans and non-viewers of the show, and develop a demographic profile of the fans as well as non-viewers. This will provide a description and comparison of its fan base and an explanation of its appeal.

1   Write one or two research questions you would like to examine in your study.

2   Design a survey questionnaire that is comprehensive and includes both open- and closed-ended questions related to various topic areas that can answer your research questions. Follow the principles of survey research and guidelines discussed in the chapter, with respect to survey design, sampling and administering of the survey.

3   Make note of relevant issues of validity, reliability and measurement involved when designing the survey questions.

The following guidelines will help you design suitable survey questions and their respective response categories. Feel free to add any others if you wish to.

$\longrightarrow$

4   Design survey questions to collect data on the various demographic groups the respondents belong to, such as age, sex, where they live, level of education, profession and income level. You could also collect data on: other programs watched; time spent watching TV; how often the respondents have watched the program (regularly, often, sometimes, rarely, never); how they watch the show (alone at home, with family, with other residents of your household, with friends at a specific venue etc); what they do while watching (have snacks, dinner, socialise etc); whether they record the program if they cannot watch it at the time of broadcast; and whether they record it anyway and watch again later or record it for others.

These data should help you examine the demographic differences and similarities between fans and non-viewers of *Kath & Kim* and how viewers appear to be consuming (watching) and enjoying the process of watching the show—in addition to enjoying just the program. You may want to compare the characteristics of the show's fans (regular viewers), occasional viewers and those who have never watched the program; if so, that also needs to be measured. Remember to use filter questions and contingency ordering, as applicable, to fit those who do not regularly watch it or have never watched it.

5   Design a few open-ended questions to ask why they watch it or why they don't.

6   Design a few questions to examine: which character is their favourite; what their favourite storyline or episode is and why; what aspects of the show do they find most funny; what they most and least like about the show; who their favourite celebrity guest stars are etc.

7   Design survey questions that may help you to explain why it is so popular based on what fans say they like about it.

Note: You may substitute *Kath & Kim* for another popular program of your choice—produced locally or overseas. It is best to choose a program you watch regularly and are a fan of because you will then identify many additional and relevant areas and factors that can be examined in the survey.

Further reading

Fowler, F J 1990. *Standard survey interviewing: Minimizing interviewer related error*. Sage, Newbury Park, CA.

Sapsford, R 2006. *Survey research*, 2nd ed. Sage, Thousand Oaks, CA.

Stacks, D W 2002. *Primer of public relations research*, Guildford Press, New York.

Sue, V M & Ritter, L A 2007. *Conducting online surveys*. Sage, Thousand Oaks, CA.

Weaver, D H & Wilhoit, G C 1992. *The American journalist in the 1990s: A preliminary report of key findings from the 1992 national survey of US journalists*. The Freedom Forum, Arlington, VA.

Wilhoit, G C & Weaver, D H 1990. *Newsroom guide to polls and surveys*. Indiana University Press, Bloomington, IN.

Content Analysis

In Chapter 8, we discussed the quantitative research method of surveys. This chapter is devoted to content analysis—the other quantitative research method covered in this book.

Just as when reading the chapter on surveys, this chapter also requires you to be familiar with sampling (Chapter 6) and measurement (Chapter 7) as well as surveys (Chapter 8), as the procedures followed in the survey method share many similarities with content analysis.

This chapter examines the following:

o everyday applications of content analysis

o functions of content analysis

o manifest and **latent content** of messages

o how to conduct a content analysis

o practical uses of content analysis

o limitations of content analysis

o lists of archives of media content

o applications of content analysis in journalism, media and communication, and public relations.

EVERYDAY APPLICATIONS OF CONTENT ANALYSIS

You may be new to the concept of content analysis as a research method, but its applications in everyday life are familiar to all of us. For example, each time you carry out a Google search using keywords or phrases in a sequence, or use the 'Find' function in word processing to search for a word or phrase in a document, you benefit from of an application of content analysis. Similarly, every time you search a library's electronic or other catalogue using the keyword, title, or author search you are utilising an application of content analysis.

Try this …

Carry out a Google search under your name, or of someone you know who is not famous, to find where that name has appeared in published form. You will be surprised with what you find! See how many of the entries (if found) are linked to that person and how many are not.

APPLICATIONS IN SURVEILLANCE

In the film *The Bourne ultimatum* (Gilroy, Burns & Greengrass, 2007), there is a scene where the journalist from the UK's *Guardian* newspaper, Simon Ross (played by Paddy Considine), speaks on his mobile phone referring to 'Blackbriar'—a secret training program of the CIA. Immediately, the computer surveillance system at the CIA headquarters becomes active because it has been programmed to detect any mention of the word. In an era of war on terror, such voice recognition and other software are widely used by law enforcement agencies to track mobile and landline phone conversations, email or chat-room discussions in which suspected individuals, convicts in prisons and others participate.

Credit card companies also use computer software to detect unusual spending with individual credit cards, indicating theft or fraud by unauthorised users. This system uses the principle of content analysis.

Case Study 9.1 CONTENT ANALYSIS IN FORENSIC LITERARY STUDIES

Content analysis was used in forensic literary studies (or forensic linguistics as authorship studies or attribution studies) to uncover the real author of the novel *Primary colors* (Anonymous, 1996) published as 'Anonymous' by Joe Klein, a journalist with the *Washington Post*. Don Foster used '**Stylometrics**' to compare and match the stylistic aspects of the novel with the author's known work. The novel is a fictionalised version of Bill Clinton's 1992 presidential primary election campaign and was made into the 1998 film with John Travolta as presidential candidate Jack Stanton. Forensic literary studies are often used by law enforcement agencies to check the authenticity of various documents and attribution of their authorship (Vickers, 2002).

Handy Hint

Content analysis is the research method used in analysing mass media or other messages or texts in a systematic, objective and quantitative manner to measure and compare variable categories of the message characteristics. It uses specific and uniform rules and scientifically selected samples of texts.

These rules are set out in the **coding manuals** designed using clear operational definitions of categories.

FUNCTIONS OF CONTENT ANALYSIS

Content analysis is probably the most commonly used research method of examining media messages. This technique or research method is useful because it can:

- describe the content of media or communication messages—this could be as a **longitudinal study** (see Chapter 6) examining how coverage of specific groups (for example, women or minorities) or issues (for example, poverty or unemployment) have changed over time or remained the same. Other elements, such as interpersonal interactions between professionals and clients, can be examined for areas for improvement.
- examine research questions or test hypotheses—for example, 'How did the Australian media cover the 2008 Beijing Olympics, with reference to the Australian team and their performance?' (research question); and 'The Australian media's coverage of the 2008 Beijing Olympics was exclusively concentrated on the Australian team and their successes' (hypothesis).

- Compare media representations of groups, issues and events to their real-world occurrences—using statistical figures, content analysis compares the media and real-world occurrences of particular groups, issues and events. For example, in TV programming, professionals such as doctors, lawyers and media workers far outnumber their real-life figures; portrayal of minorities in TV or films is well below their population figures; and the incidence of violent crime is much higher in media portrayals in comparison with real-life statistics.

MT THOMAS: THE 'CRIME CAPITAL OF AUSTRALIA'   Case Study 9.2

The popular Australian TV police drama *Blue Heelers* (1994–2006) was set in the fictional, rural Victorian town of Mt Thomas. An actor playing a female police officer said that her friends who are real-life police officers call Mt Thomas 'the crime capital of Australia' due to the violent and unusual crime scenarios depicted in its storylines. This is common in TV or films and is designed to create dramatic effect and audience appeal. Content analysis can examine and compare its depictions of violent crime with real-life crime statistics for a town similar to Mt Thomas.

- Examine the images of specific groups in society in media messages—generally applied to marginalised, powerless or stigmatised groups. Content analysis examines how these groups are depicted in media images and if changes have occurred across time; for example, examining how gays have been represented in Hollywood films across time and the correlation of these representations with laws and public attitudes towards gays at various times in history.

FILE TAPES OF 'ABORIGINALS DRINKING' AND QUEENSLAND TV NEWS Case Study 9.3

Using a content analysis of file tapes, Peter Putnis (1994) examined how Queensland TV news programs depicted Aboriginal people, which was predominantly negative. The people were often shown sitting in groups under a tree, walking around or generally doing nothing. The tape librarian at one TV station had created a category of 'Aboriginals drinking' for classifying video clips, because she was always asked for such visuals.

- Serve as a starting point for researching media effects—results obtained from a content analysis of media messages can be used for future studies to examine media effects. This is because media content analysis can only describe what is depicted—not predict what it can do to audiences. Content analysis can also only describe what media messages were 'transmitted' and not if audience members actually 'received' or 'reacted' to them in anyway. Therefore, further studies using depth interviews, focus groups, field studies, surveys or case studies are carried out to examine what audience members think about specific media messages or the groups, issues and events depicted in the media—and the match between what is depicted and what audiences think. In other words, content analysis can lead to research examining the relationships between the media agenda and the audience agenda.

Case Study 9.4 EFFECTS OF VIEWING *THE COSBY SHOW*

A longitudinal study of a content analysis of African-American families depicted on US TV indicated that they have become more positive, culminating with *The Cosby show* (1984–1992), where the lead couple were wealthy professionals—a doctor and a lawyer.

In a further study examining the effects of such positive portrayals of minorities using focus groups of white people, Sut Jhally and Justin Lewis (1992) found that some subjects saw the Cosbys' success as due to Affirmative Action policies adopted since the Civil Rights Laws of 1965 eliminating barriers to minority advancement. Some subjects argued that, therefore, if any African-Americans are still poor and disadvantaged, it must be due to their own fault of being lazy, rather than due to continued discrimination or lack of opportunities.

On the other hand, in apartheid South Africa, whites watching *The Cosby show* began to question the assumption in their society about blacks being inherently less intelligent and incapable of professional success or higher education, which had justified the black population's marginalised status and state-imposed apartheid policies (de Klerk, 1998).

These examples indicate that audiences interpret a given media message in different ways and media effects are not unitary for the same messages.

MANIFEST VS LATENT CONTENT OF MESSAGES

Content analysis can be both quantitative and qualitative. Quantitative content analysis involves the examination of **manifest content**—the literal, denotative, generally accepted and shared meanings of a message, such as of a word, phrase, speech, advertisement or other media message. Quantitative content analysis involves 'counting' to describe the manifest content and measure the 'amounts' of the categories of variables empirically and systematically. That means examining a systematically selected sample of messages using our senses of sight and hearing rather than anecdotal evidence.

Large organisations, such as corporations or government departments, hire a **media monitoring** company to content analyse media portrayals of their organisations and to have them grouped into positive, negative and neutral depictions to 'track' them for public relations purposes. (See www.mediamonitors.com.au for examples of how they operate.)

The latent content of a message is the hidden, implied, connotative meanings of the message and is analysed qualitatively using rhetorical analysis, narrative analysis, discourse analysis, structuralist or semiotic analysis, interpretative analysis, conversation analysis and normative analysis (Neuendorf, 2002). Some of these qualitative methods are discussed under textual analysis in Chapter 14.

HOW TO CONDUCT A CONTENT ANALYSIS

The procedure followed in conducting a content analysis consists of ten steps (Wimmer & Dominick, 2006), which are somewhat similar to those of survey research. Content analysis involves the preparation of a coding instrument, sampling, the levels of measurement such as nominal, ordinal, interval and ratio, data coding and data analysis. The ten steps are:

1   formulating research questions or hypotheses
2   defining the **universe**
3   sampling
4   selecting the unit of analysis
5   constructing content categories
6   levels of measurement of items and their coding categories
7   training coders and conducting a pilot study
8   coding the content and conducting **reliability checks**
9   analysing data
10 interpreting results, making conclusions and reporting the findings

Next, these steps are illustrated using a real example of a content analysis of news-paper coverage. As the principles of content analysis across media are the same, the method used in analysing newspaper content can be adapted to fit other media texts—such as magazines, TV, radio, websites, blogs, video blogs and networking sites like MySpace—as applicable.

FORMULATING RESEARCH QUESTIONS OR HYPOTHESES

A research study involving a content analysis needs good research questions or hypotheses to develop accurate and sensitive coding categories and gather the necessary data.

> **Handy Hint**
>
> A content analysis generally involves some form of comparison and should be kept in mind when designing a research study and the research questions or hypotheses to be examined.

THE CONTENT ANALYSIS OF THE COVERAGE OF THE
LOS ANGELES RIOTS BY THE *LOS ANGELES TIMES*

Case Study 9.5

On 29 April 1992, the four white officers from the Los Angeles Police Department (LAPD) accused of the widely televised beating of black motorist Rodney King were found not guilty by an all-white jury. That evening, many black residents of impoverished South Central Los Angeles took to the streets and rioted, burning and destroying property. The Los Angeles police force was conspicuously absent to enforce law and order, and the riot went on unchecked until the California Governor called the National Guard. Rioters attacked the white truck driver Reginald Denny, which was also televised live.

The following five research questions were examined in a content analysis that examined the coverage of the Los Angeles riots by the *Los Angeles Times* newspaper.

1   What was the volume of news coverage devoted to the riots from their outbreak to their conclusion?

2   What was the amount of coverage devoted to hard news, commentary, analysis, human interest and features during the riots?

3   What specific sources were most frequently relied upon in reporting the riots to local and national readers?

4   What was the incidence of photographs accompanying news stories (accounts) of the riots?

5   What were the topics that received major emphasis in the *Los Angeles Times'* coverage of the riots?

Refer to this book's Online Resources Centre (www.oup.com.au/orc/weerakkody) for the study's report in Atwater and Weerakkody (1994).

Reviewing the literature A review of literature needs to be carried out to examine content analyses of similar or comparable situations to obtain ideas for research questions, relevant current issues, conditions, practical problems and sources of content (texts) to be analysed in a new study. For example, anyone who desires to examine and compare the coverage by Australian broadcast TV—Channels 7, 9 and 10, ABC (Australian Broadcasting Corporation) and SBS (Special Broadcasting Corporation)—of the 2005 Cronulla riots or the 2007 APEC protest marches in Sydney will benefit from the study of the Los Angeles riots coverage of Atwater and Weerakkody (1994). The literature search will also identify the theories applicable to the new project; for example, **agenda setting** (McCombs & Shaw, 1972).

DEFINING THE UNIVERSE

Defining the universe is analogous to identifying the 'target population' or sampling frame in survey research (see Chapter 8) and sets the 'boundaries' for the content to be analysed. This stage identifies the applicable and suitable operational definitions for the relevant 'population' and study; for example, which newspapers are to be analysed is decided using circulation figures for that nation or state, selecting the newspaper with the highest circulation within the specific market.

With TV, a decision is made about what is defined as 'TV' for the study. For example, does it only include broadcast TV? Do you include pay TV (news programs such as *Sky News* and *Fox News*), video or DVDs of TV programs (for example, the TV documentary *OutFoxed*), mobile telephone TV, or webcasting and streaming TV? Do we analyse all news bulletins of a TV channel for each day or is it only the main evening bulletin? It's important to focus the study by narrowing the period and the data sources to be analysed to an optimal level, so that time and resources are not wasted on data unrelated to the research questions.

Case Study 9.6 OPERATIONAL DEFINITIONS OF THE LOS ANGELES RIOTS STUDY

In the Los Angeles riots study, the *Los Angeles Times* newspaper was selected as it is the largest circulation, prestige (broadsheet) newspaper in Los Angeles with a national standing. The number of days for the content analysis was decided using 'Facts on File', which indicated 29 April as the day the riots began and 3 May 1992 as the day they officially ended.

SAMPLING

Note that concepts discussed under sampling (Chapter 6) are as applicable to content analysis as they are to survey research. In content analysis, a researcher follows the multistage sampling method to select:

- the sources of the content (for example, which newspapers to analyse)
- dates or the time period for analysis
- the sample of messages from the 'universe' of the content.

Content analysing a census of all content relevant to the study (analogous to the sampling frame for people) would be an ideal. But if the census is too large—especially if the time period under analysis spans months or several years—a sample is selected.

A sample is selected considering the relevant content sources and relevant dates or time period examined. Relevant content sources are based on which newspapers, websites and TV and radio stations are to be selected, and from which state, city or town. You may choose a broadsheet and tabloid newspaper from the same market for comparison of how the same event, issue or topic was covered by each; for example, *The Age* (broadsheet) and the *Herald Sun* (tabloid) in Melbourne, Victoria.

Relevant dates or time periods for the content analysis are selected based on the research questions and the issue, topic or event under study. For example, the dates of the actual Los Angeles riots were the dates selected for the news coverage to be examined; that is, 30 April to 4 May 1992, as the riots took place between 29 April and 3 May.

If the content analysis involves a phenomenon that spanned a long period of time—say portrayal of women in the long-running Australian soap operas *Neighbours* and *Home and away*—a two-year period may be suitable for examination. A composite week per month of episodes may be selected by randomly choosing a Monday, Tuesday, Wednesday, Thursday and Friday in each month to obtain a manageable sample of texts. Composite samples are better for content analyses than random ones.

If the subject matter selected is related to a topic or issue of a group that's rarely covered in the media (for example, human rights in China), a longer period such as several years is needed to obtain a large enough sample.

Purposive sampling is the basis of content analysis, as the examined characteristics should be present in the content analysed.

THE PURPOSIVE SAMPLING OF UNITS OF ANALYSIS IN THE LOS ANGELES RIOTS STUDY — Case Study 9.7

The Los Angeles riots study selected a purposive sample of all coverage—news items, commentary, editorials, features, letters to the editor and announcements—related to the Los Angeles riots that appeared in the *Los Angeles Times* from 30 April to 4 May 1992. (The riots started in the evening of 29 April and officially ended on 3 May 1992.)

PURPOSIVE SAMPLING — Case Study 9.8

To examine how the Chinese Government presented its image of Chinese women to the world from 1956 to 2003, Yunjuan and Xiaoming (2007) selected the covers of the only official English-language women's magazine in the country—*Women in China*—for analysis for the entire period. They excluded the covers that had no women on it (that is, children or men) and obtained a 352-cover sample. The magazine is state-owned, so is published by the Chinese government.

In spite of all precautions taken in selecting the sample, **systematic biases** in the content can occur due to unexpected factors.

Case Study 9.9 SYSTEMATIC BIAS IN DATA COLLECTION: THE GAS EXPLOSION

In the early 1990s, a content analysis was conducted on the coverage of New Jersey news in the news bulletins of New York City and Philadelphia commercial TV stations. A non-profit group funded the project to examine if New Jersey—a small but prosperous state sandwiched between the two large TV markets of New York City and Philadelphia, but with no commercial TV stations of its own—was being adequately served by these TV stations. New Jersey residents were able to receive the broadcasts from both cities, but the group wanted to see if they should lobby the government for a new commercial TV licence for New Jersey.

The project had randomly selected a two-week period to collect the data from the main evening newscasts of all the TV stations. These broadcasts were to be examined to select each story related to New Jersey, which would serve as the unit of analysis. Unfortunately, on the third day of the data collection, a gas explosion occurred at a large apartment complex in New Jersey, which received blanket coverage from all the TV stations, thereby systematically biasing the data collection. Therefore, the researchers decided to extend the data collection by another week, allowing the first week's data to be discarded.

SELECTING THE UNIT OF ANALYSIS

Selecting the unit of analysis is the most important step in a content analysis. Therefore, it should be clearly defined and decided on *before* the coding manual is designed. Take a look at a sample of the content to be analysed before deciding on the unit of analysis with reference to the research questions or hypotheses examined.

Case Study 9.10 THE UNIT OF ANALYSIS IN THE LOS ANGELES RIOTS STUDY

In the content analysis of the Los Angeles riots coverage, the unit of analysis was each news item, analysis, feature, commentary, editorial, letter to the editor etc that addressed any issue or topic related to the riots.

Handy Hint

The unit of analysis is the smallest element of the message examined in a given content analysis.

- In print or written media, it can be a word, symbol, phrase, theme, photograph, cartoon, illustration, newspaper article, feature, letter to the editor, editorial, commentary etc.
- In audio messages, it can be a radio news clip or an entire hourly news segment, talkback discussion, telephone conversation, recorded song, conversational turn between people etc.
- In TV, films or other audio-visual media, the unit of analysis can be a character (for example, a teen or female), an act (for example, of violence), a specific scene, an advertisement, an entire episode of a TV program, an entire film, a single news story in a newscast or the entire news broadcast.
- When analysing internet messages, the unit of analysis can be a pop-up advertisement, an entry in a blog, a moblog, a video diary, chat-room discussion, a personal webpage, a commercial media webpage, an email message, an online news item, a message board, a political campaign website, a political party or candidate's webpage, or MySpace, Facebook or YouTube content.

However, note that ethical issues of privacy and informed consent may arise when content analysing private sites (those not open to everyone) such as MySpace or Facebook.

Sample size   The sample size should be sufficient and manageable. To examine general news coverage or programming, the performance of a daily newspaper or TV news broadcast, or TV advertisements in a given time slot such as prime-time or children's programming, a two-week period is manageable and sufficient.

Searching the existing literature of content analyses that use the same media forms (for example, films, TV programs and newspapers) and units of analysis will provide useful guidelines on the sample size for a new study. The average sample size in a content analysis of films is around 40 films chosen purposively (Stern, 2005) and as a stratified sample (Beeman, 2007).

SAMPLE SIZE IN THE LOS ANGELES RIOTS STUDY   Case Study 9.11

In the Los Angeles riots coverage study, the purposive sample of all the riots related items for the five-day period that appeared in the *Los Angeles Times* newspaper ended up as 247 news stories or units of analysis. This in fact was also a census or the sample frame for that content.

CONSTRUCTING CONTENT CATEGORIES

Constructing content categories for a content analysis is done with the development of a coding instrument. Again, the research questions or hypotheses of the study will guide the process to identify the topic areas that need to be content analysed as coding categories.

Types of coding categories   The list of items and their coding categories included in a coding manual are of two types:

1   **a priori coding categories**—where an item and all its coding categories are designed before the coding begins and obtained from prior research or theorising; for example, story types as hard news, commentary, features and human interest.

2   **emergent coding categories**—where additional categories are added to the coding manual during the coding when new categories emerge from the content. For example, the list of topics emphasised in a news item is expanded when new topics emerge from the content. (The coding manual, **instructions to coders** and the coding sheet are revised accordingly to include these new categories.)

DEVELOPING CONTENT CATEGORIES IN THE LOS ANGELES   Case Study 9.12
RIOTS STUDY

The first research question of the Los Angeles riots (see Case Study 9.5) coverage study was, 'What was the volume of coverage devoted to the riots from their outbreak to their conclusion?' This means the length of each news item or unit of analysis in column centimetres needed to be coded. The study also examined on which page each coded unit of analysis appeared, because front page news is what the editorial staff considers as the most important stories of the day.

Research question 2 was, 'What was the amount of coverage devoted to hard news, features and analysis during the riots?' This meant each unit of analysis was coded under its type of story—that is, hard news (time bound

---------->

Case Study 9.12

spot news), commentary or analysis (stories that provide context and perspective, furnish background information and give more reflective accounts), human interest or features (items that are not time bound and that relate to the human side) or the 'other' category (for example, letters to the editor). The operational definitions used in developing these categories of news coverage were adapted from past studies such as Meeske and Jevaheri (1982).

Literature reviews of previous studies that dealt with news coverage of other crises such as the Iran Hostage Crisis (Larsen, 1986); the Yellowstone forest fires, the Exxon Valdez oil spill and the Loma Prieta earthquake (Smith, 1992); and media and the politics of crisis (Raboy & Dagenais, 1992) were used to seek suitable operational definitions and guidelines for developing the coding manual.

Research question 3 was, 'What specific sources were most frequently relied upon in reporting the riots to local and national readers?' To obtain data to answer this question, the information sources cited in each unit of analysis were coded under seventeen categories, such as local journalists, national/international journalists, police officers/spokespersons; fire fighters; National Guard or army officials and spokespersons; store owners; and community leaders. Each of these was coded as yes or no.

For research question 4—'What was the incidence of photographs accompanying news accounts of the riots?'—the coding manual included 'If a photograph appears with the story' with the responses yes or no.

'What were the topics that received major emphasis in the *Los Angeles Times*' coverage of the crisis?' was research question 5. The coding manual used the items 'the most emphasised topic', 'the second most emphasised topic' and 'the third most emphasised topic' to identify them from the content. Some of these topics were listed as a priori (in advance) categories in the coding manual such as the Rodney King trial, looting and related violence, repercussions of civil disturbances; Reginald Denny assault and crimes against Korean-owned businesses because they were well known. Others arose from the data as emerging categories and were added to the coding manual as the coding proceeded.

An 'other' category was also added to accommodate unusual ones or the 'odd ones out'. In all, the coding manual included thirty items and their categories.

Source: Atwater & Weerakkody (1994).

Preparing the coding manual, instructions to coders and the coding sheets The next step of the content analysis is to prepare a detailed coding manual, instructions to coders and a coding sheet to be used during the actual coding. This involves constructing the coding categories by looking at a sample of content to be analysed; searching and reviewing the literature for comparable studies (for example, crisis coverage) and coding categories; and developing relevant operational definitions.

The example of a coding manual provided in this chapter is designed to analyse samples from three newspapers (*Los Angeles Times, New York Times* and *Washington Post*) and shows how it is prepared for coding units from more than one source and involving up to a 1000 units of analysis (see Atwater & Weerakkody, 1994).

Need for comprehensive and mutually exclusive categories Just as when preparing a survey questionnaire, a coding manual also must make the categories comprehensive or exhaustive by including 'other', 'not clear', 'not applicable' or 'mixed' categories in the coding manual. However, these 'other' or 'mixed' categories should not exceed 10% of the total units of analysis coded. A higher percentage indicates that more coding categories are needed for that item. It is better to have more categories under an item than less, as categories can be easily combined but breaking up categories incurs re-coding of a unit of analysis.

The categories of an item in the coding manual should be mutually exclusive; that is, a unit of analysis should fall only into one category. Including a 'mixed' category will accommodate any units of analysis that appear ambiguous or falling into more than one category.

The coding manual for the Los Angeles riots study

The following is the thirty-item coding manual prepared for the content analysis of the *Los Angeles Times'* coverage of the Los Angeles riots coverage by Atwater and Weerakkody (1994).

COVERAGE OF THE LOS ANGELES RIOTS BY THE MAINSTREAM PRINT MEDIA

1 ID Number of article (unit of analysis) coded: 0001 to 1000
2 Newspaper analysed:
  1 *Los Angeles* Times
  2 *New York Times*
  3 *Washington Post*
3 Date of issue: day/month

Origin of story

4 Section
5 Page number
6 Length of story (to the nearest column cm)
7 If photograph appears with story
  1 Yes   2 No
8 Story type
  1 Hard news
  2 Commentary/analysis
  3 Human interest/feature
  9 Other (it's customary to label the 'other' category as 9, 99 etc.)

The three main topics emphasised (items 9–11)

9 The most emphasised topic
10 The second most emphasised topic
11 The third most emphasised topic

The categories or list of topics applicable to items 9–11 are:
  1 Rodney King trial
  2 Looting and related violence
  3 Repercussions of civil disturbances
  4 Maintaining law and order
  5 Reginald Denny assault

6 Related civil disturbances in other US cities
7 Reaction of social groups
8 Reactions of US govt. and political sources
9 Reactions of Rodney King and his family/friends
10 Reactions of foreign dignitaries
11 Reactions of domestic and international press
12 Los Angeles Police Dept's (LAPD) handling of the riots
13 LAPD's defence against criticism
14 Reconstruction of Los Angeles
15 Apprehension and prosecution of looters and rioters
16 Safety and protection of residents
17 Crimes against Korean-owned businesses
18 Antecedent conditions/causes for the riots
19 Improvement/resolution of racial tensions
20 Calm returns
99 Other (it's customary to number the 'other' or 'not applicable' categories as 9, 99 etc.)

(More categories may be added as new ones are encountered (emerge) during the coding.)

EXAMPLE 9.1

EXAMPLE 9.1

Sources cited in the news story (items 12—30)

(This refers to people interviewed by journalists for their reports.) The coding categories are:

1   Yes   2   No

12   Local journalists (Los Angeles and California)

13   National and international journalists

14   LAPD officials/spokespersons

15   Fire fighters

16   National Guard or Army officers/ spokespersons

17   Los Angeles city officials/ spokespersons

18   California state officials/spokespersons

19   Federal officials/spokespersons

20   Eyewitnesses (not victims)

21   Riot victims

22   Community leaders

23   Store owners

24   Residents of Los Angeles

25   California residents outside of Los Angeles

26   State prosecuting officials

27   Defence attorneys for police officers accused in Rodney King beatings

28   Proponents of the Los Angeles Police Department (LAPD)

29   Opponents of LAPD

(Items may be added as new ones emerge)

99   Others

(It is customary to label the 'other' category as 9, 99 etc.)

Instructions to coders   The coding manual needs clear and unambiguous explanations about what should really be included under each category when coding a unit of analysis. This is provided as 'Instructions to coders' and helps maintain the reliability and validity of the coding process. Examining a few units of analysis provides an understanding of what sort of explanations may be needed in the Instructions to coders. Example 9.2 provides such explanations, in a partial list of instructions to coders, to illustrate how to prepare them.

Coder subjectivity   Often, researchers seek to code a media message's 'valency' as being positive, negative or neutral when reporting on a person, group, issue, phenomenon etc. For example, criticism of the obvious failures of the Los Angeles Police Department (LAPD) in handling the riots in its initial stages can be coded as negative of the LAPD, while pointing out their being outnumbered and unprepared for such a situation—and the obvious threats to LAPD officers in the context of the Rodney King verdict and hence being justified in staying in—may be coded as neutral. Pointing out that the LAPD going out to quell the riots would have made things even worse and hence staying in was the right thing to do may be coded as positive of the LAPD.

When coding an item's valency, a certain amount of **coder subjectivity** comes into effect. Therefore, detailed guidelines about how to code such items must be provided to coders, and some coder training and practice runs carried out, before the coding proper begins.

Instructions to coders for the content analysis of the Los Angeles riots coverage

EXAMPLE 9.2

(This is a partial list of items in the coding manual provided in Example 9.1.)

1 ID number of article
   Assign a number ranging from 0001 to 1000 to every unit of analysis coded, following the order in which they were content analysed.

2 Newspaper
   1 *Los Angeles Times*
   2 *New York Times*
   3 *Washington Post*
   Self-explanatory

3 Date of issue from 30/4/1992 (coded as 304) to 5/5/1992 (055).

Origin of Story

4 Section
   • Enter the section of the newspaper in which the article originates as A, B, C etc (as they are done with the *Los Angeles Times*).
   (Some Australian newspapers may use section names such as Business, Insight, Opinion and Analysis, which may require you to label them accordingly.)

5 Page number
   • Enter the page number in which the article originates within the section entered above. Use two digits as 01, 02, 03 etc.

6 Length of story
   • Measure the unit of analysis (newspaper article) including headline, accompanying photographs, maps, charts, graphics or anything else to the nearest column cm.

7 If photograph appears with story
   1 Yes   2 No
   • Self-explanatory

8 Story type
   1 Hard news—items of news that are time-bound and are stories reported directly. Spot news etc.
   2 Commentary/analysis—stories that focus on a particular aspect and provide background information or

views from particular perspectives. It is a more reflective coverage of the news as they sometimes discuss the consequences or implications of an event/issue under discussion.

3 Human interest/feature—items dealing with softer news topics or items that are not time-bound. Such topics deal with an issue from the human aspect. They profile an event such as a store owner's loss of his livelihood, with his personal history of hard work and perseverance. This type of item spotlights the individual and is more positive in nature. It's a feel-good piece.

9 Other
   Any item that does not fall under the above three categories; for example, editorials and letters to the editor.

The three main topics emphasised (items 9–11)

9 The most emphasised topic
   • Read the entire news story and determine the most dominant topic or theme addressed (for example, the Rodney King verdict) and find the category it falls under from the list of categories provided. Use two digits (01, 02, 03 etc) up to 99 for 'other'.

10 The second most emphasised topic.
   • Same as item 9 but select the second most dominant topic or theme addressed.

11 The third most emphasised topic.
   • Same as item 9 but select the third most emphasised topic. (Note that only two topics from a total of 21 are listed below.)

1 Rodney King trial
   • Any details about the beating, trial, verdict, details about the jurors, the accused police officers etc.

EXAMPLE 9.2

2 Looting and related violence

- Include fatalities, injuries, and attacks on journalists and media organisations in addition to actual rioting, looting, arson and activities of gangs.

(Detailed explanations continue for remainder of list of topics.)

Sources cited in news story (item 12–30)

12 Local journalists

   1   Yes   2   No

Journalists based in LA and California and working for media organisations in LA and California.

13 National or international journalists

All other journalists who do not fall under item 12.

(Items are added as new ones emerge.)

99 Others

Any sources that do not fall under Items 12–29.

(Note that only three items—12, 13 and 99—under 'sources cited' are listed.)

Coding sheets   A coding sheet is a shorter version of the coding manual to be used by each coder when coding the units of analysis in the sample. Each unit of analysis can use one sheet that will code the relevant categories under each item. This sheet can be used when entering the data in **SPSS** (Statistical Package for the Social Sciences) or Excel (from Microsoft Office) files for statistical data analysis (see Chapter 15). The number of spaces (_ _ _) indicates the number of digits assigned to the coding category under an item.

EXAMPLE 9.3

Coding sheet for the content analysis of the Los Angeles riots coverage

Name of coder:_____

Date of coding:_____

Title (headline) of article/subject/topic: _____

1   Article ID Number (for example, 0001 to 1000)   _ _ _ _

2   Newspaper (1, 2, 3 etc)   _

3   Date of issue (304, 015, 025, 035, 045 etc)   _ _ _

ORIGIN OF STORY (ITEMS 4–8)

4   Section   _

5   Page number   _ _

6   Length of story (nearest column cm)   _ _ _

7   If photograph appears with story   1 Yes   2 No   _

8   Story type   _

THE THREE MAIN TOPICS EMPHASISED (ITEMS 9–11)

9   Most emphasised topic   _ _

10 Second most emphasised topic   _ _

11 Third most emphasised topic   _ _

SOURCES CITED IN NEWS STORY (ITEMS 12—30)

12 Local journalists   _

(Items may be added as new ones emerge)

99 Other   _

LEVELS OF MEASUREMENT OF ITEMS AND THEIR CODING CATEGORIES

The coding categories listed under an item in a coding manual belongs to one of the four levels of measurement: nominal, ordinal, interval or ratio (see Chapter 7). For example, in the coding manual for the Los Angeles riots coverage, item number 2 ('Newspaper') is a nominal measurement, as it refers to the name of the newspaper being content analysed. In item 6, the 'Length of the story' measured to the nearest column cm is a ratio measurement.

When examining a photograph of women in an advertisement, the type of clothing worn by a model can be measured on an interval scale measurement of 1 to 5 with 1 being modest and 5 being very revealing.

Very modest 1   5 Very revealing

An ordinal measurement can be used when coding the same advertisement and the clothing worn by the model as:

1 Very modest   2 Modest   3 Neither modest nor revealing   4 Somewhat revealing   5 Very revealing

Coder subjectivity   Ordinal and interval measurements involve coder subjectivity, which negatively affects the validity and **inter-coder reliability** of the content analysis. Therefore, detailed instructions to coders and clear operational definitions are used when a content analysis involves these two types of measurement (Wimmer & Dominick, 2006).

TRAINING CODERS AND CONDUCTING A PILOT STUDY

As content analyses need validity and reliability, it is very important for all coders to familiarise themselves with the coding manual and instructions to coders before the actual coding begins. The researcher or the primary research assistant should spend some time training the coders and conduct a pilot content analysis with them, using a number of units of analysis with diverse characteristics, to help them understand how to identify the coding categories correctly.

For example, in the Los Angeles riots study it was useful to select a few articles that were hard news, commentary, features, human interest and editorials to show the coders how they differed from each other. Thereafter, a few units of analysis were chosen and the coders asked to code them individually and compare each other's coding sheets to check the levels of agreement between them. A discussion on why individuals coded them differently shed light on ways to eliminate ambiguities in the instructions to coders and coding categories.

One coder or many?   One might think that having just one coder would then be the ideal, as it eliminates inter-coder reliability issues. But different coders provide different perspectives and operational definitions on subjective measures such as levels of violence and sexual content. Views and interpretations of these different coders can be used to fine-tune or revise the coding manual after the pilot or the trial run. A single coder, on the other hand, will carry his or her personal subjectivity into the entire coding without anyone realising it has taken place.

Choosing coders from the target audience   Using coders who belong to the target audience of the content under analysis in the pilot study will make the process of designing and revising the coding manual more efficient (Wimmer & Dominick, 2006).

This is analogous to giving a draft survey questionnaire to a few people from the target population of the survey as a pilot run, before finalising and administering it.

CODING THE CONTENT AND CONDUCTING RELIABILITY CHECKS

Using a coding sheet per each unit of analysis, coders will content analyse the units of analysis following the coding manual and instructions to coders. Coders must be encouraged to consult with the researcher or the principal research assistant in case of ambiguity or lack of clarity during the coding.

Reliability checks   Once the coding has been completed, 10% of units of analysis coded by each coder should be recoded by another coder and their agreement calculated. This is called the inter-coder reliability. The agreement between coders should be at least 80%. If only one coder was used in the content analysis, this coder must recode a randomly selected 10% of the units of analysis and recode them at a later time and arrive at an agreement of at least 80%. This is called intra-coder reliability.

ANALYSING DATA

The coding sheets carry the numerical values for the relevant categories of content under each item coded assigned to each unit of analysis (see Example 9.3). These values can be entered into a data file in SPSS or Excel software. Each row in the data file is dedicated to each unit of analysis and a column is set up for each item coded (see Chapter 15— 'Data Analysis'). Statistical tests can then be run to calculate the **frequencies**, **percentages**, mean, median, mode and range for describing the various items coded (See Chapter 8— 'Measurement').

Cross-tabulations are used to examine the breakdown of media content categories. For example, in the Los Angeles riots coverage study, a breakdown between the days of the coverage and the most emphasised topic indicated how the topics changed from one day to another.

Using computer software in content analysis   Computer-aided content analyses can be carried out using TextSmart by SPSS, which automatically analyses keywords and groups texts into categories. It sorts words into frequency and alphabetical lists, and produces graphic elements such as bar charts. Computer software can be used even for inter-coder reliability checks (Skalski, 2002). However, Conway (2006) warns that computer-aided content analysis is not suitable for all contexts and data—especially those involving coder judgments.

However, computer software simply makes an analysis faster and more efficient. The thinking behind the analysis and the development of categories of items still needs to be done by the researcher, especially if the coding involves judgments such as type of story among hard news, human interest etc. In other words, using computer software in research data coding and analysis instead of doing it manually is analogous to using a computer to write a best-selling novel instead of writing it by hand. The ideas and creativity still need to come from the author!

INTERPRETING RESULTS, MAKING CONCLUSIONS AND REPORTING THE FINDINGS

Content analyses are mainly about providing descriptive data. For example, in the Los Angeles riots coverage study, the researchers examined if newspaper articles were citing more official rather than unofficial sources. The findings indicated that they did so at the beginning of the riots, but changed to using more unofficial sources as the riot progressed.

The study also calculated the percentages of stories in the coverage that were on a specific topic such as the Rodney King trial (17%) and the total column cms devoted to the riots coverage for the period analysed (a total of 27,000 cm). These findings were illustrated with tables when reporting the results.

Testing hypotheses   If a content analysis is carried out to test hypotheses, the data analysis will provide data and findings that will either support or not support them, allowing the researcher to make conclusions and generalise the findings to the 'universe' of the message content.

Comparison with earlier studies   A researcher can report the findings based on how they are consistent with or deviate from earlier findings of analyses of similar content; for example, crisis coverage or violence in the media. In the Los Angeles riots study, it was concluded that the coverage often addressed antecedent conditions (historical factors behind the riots) and, therefore, the *Los Angeles Times* had avoided the familiar criticism made against media of not doing so in the coverage of crises.

Practical uses of content analyses

- Content analysis is used in media monitoring either by an organisation to keep track of media reports about it and its staff, and to check if the coverage about them was negative, positive or neutral, for public relations purposes.

- The leading organisations carrying out media monitoring in Australia are Media Monitors (www.mediamonitors.com.au) and the Australian Associated Press (AAP; http://aap.com.au).

- Neilsen/NetRatings (www.nielsen-netratings.com) monitors content, product placement and the most popular content of a client's website, under its SiteCensus and Market Intelligence Analysis functions.

- HitWise (www.hitwise.com) is an internet monitor whose Online Intelligence Analyst examines the keywords most used by users of ISP (internet service provider) networks. Their findings help website designers to use keywords in order to optimise their access by users.

- Scholarly researchers are hired by various advocacy groups in society (for example, women's groups and gay rights organisations) to keep track of: media content to see how the groups they represent or advocate for are portrayed; harmful content such as violence; false or offensive advertising; and sexual content on TV unsuitable for children.

- The negative media representations of various groups are also content analysed by scholarly researchers taking the cultural studies and critical theory perspectives to track patterns in:

  1 **stereotyping**—using specific and often negative characteristics as generalisable to a specific group

  2 **marginalisation**—portraying various groups in society such as minorities in powerless positions, such as only being employed in menial jobs

  3 **ghettoisation**—asking women or minorities to comment on or be represented in situations and roles that are specifically relevant to them, such as the glass

ceiling or racism respectively, and not issues relevant to the wider society like the economy or politics

4 **tokenism**—using minority members or women in media portrayals as the only members of their group in a given situation and generally with little say or power, in order to say they were included

5 **exclusion**—completely excluding certain groups from media representations as if they do not exist, leading to their **invisibility**; referred to as **symbolic annihilation**.

With internet-based content such as electronic archives, obtaining content for analysis has become faster and more convenient with search engines such as Yahoo and Google or databases such as Lexis-Nexis or Factiva (for newspaper articles). They can be accessed and coded electronically without having to save or print them.

Limitations of content analysis   A content analysis has the following disadvantages:

- It is time consuming and expensive to conduct.
- It can only describe the content rather than predict or explain effects.
- It is shaped by the coding instrument designed by the researcher, which could be subjective due to the specific coding categories, operational definitions and levels of measurement used. Therefore, comparing different content analyses of the same content is not always possible, if they have been analysed differently.
- Content from older sources—for example, past issues of newspapers and old films or TV programs—may not be available or accessible for analysis unless they have been archived (old newspapers as microfilm and microfiche). If required in large volumes, they will be too expensive to obtain by an unfunded researcher.
- Internet-based content is difficult to sample in a systematic manner if the sample frame is not available as a directory of websites on a given topic.
- Website content is not permanent as it changes without notice or completely disappears, hindering later checking of the content for inter-coder or intra-coder reliability. This means the content under analysis must be saved electronically or print-outs made.

APPLICATIONS OF CONTENT ANALYSIS IN JOURNALISM, MEDIA AND COMMUNICATION, AND PUBLIC RELATIONS

Content analysis is applied in various disciplines, both for media messages and messages created during communication acts or human interactions. These disciplines include:

- social work—where they monitor events and interventions involving interpersonal communication between social workers and their clients to evaluate and improve their practices.
- medicine—where content analysis is used to examine doctor–patient interactions or the image of medical professionals on TV (Turow, 2006).
- organisational communication—where consultants carry out content analyses of recorded messages such as email and memos in communication audits that trace the flow of communication within an organisation (Neuendorf, 2002). (However, this leads to ethical issues related to privacy and informed consent of those whose communications are audited.)

Journalism   Journalism often uses content analysis to monitor itself on issues such as credibility or accuracy (Maier, 2005). The *Journalism and Mass Communication Quarterly* (formerly *Journalism Quarterly*) routinely publishes research based on content analyses of media coverage on specific issues such as plastic surgery (Cho, 2007) or gender issues in political campaign coverage (Fico et al., 2006).

Many scholarly research in journalism is based on analysis of media coverage of various natural disasters such as earthquakes and hurricanes (Hornig et al., 1991); crises such as school shootings (Muschert & Carr, 2006); high-profile crimes (Carpenter et al., 2006); the military invasions of Granada by the US (Cuthbert et al., 1987) and Afghanistan by the Soviet Union (Kristiansen et al., 1982); the Persian Gulf and Iraq Wars (King & Lester, 2005); social protests (Boyle et al., 2005; Jha, 2007); and political controversies (Schiffer, 2006).

With new media technologies used in news production (Reich, 2005) and the emergence of blogs as news (Trammel & Keshelashvili, 2005), content analysis appears poised to become even more commonplace in the field of journalism-related research.

As the mainstream media is often accused of neglecting to address issues related to minorities, a newspaper may request a journalism scholar to carry out a content analysis examining their coverage of minority-related events to see if the accusations are valid and, if so, how the situation may be rectified. Marketing professionals working for a newspaper may carry out a content analysis of its coverage of news and compare it with that of local TV news stations—who are its competitors for the same audience—to gain insights (Neuendorf, 2002).

Media and communication   Violence on TV is probably the most well-known research in media and communication that uses content analysis (Signorielli, 2005). In the past, researchers examined the type of violent acts portrayed, their frequency, why the violence was committed (for personal gain, in anger or retaliation) and how perpetrators and victims are portrayed. With new media such as video games and the internet, this area of research has widened even further.

Gender roles for males and females in media messages, sex stereotyping (Marcellus, 2006) and body images of women are also areas of research using content analyses. So is depiction of minorities (Lee & Joo, 2005) or their invisibility, which extends to advertising (Knobloch-Westerwick & Coates, 2006). In political communication, content analysis examines negative campaign advertisements, and the use of websites and the internet such as the YouTube or MySpace by political candidates or parties. News coverage of political issues in the media is content analysed to examine theories of agenda setting (McCombs & Shaw, 1972) and **media consonance** (Noelle-Neumann & Mathes, 1987; Neuendorf, 2002).

Potter and Riddle (2007) have content analysed the media effects literature in sixteen scholarly journals published between 1993 and 2005, examining the specific medium tested, type of content analysed, use of theory, methods and type of effect studied.

Public relations   Content analysis is an important research method with useful applications for public relations due to the profession's reliance on media monitoring. An organisation will commission an independent media monitor to keep track of the exposure the organisation receives in the media, about what or whom the coverage relates to, and whether it is neutral, positive or negative. For example, a university's media office will issue a news or media release about its staff research activities. This may be picked up by media outlets and journalists to report upon it and may lead to in-depth interviews or features with relevant staff, giving additional publicity to the university. Media monitoring will indicate how effective this news or media release was in terms of the volume and valency (positive, neutral or negative) of the coverage.

Share of voice   Media monitoring also uses content analysis to calculate the 'share of voice'—the proportion of media exposure given to your organisation in comparison with others. It also 'tracks issues' or examines if the messages disseminated by the media about the organisation were what the organisation intended or desired.

Case Study 9.13   ADVERTISING VALUE EQUIVALENCE OR THE RATE CARD

A controversial use of media monitoring is 'advertising value equivalence', which refers to the free airtime or (print) space gained as a result of media releases and related exposure by an organisation (mentioned as share of voice), and is calculated using the 'rate card' (the number of viewers, listeners or readers of the message). In other words, it estimates how large an audience would have been exposed to these media messages about the organisation (based on ratings or circulation figures) and how much it would have cost the organisation had it been

bought as advertising. Here the coverage is not examined as positive or negative for the organisation.

The Public Relations Institute of Australia (PRIA) and many media organisations disapprove of this practice, calling it an 'uncontrolled medium' of journalistic editorial content. On the other hand, paid advertising is 'controlled media' as the organisation decides the content of its message. (See www.pria.com.au/resources/cid/262/parent/0/t/resources for the statement by the President of PRIA, Rob Masters, in 2005.)

Summary

This chapter examined the everyday applications of content analyses; its functions as a research method; manifest and latent content of messages; conducting a content analysis; practical uses and limitations of the method; archives of media content; and applications of the content analysis method in journalism, media and communication and public relations.

The next chapter examines the qualitative research method of depth interviews.

Try this ...

1   Design a research question or hypothesis related to the mass media you would like to examine using the content analysis method (for example, coverage of an event or issue in newspapers, TV news bulletins or your favourite TV series or website) for its depiction of a particular group or issue.

a What is your rationale for carrying out this study? What is your 'universe' (sampling frame) and sample, and what sampling method will you use? What will be your unit of analysis?

b What are your operational definitions?

c Prepare a comprehensive coding manual, instructions for coders and a coding sheet to analyse its content, using the examples and guidelines provided in Chapter 9.

Hint: Take one issue of the newspaper (or TV news bulletin, episode of your favourite TV program or webpage) and create a coding manual to analyse its content. Once the basic or a priori coding items and their categories have been developed, the other emergent items and their categories can be added by looking at other units of analysis to fine-tune it. Be sure to include a mix of measurements (for example, nominal, ordinal, interval or ratio) for the items and their categories in your coding manual.

Further reading

Cantor, M 1991. The American family on TV: From Molly Goldberg to Bill Cosby. *Journal of Comparative Family Studies, 22*(1), Summer.

Field, A 2005. *Discovering statistics using SPSS for Windows,* 2nd edn. Sage, Thousand Oaks, CA.

Riffe, D, Lacy, S & Fico, F G 2005. *Analysing media messages using quantitative content analysis in research.* 2nd edn. Lawrence Erlbaum Associates, Mahwah, NJ.

Additional resources

List of archives for media content

Australian TV news and current affairs—RMIT University's Informit Media for access online or RequestTV for DVDs (www.rmit.edu.au).

International newspaper articles—Lexis-Nexis database (www.lexisnexis.com/news).

International literature and references (free)—Project Gutenberg (www.gutenberg.org).

International TV news reports—CNN *World Report* TV archive, Texas Tech University (www.orgs.ttu.edu/CNNworldreport)

US Film, TV programs and TV commercials—UCLA Film and TV Archive (www.cinema.ucla.edu).

US political campaign TV and radio ads—Julian P Kanter Political Commercial Archive, University of Oklahoma (www.ou.edu/pccenter).

US TV news—Vanderbilt University TV News Archive (http://tvnews.vanderbilt.edu).

Consult your university library's electronic resources for databases such as Factiva that allow for searching and accessing newspaper articles.

Leading media monitoring organisations in Australia

Australian Associated Press (AAP)—National news agency (www.aap.com.au/mediamonitoring.asp).

HitWise—Online intelligence analyst service (www.hitwise.com).

Media Monitors—Analyses newspapers, popular trade and other magazines, radio, TV and the internet (www.mediamonitors.com.au).

Nielsen/NetRatings—Ratings for websites (www.netratings.com).

Part

3

Research Approaches: Qualitative

10 Research Interviewing

In Chapters 8 and 9, we examined the quantitative research methods of surveys and content analysis. This chapter explores the qualitative research method of depth interviews.

Depth interviews allow a researcher to collect data from respondents (often interchangeably referred to as interviewees, research subjects or informants) when the phenomenon under study cannot be a directly observed or measured. Interviewers ask people questions to obtain their opinions, feelings, values, motivations and recollections of incidents or experiences, and provide verbal and non-verbal data relevant to a given research project.

This chapter examines the:

o different styles of research interviewing, such as structured, semi-structured and **unstructured interviews**

o types of interview questions posed (descriptive, structural and contrast)

o procedures followed in research interviewing

o genres or types of qualitative interviews.

These are examined with reference to the issues related to:

o sampling and sample sizes used

o advantages and disadvantages of research interviews

o issues of credibility (accuracy), confirmability (validity), dependability (reliability) and transferability (**generalisability**) of interview data and their resulting findings.

Thereafter, a few real-life examples are discussed where research interviewing has been used in journalism, media and communication, and public relations.

STYLES OF RESEARCH INTERVIEWS

Research interviews can be of three types:

- structured
- semi-structured
- unstructured.

These classifications relate to the list of questions or the **interview protocol** or **interview guide** prepared by the researcher and used by each interviewer. They indicate the freedom and flexibility available to the interviewer when asking questions from respondents.

STRUCTURED INTERVIEWS

Structured interviews are used in survey research when they are posed to a respondent by the researcher—face to face, over the phone or by other method. All respondents are asked the same set of questions prepared by the researcher, which are read out using the same wording and in the same order with the interviewer noting the answers.

The questions posed can be close-ended, where the interviewee selects the applicable answer from a list of responses provided, or open-ended, where all respondents are asked the same questions and the answers are written down by the interviewer.

Structured interviews are generally used in quantitative research and carry the researcher's point of view and language rather than those of the respondents. When using structured interviews, researchers know exactly what they are looking for, and collect data accordingly.

Advantages and disadvantages of structured interviews   Even with open-ended questions, structured interviews:

- provide data that are limited in depth and richness
- comprise rigid questions, which means the interviewer is unable to vary the questioning to suit different respondents and their unique circumstances or characteristics.

Structured interviews are best for:

- obtaining direct answers to questions
- when the researcher needs to compare findings between respondents, such as based on demographic factors of sex, age, ethnicity, level of income or education, and comparing the frequency of the occurrence of an opinion between groups of respondents.

Structured interviews on digital TV adoption

EXAMPLE 10.1

In examining digital TV adoption in Australia, the open-ended questions in a structured interview can ask why a person has adopted or not adopted digital TV, and the responses can be compared within and between different sexes, age groups, ethnicity, level of income, education or type of TV programs watched.

In other words, the researcher will be able to examine if higher-income males in their thirties who prefer sports programs are more likely to have adopted digital TV than females of the same age group and level of income who prefer non-sports programming.

SEMI-STRUCTURED INTERVIEWS

Semi-structured interviews are more suitable when the researcher's interest is limited to specific topic areas and they have some idea what they are looking for. Semi-structured interview protocols include a list of open-ended questions prepared by the researcher that are posed to all respondents.

However, the interviewer has the freedom and flexibility to add other questions or vary the wording or order of the questions posed from the list, if the respondent's unique characteristics or circumstances make it necessary or useful. These additional questions further explore any interesting points made by a respondent. In other words, semi-structured interview data carry a mixture of both the respondent's and researcher's points of view.

EXAMPLE 10.2

Adding questions during a semi-structured interview

During an interview on digital TV adoption, if a respondent says he or she has not adopted digital TV due to its cost, the interviewer using the semi-structured interview method can include additional questions to query it in more depth by asking the person to explain or elaborate it further. For example, the interviewer can ask how much the respondent thinks the adoption is going to cost and why the respondent thinks it is not worthwhile to do so.

Advantages of semi-structured interviews   Semi-structured interviews can still provide qualitative data that allow for comparisons between respondents (as with structured interviews) because they have still posed the same basic questions and covered the same basic topics with every respondent.

However, the researcher can still calculate the frequency of occurrence of specific opinions and themes between and within respondents—as with structured interviews.

UNSTRUCTURED INTERVIEWS

Unstructured interview protocols (lists of questions) only contain suggestions or topic areas to use when interviewing respondents for a given research project. The interviewer is free to use any form of wording or question order during the discussion and add any topic area to the list as he or she sees fit.

This means each respondent's unique characteristics and circumstances can be taken into account to obtain qualitative data that are rich, in-depth and mainly from the point of view of the respondent. They are most suitable for field studies and inductive research, where the researcher does not know what he or she is looking for.

EXAMPLE 10.3

Unstructured interviews on digital TV adoption

An unstructured interview can be used to ask respondents who had adopted digital TV in their homes, via pay TV digital interactive, to show researchers how they use the various functions of the technology and explain things to them.

While explaining the procedures, the researcher can ask questions about its interactive functions to suit the respondent's age etc, such as asking young people about the video games they play and their parents to discuss the use of the 'pause' function when interrupted during TV viewing.

Types of qualitative interview questions   An interview protocol for a semi-structured interview is designed to be a guide for planning and conducting the interviews. It is not a 'script' to be used by interviewers. A qualitative interview protocol uses three types of interview questions:

- descriptive
- structural
- contrast.

The types of structured interview questions and the interview protocols used in quantitative research relate to survey questionnaires and are discussed in Chapter 8.

Descriptive interview questions   Descriptive interview questions posed to respondents seek to collect their opinions using their own words, providing a general description or a 'general grand tour' of the topic or phenomenon under study. These are often posed at the beginning of the interview, as they are easier to answer than others.

A 'general grand tour' question on digital TV adoption

When interviewing a respondent from a household that has adopted digital TV, a semi-structured interview will ask them, 'Can you tell me how your family decided to adopt digital TV?', describing it in their own words.

EXAMPLE 10.4

A 'specific grant tour' question will ask for respondents' opinions related to some aspect of the topic under study or discussion.

A 'specific grand tour' question on digital TV adoption

When interviewing a respondent from a household that has adopted digital TV, a semi-structured interview will ask them, 'What changes have you noticed in your TV viewing experience since you adopted digital TV?'

EXAMPLE 10.5

A 'guided grand tour' or 'task-related grand tour' question posed during a semi-structured interview will ask the interview respondent to 'show' the interviewer how 'something is done'.

A 'guided grand tour' or 'task-related grand tour' question on digital TV adoption

When using a 'guided grand tour' or 'task-related grand tour' question in a semi-structured interview on digital TV adoption, a respondent can be asked, 'Can you show me how your digital TV set-up works?'
    The respondent is asked to explain in his or her own words how it is done and demonstrate how to operate it.

EXAMPLE 10.6

'Experience questions' are another type of descriptive question posed to a respondent taking part in a semi-structured interview. They will ask the respondent to recall something he or she remembers that's related to the topic under discussion.

An 'experience question' related to digital TV adoption

During a semi-structured interview, a respondent is asked, 'Can you describe an experience with digital TV that showed your family had made a good decision when adopting it?'
    The respondent then recalls: 'My mother was not very keen to get this set-up (large, wide-screen plasma TV with the digital converter) because of the cost. She thought maybe

EXAMPLE 10.7

EXAMPLE 10.7

we should get new curtains for the house instead … But then she watched her favourite travel program on the new set-up for the first time … She was so happy … I mean it has great sound and a fantastic picture … She said, "Oh, I am so glad you guys didn't listen to me … This is much better than velvet curtains." … I think that's the first time she realised it was a good decision …'

Semi-structured interview protocols may also include 'natural language questions', where the respondent is asked to explain something in his or her own words. For example, the respondent could be invited to comment on the advantages of adopting digital TV, which is related to the research topic.

EXAMPLE 10.8

A 'natural language question' related to digital TV adoption

Towards the end of a semi-structured interview on digital TV adoption, the respondent is asked to comment, in his or her own words, on the following: 'In your opinion, what is the best thing about your digital TV set-up?'

To this, the respondent (whose household has the digital interactive service) says 'Oh, with this set-up, we don't need so many remote controls … Everything can be done with one remote now … For me, that is a blessing.'

Structural questions   Structural questions included in the interview protocol of a semi-structured interview refer to those looking for 'specific details' about an area of interest to the researcher and the study. The researcher could be interested in finding out what types of programming are most popular with digital TV viewers, as well as the demographic details of those in homes that had adopted the technology.

EXAMPLE 10.9

Structural questions on digital TV adoption

'What are the most popular programs for members of your household?', 'Let's start with yourself' and 'How about your father?' are structural questions that can be posed to a respondent of a semi-structured interview on digital TV adoption.

These data can help examine patterns of favourite programs of digital TV adopters across sex, age, level of income etc of respondent households.

Contrast questions   A contrast question asks respondents of a semi-structured interview to compare two aspects related to the research area under study and comment using their own words, so that researchers can learn what they mean for different respondents.

EXAMPLE 10.10

A 'contrast question' on digital TV adoption

In the semi-structured interviews held with digital TV adopters using pay TV, the respondents are asked 'What is the difference between adopting digital TV via pay TV digital and pay TV digital IQ services [in Australia]?'

A respondent explains that pay TV digital IQ has interactive functions such as pause, fast forward, rewind, different camera angles during live sports broadcasts, recording one program while watching another, and recording programs on the hard disc of the set-top box, which makes a DVD recorder unnecessary.

He further explains that these functions are not available on regular pay TV digital service and that the IQ (interactive) service charges a higher subscription fee than the other.

The above details should help you with preparing an interview protocol for any research study that involves qualitative interviewing.

CONDUCTING RESEARCH INTERVIEWS

The most important aspect of being an effective interviewer is to be able to listen to the interviewee. The use of verbal and non-verbal cues that indicate an interest in what the respondent has to say is also essential. The interviewer should also gain some background knowledge of the subject matter under discussion, while at the same time be keen to learn more in depth about it from the respondents. There are fourteen elements in the interview process:

1 preparation
2 equipment needs
3 training
4 locating and identifying suitable respondents
5 choosing the sample
6 conducting the interview
7 developing rapport with interviewees
8 duration of interviews
9 changing topics during an interview
10 being inclusive of 'others'
11 after the interview
12 analysis of interview data
13 reporting of findings
14 accuracy, validity, reliability and generalisability of interview data and their findings.

PREPARATION

In a semi-structured qualitative interview, the researcher will prepare the interview guide or protocol with ideas gained from the literature review on the topic and the research questions examined in the study. The background information will indicate which topic areas need to be examined while the research questions will suggest what specific information and data need to be collected from the respondents.

Do not forget that ethics clearance will be required and consent forms and other documents organised before you begin interviewing your respondents (see Chapter 5).

AN INTERVIEW PROTOCOL FOR THE DIGITAL TV
RESEARCH PROJECT

Case Study 10.1

In the research study *Examining measures to improve digital TV adoption in Australia* the following served as the interview protocol.

Case Study 10.1

For end-users or householders who had already adopted digital TV

1 What made your household decide to get digital TV?

2 Whose idea was it mainly?

3 Which system are you using: set-top box, built-in converter, pay TV digital or pay TV digital IQ (interactive)?

4 How much did/does the technology cost you? (For the set-top box to convert the analogue signal/the monthly subscription and installation fee if pay TV.)

5 What do you know about digital TV? (For example, what it can do and the cut-off date for the analogue signal.)

6 How did you learn about it?

7 What do you like about digital TV?

8 What do you dislike about digital TV?

9 What improvements would you like to see added to your digital TV services in the future?

10 Can you show me your digital TV set-up and how it works?

Demographic information:

11 What is your age group? (15–20 years, 21–30 years, 31–40 years, 41–50 years, 51–60 years, 61 years and over)

12 What is your level of education? (some high school, completed high school, some university, university graduate, trade certificate, postgraduate, other)

13 What is your household income? (below $30,000 per year; $31,000–40,000; $41,000–50,000; $51,000–60,000; $61,000–70,000; $71,000–80,000; $81,000–90,000; $91,000–100,000; $101,000 and over)

14 What is your profession? (technical, trade, service, professional, administrative)

15 What are the ages of any children (under 18 years of age) in your household?

Source: Weerakkody (2006a).

EQUIPMENT NEEDS

The necessary recording equipment, such as audio or video recorders, and a quiet room for interviews need to be arranged. (The digital TV interviews discussed above were conducted at the respondents' homes because they needed to show the researcher their set-up and talk about its functions and operations.)

If video or internet images are to be shown to the respondents during the interview, this equipment also needs to be arranged for. Once recorded, the interviews have to be transcribed and a 'transcriber' (with headphones to listen to the tape and the function to control the speed in which it is played to suit the typist) needs to be booked from your university's audio-visual unit or hired for the purpose.

Some digital audio recorders allow for the USB memory stick (which has the interview recorded in it) to be connected to the computer, where the interview can be played while the typist transcribes it. Software may allow for the direct transcribing of interviews from digital audio recordings, but they are still in the process of being perfected to correctly decipher different accents or individual pronunciations of words. (See the website of Dictation Solutions Limited for suitable digital voice recorders and digital and analogue dictation equipment such as the Dictaphone, WinScribe and SmartMedia reader/writer: www.dictationsolutions1.co.uk.)

Audio or video tapes for the recordings if you are using standard audio recorders and/or computer USB memory sticks for saving the recorded and transcribed interviews need to be purchased.

TRAINING

The researcher and others conducting the interviews need to test the interview protocol and their interview skills with a few practice interviews with people who are similar to your respondents to see if the protocol needs fine-tuning. After playing back the tapes and observing the interviews as they take place, interviewers can provide feedback to each other on areas that need improvement.

LOCATING AND IDENTIFYING SUITABLE RESPONDENTS

Your search for interviewees needs to be publicised to attract a wide array of respondents from which you can choose your sample. You can use newspapers or other media advertisements or post advertisements on notice boards in public places such as community centres or public libraries. It is polite to seek permission from the management of these centres before you do so. For a study on ethnic communities, I was able to telephone the management of various ethnic community centres in the region who agreed to have the mailed notices posted on their notice boards.

Once the prospective interviewees have responded to the advertisement, you can identify suitable individuals and select, contact and recruit those you want. They should be provided with the Plain Language Statement from ethics clearance, which explains what the study is about, what questions they will be asked, and what their rights and protections are.

Respondents will feel more comfortable and empowered if they are given the chance to choose a convenient date and time for the interview and have a choice of locations; for example, their home or workplace, your office (if suitable for the study) or another location of their choice.

CHOOSING THE SAMPLE

Qualitative interviews use small, non-random, purposive samples drawn from the targeted population of the study, taking care to make the sample representative of the various demographic groups in that population. The 'sample size' has no specifications but a rule of thumb is to continue interviewing different informants until a 'saturation point' is reached where additional respondents do not provide any new information. However, where an honorarium is offered to interviewees, the number of people interviewed will be limited by the funding available.

PURPOSIVE SAMPLE OF RESPONDENTS FOR THE DIGITAL TV STUDY   Case Study 10.2

The research project *Examining measures to improve digital TV adoption in Australia* was funded by a grant that provided the honoraria for respondents, along with funds for transcribing of interviews and the cost of equipment such as for audio tapes, USB memory sticks and batteries (for the recorder).

The study interviewed ten individuals from households that had adopted digital TV via a set-top box, five that had adopted pay TV digital and five that had adopted pay TV digital IQ. The sample of householders was selected to represent the various demographic groups based on sex, age group, race, ethnicity, level of education, income etc.

Ten other respondents were selected to represent the various stakeholder groups other than end-users (householders) of digital TV in Australia. They were sales staff at leading

⌐⌐⌐⌐⌐⌐⌐>

Case Study 10.2

digital TV equipment dealers; academics researching digital TV; executives of lobby groups promoting digital TV; executives from Digital Broadcasting Australia; persons in charge of digital media with free-to-air broadcasters and pay TV digital services; journalists reporting on digital TV related issues; and public servants involved in the policy making and regulation of digital TV.

Source: Weerakkody (2006a).

CONDUCTING THE INTERVIEW

It is essential that respondents are treated fairly, with respect and politely during the entire research process. You should present as being honest, trustworthy, reliable and open in the minds of the interviewees—remember that they will judge you, the research process and your institution and profession based on their experiences of this interview.

With professional and high-status interviewees, it is best to be formal in dress and manner, especially if you visit their offices for the interviews. With others, you still need to dress and act in a semi-formal manner to indicate the importance and seriousness of the research, but not be too formal as you might intimidate them. In other words, maintain the formal–informal balance depending on the situation and the type of interviewee. Be sensitive to and knowledgeable about the cultural aspects of interviewees if they belong to a group different from your own.

DEVELOPING RAPPORT WITH INTERVIEWEES

Creating a friendly relationship with each interviewee from first contact will help to develop a rapport with a respondent during the interview. Making small talk or 'breaking the ice' before the interview begins helps smooth the process. For example, if interviewing ethnic minority members about their experiences as migrants, you might visit many homes of interviewees from various age groups and ethnicities. Photographs of their family and art works or souvenirs from their homelands displayed in the home could be useful topics to 'break the ice' in these situations.

When interviewing members of the public or those who are not specialists in the topic area under discussion, use simple language and reassure them that you are interested in their own ideas and opinions and that there is no right or wrong answers to the questions you ask them. Give the interviewees (respondents or informants) the freedom to speak freely and take their time, as they are the 'experts' in this situation. If they become silent at the end of a sentence, giving them non-verbal indications such as waiting patiently and looking at their face in anticipation will encourage them to continue.

Use probing questions such as 'Why do you think so?' and 'Can you give me an example?' to obtain more details. Using the exact words and phrases the interviewee just mentioned in a response will help the interviewer to 'dig deeper', as well as show you have been listening intently to their words. For example, 'You said that with digital TV, you only have to use one remote control now. Can you tell me what it was like before?'

DURATION OF INTERVIEWS

Qualitative interviews can take between thirty minutes to six hours at a stretch. Some interviews will be one-off, taking one to two hours while others may be carried out on several occasions in smaller one- to two-hour segments, based on the topic and the detail required for the project. Be considerate of the person's age or discomfort during the interview and make sure he or she takes a break for a drink of water or coffee if he or she appears distracted or tired after a while.

CHANGING TOPICS DURING AN INTERVIEW

It is necessary to carefully change from one topic to another during an interview in order to cover all areas listed in the interview protocol or guide. When the answers become repetitive or there are too many pauses, it indicates the topic has been exhausted and it is time to move on to another. However, it is equally important to be flexible and adaptive and allow respondents to talk about a new topic they had introduced, even if it is not on the interview protocol, as it may lead to useful information.

BEING INCLUSIVE OF 'OTHERS'

It is quite common for researchers to only use respondents who can speak the researcher's own language as it is convenient. But in a multicultural society, every citizen's opinion counts and these 'other' viewpoints may provide additional insights, points of view and unusual opinions that can enrich the project.

Therefore, make it a point to recruit ethnic minority or 'other' informants or interviewees into your sample and use a speaker of their language to translate the interview protocol, conduct the interview and translate the interview into the researcher's language, which can then serve as the interview transcript for data analysis. These costs can be included in the budget of your research project. You may also be able to find friends or acquaintances who speak other languages and are willing to help if the project is not funded. See Cunningham and Sinclair (2000) for more on bilingual media and communication research.

Some interviewees who volunteer to take part may be able to speak your language, but might feel self-conscious about making mistakes and later try to avoid taking part. Therefore, it is the interviewer's role to put them at ease and help them get their ideas across. Interviewees who indicate misgivings about their language ability in a second language tend to forget about it once the interview begins. Tell them to ask you to explain any words they do not understand. Conduct the interviews more like everyday conversations with a new acquaintance. Use simple and standard language, which is how qualitative research interviews should be conducted anyway.

AFTER THE INTERVIEW

Once the interviewer has exhausted the topics and questions listed in the interview protocol, they can ask each interviewer to add anything they would like, or can think of, that may be relevant. Summarising the topics that were discussed can help in this process.

Thank the interviewee for their time and ask if you can contact them by phone if anything needs clarification or if you need further details. This will be much easier if the interview was conducted in a cordial manner and ended well. Remember these respondents can help you find others for the same project (as in snowball sampling—see Chapter 6) or be useful contacts for the future, especially if they were interviewed in their professional capacity.

Case Study 10.3 REFRESHMENTS AFTER THE INTERVIEW

During my research project interviewing ethnic minority members, when visiting homes of interviewees I found that some had prepared refreshments to offer me after the interview. I would always accept them because in some cultures (such as in South Asia, which has highly stratified social structures) it would be considered an insult for someone to refuse food and drink from another, as eating together and offering and accepting food is only done between social equals. Refusing to do so may say 'we are not equal'.

I also asked them to prepare the coffee or tea exactly the way they have it. It gave me an insight in to some of their cultural aspects and to taste some wonderful home-cooked ethnic food and coffee. Some interviewees showed me their photo albums with photos of themselves from the past and books about their country that helped me obtain some additional information about them and their original homelands. Another showed me some traditional craft work she specialises in. One had made a copy of a local newspaper article published a few years ago (for me to take home) that was about her community.

ANALYSIS OF INTERVIEW DATA

Data collected from semi-structured or unstructured interviews are qualitative in nature and need to be analysed accordingly. The open-ended questions from structured interviews also provide qualitative data. The interviews need to be transcribed and the opinions expressed by various interviewees analysed according to common themes and sub-themes of opinions, either manually using 'pattern coding' (Miles & Huberman, 1994) or using software such as NVivo (see Chapter 15).

Transcribing of interviews is done with the interview text typed verbatim (that is, word for word) and as a single vertical column at the centre of the page taking one-third or half of the width of the page. The margins on the sides are used to write comments to help the researcher during the data analysis later on.

Some scholars advise that the researcher—or the person carrying out the data analysis of the research interview data—should avoid transcribing the tapes as too much familiarity with the data can hinder the analysis. Transcribing is a time-consuming and routine activity and is better carried out by someone else, so that the researcher's (or data analyst's) time can be utilised in a more productive manner. However, the cost of paying someone to do the transcribing can be an issue for unfunded research projects, and might necessitate the researcher doing his or her own transcribing.

REPORTING OF FINDINGS

Projects using interview findings are reported in the same manner as other qualitative research, using the realist, confessional or impressionist tales (van Maanen, 1988) discussed in Chapter 3. However, as the realist tale is the style used in scholarly writing, it is the one discussed here.

In a realist tale or standard research article, findings are reported under themes and sub-themes with direct quotes from interviews to illustrate them and support any arguments, inferences and conclusions made by the researcher. As a rule, about half the length of a qualitative research report should consist of such quotations.

ACCURACY, VALIDITY, RELIABILITY AND GENERALISABILITY OF INTERVIEW DATA AND THEIR FINDINGS

As in any research, the issues of accuracy, validity, reliability and generalisability are important in qualitative research using interviews.

- Dependability or *reliability* of data is maintained by keeping proper and detailed records of all research activities, and maintaining and archiving the recordings of interviews and their transcripts. Researcher's notes, field notes and journals about who was interviewed when and their correct details (as well as all signed consent forms) should be filed for future reference and clarification.
- Confirmability or *validity* of the project is maintained by using suitable interview guides prepared for and used in the project to answer its research questions. Having a sufficient number and diversity of interviewees is also helpful in this process. Use of methodological triangulation or additional methods of data collection can improve this aspect of the research project.
- Credibility or *accuracy* of findings is maintained by making sure the conclusions are accurate and supported by the data. This relates to honesty and integrity of the researcher. A reliability check will improve the credibility of the data when the interviews are repeated with the same or similar informants on the same topics.
- Transferability or *generalisability* of findings to populations other than the 'sample' used is likely to be low, as with all qualitative research. The low number of interviewees or 'small' sample size adds to issues of low transferability of findings. However, as the interviewees are selected from a diverse array of people, and speak in their own words, in detail and in depth, the data collected can be rich and provide useful insights of the issues under study.

ADVANTAGES OF RESEARCH INTERVIEWS

Qualitative research interviews are best suited to discuss controversial, sensitive or confidential issues, such as with survivors of rape or incest, and for busy subjects who may not bother to answer surveys. Many novels, biographies and scripts for films, TV dramas and documentaries are written using qualitative interviews with a purposive sample of relevant informants. Journalists use interviews—even though of much shorter duration—using the same principles when obtaining information from their sources.

DISADVANTAGES OF RESEARCH INTERVIEWS

The data collected with qualitative interviews can be easily contaminated due to:

- interviewer bias, such as using loaded or leading questions, and giving negative non-verbal cues, including pitch and tone of voice, hints of uninterest and negative body language such as unconscious smirks or intimidating attitudes.
- sarcasm or embedding their own opinions in follow-up questions, which can easily lead interviewees to being guarded in their opinions expressed (or to not express them at all).
- the social desirability effect; that is, interviewees trying to make themselves sound good or trying to give opinions they think the researcher wants to hear.

The effects of these factors are not easy to detect, estimate, measure or account for during the data analysis stage, and affect the validity, reliability and credibility of the findings. Interviews are also time-consuming and expensive to conduct due to the time required for interviewing, transcribing and data analysis.

TYPES OR GENRES OF QUALITATIVE RESEARCH INTERVIEWS

We have so far examined the types of interview protocols used (structured, semi-structured and unstructured), the procedure followed in interviewing and the advantages and disadvantages of qualitative research interviewing as a method of research data collection.

Let us now examine five of the different types or 'genres' of qualitative interviews that are commonly used in social s science research today (Baxter & Babbie, 2004):

- **ethnographic conversations** (in field studies and participant observation)
- depth interviews
- group interviews or focus groups
- **narrative interviews** (**life histories** and **oral histories**)
- **postmodern interviews** (giving a voice to the marginalised).

ETHNOGRAPHIC CONVERSATIONS

The generally unstructured qualitative interviews conducted by a researcher in a field study setting (see Chapter 12) are called ethnographic conversations. These 'casual conversations' take place between the researcher and individual members of the field study setting during covert or overt, or participant or non-participant observations.

Even though they are formal interviews, ethnographic conversations take the form of informal discussions during interactions with 'native' informants (members of the local population being studied) on a topic of interest to the researcher. These generally take place over a long time throughout the researcher's stay in the setting and aim to collect opinions from the point of view of the 'native' or the informant. They are carried out in conjunction with other methods of data collection in field studies, such as field notes and journals.

DEPTH INTERVIEWS

Depth interviews are often used in media and communication research. They generally use the semi-structured format and are carried out more formally than ethnographic conversations. They are also called 'long interviews' (McCracken, 1988). Depth interviews attempt to obtain the point of view of the respondent on a topic, phenomenon or subject under study and seek as much detail as possible about the research subject's views on the topic via their opinions expressed. This in-depth nature of the examination of a topic gives rise to its name of 'depth interview'.

A depth interview can last between 30 minutes and several hours, depending on the purpose of the interview and research topic. Today, depth interviews can be conducted face to face, over the phone, via video/audio conferencing and on email or the internet, allowing for the inclusion of subjects or informants from across the globe. In a depth interview, the respondent speaks to the interviewer who is free to probe any new lines of inquiry or topics of interest introduced by the interviewee, even though they will follow the interview protocol in terms of covering the same main topic areas with all respondents.

GROUP INTERVIEW OR FOCUS GROUPS

A focus group interview allows a researcher to gather data from several respondents or subjects at the same time, using a moderator to direct the discussion. The group interactions and dynamics provide an added element to the discussion. Due to the group dynamics involved and their effects on the focus group discussion, the unit of analysis of a focus group is the group discussion, not the individuals taking part in it. Focus groups are discussed in detail in Chapter 11.

In market research, the structured interview format is used in focus groups as the aim is to narrowly cover as many topic areas or questions as possible, as quickly as possible. Here the participants speak to the moderator rather than to each other (unlike in a research focus group) and the moderator strictly keeps the discussion on the specified topic or topics, without exploring any additional ones introduced by the participants. However, all participants will be encouraged to express an opinion on each question posed or topic introduced to the discussion by the moderator.

NARRATIVE INTERVIEWS

The term 'narrative' roughly means 'a story'. Therefore, narrative interviews seek interviewers to collect their 'stories' on a given topic of interest to the researcher. Often used in biographical studies, narrative interviews can be conducted as 'oral histories' or 'life histories'. These interviews are often used when researching for documentaries or docudramas for TV and films, as well as written biographies or 'bio-pics' (biographical feature films). Even in academia, famous media and communication theorists such as Marshall McLuhan (1911–80) had his life history written by other scholars, such as W Terrance Gordon (Gordon, 1997), who incorporated McLuhan's work with his life history and used interviews with many people who knew the theorist and scholar at different times to create a coherent biography.

'Life histories' as qualitative interviews are aimed at tracing a specific individual's chronological life history, from birth to date (if still alive) or from birth to death. They use the semi-structured or unstructured interview formats to gather data about the person under study and examine it in the larger context within the cultural and societal themes and conditions of the time the person lived.

WRITING LIFE HISTORIES: *JOHN WINSTON HOWARD— THE BIOGRAPHY*   Case Study 10.4

The unauthorised biography of John Winston Howard (Errington & van Onselen, 2007), the second-longest serving and 25th Prime Minister of Australia (1996–2007), was written by Australian academics Wayne Errington and Peter van Onselen and released in an election year to coincide with Howard's 68th birthday on 26 July 2007.

The authors had interviewed the Prime Minister himself, his wife Janette, two of his three brothers and many Cabinet members, including his deputy—Treasurer Peter Costello—who was seen as Howard's most likely successor and whose frustrated aspirations for leadership were well known. The interviewees also included Tony Abbott, the Minster of Health, and Arthur Sinodinos, Howard's former Chief of Staff, both of whom were his political supporters. Other interviewees included many of Howard's family, friends and supporters, as well as detractors.

Case Study 10.4

The authors gained access to crucial respondents for their 77 on-the-record and more than 30 off-the-record (not to be attributed) interviews in part because co-author van Onselen was a former staff member of Howard's Liberal Party and a friend of Howard's son, Richard.

The book helps the reader understand how Mr Howard developed his political views from his parents and how his mother Mona thought that it was 'consumption not income' that needed to be taxed. This view corresponds with Mr Howard's policy of introducing the current Goods and Services Tax (GST) and reducing income tax on high earners. The biography also presents Howard as a devoted family man. The authors conclude that Prime Minister Howard was the first professional politician the country had seen and they provide analyses to help the reader to understand how 'Team Howard' operated, and why it was so successful.

'Oral histories' follow the procedure of a researcher conducting interviews with respondents to collect their memories of specific events or periods in their own life— or the lives of many like them in the same situation. For example, a researcher can interview migrants from southern Europe who arrived in Australia in the early 1950s about their lives and experiences with respect to their migration and settlement. With reference to media and communication, an oral history research project can interview a group of older people about how they spent their evenings before TV was introduced and widely diffused in Australian homes, and how their life and leisure time has changed after TV.

Selecting a fixed period of history for an oral history makes the research more focused. Instead of a time period, a particular topic could also be chosen for an oral history project, such as the detention of terror suspect David Hicks (Sales, 2007).

Case Study 10.5   WRITING ORAL HISTORIES: *DETAINEE 002*—DAVID HICKS AS A TERROR SUSPECT

David Hicks is an Australian citizen who allegedly fought with the Taliban in Afghanistan. After the 11 September 2001 events, he was arrested by coalition forces once they invaded Afghanistan in early 2002. Hicks spent five years at Guantanamo Bay prison in Cuba under the US military. He pleaded guilty to his charges, which saw him returned to Adelaide, South Australia in early 2007 to serve a nine-month jail sentence, which ended in December 2007. His return to Australia was hastened once public opinion on his incarceration changed from the Australian Government's stance of his being 'given due process by the US' to that of being 'held without charge for too long'.

Leigh Sales' book *Detainee 002* (Sales, 2007) is based on interviews with David Hicks' family and friends, and those who knew him in Afghanistan and Guantanamo Bay, to describe what type of person he was from their points of view. David Hicks was not in a position to be interviewed at the time (nor since being freed). These interviews were combined with many other source materials such as newspaper articles and official documents.

Learning background information   When carrying out oral histories or life histories, researchers or interviewers are expected to familiarise themselves with the background information about the historical period and its significant events and people, so that they can ask better questions from the respondents. This can also help older interviewees to remember the names or dates and check if their recollections are accurate or incomplete.

Cross-checking the information   A researcher is strongly advised to cross-check all information provided by interviewees related to events, dates, institutions, organisations etc for accuracy. This is because a person's memory can be selective, incomplete or even misleading. For example, check a person's date of birth using his or her birth certificate or official records such as educational diplomas or enrolment records of schools or universities. Death certificates can be checked for date and cause of death of a person; court records for divorces, convictions and prosecutions; newspaper articles for significant events in an era and geographic location and the dates of their occurrence; and archives of historical societies, museums and reference books are other sources of information and authentication of facts.

Immigration departments worldwide use such records to verify claims by applicants for refugee status or of persecution in their own countries. They may even use weather reports from the past to cross-check the authenticity of the accounts of applicants to see if the climatic conditions of the time period and location in question match the applicants' stories. However, many refugees who flee traumatic situations where their homes and villages were destroyed will be unable to provide official documentation and can easily make mistakes with events and dates recalled years later.

Differences between life histories and oral histories   The main difference between a life history and oral history is that a life history examines the entire chronological life history of a person, is autobiographical and only a few other people will be interviewed (even though in depth) to gain insights into that person's life. An oral history, on the other hand, only examines a specific aspect or period in life of a person or group of people. Apart from that, both life histories and oral histories have their interviews conducted and data analysed the same way as other qualitative interviews.

Differences between oral histories and depth interviews   Oral histories have some historical aspect attached to them and are conducted some time after the events have occurred. Thereafter, those events are examined for reflections and analysis from the point of view of those who experienced that time period and events in history. These life histories can also be examined to see how the events have undergone changes in people's memories. In contrast, depth interviews only need respondents who fit the purpose of the study by being able to provide opinions on a specific area of interest or topic. They may be interviewed on any topic or issue relevant to the researcher.

THE POSTMODERN INTERVIEW

Postmodern interviews and how they are reported differ from other types of qualitative interviews because postmodern ones follow the critical theory perspective or paradigm. They aim to provide a voice to marginalised or powerless subjects and groups in society to tell their own stories in their own voices and from their own points of view.

This theoretical perspective sees the research process and the interview situation as carrying an inherent power imbalance where researchers are in a dominant position in relation to the interviewees. They are able to write the report according to their wishes or subjective points of view, even though they claim to be objectively conducting the research or reporting from the informants' points of view. It is not possible for any researcher to completely shed his or her subjectivity during the research and reporting process because the researcher may have different and more privileged life experiences in comparison to those of the marginalised respondents.

EXAMPLE 10.11

Power imbalance between the researcher and researched

A researcher from a developed country visiting a remote, impoverished village in a developing country to carry out field study research automatically occupies a dominant position due to his or her membership in a privileged society, dominant racial or ethnic group membership, and higher socio-economic status and education.

Some may argue that this gap should be eliminated once the researcher is 'accepted' into the setting and the group and had lived there for a while under the protection of the group. However, the more dominant aspects of the researcher, such as his or her education, prior life experiences, privileged social status and powerful contacts outside the setting, will still remain. For example, a researcher can seek and receive help from his or her family and contacts overseas or the diplomatic mission of his or her country in the research location in case of a problem, which is unavailable to a 'local' or 'native' facing a similar crisis.

Postmodern interviews are unstructured and try to empower the research subjects who are from marginalised groups or victims of the existing social system and circumstances. The researcher endeavours to collect data or opinions from a diversity of subjects from the group under study to obtain as many perspectives as possible, while imposing minimal influence on them. In the final report, the researcher will discuss any problems faced during the research process.

Civic or public journalism uses this method of interviewing, where respondents are allowed complete freedom to discuss their experiences. The report tries to provide a candid look at the lives led and issues faced by these marginalised research respondents.

Case Study 10.6   POSTMODERN INTERVIEWS: GIVING VOICE TO THE VOICELESS—THE LIVES OF REFUGEES ON TEMPORARY PROTECTION VISAS IN AUSTRALIA

The book *Lives in limbo: Voices of refugees under temporary protection* by Michael Leach and Fethi Mansouri (2004) is based on interviews with thirty-four refugees or boat people from Afghanistan and Iraq who were found to be genuine refugees, but were issued with three-year Temporary Protection Visas (TPVs) instead of permanent residency. At the time of the interviews, there were 9000 such TPV holders.

These individuals face the threat of deportation if the conditions in their country of origin are evaluated by the Australian Government as safe for them to return. They are not allowed to travel overseas or bring their families over. They also face many other restrictions and are limited in their rights and privileges available. One interviewee calls the 'P' in TPV as standing for 'punishment'.

The book has its first three chapters devoted to the background of the arrival of boat people and the establishment of the TPVs in Australia.

Thereafter, the stories of these refugees who lead precarious lives are told in their own words with direct quotes from the interviews.

APPLICATIONS OF THE QUALITATIVE INTERVIEW METHOD IN JOURNALISM, MEDIA AND COMMUNICATION, AND PUBLIC RELATIONS

The above case studies indicate how the qualitative interview method is used in their various genres in scholarly research. However, just as with other social research methods, qualitative interviews are increasingly being used in the disciplinary areas of journalism, media and communication, and public relations in everyday applications.

QUALITATIVE INTERVIEWS IN JOURNALISM

Social research methods are an extended form of journalism (even though with different aims) in many ways because both follow the same processes of observation, recording, analysis and reporting of findings. Interviewing significant people in journalism is compared with conducting oral and life histories or narrative interviewing, even though journalists only use some of the data collected in their reports. But they could still record, transcribe and archive these interviews for future reference—just as scholarly researchers do (Coleman, 2004).

Public or civic journalism's use of interviews with ordinary people as sources, in addition to the usual official sources, is seen as postmodern interviewing, as the interviews give a voice to the powerless.

POSTMODERN INTERVIEWING IN JOURNALISM: THE FORMER STAFF OF THE WOOMERA DETENTION CENTRE
Case Study 10.7

Journalist Catherine Carey interviewed a significant number of former staff at the Woomera Detention Centre, which detains illegal immigrants in Australia. These staff talked about the 'trauma' experienced by seeing the plight of the detainees. Some former staff had become suicidal and many suffer from post-traumatic stress disorder (PTSD). She also interviewed a doctor and a psychologist who served at this detention centre who recalled having treated large numbers of the centre's staff for the condition.

The article (Carey, 2007) reports on how the staff at the centre had come from all parts of the country looking for a well-paying job but were inexperienced and untrained for the jobs assigned; and how this centre was run like a prison—even though it was not, in legal or administrative terms.

The article quotes several staff at length about their situation and what they saw as harsh treatment of detainees. It indicates that these staff had been as powerless in the situation as the detainees, and had suffered and continued to suffer the after-effects of being in a detention centre—just like the detainees.

MEDIA AND COMMUNICATION

Depth interviews and life histories or oral histories can be used when researching for novels, scripts for films and TV programs.

Case Study 10.8 QUALITATIVE INTERVIEWS IN MEDIA AND COMMUNICATION: SCHOOL SHOOTING IN *NINETEEN MINUTES*

Depth interviews are widely used in writing best-selling novels—especially when they are based on actual events, as Jodi Picoult has done with most of her 12 books. In writing her latest book *Nineteen minutes* (Picoult, 2007), which is based on a school shooting, she interviewed many informants related to the Columbine High School shooting in 1999 in Colorado, USA.

Her interviewees or informants included police chiefs, grief counsellors, bereaved parents, survivors of other school shootings, two teachers from Columbine High School and a young man whose friend died in the shooting. Her interviewees recalled how the air vents in the buildings were prised open so that students could crawl into them, how kids ran away leaving their shoes behind and how there were abandoned sandwiches in the cafeteria—all details she included in the book.

Such details are also useful when writing scripts for films or docu-dramas, to create authenticity and provide a realistic portrayal of events and the setting.

PUBLIC RELATIONS

Depth interviews are much less used in public relations (PR), and when they do it is to obtain the perspectives of someone who is an expert on the subject, in a position of power or an opinion leader. PR professionals may also use depth interviews when trying to understand how decisions are made in a government organisation by interviewing someone who works there, rather than as a regular method of data collection in research.

A '**public relations audit**' may use depth interviews when examining what an organisation (or its leaders) think about a particular issue and comparing it with how the public thinks about the same issue, in an effort to close the gap between the two.

Summary

This chapter provided detailed explanations about the types of qualitative interviewing using structured, semi-structured and unstructured interview protocols, and discussed the procedures followed in carrying out qualitative research interviews. Thereafter, it examined the different genres of qualitative interviews such as ethnographic conversations, depth interviews, focus groups, narrative interviews and postmodern interviews. These discussions were illustrated with examples and case studies from real life. The applications of the qualitative interview method in journalism, media and communication, and public relations were also discussed using suitable case studies.

The next chapter examines the qualitative research method of focus groups.

Try this …

Design four different research studies where each involves one of the qualitative interviews of the following genres or types:

1   an ethnographic conversation (during a field study or participant observation)

2   depth interviews (individual opinions on a the topic under study)

3   narrative interviews (life histories or oral histories)

4   postmodern interviews (giving a voice to the powerless).

In each study, indicate the population involved; characteristics of the 'sample' selected; what equipment and budget you will need; how you would locate, identify, select and recruit your respondents; what background information you will need to gather before the interviews; and discuss how you will maintain the dependability (reliability), confirmability (validity), credibility (accuracy) and transferability (generalisability) of the data collected.

Prepare a suitable interview protocol (structured, semi-structured or unstructured as applicable) that can be used by the interviewer in each study.

Further reading

Podber, J J 2008. Television's arrival in the Appalachian mountains of the USA: An oral history. *Media History*, 14(1), 35–52.

Rubin, H J & Rubin, I S 2004. *Qualitative interviewing: The art of hearing data*, 2nd edn. Sage, Thousand Oaks, CA.

Silverman, D R 1999. *Doing qualitative research: A practical handbook*. Sage, Thousand Oaks, CA.

Willis, G B 2004. *Cognitive interviewing: A tool for improving questionnaire design*. Sage, Thousand Oaks, CA.

11

Focus Groups

In Chapter 10, we discussed depth interviews in detail. This chapter examines focus groups, which involves group interviewing and is another popular method of qualitative research. Often used in marketing, advertising, political campaigns, public relations and media and communication, focus groups identify the opinions and attitudes of interviewees, who are selected as a purposive sample from the target population.

Focus groups examine a range of subjects or issues during a 'focused' discussion for a given research study. They generally examine what the six to 12 subjects in each group like and dislike about an issue or topic under study, or compare the attributes of two or more issues or matters under examination. Their findings provide valuable insights as a pilot study or lead to further in-depth research using other methods such as surveys, depth interviews or case studies.

This chapter examines the:

o   design, planning and conduct of focus group interviews

o   their advantages and disadvantages

o   issues related to **group dynamics** affecting the data collection

o   applications in journalism, media and communication, and public relations research.

Handy Hint
Focus groups can only examine 'What's going on?' in a given situation. Their data should be used in combination with data from other methods because focus group findings—like all qualitative research—are not generalisable to the targeted population.

Case Study 11.1   POPULARISING ASIAN VEGETABLES

Most lifestyle TV programs and magazine articles in Australia cover Asian cuisines as they are popular with Australians. Any Australian supermarket will have an Asian food section and many Anglo Australians enjoy Asian foods at ethnic restaurants or prepared at home using recipes provided in the media. However, some supermarkets and growers of specific Asian vegetables, such as okra, snake beans and bitter melon, found these vegetables as only attractive to the niche market of Asian Australians, even though they are nutritious and tasty when cooked. Therefore, some supermarkets, greengrocers and growers' associations joined together to seek help from a food technology company specialising in solutions to such problems. They wanted suggestions on how to popularise these vegetables with mainstream Australians, to reach optimum sales and a wider market.

The food technology company commissioned a professional chef specialising in Asian cuisine to develop several recipes using each of these three vegetables. A research company was engaged to conduct focus groups to test the dishes and discuss what the subjects thought of the vegetables, then get them to compare the dishes and their preparations, and explore how they may be encouraged to buy and consume these vegetables in the future.

The research company conducted six focus groups with Anglo Australians: three with each sex drawn from the 18–25 years, 26–40 years and over 41+ years age groups. They recruited subjects by randomly calling them by phone (selecting names from the phone directory), and included a diverse array of educational, income and professional groups to represent the general population. Only subjects who did not currently cook, consume or purchase these vegetables were selected for the focus groups, using a 'screener' survey interview over the phone. Each subject was offered $100 for a two-hour discussion.

The interviews were held at a professional research facility with a test kitchen. On the day of the interviews, a hostess provided by the facility met and greeted the interview subjects, while a professional **moderator** conducted the focus groups. The interview table had bowls of these three raw vegetables displayed for the subjects to see, touch, smell and even taste if they wished to. The room had a one-way glass window to the next room where the researchers watched and listened to the discussion. The moderator used a '**moderator's discussion guide**' when conducting the focus groups.

After preliminary introductions and an explanation of the purpose of the research and the focus group, the moderator invited the subjects to express their opinions and impressions of the three vegetables in their raw form and asked if they had seen them in supermarkets. Thereafter, the chef brought in attractively presented trays of one of the vegetables prepared in three different ways— such as a curry, sweet and sour and stir-fry with steamed rice—for tasting. The moderator also tasted them and they discussed what each subject thought about the vegetable and compared the three preparations as to what they liked or disliked about each. They also indicated what would make them want to buy and prepare the vegetable at home or order dishes made with them at a restaurant.

This process was continued with the other two vegetables, and then all three vegetables, and their preparations were compared in the discussion. The focus groups were videotaped with the subjects' permission for researchers to analyse the verbal as well as non-verbal data collected.

Once all six focus groups were completed, the researchers and the moderator had a discussion about their experiences and observations made, which was also taped for later use by the researchers. The researchers submitted their report on the aspects the subjects liked or disliked about each vegetable. The supermarkets, growers and wholesalers later used this information for their promotional, marketing and advertising campaigns consisting of information and recipe cards provided free to shoppers at supermarkets.

The professional chef used the researchers' reports of summary opinions and suggestions as guidelines when introducing these vegetables in the dishes he prepared in his TV cookery show and his magazine columns for recipes.

CONDUCTING FOCUS GROUP INTERVIEWS

Just as in other research methods, focus groups need to follow several steps that will maintain the reliability and validity of the data collected. There are nine steps to follow when using focus groups:

1 defining the research problem
2 selecting a sample
3 recruiting focus group interviewees
4 choosing a suitable location for the interviews
5 understanding the role of moderator
6 understanding the role of researcher
7 preparing focus group materials
8 collecting and analysing the data
9 preparing the summary report of findings.

DEFINING THE RESEARCH PROBLEM

Before starting on the data collection with focus groups, a researcher must define a research problem to be examined based on the requirements of the project for applied or sponsored research, or based the existing literature if for scholarly research. For example, the project *Examining measures to improve digital TV adoption in Australia* (Weerakkody 2006a) was conducted because the adoption of digital TV in Australia has been sluggish since its introduction on 1 January 2001, even though the rates of adoption and diffusion for other contemporary technologies such as DVD (Digital Versatile Disc) players and mobile phones have been very high. The basic digital converter required for the conversion of the existing analogue signal to digital for a home TV set was as low as $99 at the time.

SELECTING A SAMPLE

The sampling method used for focus groups are purposive; that is, the interviewees must fit the 'purpose' of the study and be drawn from the targeted population. Therefore, individuals from households that had more than one working analogue colour TV set but no digital TV were chosen for the focus groups on digital TV adoption. This was because these households were assumed as able to afford the cost of a basic converter.

A focus group consists of six to 12 people and two to four focus groups are recommended for each topic under study. The composition of each group should be **homogeneous** in terms of sex, age group, race or ethnicity, political views, level of education, professional status and income, allowing for members to feel more comfortable and free to express their opinions with strangers. However, a diverse group may be more suitable depending on the topic under discussion; for example, the comparison of views between men and women or young and old on the same issue.

RECRUITING FOCUS GROUP INTERVIEWEES

About two people above the number required for each focus group should be recruited to allow for 'no shows', even where reminders are made to the participants a day or two before. To facilitate free discussion, a focus group generally consists of people who are not previously known to each other. However, sometimes if the focus group is conducted in a small community, or the sampling frame is a small one (for example, staff of a small workplace), it may not be possible to find groups of total strangers. If the research design requires focus group members to be strangers to each other, but one participant appears to be known to several people in the group, that person may be paid the honorarium promised but excused from the discussion. Recruiting more people than necessary will help in such a situation.

Participants for focus groups are recruited via advertisements or by getting a research company to select people from their database of interested people that belong to the target population. Sometimes, random digit dialling of telephone numbers is used to contact people. Using a screening questionnaire, those who fit the profile of the required sample are selected and invited to participate.

Selecting suitable focus group participants

EXAMPLE 11.1

When selecting and recruiting participants for a focus group on digital TV adoption in Australia, the prospective subjects were asked if they currently had no digital TV at home, but had two working analogue colour TVs. (This was under the assumption that a household with two working colour TV sets could afford a $99 digital converter but had not done so.) The individual focus group members were selected according to the number of participants needed for each focus group and research sample, based on their sex, age group, education, race or ethnicity, income level etc.

Generally, focus group participants are paid an honorarium for their time and to cover other related expenses such as travel, parking, child care or time off work. The payment can vary from $50 to $1000 or even higher for a two-hour interview, depending on the type of focus group and the specialised nature of the topic, particularly if it requires highly paid professionals such as lawyers and doctors.

CHOOSING A SUITABLE LOCATION FOR THE INTERVIEWS

Most focus groups in academic research are conducted in university social science research labs, meeting rooms or even the dining room at the researcher's home if the research is not funded. However, commercial research companies working for corporate clients hire rooms specifically set up with a one-way window leading to a room that allows researchers to observe the focus group in progress. Some provide test kitchens and audio-visual equipment for recording the interviews and the playing of audio-visual materials to the group as 'stimulus materials'.

These rooms may be hired (at an additional cost) with a host or hostess to receive the participants and take care of their refreshments and other needs, operate the audio-visual equipment, attend to consent forms and make payments to participants. In academic research, the researcher or a research assistant—generally a postgraduate student—will serve this function.

UNDERSTANDING THE ROLE OF MODERATOR

The moderator conducts the focus group, serving as discussion leader to get the members talking about the issues related to the research project. The moderator is briefed by the researcher and provided with a 'moderator's discussion guide'. Good moderators may earn from $200 to $1000 per focus group based on their skills and the type of project. The moderator can be of either sex because their skill and experience generally is the most important factor. However, some sensitive topics such as contraceptives or family planning may be better discussed by a moderator of the same sex and age group to make participants feel more at ease.

In most scholarly research, a member of the research team serves as the moderator of the focus group—again to reduce costs. However, in such cases, the researcher who may be knowledgeable about the subject under discussion is advised not to appear to take a position on the topic or issue under discussion. Instead, he or she should be patient and neutral, and listen to and treat all opinions—however bizarre—as valid to avoid biasing or skewing the data collected.

EXAMPLE 11.2

Putting the group members at ease

Sometimes, focus group members may feel intimidated by the research process and feel they do not want to say the wrong thing and 'lose face' in front of the group or the moderator. Therefore, the moderator should explain to the group before the discussion begins that: 'There is no right or wrong answer to questions or issues we will be discussing today. So feel free to say what your own opinion is because that is what we are looking for: your individual opinions.'

Once the group has gathered in the discussion room, the host or hostess should provide the participants with refreshments and see if they need anything else, such as using the restrooms or making a phone call. The moderator should then introduce him- or herself and the group members to each other to create a friendly environment for open and lively discussions.

Generally, group members and the moderator will be wearing name tags indicating their first name or have a name tag placed on the table before them. The moderator is advised to mention each member by name when addressing him or her and ideally be able to remember their names without having to check the tag.

Good moderators will create a lot of energy and a good feeling within the focus group, encouraging the members to speak freely. They will know when and how to probe a topic further when an important or interesting point is made by a participant. Sometimes, a moderator can probe these points by using the same words and phrases used by the member.

EXAMPLE 11.3

Probing further

During a focus group discussion on digital TV, a subject might mention that there is no incentive to get a converter or a new digital set. The moderator can then probe this further by saying 'Geoff, you think there is no incentive to convert to digital TV. Why is that?'

It is also the role of the moderator to: encourage the quiet ones to speak by giving them opportunities to contribute; politely and diplomatically keep those dominating the discussion from monopolising it; and keep the discussion from moving too far from the topics under discussion.

Getting the quiet ones to talk and moving the discussion back on track

EXAMPLE 11.4

In most focus groups, some members will speak more than others. Sometimes one or two members will remain very quiet while one or two will dominate, discouraging others or preventing them from contributing their input. In such situations, the moderator can address a quiet one and say, for example, 'John, I am sure you have some experience in this area. What is your opinion?'

If a dominant member has moved the discussion elsewhere, the moderator can say, 'Well, David, what you said about the reality TV programs you saw last week is very interesting. I hadn't thought of them that way before, hmmm … OK. … So let's go back to why each of you had not adopted digital TV yet. What would make you get a digital converter for your analogue TV at home in the near future? George, would you like to go first?' Here, George will be a quiet one, who gets first chance to speak on the topic before the more talkative or dominant ones contribute.

When conducting focus groups, sometimes group activities are used to get the members feel more at ease with each other and the process, get better acquainted with each other and be energised (Robert, 2006). These are often suitable with young people.

Group activities

EXAMPLE 11.5

At the beginning of the discussion, it's useful to create a friendly atmosphere between group members who are strangers to each other. The moderator can, for example, ask group members to talk to the person sitting on the left or right to them, exchange information such as their name, what they do and where they live, and then introduce that person to the group.

Halfway through the discussion, the moderator can also ask members to write a question on the topic under discussion that they would like the group to answer, and get each member to pose this question to the group and carry out its discussion. This will provide a break for the discussion and give the members a chance to think of a new issue or area that may be useful to the study.

When looking at print advertisements or other stimulus materials that are to be discussed, group members can be asked to do them in pairs and talk about them between themselves. Once the discussion resumes, these pairs can tell the group what they thought about the materials. Group members can also be asked to suggest remedies to the situation under discussion, such as 'What do you think should be done to encourage digital TV adoption in Australia?' by discussing it as pairs and then presenting their views to the group.

Once the moderator has posed all the questions and areas listed in the moderator's discussion guide to the focus group, he or she can recap the issues and topics discussed and request members to suggest additional ones.

The above group activities will give the group a feeling of 'ownership' of the discussion and issues examined as they were able to shape the discussion as a two-way process.

Source: Robert (2006)

The moderator should also know when to change the subject during the discussion by closely observing the non-verbal cues of the group members, such as feeling bored, uneasy, distracted or restless. When members come up with the same answers or say 'I also think the same as the others', it means that saturation point has been reached and it is time to move to a new question.

UNDERSTANDING THE ROLE OF RESEARCHER

Irrespective of whether the researcher moderates the focus group discussions, the role of researcher involves many preparatory and other activities. These include:

- obtaining ethics clearance for the project
- identifying and recruiting suitable focus group members (research subjects)
- booking the facilities
- hiring and briefing the moderator
- preparing the focus group materials such as the **screener questions**, stimulus materials and the moderator's discussion guide
- making payments
- coordinating the conduct of focus groups and the collection of data via audio or audio-visual recordings
- analysing the data
- preparing a summary report of findings.

PREPARING FOCUS GROUP MATERIALS

Focus groups need some materials prepared beforehand by the researcher:

- screener questions to select suitable participants
- stimulus materials for the group to get the subjects talking
- moderator's discussion guide
- other relevant materials as needed.

Screener questions   Screener questions are a short list of questions for the person who is contacting prospective focus group members to identify those who fit the sample characteristics needed for the project. This is also a type of script used by the person calling the subjects. The following is a screener questionnaire to select members for focus groups on digital TV in Australia.

Case Study 11.2   SCREENER QUESTIONS FOR THE DIGITAL TV STUDY

Hello, I am _____ from _____ University / a market research company. This is not a sales call, but we are looking for paid participants who are willing to take part in a focus group on digital TV and wonder if you could give me a few minutes of your time. That's good.

1   Do you have digital TV in your home with a set top converter, digital TV set or Foxtel digital for pay TV? (If yes, terminate and say) Thank you very much.

Explanation: Note that we are looking for those currently without digital TV in their homes.)

$\dashrightarrow$

2   How many working colour TV sets do you have in your home at the moment? (If less than 2, terminate and say) Thank you very much.

Explanation: We are looking for those with two ore more working colour TV sets in the home as we assume they can afford the $99 needed for a basic set top converter, but have not got one, therefore not adopting digital TV.

Can I now ask you a few questions about your age group, education, etc.? Thank you.

3   Are you between the ages of:

☐ 15–20 years   ☐ 21–30 years   ☐ 31–40
☐ 41–50   ☐ 51–60   ☐ 61 and over
(Please recruit a mix of age groups)

4   Your level of education is :

☐ some high school
☐ completed high school
☐ some university
☐ university graduate
☐ trade certificate
☐ postgraduate
Other_____
(Please recruit a mix of education levels)

5   Your current profession is:

☐ Technical   ☐ Trade   ☐ Service
☐ Professional   ☐ Administrative
☐ Student   ☐ Home maker   ☐ Retired
☐ Not in paid employment
Other_____
(Please recruit a mix of professions)

6   What is your household income before taxes?

☐ Below $30,000   ☐ $31–40,000
☐ $41–50,000   ☐ $51–60,000
☐ $61–70,000   ☐ $71–80,000
☐ $81–90,000   ☐ $91–100,000
☐ $101,000 and over
(Please recruit a mix of income groups)

7   Note if this person is male or female or ask 'For the record, can you tell me if you are male or female?'

1 Male   2 Female
(Explanation: Some voices may sound different over the phone making it difficult to gauge their sex.)

General: The mix of demographic groups are sought to maintain some sort of representativeness of the population in the focus group sample.

8   Can I have your name, address and a contact phone/fax number and email address so that we can contact you about the date, time and other details for the focus group?

Name of subject: _____
Address: _____
Contact phone number: _____
Fax: _____
email: _____

Thank you very much. Bye.

Note: Once the researchers have the entire list of prospective focus group members who are willing to participate and have been initially contacted, they will choose the sample for the number of focus groups to be conducted and mail, email or fax them the Plain Language Statement (approved by the relevant ethics committee) that includes details about the research project, the questions to be posed to them and the payment details. They will also be informed about the location, date, time and other details about the focus groups.

Stimulus materials   Stimulus materials are prepared by a researcher to show each focus group at the beginning or during the discussion. They are designed to provide a common experience the entire group can relate to plus a starting point for the discussions on the specific topic.

EXAMPLE 11.6

Stimulus materials for the digital TV study

The focus groups conducted for the digital TV project were shown brochures and a DVD containing promotional information about digital TV technology that was produced and distributed by Digital Broadcasting Australia (DBA)—an industry lobby group. DBA had sent out these to dealers of TV equipment, such as digital set-top converters and wide-screen TV receivers.

The DVD explained what digital TV is, what Australian audiences can expect from the technology, how broadcast TV networks have adopted digital TV and what benefits users can expect from the technology.

Moderator's discussion guide   The moderator's discussion guide provides a brief overview of the aims of the study and sets out a list of semi-structured interview questions for the moderator to use as a guide. These questions should indicate what each group needs to discuss. The moderator is free to add other relevant questions or examine or probe any areas or topics mentioned by the group that may appear useful to the study.

Case Study 11.3   MODERATOR'S DISCUSSION GUIDE FOR THE DIGITAL TV STUDY

Aims of the study

The aims of the project are to ask Australians what they know about digital TV, where they heard or learned about it, if they have digital TV sets or set-top boxes in their homes or plan to do so in the future, and what they think about the new technology and its capabilities. Digital TV was introduced to Australia on 1 January 2001 and so far has only a limited number of households buying the set-top boxes, new digital TV sets or subscribing to the pay TV service Foxtel digital. Because digital TV is the next step in the development of TV as a technology, it needs to be popular with the public so that Australia can remain competitive in the global marketplace, as digital TV can bring the internet and other services and functions to the home via TV in the future.

Notes to the moderator about the study and DTV technology

The study has involved depth interviews with those who have already adopted digital TV and a survey with a wide sample of the general population. The focus groups are the third part of the data collection and is carried out with those who do not have digital TV at home (with a set-top box, a digital TV set, Foxtel digital or Austar pay TV services), but live in a household with at least two working colour TV sets, as they are assumed to be able to afford the basic digital converter priced at $99. The high end of the converter is about $1500.

Probing

Any discussions about plasma TVs could be helpful as many buyers of these sets appear to be buying a digital converter at the same time or they buy a set with a built-in converter. Sports appear to be the most popular genre of TV that encourages digital conversion.

In areas where the analogue signals for Australian Broadcasting Corporation (ABC) and Special Broadcasting Service (SBS) TV channels are weak, digital TV converters help them receive the signals in digital format, and this is why some people have purchased converters. The idea of a mandated converter (tuner) inside all new TV sets above a certain screen size is raised from time to time. This might increase the cost of the set by about $200, and therefore it is opposed by dealers who worry it would reduce

..........>

their sales. This requirement was made law in the US recently as they, too, have the problem of low conversion rates for digital TV.

Suggested guidelines

Stimulus materials

Before the discussion begins, please screen the DVD, which is about digital TV, and show them the brochures provided, both of which are from Digital Broadcasting Australia.

List of semi-structured focus group questions

1 What is the main reason your household has not yet bought a set-top box, a digital TV set or subscribed to Foxtel digital to convert your analogue TV signal to digital?

2 Did you know about digital TV and its functions before today? What did you know?

3 Now that you have seen the DVD about digital TV and its functions, do you like to get a converter for your home TV?

4 Have you heard about the proposed analogue signal cut-off date after which only digital signals will be broadcast? (It is 2010 for metropolitan areas and 2012 for all other areas.)

5 When you visit shops selling TV equipment, have you seen digital TV set-top boxes (converters) displayed for sale or advertised in their catalogues or in newspapers?

6 Does your home receive ABC and SBS signals clearly? (If they do, it means they have lost an incentive to convert.)

7 What type of programming do you watch the most in your households? (Examine if they are sports fans or not.)

8 Is there anything that would encourage you to convert to digital TV in the near future?

9 Do you like the idea of all new TV sets above a certain screen size having a mandated converter or tuner fixed inside the TV set (integrated), so that they will be digital? (This will add to the cost of the TV set.)

Other materials   Sometimes, interviewees may feel awkward about expressing an opinion that is opposed to that of the rest of the group and may feel obliged to maintain a consensus: they may remain silent, not express their real views or simply express an opinion that agrees with the rest of the group.

Therefore, before the discussion begins it is helpful to ask all participants to write down their answers to one or two main questions that will be posed to the focus group (Stewart & Shamdasani, 1990). This will force them to stick to and express their original opinions on the subject since they know they have already committed to them on paper. The researcher will also be able to compare these answers with the participant's opinions expressed during the interview.

QUESTIONS TO ASK FOCUS GROUP MEMBERS TO ANSWER IN WRITING, BEFORE THE DISCUSSION BEGINS

Case Study 11.4

Please provide your answers to the following questions.

Name: _____

1 What is the main reason (or reasons) your household has not yet adopted digital TV (via set-top boxes, integrated TV sets with

an inbuilt converter, or pay TV such as Foxtel digital)?

_____

_____

_____

_____

Case Study 11.4

2   What would make you/your household
    decide to adopt digital TV (via set-top boxes,   _____
    integrated TV sets or pay TV such as Foxtel   _____
    digital) in the near future?   _____
                                                         _____

Analysing focus group data   Once the focus groups have been completed, the discussions of the focus groups with the moderator, and the moderator's discussions with the research team, are transcribed. The transcripts should carry the date and location of the focus groups and the name of the project for future reference. The interviews should be typed in double space in a centred single column about one-third to half the width of the page, allowing the researcher to make notes and comments in the margins during the data analysis.

Case Study 11.5   TRANSCRIPT OF A FOCUS GROUP DISCUSSION

Digital TV focus group 1

Females, age group 15–30 years old

29/5/2007, Meeting Room 2,

Moderator: Kelly

Interviewer/moderator:
We just saw the DVD from Digital Broadcasting Australia. Did you know about digital TV before today?

Mary:
I have seen digital TV at my neighbour's place. She explained to me about the box they had on the TV set.

Janette:
I saw it at my sister-in-law's place. She has a large plasma TV and they had bought a converter box, too.

COLLECTING AND ANALYSING THE DATA

Focus group interviews are analysed the same way as other qualitative data in terms of the themes and sub-themes of opinions expressed during the discussions. The themes and sub-themes arise from the data itself, but a researcher can subjectively code them into various groupings based on the similarities within, and differences between, the themes of opinions expressed by the participants, and give them each a label that explains or summarises the theme or sub-theme (see Chapter 15).

CODING OF OPINIONS INTO THEMES AND SUB-THEMES   Case Study 11.6

The opinions expressed by focus group participants are qualitatively analysed and then represented in quantitative terms as the frequency of their occurrence.

Qualitative analysis

The opinions expressed by the focus group participants as to 'Why they or their households have not yet adopted digital TV' can be identified as a theme in the analysis of all the focus group data. Thereafter, the specific reasons given by the participants can be discussed under the sub-themes labelled as:

1 'cost of the technology' (to convert)

2 'lack of incentives in terms of programming' (available with digital conversion for broadcast TV)

3 the 'deadline for the conversion is too far away' etc.

The title given to a theme or sub-theme should represent the 'essence' (the reality underlying the phenomenon) of the group of opinions that make up that theme or sub-theme (Lincoln & Guba, 1985).

The opinions expressed under each theme and sub-theme can be summarised to provide a description of how these themes and sub-themes were framed by the sample of focus group participants interviewed (See Chapter 15). Computer software such as NVivo can be used in this analysis of opinions expressed into themes and sub-themes, while 'pattern coding' is a manual method of carrying out the same analysis of opinions (Miles & Huberman, 1984; Lincoln & Guba, 1985; Weerakkody, 1999) (see Chapter 15). Both follow the same principle but the use of computer software makes the analysis faster.

Quantitative analysis

The data can be represented quantitatively by counting the number of themes identified, the number of sub-themes under each theme, and the total number of opinions expressed under each theme and sub-theme, plus their percentage of the total number of opinions. This will help the researcher to identify which themes and sub-themes of opinions were the most common or most often expressed.

PREPARING THE SUMMARY REPORT OF FINDINGS

Once the data have been analysed into themes and sub-themes of opinions expressed by the focus group participants, they are reported as summaries of findings. The qualitative findings are reported as various themes and sub-themes with direct quotes from various focus group members cited to illustrate them.

The quantitative findings are represented as charts or tables to indicate the number of opinions expressed and their percentages under each theme and sub-theme. For a more detailed description, tables can be compiled indicating the cross tabulation of opinions expressed under each theme, broken down by the sex, age group, education, income level etc of the focus group members in the sample (see Chapter 15). This will indicate any patterns in the frequency of opinions expressed. For example, more women (60%) than men (40%) from the 15–20 age group have expressed opinions under the sub-theme 'cost of the technology'.

Case Study 11.7 REPORTING THE FINDINGS

Findings can be reported as both qualitative and quantitative analyses, in separate chapters or sections.

Qualitative findings

Under the theme 'Why they or their households have not yet adopted digital TV' a sub-theme that was identified was 'the current set is good enough'. Under this sub-theme, Cam (a 19-year-old male who is a high-school graduate from a household earning $71,000 to $80,000) said 'We got a new TV recently … probably in the last two years … it's got pretty good colour and sound … Unless we were probably replacing the TV (if broken), we probably wouldn't really go out of our way to go do it (convert to digital)'.

Quantitative findings

Quantitative findings can be reported indicating how many opinions were expressed under each theme and sub-theme in terms of numbers as well as percentage of the total number of opinions. For example, the theme 'Why they or their households have not yet adopted digital TV' had 335 opinions (26.0%) of a total of 1284 relevant opinions expressed by the 60 focus group participants for the study.

The four main sub-themes of this theme were:

1 'cost of the technology' (to convert) (113 opinions or 8.8% of total)

2 'lack of incentives to convert in terms of programming' (available with digital conversion for broadcast TV) (87 opinions or 6.7% of total)

3 'the current set is good enough' (81 opinions or 6.3% of total)

4 the 'deadline for the conversion is too far away' (54 or 4.2% of total).

Note that the number of opinions and their percentages for the sub-themes 1 to 4 add up to 335 opinions and 26%.

ADVANTAGES OF FOCUS GROUPS

There are several advantages of using focus groups in media and communication, as well as other social science research. The main advantages are that:

- they can be conducted in a very short time, where up to 12 people are interviewed in about two hours
- several groups can be identified, recruited and interviewed within about a week
- within an academic setting, they are affordable, as most costs, apart from honoraria and transcribing expenses, are borne by academic researchers using their time and institutional resources
- a good moderator is able to gather valuable data by energising the focus group members.
- Today, focus groups can be conducted as online discussions or as webcasts, which means group members need not be present in the same location (Wilcox et al., 2007).

DISADVANTAGES OF FOCUS GROUPS

The main disadvantages of focus groups:

- They cannot be used to discuss controversial issues as they can lead to disagreements causing unpleasantness or conflicts between group members.

- What group members say in public in the company of others—especially strangers—can be very different from what they actually think or say in private or when among their friends and family.
- They lack the naturalness of everyday conversations, even though they are expected to gather people's opinions and attitudes in everyday conversations.
- Members may express extreme views they normally won't express due to being carried away by the discussion or the captive audience.
- They involve volunteer subjects who may not be representative of the population, even if selected as a purposive and stratified sample based on their demographic characteristics.
- Using audio-visual technology to record the discussions can distract members or lead to **reactivity** of participants, in which they behave in a way different from normal.

Group dynamics and focus groups   Other shortcomings of focus groups are related to the group dynamics between focus group members, which can hinder the data collection or contaminate the data. These include the:

- group leader effect
- false consensus effect
- group think syndrome
- **positive self-representation**
- effects of the '**spiral of silence**' (Weerakkody, 2002).

The group leader effect   **The group leader effect** is created when a self-appointed leader of a focus group who is talkative and aggressive dominates the discussion, imposing his or her own opinions and thereby silencing any minority views within the group. This can lead to this person or persons not giving sufficient opportunities, or not providing a suitable climate, for others to speak, even if the moderator tries to intervene to rectify the situation.

The false consensus effect   During a focus group discussion, some participants may assume that everyone in the group thinks the same way on a given issue and speak accordingly.

The group think syndrome   **The group think syndrome** is a situation where group members—just as in everyday life—may consciously suppress their disagreement on an issue or others' opinions, in order to maintain a consensus and group cohesiveness. This leads to opinions contradictory to those dominant in the discussion going unexpressed, or ignored or overlooked. This situation can be somewhat remedied by getting focus group members to write their answers to starter questions provided before the discussion begins (Stewart & Shamdasani, 1990) discussed earlier. Therefore, a researcher will be able to examine members' real opinions on the subject if the group think syndrome results in their real opinions being suppressed.

Positive self-representation   Positive self-representation occurs when focus group members express socially desirable opinions rather than their real views in order to sound good, create a positive impression of themselves within the group, and/or hide their real but not-so-desirable opinions and attitudes.

The 'spiral of silence'   The 'spiral of silence' (Noelle-Neumann, 1974, 1985) occurs when group members (just as in society) become afraid to express views that conflict with the prevailing dominant view, even if the dominant view may be wrong or unfair. This is due to the members' fear of 'losing face' (Goffman, 1967) or being humiliated, ostracised or isolated within the group or by the dominant individuals. This can lead to members self-censoring their opinions in order to conform to the group norms. This can lead to the '**bandwagon effect**', where members think their role within the group is to build consensus and resolve issues by mutual agreement.

This is similar to a situation such as at a meeting where a person abstains from voting on an issue when he or she disagrees with the dominant or majority view but is afraid to oppose it.

Rectifying the effects of group dynamics   To rectify situations where group dynamics appear to have negatively affected the data collection, or contaminated the data from focus groups, the researcher could contact the group members after the interview by phone and ask them to express their opinions on the affected subject or topic.

Case Study 11.8   'IS THE ALIEN THE PROBLEM?': THE EFFECTS OF GROUP DYNAMICS, CENSORING AND THE 'SPIRAL OF SILENCE' ON A FOCUS GROUP DISCUSSION

During an all-male focus group interview in Los Angeles, California for a research project on the 1992 US presidential campaign, the subjects were asked to discuss the three most important issues to them within the context of the election. Jesse, Howard and Colin were discussing the issues of abortion, violence on TV and morality when Howard suddenly introduced the issue of immigration.

Howard: I haven't heard them [the Republican Party candidates] talk about the illegal aliens coming in [sic] this country. They don't talk about that or crime. I mean ...

Jesse: You have to build a fence you know, a hundred feet high, just to keep them out, you know. And let's face it. The alien ... it's a major, major problem. But how do you stop it? What do you do?

Howard: But the big companies like it, because it is cheap labour to them.

Colin: But is the alien the problem? My wife is an alien. [She is from Western Europe.]

Jesse: I don't believe the alien is a problem at all.

Colin: I think wouldn't it be fair to say that the problem is the aliens who come into this country to take advantage of this country, versus the aliens who are coming in for legitimate reasons?

Jesse: Well, we are all aliens. We all come from alien people, one way or another.

Larry: Right. This country is a melting pot. The majority of us are children of aliens.

Moderator: Let's talk one at a time here. Ken?

(The moderator moves the discussion to another participant, Ken, giving him the chance to state the most important problem to him and keeping the focus group on track, as well as ending the awkward discussion on aliens.)

Note how Jesse had to make a complete turnaround of his opinions, indicating the existence of the 'spiral of silence'. Censoring was also imposed by Colin on the group as he had a personal interest in the topic under discussion. When Colin challenged Jesse, he immediately became the dominant member of the group, which had been criticising an issue close to him.

Jesse probably was carried away by the discussion when he talked about a 'fence a hundred feet high'. Jesse appears to have assumed a **false consensus** within a perceived homogeneous group when speaking about aliens, as the group consisted of white American citizens unlikely to be offended by opinions on aliens. Once Jesse retracted his negative views on aliens, Larry, who was not involved in the offending discussion, expressed a neutral view on aliens and brought the discussion back to equilibrium, indicating the group dynamics in action (Weerakkody, 2002: 53–4).

Now that we have discussed how to conduct focus groups and examined the various issues related to them, we can consider how focus groups are used in research related to media and communication, journalism and public relations.

APPLICATIONS OF FOCUS GROUPS IN RESEARCH IN JOURNALISM, MEDIA AND COMMUNICATION, AND PUBLIC RELATIONS

Focus groups are a very popular method of data collection in media and communication and public relations and to a lesser extent in journalism. Let us look at a few case studies.

Journalism   In journalism, newspapers increasingly use focus groups, panel discussions, town meetings and social gatherings such as newspaper-sponsored barbecues to understand the views of citizens and the local community, and the issues that are important to them. These make up parts of their news-gathering process in civic or public journalism (Willey, 2004).

However, focus groups in journalism are not conducted in as stringent a manner as in the social sciences. But they still use research questions, consider target populations and conduct the interviews in a friendly environment. Just as in social science research, journalism uses focus groups supplemented by other forms of data collection, research or news-gathering methods.

Journalists can use focus groups to identify suitable individual sources of information, who they may interview in depth later. Journalists also name their participants (or sources) when quoting their opinions expressed in news stories if the interviews were 'on the record', rather than 'off the record' or 'not for attribution'. In the social sciences, however, researchers maintain confidentiality and anonymity of participants.

Knowledge so gathered by journalists is often applied as action research and investigative journalism (which takes the critical perspective as the research paradigm and is grounded in the principle of social justice) to report on or expose unfair, illegal or unethical situations. Journalists thus seek to encourage participation by the marginalised to obtain positive social change.

Journalists are seen as combining focus group techniques and action research as a 'hybrid' in their news-gathering techniques (Willey, 2004: 82).

Media and communication   Focus groups are often used in media and communication research to test and collect opinions of audience members about pilot episodes of new TV series, film titles, characters, actors in specific roles, alternative endings, storylines, ideas for sequels or prequels etc.

Case Study 11.9   *STAR WARS* AND LUKE STARKILLER!

In the first *Star wars* film (1977), the character played by actor Mark Hamill had been originally named 'Luke Starkiller', while the film's working title was *'The star wars: From the adventures of Luke Starkiller'* (www.imdb.com/title/tt0076759 accessed 3/07/2007).

After a focus group indicated their dislike of the name 'Starkiller', it was changed to Luke Skywalker. The scene where the character introduces himself to Princess Leia was re-shot.

Focus groups had been used in marketing research since the 1920s and in the social sciences since the 1970s. In the advertising and marketing of new products, and the testing of advertising campaigns, focus groups are routinely used and their feedback obtained as to what the test audiences like or dislike about them and what improvements they would like to see.

Public relations   Focus groups are one of the most often used research methods in public relations, usually in the planning stages of a campaign to explore issues and pre-test ideas to examine what strategy is likely to work, what will not and what is the best and most effective way to communicate with a particular target public.

A focus group in public relations generally consists of about 12 interviewees and the number of focus groups conducted depends on the budget available. The research will be commissioned to an independent researcher and each focus group costs up to $10,000, depending on the type of interviewees, effort required to recruit suitable subjects, travel involved for the researchers if conducted in a country location and other factors.

Case Study 11.10   EFFECTS OF NEW INDUSTRIAL RELATIONS LAWS ON YOUNG PEOPLE

In July 2006, the Australian Government introduced new industrial relations (IR) laws and workplace agreements that were widely perceived as exploitative of casual, younger and lower-paid workers. In the lead-up to the federal elections on 24 November 2007, the Government introduced an aggressive public relations campaign to dispel the 'myths' about these laws, as they were considered an election issue.

The issues addressed in the campaign were identified using focus groups with different segments of the public on their concerns with IR laws. They found that parents were worried about these laws making their teenage children vulnerable and open to coercion and exploitation by employers.

As a result, several advertisements stressed that a child under 18 years of age is required to have their workplace agreement signed by a parent or guardian and that the Workplace Ombudsman was available to 'protect their rights'.

FOCUS GROUPS IN INTERNAL COMMUNICATION

Focus groups can assist organisations to get detailed responses from staff about internal workplace issues.

LOW MORALE AND HIGH JOB DISSATISFACTION
IN THE WORKPLACE

Case Study 11.11

An organisation commissions an internal staff survey to examine various issues within the
organisation finds that its staff indicated low levels of morale, high job dissatisfaction and
a perceived lack of equitable opportunities for professional advancement.

In a bid to examine the factors that may be causing them and to seek ways to rectify the
situation, the management commissions a research company to conduct confidential focus
groups with staff who are willing to be interviewed to obtain detailed opinions on the issues
and devise possible responses.

Summary

Focus groups are used as a quick method of collecting qualitative data for pilot
and exploratory studies in many disciplinary areas, including research in marketing,
advertising, media and communication, journalism and public relations. They collect
subjects' opinions on and attitudes towards a given issue or topic under discussion.
A group of six to 12 people are interviewed by a moderator on a 'focused' topic using
a semi-structured discussion guide. The interviews are audio or video recorded and
the data analysed into themes and sub-themes of opinions expressed by the focus
group members. The main disadvantage of focus groups is the contamination of data
collected that is caused by the effects of group dynamics within the groups.

The next chapter addresses case studies as a research method.

Try this ...

Design a focus group research project to test one of the following:

1 the pilot of a new TV series
2 a new film before its release
3 a TV ad campaign for a political candidate
4 a new consumer product (of your choice)
5 ideas for the sequel of a popular action film.
   (You may use a real situation or a fictitious one to help you with the process.

   Consider the following steps in your design.

- Define the research problem you want to examine.
- Select a sample, decide how many focus groups will be needed, their composition,
  how many participants there will be in each and in total, and their demographic
  characteristics.
- Decide who, and what will be the subjects, sample and population to be studied.
- What preparations will be necessary for the study mechanism?

- What focus group materials will be required? (For example, screener questions, stimulus materials, moderator's discussion guide and other materials.)
- How much will the focus groups cost and for what specific items?
- How will you conduct the session and what resources and facilities will be needed?
- How will you conduct the interviews?
- How will you analyse the data and report the findings?
- What will be the ethical issues involved in the study and what precautions will you take to protect against them?
- What precautions will you make to avoid or reduce contamination of the data due to various effects of group dynamics within the focus groups?

Further reading

Greenbaum, T L 2000. *Moderating focus groups: A practical guide for group facilitation*. Sage, Thousand Oaks, CA.

Kahle, R 2007. *Dominators, cynics, and wallflowers: Practical strategies for moderating meaningful focus groups*. Paramount Market Publishing Inc., Ithaca, NY.

Morgan, D L 1998. *Focus groups as qualitative research*, 2nd edn. Sage, Thousand Oaks, CA.

Field Studies

12

In Chapter 10 (Research interviewing) and Chapter 11 (Focus groups), we examined two of the qualitative research methods covered in this book. This chapter discusses the third such method. Field studies or **field observations** collect qualitative research data and are carried out in their natural settings. This method originated in sociology and anthropology (as ethnography) with Bronislaw Malinowski (1884–1942), a Polish–British anthropologist considered its pioneer. His work in the Trobriand Islands published as *Argonauts of the Western Pacific* is a landmark study (Malinowski, 1922/1961).

HISTORY OF FIELD STUDIES

Early ethnography was about studying remote or 'exotic' cultures, but later sociologists examined contemporary urban cultures using the same methods. In ethnography, a researcher takes an interpretive perspective. Since the 1980s, field studies are used in **media ethnography** to study media organisations and audiences. It is also the principle that underpins 'new' or gonzo journalism and **citizen journalism**. Today field studies are used in diverse disciplines such as administration, management, criminology, labour relations, social work, nursing and education.

AN AUSTRALIAN GEISHA
Case Study 12.1

On 19 December 2007, Dr Fiona Graham—a social anthropologist from Melbourne, Victoria—made her debut as a fully fledged geisha with the professional name of Sayuki in the Asakusa district near Tokyo, Japan. She was the first Westerner to be admitted as an insider to the mysterious, 400-year-old institution.

Dr Graham had graduated from a Japanese high school and attended Keio University as an undergraduate. She began her geisha training in April 2007 and mastered the necessary skills of the tea ceremony, small talk, traditional dancing and entertaining, and playing the drum and the bamboo flute.

Dr Graham plans to explain the geisha world when she leaves and will film her life through the different seasons of the year. Even though several other women anthropologists and journalists in the past have written about the geisha world from the inside, none had attained full geisha status (Ryall, 2008).

CONDUCTING FIELD STUDY RESEARCH

This chapter examines how field studies (field work, participant or field observations) are conducted in social science research (Lofland & Lofland, 1995). The main topics examined are:

- the role of researcher in field studies
- data collection methods
- types of field studies
- conducting a field study
- data analysis in field studies
- reporting field study research
- field studies as media ethnography
- field studies in journalism
- field studies in public relations.

THE ROLE OF RESEARCHER IN FIELD STUDIES

Just as in other qualitative research, the researcher in field studies is the instrument that collects, measures and analyses the data. (In quantitative research, such as surveys or content analysis, the researcher prepares the relevant questionnaires and coding manuals used in the process.)

The researcher's relationship to the research setting   Most often, the researcher in the field study is unfamiliar with the setting or the group being observed. However, sometimes the researcher is a member of the same setting but observes it from the point of view of an objective insider. A researcher could also be a member who had been away from the setting for some time and has returned to formally study it. For example, a researcher who was born and raised in a setting—but has been away for higher education and employment elsewhere—can return to the setting to study it, but with a different perspective thanks to her life experiences outside the setting.

DATA COLLECTION METHODS

The main methods of data collection used by researchers when carrying out field studies are:

- **intensive interviewing**
- **group interviewing**
- field observations.

A specific field study may last days, weeks, months or even years with the researcher making comprehensive and analytical observations. The researcher takes extensive written **field notes** and records observations or interviews members using audio-visual technologies.

Intensive interviewing   Intensive interviewing is carried out by the researcher with members of the setting under study. These interviewees are called '**informants**' rather than subjects. The interviews are long and may be unstructured; that is, they are flexible about the questions posed to each person (see Chapter 10). The researcher makes conversation with an informant about the setting and its everyday life. These interviews are carried out on several occasions with the same informants.

The chief informant of the researcher in a field study is the member of the setting who will be the most useful to the researcher. He or she may be an official or unofficial leader of the group or popular within it, and helps the researcher to break down barriers when gaining '**access**' (permission to study them). This informant can introduce the researcher to other members and encourage them to open up to the researcher.

THE ROLE OF INFORMANTS   Case Study 12.2

An overseas researcher, who desires to study an Aboriginal group and its lifestyle in Australia, approaches a colleague or friend who is a member of that group seeking help to gain access to them for a field study. In this case the Aboriginal friend serves as the chief informant and answers any questions posed by the researcher. He speaks to the elders of his group and obtains access for the researcher, finds him a place to live and introduces him to community members so that the members feel the outsider is trustworthy. The chief informant also briefs the researcher on the basic rules and **taboos** in the setting and identifies or suggests other useful informants for interviews.

All informants help the researcher understand the everyday activities of the group by answering the researcher's questions. After spending some time in the setting, the researcher interviews several individual informants and conducts a few group interviews with members of similar demographic groups to gain more insights on matters the researcher finds interesting. (For perspectives on Indigenous media audience research in Australia, see Meadows, 2002.)

The researcher makes extensive notes of her observations of the setting and the daily life of its members; records her own insights and comments alongside them; records the individual and group interviews carried out; and takes photographs, makes sketches, draws maps and video records their activities.

Group interviewing   Group interviews carried out during field studies involve several informants to help the discussion to take place in a livelier environment, allowing the researcher to obtain a diversity of views within a group setting. However, group interviews are only suitable to discuss topics that are 'safe' or neutral, where confidential or embarrassing information—or topics 'taboo' within the setting—are not involved.

Acceptable and unacceptable topics for group interviews

EXAMPLE 12.1

A researcher should not discuss issues related to, say, pre-marital sex in a setting where it is not an acceptable practice. But marriage ceremonies and what each of the **rituals** involved mean to the group can be acceptable.

Field observations   Field observation involves observing, looking, listening, watching and asking questions about what the observed activities mean to the members of that setting. However, the researcher might face barriers that obstruct the objective observation and analysis of the setting. These are related to the researchers themselves, the subjects or the nature of the setting. They are due to:

- demographic and other differences between a researcher and the research subjects—for example, age, race, ethnicity, class, education, nationality, values, ideology, attitudes, individual subjectivity and life experiences.
- the nature of the setting or the group—for example, a terrorist, criminal or extremist group such as Al Queda, the Mafia or the Ku Klux Klan, can make a field study difficult and dangerous.
- ethical issues—for example, not reporting illegal or antisocial activities in the setting, or being legally forced to divulge one's research data and information to authorities. Reporting illegal activities may violate the trust and promises made before gaining access to the setting and the group, while ethical issues related to confidentiality, anonymity and harm to subjects can arise in divulging the information. There are recorded instances of researchers been imprisoned for contempt of court when they refused to provide details of the setting's activities and identity of members. (This situation is analogous to journalists being jailed for contempt of court when they refuse to divulge their news sources.)

Case Study 12.3   BARRIERS TO ACCESS TO A SETTING AND THE CONDUCT OF FIELD STUDIES

Sue-Ellen is a young, single, Western woman who wants to carry out a field study in a highly patriarchal and conservative society in a remote village in a developing country. She is introduced to the setting by one of her male colleagues with contacts within the group. However, first she had to meet the strict requirements for visas issued to the country and this remote region by its government—especially for researchers, as it suspects Western 'outsiders' as trying to impose a new form of cultural colonialism by converting people to Christianity in poor nations.

Once granted access, she finds that her independent, single lifestyle is a barrier to her interviewing its males or moving freely within the setting. The young women in the setting are discouraged from associating with her as the group see her as a 'bad influence'. She also finds that some of the practices of this group—including its food, accommodation and the traditional roles of women—are 'primitive' and not compatible with her Western standards, which makes it emotionally stressful. She also suspects that a few individuals in the neighbouring village are involved in growing marijuana and have links with criminal groups outside the setting.

However, she manages to get used to the life in the setting, is very courteous towards its members, and makes friends with the older men and women who then let her associate with their young people and move about the setting freely. She tries to respect their rules and social practices, follow their lifestyle as much as possible, and help in their everyday chores. She tries to stay clear of the marijuana growers and acts in ways that they will not see her as a 'spy' for law enforcement.

TYPES OF FIELD STUDIES

There are four types of field study research. They differ based on the researcher's presence being covert (where the true nature of the researcher's presence is hidden from the group under study) or overt (where the group is informed about the researcher's purpose for being there).

Depending on the researcher's involvement in the activities of the setting and the group, it can be either participant observation (where the researcher takes part in all the activities of the setting just as its members) or non-participant observation (where the researcher simply observes what goes on in the setting). Both these can be either overt or covert. **Auto-ethnography** is another aspect of field studies, which is discussed below.

Participant observation   In an **overt participant observation**, the researcher observes and takes part in all activities of the setting, while openly taking notes, recording events audio-visually, interviewing members individually or in groups at length, and directly asking questions to have things clarified. In a **covert participant observation**, the note-taking will be done later and questions asked from individuals and groups without giving rise to suspicions or curiosity from the members.

Overt participant observation occurs when actors 'research for a role' while working or living in a relevant setting; for example, actor Brett Tucker worked with a country veterinarian to prepare for his role as a vet in the popular Australian TV drama *McLeod's daughters* (Graeme-Evans & Zwicky, 2001–08).

Participant observation in non-research everyday settings

EXAMPLE **12.2**

Even though field studies or **participant observation** is a formal research method, many everyday, non-research situations involve the same principles. A common example of an overt participant observation is the practical training in hospitals received by medical students or interns immediately after graduation. Other types of internships are carried out by journalism or other students in their respective professional settings, which are overt participant observations.

An example of a covert participant observer is that of a 'spy', such as those working for government intelligence services such as the ASIO (Australian Security Intelligence Organisation) and the CIA (US Central Intelligence Agency). Another example is undercover law enforcement officers working with an organised crime group or a protest group, observing and reporting on the group's activities.

In the popular Hollywood film *Donny Brasco* (1997), actor Johnny Depp plays the title role of real-life FBI (US Federal Bureau of Investigation) agent Joseph D Pistone, who infiltrated the Mafia in a covert participant observation.

Overt field studies or participant observations carried out by academic scholars and funded by the US government in Indo-China during the early 1960s prior to the Vietnam War and in Latin America created a scandal in the field when their data and research findings were used by the US government for intelligence purposes.

Case Study 12.4   COUNTERING THE TALIBAN: 'EMBEDDED SCHOLARS' OR 'MERCENARY ANTHROPOLOGISTS'?

Anthropological and other social researchers were attached to combat teams of the US military in Afghanistan as 'a new weapon in counter insurgency operations' in 2007. These research scientists were to understand the cultural aspects that had previously allowed the Taliban to flourish in isolated areas. For example, a female anthropologist observed a large number of widows in one village placing pressure on their sons to provide for their families by joining the well-paid insurgents.

So the US military developed job-training programs for widows, called 'armed social work', to counter this situation.

However, some academics denounce this practice as 'mercenary anthropology', which exploits social science for political gain. They fear the researchers will be seen as gathering intelligence for the military. However, the adviser to the program described it as 'anthropologising the military' (Rohde, 2007).

In covert participant observations, the researcher may find it difficult to ask too many questions from members of the setting without arousing suspicions. However, some groups and settings may only be studied as covert participant observations due to the nature of the group and their activities, such as deviant, extremist or criminal groups who do not allow 'outsiders' access to their secret settings or activities.

Non-participant observation   A researcher can be a **non-participant observer** where they simply observe if overt or pretend to be doing something else while observing if covert. Accessing a public or open setting for non-participant observations is easier and therefore often used by students and beginning researchers. The deception involved in such as situation is 'by omission' (failing to inform) rather than 'by commission' (misleading or deceiving the subjects). Some argue that this involves fewer ethical issues if 'no harm is done to subjects' and confidentiality and anonymity have been maintained.

EXAMPLE 12.3   Covert and overt non-participant observations in real life

An example of an overt non-participant observation—even though not related to scholarly research—is the 'work experience' of Year 10 students in Australia, who spend a week at a designated workplace related to a profession the student is interested in following.

Covert non-participant observation takes place when a person pretending to be reading a newspaper is actually observing the setting in a public place, such as an airport lounge or railway station.

Auto-ethnography or autobiographical sociology   Auto-ethnography or **autobiographical sociology** is about a researcher telling 'personal stories' where his or her own experiences are examined in detail. It is an exercise in self-reflexivity where the researcher looks at him- or herself through other people's eyes. This allows for useful findings, analysis and researcher's own interpretations of certain phenomena or experiences.

AUTO-ETHNOGRAPHY OF INTERNATIONAL STUDENTS IN AUSTRALIA

Case Study 12.5

Seven years ago, Megumi arrived alone in Australia from Japan to begin Year 10 in high school. She continued her education after Year 12 and obtained a four-year honours degree from an Australian university. At the time she arrived, she spoke very little English. For her honours thesis, she examined how Australians perceived her or assigned her an 'identity' based on her appearance and fluency in English.

In class, she was not seen as an international student, as the lecturers and classmates assumed her to be Australian-born, due to her fluency in English and Australian accent. Some lecturers would not ask for her experiences or views for cross-cultural comparison, when her few other international classmates were. When she insisted on speaking up, a lecturer asked, 'How can you speak English so well, when you are Japanese?'

This contrasts with the auto-ethnographic experiences of Yen Chi, a Malaysian-born Australian citizen who migrated to Australia as a four year old. Yen Chi was always assumed to be 'an international student' by Australians because she spoke English with a slight Chinese accent picked up from her parents and because the majority of her ethnic classmates were internationals.

Megumi and Yen Chi therefore examined how stereotypical perceptions of 'others' led to their teachers to assign identities to them.

Blog, moblogs and vblogs   Practical everyday applications of the phenomenon of recording and interpreting one's own everyday life experiences are personal blogs (internet or web logs), moblogs (mobile phone logs) or vblogs (video web logs), where individuals record their everyday experiences and thoughts on these blogs and make them available on the web for others to access.

Life logging   The latest research data collection process in auto-ethnography is life logging, where sophisticated recording equipment carried by a researcher or an individual at all times automatically activates to record every conversation or movement of the person—and those who come into contact with that person—in their everyday life. The data collected is used to analyse and interpret interpersonal interactions and everyday conversations, especially for 'conversation analysis' of **encounters** between the researcher and others.

This raises legal and ethical issues as the other participants in the conversations are not aware of this activity going on and have not consented to it. It could lead to issues of privacy, informed consent, confidentiality and anonymity. When such recordings are carried out by non-researchers simply to record their everyday life, they, too, raise similar legal and ethical issues.

Criticisms of auto-ethnography   Some scholars advise that 'a person should not study oneself' and that such research reports will simply be 'complaints' of people with a 'chip on their shoulder' about perceived injustices or 'vain' exercises of 'self-promotion'. They think beginning researchers will make subjective interpretations of one's own experiences. However, many travel writings including in journalism or experiences of 'outsiders' in a given setting qualify as auto-ethnography as the writers report on their experiences as participant or non-participant observers.

CONDUCTING A FIELD STUDY

A field study research needs to follow several steps::

- choosing a suitable topic
- choosing a suitable research site
- examining the ethical issues
- gaining access to the site
- data collection
- exiting the site.

The subsequent steps of data analysis and writing the research report are dealt with separately in the following sections.

Choosing a suitable topic   Field studies begin with the selection of a research topic or area of study. Ideally, the topic area should be of interest to the researcher to help them to maintain enthusiasm and relevance during the potentially difficult and laborious process of data collection.

Research topic and self-reference   Field studies often relate to the demographic groups the researcher belongs to, or those related to the researcher's life experiences (self-reference or autobiography) and interests. In other words, the topic selected for study is often related to the researcher's personal history or remote (past) as well as current biography. For example, a female researcher who is a member of a minority ethnic migrant group in Australia may decide to study an issue related to women of that group. However, a researcher may not always indicate this connection in reports if it is not required (say, if no conflict of interest exists) or the researcher thinks it is irrelevant to the topic under study. This selection of the group and setting could simply have been shaped by her links with the group that allowed her easier access and cooperation than others.

Choosing a suitable research site   In a field study, a researcher needs to spend a prolonged period of time observing and familiarising with the site. Data are collected by making (field) notes, by making personal contact with subjects or informants and by doing interviews to understand the everyday life of the group in their natural setting.

To maintain the validity of the observations, researchers must examine if the chosen setting is suitable to provide the observations needed to answer the research questions. They should also familiarise themselves with the site before the actual data collection begins.

Case Study 12.6   MAINTAINING THE VALIDITY OF DATA COLLECTION IN A FIELD STUDY

A researcher planning to examine 'how team-teaching is carried out in a particular subject at a university' needs to observe how the team members:

- communicate with each other
- conduct meetings (to discuss lesson plans)
- assign roles and functions to members
- prepare unit materials (for example, study guides)
- coordinate class room activities (to maintain structure and consistency)

- standardise assessment instruments and processes such as preparing marking guidelines
- moderate across markers to maintain reliability or uniformity of the assessment process
- teach the subject in the classroom.

A field study examining how the university department offering this subject conducts its everyday administrative activities unrelated to teaching and observing its general staff meetings will not provide the necessary data for the study, as such activities do not relate to the team-teaching of a particular unit.

Examining the ethical issues   In a field study, a researcher must examine the ethical issues related to informed consent, voluntary participation, deception, confidentiality, anonymity, objectivity, honesty and integrity, and 'no harm to subjects'. This relates to deciding whether to use covert or overt methods and participant or non-participant observation based on the nature of the study, the type of setting (open and public or closed and private) and the cooperation available from the setting and its subjects for an overt study.

Some argue that ethical issues are less problematic in a covert participant observation if the researcher had been a member of the setting for a while, and then decides to observe the setting as a research study (Lofland & Lofland, 1995). However, not everyone agrees with this.

STUDYING A REFUGEE ADVOCACY GROUP   Case Study 12.7

An academic who is a long-standing and active member of a refugee advocacy group decides to study its activities and protest marches as a formal field study. Will she need to obtain permission from the group's leaders and members to do so? A covert research may give a 'spy' or 'mole' quality to the researcher and raises moral issues. The researcher also may be bound by the ethics requirements of her institution, which may require that voluntary participation and informed consent is obtained from the setting and its subjects.

'THE MOBILE CONFESSIONAL'   Case Study 12.8

For 10 years, Marianne has been an employee of an organisation that operates several branch offices in different parts of the state. She often travels to the head office and car pools with colleagues from her own or other departments travelling there the same day.

Over the years, she found that during this three-hour return trip the passengers in the car used the time and the opportunity to talk about various topics, including office and national politics, news and current affairs, office gossip, their own families and their past. They also used this opportunity to vent their frustrations with their jobs, supervisors, colleagues and clients. One staff member referred to this journey as a 'mobile confessional'.

Marianne noticed that people were more likely to talk about their private and personal affairs when they were alone with her in the car, and office politics when the other passengers came from outside their own department. She saw these discussions as informal, individual and group interviews.

She wants to use this situation and the conversations in a research project. She assumes she does not violate any ethical rules because:

Case Study 12.8

1   the data were not collected for a research study

2   she will not divulge the identity of the speakers and will maintain confidentiality of the personal information discussed

3   she was only going to examine the categories of topic areas discussed in general rather than specific views expressed by her colleagues

4   the site was a public and open space (even though some may argue it is private and closed).

However, she realises that she may not be able to recall the data accurately and comprehensively as she has not taken any notes at the time and fully depends on her memory.

What do you think about this proposed research project in terms of data collection and the ethical issues involved? Could it be carried out as auto-ethnography? If so, what research questions should be examined?

Gaining access to the site   Once a suitable site or sites have been selected for a field study, a researcher needs to gain access to it by seeking permission from the relevant authorities or individuals. This process becomes easier if the researcher has a prior connection with the setting or its members, which helps to circumvent gatekeepers. When seeking access, researchers must also provide a suitable '**account**' or explanation of what the research is about and why they are doing it.

Case Study 12.9   ACCESSING THE SITE

An honours student at a university writing her thesis sought to interview general practitioners (GPs) of family medical centres about their use of the websites of pharmaceutical companies to learn about new medicinal drugs. She was able to get access to several GPs for interviews via personal contacts of her father—a pharmaceutical salesperson. As these interviews take time away from the busy schedules of doctors, she found the doctors were helping her as a personal favour to her father and that he had already provided her informants with an 'account' of why she was doing the research.

Balance between 'knowing it all' and 'knowing nothing' about the researched   It is also helpful to have some basic knowledge and understanding of the publicly available information and facts about the setting and your informants before the interviews. This means that basic questions about the person's well-known past achievements, life history, status or standing in the setting or society are not posed to them. This gives an impression of preparedness on the part of the researcher when interviewing busy, important or high-status informants.

This prior knowledge also alerts the researcher when informants indicate the 'social desirability effect' or blatantly lie or exaggerate facts to 'make fun' of the researcher who is an 'outsider'. For example, decades after the fact, the young female informants of the famed anthropologist Margaret Mead (1901–78) admitted lying to her about their 'promiscuous pre-marital sexual behaviour' during her research on *Coming of age in Samoa* (Mead, 1943).

However, a researcher is warned not to act as a 'know all' about the setting or the informants but instead to listen and query the informants about their own viewpoints, perceptions and opinions without imposing one's prior assumptions on the interview process.

Data collection   Once researchers gain access to the site and have familiarised themselves with it, they can begin to collect data via field observations and interviews with informants. In field studies, the observations made need to be recorded or logged for easy indexing (labelling and indicating their location in a given record) and retrieval (locating the specific records when needed).

Data collection with field observations   Detailed and comprehensive field notes taken on all observations—not just the important ones—will help to trigger the researcher's memory during the analysis stage. These data can include field notes of all observations and researcher comments that accompany them; recorded interviews; video-taped observations or activities in the setting; documents related to the setting; photos; maps; sketches; drawings; and tables or charts prepared by the researcher to explain what is going on in a given situation.

Field studies are time consuming and, therefore, using several observers can make it faster and easier. However, it can increase researcher subjectivity and chances of error, and thereby negatively affect the reliability of the data collected.

Making field notes   The field notes of observations should be made as soon as possible—at least by the following morning. These notes should be descriptive to indicate what the setting looked like, who was where, how many were present, when they were present and the conversations or activities that took place. If the study is overt, the notes can be made while making the observation, using suitable writing materials such as index cards or small note books.

Field notes are written in chronological order (that is, in the same order as they happened) with maps, sketches etc to indicate the points of reference between people or objects in the setting as to where everything and everyone was. Direct quotations of people should be recorded whenever possible and long conversations paraphrased. Listen, observe and make notes of your interpretations of events or conversations and compare them with those of the same informants at a later stage. Consult with the group members or informants to see if they agree with your observations and resulting interpretations.

There is no set style of writing or length specified for field notes; however, two pages of single spaced A4 paper is a guide for an hour of observations (Lofland & Lofland, 1995). It is always better to have more notes than fewer.

Data collection with field interviews   Interviews with informants carried out during field studies are less structured than those carried out in other research. These interviews are based on aspects of the setting that are not clear or 'puzzling' to the observer and therefore need clarification. It is useful to use a diversity of informants, such as those from different demographic groups, to obtain a variety of viewpoints.

Even though the interviews are unstructured, a researcher must prepare an interview guide with a few relevant questions to ask the informants. Each main question should have a few sub-questions (or **probes**) that try to describe the topic further. It is best to use neutral wording and avoid leading questions—such as 'Don't you think X should be …' or 'What do you think about X being …'—during the interviews and instead ask 'What do you think about X?' or 'What is X?'

Interview transcripts   Once interviews are completed, the transcripts are typed as a single column in the middle of the page that allows for researcher comments on the margins during analysis. The cover page of the transcript is a 'fact sheet' that includes information such as the date, time and place of interview, and demographic details such as the informant's sex, age, ethnicity and education. This prepares the researcher for the data analysis that begins immediately.

Any problems or challenges faced during the interviews and the emotions expressed or felt by both the informants and the researcher during the process should be noted on the transcripts.

EXAMPLE 12.4

An interview guide and procedure for field interviews

A researcher uses the following interview guide to examine the 'puzzling' aspects of courtship rituals and rules of a particular group.

1   At what age are young people allowed to court?
2   How do they initiate a courtship?
3   Are there any rules or restrictions about who can court whom and why?
4   Do parents get involved in courtships of their children? If so, when and how?
5   What activities are shared by a couple during the courting period?
6   Are they chaperoned (accompanied by an adult) during these courting activities?
7   How long does a courtship last before they get married?
8   What is the procedure followed if a couple or one party wants to end the courtship (or break up)?
9   If a courting couple decides to get married, what happens next?

The 'probes' for the last question can be:
o   How does the marriage proposal happen?
o   How does the couple inform the family about their intentions?
o   Do they obtain permission from parents to marry and how?
o   What happens once they decide to get married?
o   What are the arrangements to be made for the wedding?
o   Who pays for what for the wedding?
o   What rituals are involved with the marriage ceremony?
o   How long does it take?
o   What happens after the ceremony?
o   Where do they live after marriage?'

To obtain a diversity of views, the researcher can interview informants of both sexes, various ages, socio-economic levels and status such as:
o   those who are not yet of courting age
o   those of age but not currently courting
o   a few couples currently courting
o   those with experiences of a break-up
o   those engaged to be married
o   those recently married
o   those married for a few years and of different ages.

Using the same interview guide, the researcher can conduct both individual and group interviews.

Exiting the site   Once the data collection is complete, the researcher must leave the setting. Therefore, an **exit strategy** or plan must be in place including debriefing the members—especially if any form of deception was involved.

In an overt participant or non-participant observation in a public setting, exiting will not be a problem as few people would have noticed the researcher's presence or activities as unusual. In an overt field study in a private setting, this would be straightforward if all members knew the researcher's stay was temporary and why they were there. But if only those who gave permission for access knew about the researcher's presence and purpose, other members need a valid and truthful reason for the researcher leaving and why they were there, without creating feelings of disappointment, betrayal or exploitation.

In a covert participant observation, the sudden departure without an explanation may lead to member speculation about what may have happened to the person and why they were there in the first place. Members may also miss the researcher's presence, the role they played in the setting—for example, doing the chores—or their company if they were well liked. Sometimes the members may get offended and feel used when researchers declare their purpose of being there when leaving the setting.

Therefore, in any field study—be it overt or covert—the researcher must exit the setting tactfully and diplomatically, so as not to upset the members, tarnish the image of social research or destroy future chances of other researchers working there.

| EXITING THE FIELD STUDY SETTING | Case Study 12.10 |

Elizabeth Wynhausen—a journalist with the *Australian* newspaper—took nine months' leave without pay from her job to investigate the plight of minimum wage workers who carry out menial jobs in Australia. Her work resulted in several newspaper articles and the book *Dirt cheap: Life at the wrong end of the job market* (Wynhausen, 2005).

She worked as a food server at an exclusive social club, a factory worker, an office cleaner and a housekeeper at a hotel, as well as in a budget department store and an aged-care nursing home, with each job lasting two to four weeks. Her study, which took the critical perspective, found that such minimum wage workers were underpaid, unappreciated and invisible. However, her co-workers were conscientious and ready to share their knowledge, and protected her when she frequently made mistakes.

She divulged her identity to her co-workers at the end of each job but not to her employers. Some co-workers were not pleased, but none cared to ask about her project. Some could not believe anyone would want to 'write a book'— let alone read one—about their lives.

DATA ANALYSIS IN FIELD STUDIES

The data analysis categories in a field study result from the 'patterns', 'units of analysis' or '**units of investigation**' found within the data and the focusing decisions made by the researcher about them. These relate to meanings, social practices, **episodes**, encounters and **social roles**, among others (Lofland & Lofland, 1995).

Meanings as themes of data analysis   The smallest unit of investigation in field study research (similar to a 'theme' in general qualitative data analysis) is related to 'meanings' made by informants to define their own and others' actions and behaviours. These can be related to cultural norms, definitions of situations, ideology, beliefs, stereotypes, social constructions of reality and world views, and are used to justify their behaviours.

EXAMPLE 12.5

'Meaning' behind who may court whom in the field study setting

When asked by the researcher what 'the most important factor is when deciding on a suitable marriage partner', several informants responded that the couple's family backgrounds should be similar in terms of economic and social status within their society.

They explained that their group and culture is part of a highly stratified society where social and economic status defines their life experiences; how and what they eat and dress; how they live or behave; and their values, beliefs and aspirations.

Therefore, choosing someone from a different family background and socio-economic status can create problems between the couple and their in-laws at a later stage due to unmatched social and cultural practices, understandings and expectations.

The researcher also observed that this society did not allow for easy 'upward mobility' to those who are born disadvantaged, marginalised, stigmatised, powerless or poor.

Social practices as themes of data analysis　The most common social practices observed in a setting can be categorised as rituals, **fetishes** and taboos.

Rituals　Rituals are standard procedures that are followed in performing certain rites within a culture or setting, and that have symbolic meanings for them. Examples in Western cultures of rituals are saying 'break a leg' to actors going on stage, and the groom being the first to kiss the bride after the wedding ceremony to symbolise the exclusivity implicit in marriage.

EXAMPLE 12.6

Rituals related to weddings in a field study setting

A researcher finds that auspicious times set by an astrologer are followed to the letter by the wedding parties as to when the groom leaves his home for the ceremony held at the bride's home, when each party leaves their homes for the reception hall for the ceremony, and when the ceremony is to begin and end.

This guarantees that everyone keeps to the schedule, whereas in everyday life this cultural group is notorious for taking an easy attitude towards doing things 'on time'.

Fetishes　A fetish is an inanimate object held in respect and believed to bring good luck to those who own, use or wear them. These help people manage their anxiety of an event with unpredictable or uncertain results, such as exams, job interviews and competitions. The four-leaf clover, rabbit's foot and a bride wearing something old, new, borrowed and blue are examples of this in the Western world.

EXAMPLE 12.7

Fetishes in the field study setting

A researcher observes that some group members have the fetish of having a dried leaf from a sacred *Ficus religiosa* tree placed along with the religious icons and statues where they worship their gods to bring good luck to the home and its occupants.

Taboos   Taboos are prohibitions imposed on the members of a setting and relate to certain (generally stigmatised) people, actions or behaviour considered unsuitable or unlucky, either in general or on important occasions. In the Western world, the groom not being allowed to see the bride on the day of the wedding before the ceremony is a well-known taboo.

Taboos in the field study setting

EXAMPLE **12.8**

A researcher finds that divorcees (of both sexes) are not allowed to play a key role in a wedding ceremony or be greeted by the couple from the ceremonial platform along with other elders and close family as they are considered unlucky.

Study of episodes in field studies   An episode is an unusual or important event that takes place in a setting and is important to its subjects. These could be a sudden or traumatic event such as a natural disaster, crime, accident or civil disorder related to a larger phenomenon outside the setting.

The Boxing Day tsunami of 2004 qualifies as an example of such an episode, and can be studied by a field researcher over a limited or long period of time as to its repercussions involving just one, a few or a large number of subjects. Within an organisation, a major restructure that took place is an episode.

Studying the Boxing Day tsunami as an episode

EXAMPLE **12.9**

When studying the aftermath of the tsunami as an episode, a researcher could examine how people initially faced shock and grief, and then how some began to help each other while others looted shops and homes that had anything left worth taking.

The researcher also could look at how the group buried the dead and took care of the traumatised, injured and the orphaned, plus the social dynamics of camp life of the survivors and how they were gradually getting their lives back together.

Study of encounters in field studies   An encounter is where two or more individuals in a setting located within close proximity to each other carry out a conversation or an act of 'mutual involvement'. Common examples of encounters are job interviews, meetings, polite conversations between employees in the staff room, or conversations between a salesperson and customer or client and professional. The relationships between the interactants shape the nature of the encounter. Some encounters can be pleasant while others are not, depending on the function or need to carry out specific encounters.

Some encounters have 'defining features', such as carrying good or bad news. For example, a boss telling a staff member that he or she has been made redundant, or a military chaplain entrusted with the task of informing the family their loved one is dead or wounded in the battlefield, are unpleasant encounters to either one or both parties. In contrast, a chair of an interview panel informing a candidate that she got the job is a pleasant encounter for both.

Among colleagues in polite conversation, the defining feature will be maintaining cordial relationships in recognition of the need to deal with each other in the future. Therefore, individuals use various strategies and tactics to ensure the encounter is pleasant or bearable to one or both parties. For example, when announcing a redundancy, the employee may be told that he or she will be able to work for the company on a contract or part-time basis on special projects, or that the redundancy package offered is more generous than in the past.

EXAMPLE 12.10

Encounters in a field study setting

A researcher in a field study may observe and examine how a couple, or parents of a couple, whose courtship ended prior to marriage meet in public and handle the encounter. Its defining feature is 'cordiality'—they endeavour to be polite to each other and make small talk as they cannot avoid meeting altogether.

Study of social roles in a field study   In any given social setting, various individuals play specific roles:

- **ascribed roles**—assigned roles based on demographic categorisations acquired at birth; for example, as a daughter or son.
- **formal roles**—fixed roles that are linked to one's profession or job in a given context, or roles such as a mother (doing the household chores and child rearing) or a father (doing the outdoor chores).
- **informal roles**—roles that are supplementary to formal roles played by individuals in a setting. These include roles such as the 'helper', 'peacemaker', 'tattle-tale', 'manipulator', 'social organiser' (of parties etc), 'mentor', 'father figure', 'mother hen', 'whipping boy' (facing the anger and abuse of someone in power even if not responsible for a situation), 'work horse' (assigned difficult or unpopular tasks without much compensation), 'bureaucrat' (who follows rules to avoid taking risks or do extra), 'scapegoat' (the one taking the blame when something went wrong), 'shirker' (one who avoids work) or 'work to rule' (doing the minimum required).

These roles, their functions and how people play them, help to maintain the social groups they belong to.

EXAMPLE 12.11

Social roles in a field study setting

In a setting where the courtship practices and rituals of young people were studied, the field researcher found that when a male decided to end a courtship before it led to marriage, he sought help from his maternal uncle. A respected individual in the setting, the uncle served as the 'go between' and 'peacemaker' for the two families and helped the female and both families to 'save face'. The families presented a united front and publicly and amicably announced the break up, so there was no 'injured' or 'injuring party' and the two young people had their reputations intact to pursue other chances of marriage.

⌐--------->

You may notice that with real-life celebrities or those in the public eye, this informal role of the 'go between' is played by a third party, such as managers, agents or public relations consultants, who on behalf of their clients make carefully worded public announcements or issue media releases to 'manage' crises or neutralise a difficult situation.

REPORTING FIELD STUDY RESEARCH

Since field studies in the social sciences are inductive, they examine the research question 'What do I see here?' In the previous section, we examined how themes of observations are identified and developed from field study data. Just as with any other coding categories, these themes, too, need to be 'mutually exclusive' and 'exhaustive' to include all relevant data collected.

With field study data, a researcher can also develop 'other', 'miscellaneous' or 'mixed' themes (or categories) for data coding. Each of these themes is analogous to a variable in quantitative research.

Cause-and-effect relationships   By examining and analysing the data categories and themes under meanings, social practices, episodes, encounters and social roles, the researcher may suggest or make educated guesses (or conjecture) about the 'causes and effects' within the setting that are related to these findings. These will serve as the hypotheses and theories developed from the study's findings. Such conjectures need to be indicated in the report by stressing that the findings are simply 'educated guesses' made with the researcher's interpretations and inferences, and therefore not necessarily based on facts. In other words, the researcher may report the findings as: 'Based on the observations, it can be suggested that ...'

It is also important in any research findings to indicate and acknowledge that several factors rather than a single factor—such as various demographic variables— may be responsible for the observations or 'cause and effect' relationships discussed in the report.

The write-up   The descriptions of observations and analysis of the themes will consist of about 50 per cent of the report. They involve accounts (explanations given by the researcher as to why this study is done when accessing the setting), episodes, encounters, important events and incidents, and use specific observations and direct quotes of informants to support and illustrate them, whenever applicable. Apart from that, a field study report is written as a standard qualitative research report as a realist, confessional or impressionist tale (van Maanen, 1988) discussed in Chapter 3.

Having examined field studies in detail, let us now consider a few examples where the method is applied in media and communication (as media ethnography), journalism and public relations.

FIELD STUDIES AS MEDIA ETHNOGRAPHY

Media ethnography examines a particular group of people in a specific setting to observe their interactions with one or several media as a field study or participant observation; for example, 'How do female undergraduates at a university housing unit get together and watch their favourite TV program such as *Grey's anatomy*?'

James Lull set the trend for media ethnography in North America using the interpretivist paradigm and qualitative methods of field observations and interviews. He examined how families negotiate the selection of TV programs to watch, and the dominance and interaction strategies used by members in the process (Lull, 1988, 1990).

The goal of media ethnography is the holistic understanding of the meanings the activity and the media text have for the informants; for example, 'Why do these students watch the program together?'

EXAMPLE 12.12

Media ethnography

Examples of media ethnography could include why women read fashion magazines or romance novels, or how teens play video games, use the social networks MySpace or Facebook or provide content to YouTube. The researcher would examine how they make sense of these activities, how they consume or use these media, and what they think about them. These would be examined within the context of how they form networks of like-minded people, and share information or media content between their networked groups.

The settings of media ethnographies   Globalisation, convergence and interactivity of media today have blurred the boundaries between what is mediated communication and what is not. This has also resulted in our inability to accurately define what an audience for specific media content is, and where they are located. For example, websites can be accessed from anywhere in the world, so it is not easy to specifically identify the entire audience or group to be studied or what its location or setting is to be. If one is to study players of computer games, cybercafes or homes across the world could be the research setting for a group of regular players.

Audiences today   Today media audiences are content creators as well as receivers and audiences, thanks to affordable digital interactive media forms, such as digital cameras, recorders and computer software, allowing average individuals to produce content. This can be broadcast on websites such as YouTube or through multimedia messaging systems (MMS) or short messaging systems (SMS) on mobile phones to reach a large group of people.

Therefore, today we are users of media rather than 'audiences' of media. As a result, media ethnography is about examining the complex mix of the processes of production and reception, the boundaries between which are not quite clear.

FIELD STUDIES IN JOURNALISM

Field observations are the basis of news coverage even though they are not identified or acknowledged as such. A journalist covering a new story on location either for print or electronic media is involved in an overt, non-participant observation. Often journalists carry out undercover reporting using covert, participant or non-participant observations. In both situations, they interview 'sources', who social researchers refer to as 'informants'.

Field studies in journalism vs social science   The main differences between field studies conducted by journalists and social scientists are that:

- journalists carry out deductive studies using hypothesis testing as they begin with 'an angle' to the story, approved by their editor
- social scientists carry out inductive studies using research questions, trying to learn what goes on in a setting.

However, journalists also carry out inductive studies when they set out on a story on 'a hunch', while social scientists carry out deductive studies when they go about researching a popularly held belief or perception to test if it is true or not.

When writing a report, journalists may use the same themes or categories of observations such as encounters, meanings, social practices and social roles to discuss their observations and findings, without indicating they are doing so, in the same way as social scientists.

New journalism or Gonzo journalism   Field studies involving overt or covert participant observation are used in 'new journalism' or 'Gonzo journalism' (introduced by Hunter S Thompson), where the journalist's own views and opinions are introduced into the report.

GONZO JOURNALISM: OBSERVING THE HELL'S ANGELS BIKIE GANG
Case Study 12.11

Hunter S Thompson's year-long overt participant observation of the 'Hell's Angels' bikie gang gives an inside look of the realities of the group from his own perspective as well as those of the group members.

He described the initiation 'rituals' of new gang members, and the defining feature of their encounters with outsiders as 'maintaining their dignity' by proudly riding their bikes or being violent in a mainstream world where they amount to very little due to their low socio-economic status (Thompson, 1966).

This type of journalistic reporting and research is different from traditional journalism where journalists use field observations and remain 'objective' by not providing their own views or opinions in the story. They also maintain a 'balance' in the report by using a variety of sources, representing opposing viewpoints.

INSIDE THE BOHEMIAN GROVE
Case Study 12.12

Taking the critical and interpretivist perspectives, journalist Philip Weiss reported on a seven-day covert participant observation of the Bohemian Club's members and guests in July 1989, at the Bohemian Grove in California, which he described as a 'summer camp for the world's 1500 most powerful men' (Weiss, 1989). The setting is extremely inaccessible to the press and anyone other than members and their carefully selected and important guests.

The all-male, right-wing Bohemian Club has been an exclusive one since the 1930s and has a waiting list of 33 years to join. It includes many powerful US Republican Party members among its 2300-strong membership from North America. These include Republican

Case Study 12.12

administration officials, media barons, defence contractors, Hollywood celebrities, famous writers, business leaders and right-wing intellectuals. It also includes the US power class, including members of the Bush family, past Republican presidents and former secretaries of state and defence such as Henry Kissinger and Alexander Haig. The guests at the camp that year included the former Indian and the current Soviet ambassadors to the USA.

Weiss provided maps and photographs of the camp and a copy of the day's schedule for former US president Ronald Reagan who was in attendance. He describes the sexist and racist jokes of the camp, slang terms, rituals of the opening ceremony, a drag show, 7 a.m. gin fizzes, encounters between participants, guest speakers and other camp activities.

He mentions the speech of the right-wing French Prime Minister Michel Rocard, who discussed many early plans of the Europeans to remove trade barriers and adopt a common currency, long before making them public. The French public and press believed him to be on a boating holiday in the Atlantic Ocean, and his last visit to the US had been eighteen months earlier.

The camp was described as a place where many secret 'gentlemen's agreements' are made between important people, and a private gathering and decision-making place for national and international power brokers, away from the scrutiny of the press and other standard democratic processes.

Citizen journalism Today, converged media such as mobile phones with still and video camera capacities and the internet and email—used for blogs (email/internet logs), vblogs (videoblogs) and moblogs (mobile phone logs)—have given rise to citizen journalism. This is where the average person is able to capture unexpected situations on camera and provide the content to media organisations, or write news stories and opinions in their blogs.

Case Study 12.13 FIELD OBSERVATIONS AND CITIZEN JOURNALISM

The 2004 Boxing Day tsunami saw many tourists at the affected locations capture the devastation on their video or mobile cameras, sometimes providing the only footage of a crucial moment. On 7 July 2005, the London bombings were reported as blogs, mobile phone still and video footage, and digital camera photos sent by email to British media organisations.

Blogs carry opinions of their authors just as ethnographic reports. But they may provide less background information, carry inaccurate facts and opinions and implausible visuals, or be outright hoaxes. The British Broadcasting Corporation (BBC) receives large numbers of submissions from citizen journalists who record what they see in the field as overt non-participant observers. However, the organisation checks them for accuracy and copyright, as individuals often submit materials to which they do not hold copyright (Reporter's guide to citizen journalism, 2006).

The Gulf War of 2003 saw bloggers' diaries make a significant contribution to journalism. For example, *Salaam Pax* (or *Salam Pax*)—a blog perceived as written by an Iraqi civilian—provided first-hand accounts of the bombing of Baghdad in the first days of the war (Iraq Diaries, 2003). At the same time, US soldiers in Iraq were providing their own interpretations of the war, which made the US military concerned about what the blogs were saying (Wall, 2006).

FIELD STUDIES IN PUBLIC RELATIONS

Even though field studies are not a commonly used research method in public relations (PR), non-participant observation is sometimes used. PR research may study a target population's observable behaviours, which a PR campaign is hoping to change. For example, before implementing a PR campaign to accompany a plan by a local government authority to introduce a new recycling scheme, a field study using non-participant observation is conducted to examine how people currently handle their household waste.

FIELD STUDIES ON DRINK SPIKING

Case Study 12.14

A few years ago, 'drink spiking' at bars—adding the date-rape drug rohypnol or other drugs to the drinks of unsuspecting people (especially females) by other customers—became a problem in a major city in Australia.

Before a PR campaign was designed and launched on the subject, non-participant observations were conducted to observe the behaviour of customers in bars across the city to see what the unsafe practices were and what behaviour needed to be addressed.

Summary

This chapter examined field study research with respect to the role of researcher, types of field studies, data collection methods, data analysis and reporting. It also examined the application of field study method in journalism, media and communication (media ethnography) and public relations.

The next chapter addresses research case studies.

Try this ...

1 Plan and carry out an ethnographic field study on one of the following:
   a a group of people who regularly get together to watch their favourite TV program*
   b a weekly sporting or recreational activity of a group of friends*
   c a group chat on the internet (using live chat reference transcripts as data records)*
   d shoppers at a popular departmental store at a large suburban mall during a massive sale such as on Boxing Day
   e the set of a TV drama or film production*
   f rehearsals or opening night from backstage at an amateur theatre production*
   g mobile phone use by young people in public places
   h people waiting to enter a club
   i MySpace, Facebook or YouTube use by young people*
   j the daily activities of a media organisation such as a newspaper or dot.com company*

k   the university cafeteria during the lunch rush

l   a rock concert

m   activities at a video game arcade.

*Note that ethics clearance will be required unless the setting is an open, public space.

2   Follow the procedures for a participant observation and/or intensive interviews in the selected setting according to the established guidelines.

Hint: plan to spend a total of three to five hours observing the setting either in several one-hour blocks on different days and times or in one three-hour block depending on the activity of the setting. Make field notes, maps and sketches, and collect documents related to the setting such as advertisements or publicity materials.

3   Prepare an interview guide with probes for one important question that can be used in interviewing informants in your selected field study situations.

4   Analyse the data collected with your field study.

Hint. Identify the meanings, rituals, fetishes, taboos, social roles, slang or special terminology related to the setting and its members.

Further reading

Emerson, R M, Fretz, R I & Shaw, L L 1995. *Writing ethnographic fieldnotes,* University of Chicago Press, Chicago.

Gobo, G 2008. *Doing ethnography*. Sage, Newbury Park, CA.

Shaffir, W B & Stebbins, R A (eds) 1991. *Experiencing fieldwork: An inside view of qualitative research*. Sage, Newbury Park, CA.

Part

4

Other Research Approaches

13 Case Study Research

In Chapter 8 to Chapter 12, we examined the various qualitative and quantitative research methods commonly used in the social sciences. This chapter examines case studies.

This chapter examines the **case study** research method as follows:

o characteristics of a **research case study**

o what can be studied as a case study

o the difference between teaching case studies and research case studies

o types of case studies—exploratory, descriptive and **explanatory case studies** and single or multiple case studies

o the procedure followed

o advantages and disadvantages

o applications of case study research in public policy, journalism, media and communication, and public relations

CHARACTERISTICS OF A RESEARCH CASE STUDY

The case study research method uses a combination of data collection methods—both qualitative and quantitative. These methods can be surveys and content analyses (quantitative) or interviews, focus groups, field studies and document and archival analyses (qualitative).

The phenomenon examined in a case study generally has a large number of factors or independent variables, but no information available about the interactions between them or their relationships to the dependent variables. These interactions and relationships are examined within the real-life context or specific circumstances of the phenomenon, within its natural environment.

A case study uses just one or a few cases, instances or '**objects of interest**' to analyse a complex, contemporary phenomenon within specific limits of time (When?) and space (Where?), and examines it from various viewpoints to understand the **multiple realities** or diverse perspectives of the informants or research participants.

WHAT CAN BE STUDIED AS A CASE STUDY?

A case study can examine an individual, a group of people, an organisation, an event, a process, an issue or a campaign (advertising, political, public relations or marketing) as its unit of analysis. Case studies can examine neighbourhoods (for example, a depressed or affluent one), the economy of a nation (for example, a recently bankrupt or successful country), public agencies, regional planning or a business from its establishment to its demise (for example, OneTel telecommunications or Impulse Airlines of Australia).

Case study research is conducted in many academic disciplines—especially management science, organisational communication, public policy, psychology, sociology, political science, anthropology and history—and in practical fields such as urban planning, education, medicine, clinical psychology, social work, investigative journalism, and media and communication. In public relations, case studies can be exploratory and used to examine what others have done, and what worked and did not work in a given case. Thereafter, further research is carried out to check its relevance to the current situation in question and fill any gaps in knowledge and understanding.

> **Handy Hint**
>
> A case study asks the question 'What is going on here?' and tries to answer the 'How?' and 'Why?' questions related to a contemporary, practical, real-life problem or phenomenon under study.

RESEARCH CASE STUDIES VS TEACHING CASE STUDIES

Often research case studies are wrongly considered to be the same as teaching case studies and, as a result, get rejected as lacking in credibility as legitimate research. The *Harvard Business Review* regularly features a case study written in narrative form or an impressionist tale (van Maanen, 1988) featuring a specific storyline, characters and dialogue that teachers in management or organisational communication use as a teaching tool to stimulate discussion, debate and deeper understanding of various concepts. Textbooks of collected teaching case studies are popular in university courses in organisational communication (for example, Keyton & Shockley-Zalabak, 2006) and public relations (for example, Hendrix & Hayes, 2007; Fearns-Banks, 2006). Some teaching case studies are based on actual scholarly research but written in the impressionist or confessional tale formats (van Maanen, 1988). Others may be fictional cases or semi-fictionalised real cases.

By contrast, research case studies are written as realist tales and published in academic journals and scholarly books, and as research reports for non-academic settings. A research case study has to be 'real' with all evidence relevant to the study objectively and accurately reported (Yin, 1994).

A case study of the limited adoption of the intranet

EXAMPLE 13.1

The Nirogee Centre is a rural health-care organisation in Australia, run by a state government department as a residential facility for 172 intellectually disabled individuals or clients. It has 200 staff working in nine different units and is the largest single employer of the town of Guthrie (population 12,000), located 70 km from its head office.

In early 1998, the head office, which only carried out administrative functions and had a networked computer for each of its employees, unilaterally decided to provide an intranet service to Nirogee to improve communication between Nirogee and itself. Nirogee

EXAMPLE
13.1

only had 20 computers, most of which were housed in the administration building. The six residences of the clients, called direct-care units, each had a networked computer located in the manager's office. But the non-direct care units—such as housekeeping, maintenance, stores, vocational therapy, physiotherapy and hydrotherapy—were neither networked nor provided with a computer. The non-direct care catering division's existing computer was not networked. This limited implementation of the intranet was explained as being due to budgetary constraints.

Once the intranet was installed, all communications from the head office to Nirogee were sent exclusively via the intranet as emails. Policy documents and procedural manuals related to client care previously available as printed material were made available only on the department's website. The computers in direct care units located in the managers' offices were accessible only by the managers and deputy managers, who were nursing professionals. The managers were expected to print any relevant emails and documents from the website and post the emails on the unit notice boards and file the documents in the memo folders for other staff to read. The secretary in administration was expected to print them and send them via internal mail to the non-direct care units for their notice boards and memo folders.

But in reality, this did not always happen. The older unit managers of both sexes did not want to use the intranet and asked the younger deputy managers to do it. This meant they spent time on the intranet instead of nursing the clients, which increased the workloads of other direct care staff, who resented it. Due to time constraints, the secretary in administration as well as deputy managers often failed to print all emails and other documents, resulting in the non-dissemination of important information to both non-direct care as well as direct care staff. This was because the intranet had increased the e-correspondence received by both the secretary and direct care managers, with even the most routine messages previously sent by phone or passed on in person being sent as emails.

When the intranet was only provided to direct care, it became a status symbol for direct care managers and created a perception of non-direct care units and their staff as less important to the organisation. This was within the context of recent feasibility studies of outsourcing the non-direct care functions by the then state government, which was well known for its commitment to economic rationalism and privatisation.

The centre also had very few social events, resulting in an unhealthy organisational climate and lack of organisational culture. The centre's newsletter meant for staff and clients' families had ceased publication a while ago. Guthrie's newspaper often published letters to the editor and news items negative towards Nirogee. In response to these factors and others, the new director of the centre appointed a 12-member 'Communication Project Team' in August 1998 to examine the various aspects of organisational, interpersonal and mediated communication systems within this centre and to recommend suitable steps to improve its organisational communication, culture, climate and image.

The author served as consultant to this team and moderator of its meetings, which served as informal focus groups. The project team consisted of three administrative, three direct care and four non-direct care staff drawn from various levels in the hierarchy, different age groups and both sexes. The Information Technology (IT) Manager from the head office attended the first meeting of the team.

The director of the facility and a sector manager in charge of three of the six direct care units—himself a long-standing nursing staff member of Nirogee—served as chief informants for the researcher/author, who carried out a case study research of this organisation. In an attempt at **triangulation** or using multiple data sources, the author also carried out interviews with several randomly chosen members of staff at various levels (three males and three females) from both direct and non-direct care. As the third method of data collection, the author examined all intranet messages sent by the head office to Nirogee for a randomly chosen two-week period and compared them with the emails received by the secretary in administration and sent as printed emails to non-direct care units during the same period. This was to examine how many and which messages were missed by the non-direct care staff.

In the fourth method of data collection, the author examined all newspaper articles and letters to the editor related to Nirogee published in the local paper in the last two years from the centre's archives. She also examined the procedural manuals and other documentation necessary for the everyday running of the centre, which were now made available in electronic form. As a fifth method of data collection, the author 'walked around' and observed the facility's various units and their functions; the centre's layout regarding the location of various units (which are far apart and reduced informal interactions between staff in different units); their networked computers; and the notice boards where printed emails were to be posted, as an overt, non-participant observation. This was to gain an understanding of the ease of accessibility of the notice boards to deputy managers who print the emails in the manager's office, because a considerable distance between the two can be a constraint to the proper dissemination of information to other staff.

In their final report, the team recommended that a second networked computer be provided in each direct care unit and a networked computer in each non-direct care unit, as well as printers to these computers, and that training in using the intranet be provided to all staff. This was to eliminate the gate-keeping role of the secretary and unit managers that created problems in disseminating emails from the head office to staff at Nirogee.

The findings of this case study were reported and published as a research case study and a scholarly research article (Weerakkody, 2004b). It was also written as an impressionist tale and a **teaching case study** (Weerakkody, 2006b).

TYPES OF CASE STUDIES

Case studies can be of three types depending on the purposes they serve:

- exploratory
- descriptive
- explanatory.

However, a single case study may carry out all three functions.

Exploratory case studies are preliminary studies that define the research questions and hypotheses or identify areas for more detailed examination.

Descriptive case studies describe what was observed, in detail and in depth, within its context.

Explanatory case studies provide cause-and-effect relationships between variables and explain why events happened. They provide multiple interpretations of the same observations and events, and may use several theories or models—sometimes those that compete with each other—to explain the course of events that took place within the case and to provide answers to why each party in the setting did what they did.

EXAMPLE 13.2

A cause–effect explanation

One of the middle-aged, female, direct-care managers at the Nirogee Centre who refused to use the intranet explained to the researcher that her preference was to use the telephone as she considered the intranet to be 'too impersonal'.

However, further inquiry indicated that she (who was a member of the more privileged group within the organisation given access to the intranet) had missed the only intranet training session offered to the centre due to being on annual leave. Her refusal to use the intranet in favour of the telephone was actually an exercise in 'saving face' (Goffman, 1967).

EXAMPLE 13.3

Types of case studies

The Nirogee study about the effects of the limited adoption of the intranet was the follow-up, explanatory, in-depth case study of an exploratory case study carried out by a private consultancy to recommend improvements to client care at Nirogee. The consultants reported problems in communication within various units of the organisation, giving rise to the formation of the Communication Project Team to examine the phenomenon in depth.

The Communication Project Team examined the various channels of communication within the centre and provided a descriptive case study report to the management, discussing the types, advantages and shortcomings of each mode of communication at Nirogee. It described the lack of social activities and a common space such as a staff room where people could socialise during breaks. It also described how each direct care unit had its own Christmas party for the clients and their families, which did not include staff from any other units, and the need for a common Christmas party and other social activities for the entire centre to develop a positive organisational culture and climate.

It also described how the removal of the meal subsidy at the cafeteria, which led to its subsequent closure, had caused the loss of an opportunity for staff to socialise during meal times. This descriptive case study is reported in Weerakkody (2006b) as an impressionist tale (van Maanen, 1988).

The scholarly research case study that used several data sources and reported in Weerakkody (2004b) is an explanatory case study. It takes the critical theory perspective and explains the phenomena by linking the limited adoption of the intranet implemented at Nirogee by the head office, without the centre being consulted, to theories of power and hegemony (Foucault, 1974) and as reinforcing the status of the privileged or powerful. (The direct care staff who are health care professionals earn higher wages than non-direct care staff and are of higher rank within the organisational hierarchy.) The author also used the pluralist view of technology (Hirschheim, 1985) to explain how a technology is used and adopted—rather than the technology itself—creates its negative effects in terms of exclusion and marginalisation of some staff from the organisational communication process.

She also explains how a new technology limited in adoption and given access to only some individuals made them unwitting '**gatekeepers**' (Pettigrew, 1972) of the information transmitted via the intranet, as they were supposed to print and post the messages and other documents for access by other staff.

DOING CASE STUDY RESEARCH

The procedure followed in carrying out a research case study involves:

- choosing a suitable topic
- designing the case study
- developing the case study protocol
- carrying out the pilot study
- collecting data
- data analysis
- reporting of results.

These are discussed below using Stake (1995), Yin (1994, 2003), Wimmer and Dominick (2006) and Haas (2004.)

CHOOSING A SUITABLE TOPIC

A good case study chooses a significant topic or a case that is of national importance or serves the public interest. It may be useful in theory development or have practical applications with benefits to wider society; for example, the adoption of digital TV in Australia (Weerakkody, 2006a), the impact of serious and organised crime on Australian society, and a review of online gambling in Australia.

The case must be 'complete' in the sense that both its **boundaries** (terms of reference) demarcated between the phenomenon to be studied and the context within which it is examined (such as the time and place) are clearly defined. The boundaries can be both social (who is included) and physical (what is included).

The topic and boundaries of a case study: Inquiry into the Future Impact of Serious and Organised Crime on Australian Society

This report was produced by the Parliamentary Joint Committee on the Australian Crime Commission. The importance of this topic to public policy and the national and public interest is self-explanatory.

The aim of the inquiry was to examine, '[What are] the trends and changes in criminal activities, practices and methods?' and to report to both Houses of Parliament on: 'What are the changes that may be desirable to the functions, structure, powers and procedures of the Australian Crime Commission (ACC)?' (Note that these served as the preliminary research questions.)

The committee inquired into the future impact of serious and organised crime on Australian society within the boundaries (the committee's terms of reference) of:

1 future trends in serious and organised crime activities, practices and methods and their impact on Australian society [note that this refers to boundaries of 'time']
2 strategies for countering future serious and organised crime
3 the economic cost of countering future organised crime at a national, state and territory level [note that this refers to boundaries of 'space' or place]
4 the adequacy of legislative and administrative arrangements, including the adequacy of cross-jurisdictional databases, to meet future needs.

[Note that 2, 3 and 4 above refer to the boundaries on 'what' is to be examined. Organised crime is the 'who' to be examined.)

EXAMPLE 13.4

The 24 public submissions received by 18 August 2007 included those from the Police Federation of Australia; The Australian Federal Police; the State Police Forces of Victoria, South Australia, Western Australia (WA) and New South Wales; CRIMTRAC (database); Australian Customs Service; Attorney General's Department; Department of Transport and Regional Security; Commonwealth Director of Public Prosecutions (DPP); Crime and Misconduct Commission; Human Rights and Equal Opportunity Commission; Australian Institute of Criminology; Australian Crime Commission; Office of the Privacy Commissioner; Australian Mobile Telecommunication Association (AMTA); Crime and Misconduct Commission—Queensland; Australian Transaction Report and Analysis Centre (AUSTRAC); Advocates for Survivors of Child Abuse; Corruption and Crime Commission for WA; two submissions from individuals; and one anonymous (confidential) submission. These represented a wide range of stakeholder groups contributing to the case study.

The above list of submitting agencies indicated the wide array of perspectives (stakeholders) represented and their relevance to the topic under study. Members of these groups and others were called upon to give evidence to the committee during its actual hearings.

Source: www.aph.gov.au/senate/committee/acc_ctte/organised_crime/submissions
(retrieved 18 August 2007).

DESIGNING THE CASE STUDY

As with any other inductive research, a case study needs research questions or issues to be examined to probe the 'how' and 'why' of the phenomenon under study, and identify the relevant unit or units of analysis. The literature review will help to uncover the relevant units or subunits of analysis, as well as suitable research topics or issues.

Choosing cases for case study research   The research questions or issues to be examined influence how the relevant cases will be selected and what research methods will be used. The case or cases selected for a case study research need to be 'purposive' or be able to provide the data, information or documentation necessary to examine the phenomenon under study.

In addition, the accessibility of the setting and data sources, and the willingness of the informants and the setting to participate, influence the selection of the cases to be studied. The time, budget and staff resources available also influence the number of cases selected. Selecting the best case or cases from all those available to the researcher will help reduce the probability of a researcher simply selecting the most 'convenient' one for a study.

Types of cases   A researcher can also select a typical or **representative case** or an atypical, unique or **unusual case** to understand the phenomenon from different perspectives. An **atypical** case will uncover aspects or factors that are absent in **typical cases**.

Sometimes, a balance and variety of cases are selected when **multiple cases** are examined. However, a case study is about the in-depth and comprehensive examination of a phenomenon. Therefore, selecting more than four to six cases for a study could reduce the level of detail obtained, as the available resources of time, budget and personnel will be stretched by a larger number of cases.

Selecting cases

EXAMPLE 13.5

When carrying out a case study, 'The nature of the undergraduate majors in Media and Communication at Australian universities', one may select a list of universities that offer the major and are willing to cooperate by allowing free access to staff, students, classrooms, facilities such as media labs, course materials, documentation such as student attendance records, and course evaluation results.

One may look at the course offerings of each university in the list to select a typical or representative case of a course where: the required student performance at the high school certificate examination is at the middle band; no previous media experience is needed; and the students are mostly school leavers.

An atypical case would be where the students' required high school performance is very high or very low.

A **unique case** would be where: the course is very selective and enrolment small; previous media experience is required; students are selected after an interview and submission of a portfolio of work; and the course generally attracts mature-age students from the profession.

If the case study needs a diversity of cases, they may be selected from similar cases from universities in different states and those located in metropolitan, regional or rural areas.

Single vs multiple case study designs   A single case study, such as the one of the Nirogee Centre (discussed in Example 13.1), is best when the researcher can find a **critical case**, an **extreme case** or a **revelatory case** (Hass, 2004).

Critical cases   A critical case is one where all the conditions needed to test the theory are found in the case study.

A critical case: limited implementation of the intranet

EXAMPLE 13.6

The Nirogee centre was a suitable case to test the theories that:
1 the limited adoption of a communication technology may exclude and marginalise some staff from the communication process
2 there is a relationship between technology, status, power and hegemony with regard to the implementation of the intranet at an organisation.

Extreme cases   An extreme case is one that is unique (that is, one of a kind) and so warrants formal study on its own merits.

An extreme case: the fall of OneTel telecommunications

EXAMPLE 13.7

OneTel was a new telecommunication company in Australia, which had a very satisfied workforce and considerable customer base. However, the company closed down within a short time. It would be interesting and useful to examine 'how' and 'why' it happened.

Revelatory cases   A revelatory case is one that was not accessible before, but recently became open to researchers.

A revelatory case: detainees at Guantanamo Bay, Cuba

The case of Guantanamo Bay detainees arrested and moved to the prison from all over the world after the terrorist attacks on the USA on 11 September 2001 is controversial due to the secrecy involved and the restrictions imposed on those affected and everyone related to the issue. The related information and sources may become available one day and then may be studied in depth as a revelatory case.

A multiple case study design A multiple case study design is used when a researcher needs to replicate a study and its findings to obtain results from other similar cases ('**literal replication**') or to obtain contrasting results from different cases to examine predictable reasons for the phenomenon ('**theoretical replication**').

A multiple case study design

At a university in Australia, it was found that student attendance in lectures and tutorials was decreasing and had been doing so for several years. Some staff argued that it was due to the availability of detailed lecture notes and tutorial exercises on the university's web server, making attendance in class not essential.

For a multiple case study design involving literal replication, cases need to be selected that replicate each other to confirm this evidence. This may be done by selecting as cases for study several university course units that provide detailed lecture notes and see if they all record low attendance.

For a case study design to examine theoretical replication, a researcher needs to select two cases each, from units that provide:

1 detailed lecture notes
2 only the PowerPoint slides used during the lecture
3 no lecture notes at all.

The researcher would then examine the attendance figures to see if there is any correlation between class attendance and the availability of lecture notes.

However, in each situation one needs to make sure to select courses that offer similar classes, such as face-to-face lectures and tutorials rather than lab sessions with computer work, or where being in class is an essential part of their assessments; for example, TV production units that need sophisticated studio facilities and editing equipment that may require class attendance even if not compulsory when students are working on their projects.

Since case studies are in-depth examinations using several data collection methods, the research project will not be a simple exercise of looking at the website for the type of lecture notes available in each class and examining student attendance records. The researcher may need to: attend these lectures and tutes for observation; interview the lecturers and tutors about their views on, say, students working several jobs to support themselves, which affects their attendance; and ask students about why they do or do not attend class, such as due to long and expensive commutes.

Such multiple data sources will allow for comparisons between cases in terms of their replications and provide useful insights and multiple perspectives, and highlight the different realities of various respondents.

The unit of analysis   The unit of analysis of a case study may be an individual (for example, a student or staff member), a group (for example, a research team working on a grant), a department or division (for example, a faculty or school of a university), an organisation (for example, the entire university) or an entire nation (for example, all Australian universities). The unit of analysis can also be an issue (for example, low student class attendance at universities.)

Even though a researcher may identify the unit of analysis to be examined in the case study at the commencement of the project, he or she may have to modify it, based on the data collected as the study progresses. The same happens with the research questions, where a case study begins as an inductive (generate theory) study examining specific research questions, but as the study progresses and new information surfaces, these questions may develop into hypotheses to be tested, turning the case study into a deductive (testing theory) one.

DEVELOPING THE CASE STUDY PROTOCOL

A protocol is an essential part of any data collection in a research project, and a case study protocol is required before the data collection begins. This protocol helps the researchers to guide themselves in a disciplined manner and to maintain validity and reliability of the data collection. It is most helpful when several researchers are collecting the data or multiple cases are involved.

The case study protocol involves the following components (Yin, 1994):

* overview of project—includes background information of the case, study objectives, issues of importance that need to be studied, and the relevant scholarly literature
* field procedure to be followed—describes how data are to be collected and the potential sources of information and existing data that may be used
* research questions or hypotheses to be examined or tested in the project
* a guide to be followed when preparing the report once the study is completed— includes a rough guideline for the report, a format for the narrative, relevant bibliographic information and documents to be examined.

Once the case study protocol is ready, a pilot study is conducted.

CARRYING OUT THE PILOT STUDY

The pilot study helps to fine-tune the research design, research questions, interview questions posed to informants or research participants, data collection plan for content, and procedures to be followed for the case study.

If the case study is large, complex and costly to conduct, a pilot study becomes important. The case that is the most conveniently located and cheapest to conduct is used for the pilot study. However, the data collected from the pilot study should not be included in the case study proper, as they may involve inconsistencies and mistakes.

Let us now see how the actual data collection is to be conducted.

COLLECTING DATA

When collecting data for a case study, a researcher must follow some rules (Hass, 2004):

* triangulation
* creating a **case study database**
* maintaining a **logical chain of evidence**
* following standard ethics guidelines for research.

Triangulation   A case study is an in-depth study, so data collection should use all available sources of information. This is known as triangulation, which allows for multiple measures of the same phenomenon. Use of multiple sources of data provides multiple perspectives of the phenomenon under study from the point of view of various respondents or informants.

There are four forms of triangulation:

- **data triangulation**—using at least two sources of data
- **methodological triangulation**—using different research methods to confirm the findings such as interviews and participant observation, and using documentary or other evidence to verify the accuracy of information gathered
- **theory triangulation**—using alternative theoretical paradigms, such as combining interpretivism with critical theory
- **investigator triangulation**—using different researchers to collect, analyse and interpret the data to obtain alternative viewpoints.

The different sources of data used in triangulation can involve:

- documents and archival data
- interviews
- field studies
- physical artefacts.

Documents and archival data   Data sources related to documents and archives include letters; audio-visual materials such as photographs, films and clips, videos, audio recordings and news clips from TV; personal records such as dairies and journals; organisational memos, minutes of meetings, annual reports, agendas, historical records, brochures, posters, pamphlets, and advertising and promotional materials related to an organisation; newspaper and magazine articles related to the topic or case; policy documents and regulations; website content and blogs; entries in yearbooks, *Who's Who* and encyclopaedias; museum exhibits; and documented records such as birth, marriage and death records.

Archival records include service records (military or other), organisational charts and past census figures related to the phenomenon, the case and its setting.

Interviews   Survey interviews, depth interviews and focus groups can collect data for a case study. These must be corroborated by the informants (in field studies) or other respondents (in depth interviews) for accuracy.

Field studies   Field studies can be conducted within the setting of the cases using overt or covert as well as participant or non-participant observations. This could involve sitting in at meetings, attending social events or 'walking around' the setting to observe where everything and everyone is located, and how things are done on a routine basis within the setting. This is because the organisational climate and how members feel about the organisation is indicated by how individual members of a setting interact with each other, with outsiders and with visitors such as the researcher, clients and customers.

Physical artefacts   How people decorate their organisation's public areas, its landscaped surroundings, individual offices or work areas—with photos, paintings, cartoons, pot plants, ornaments and flower arrangements—provides valuable insights into the culture, climate and image of a setting.

Once the data have been collected, they need to be included in a systematic database.

Creating a case study database   A case study database is the record of all data the researcher has collected and maintained during the case study. These can be checked by others for reliability or used in future research without violating confidentiality, anonymity and other ethical issues related to the original sources of information.

In addition to maintaining a database, how the data was collected also needs to be recorded.

Maintaining a logical chain of evidence   It is essential to maintain records and evidence of the circumstances under which the case study data were collected; for example, making notes of the dates in which the interviews or data collection were carried out, when a website was accessed or how these sources were identified (such as in response to an advertisement or referral by a particular person). Retain consent forms and other documentation. Indicate the links between the questions asked from respondents in collecting data and how conclusions were made based on these responses, noting the context in which they were made.

In case study research, too, ethical issues need to be kept in mind.

Following standard ethics guidelines for research   Standard ethical guidelines related to social research also apply to case studies. Therefore, you need to follow the relevant ethical guidelines on doing research with human subjects established by your country, institution and profession. If the case examined is controversial, anonymity and confidentiality of the data collected will be of utmost importance to research participants. The safety of the investigators in a setting that is volatile or politically unstable such as a civil war also needs to be considered. Research ethics are discussed in detail in Chapter 5.

Once the data have been collected they need to be analysed.

DATA ANALYSIS

The analysis of data collected from various sources involves a process of examination, categorisation (into themes and sub-themes), tabulation (of these categories and their frequencies etc for easier understanding and better display) and analysis of the evidence to answer the case study's research questions or test its hypotheses. One should also look for rival or alternative explanations and interpretations of observations.

The information gathered is arranged in chronological order for easier description in the report. The themes and sub-themes identified or developed during the data analysis can become the individual chapters of the book or the detailed report written about the case study and its findings. If the case study is simply a report or a scholarly article, these themes and sub-themes can make up the different sections or headings.

Progressive focusing   The research process of a case study begins as an inductive examination (to generate theory), simply asking the general research question 'What's going on here?' As the data collection progresses this will be modified if specific observations make it necessary. In other words, as the data collection progresses, the case study may develop more specific research questions or become a deductive one (testing theory or specific hypotheses as true or false), in a process referred to as **'progressive focusing'**.

EXAMPLE 13.10

Progressive focusing

A case study about the undergraduate majors in media and communication in Australian universities may begin with the research question, 'What appears to be generally covered in the major at Australian universities?'

The additional questions to be examined could be:

o What level of high school performance is needed to gain selection into the major at this university (for example, standardised scores at Year 12)?

o How many hours (class time for lectures and tutorials or lab work) of contact time per week are involved at each university?

o What type of assessment tasks are set at each university?

o Is class attendance compulsory or optional?

o What is the staff–student ratio at each university?

o What is the socio-economic distribution of the student population in the major?

Thereafter, the questions are progressively focused and the hypothesis to be examined might become, 'The universities that require a high standardised score for selection into the major make it compulsory for students to attend lectures and tutorials or lab classes.'

Assertion   In case study research involving qualitative methods, making conclusions based on the researchers' own interpretation of data and observations is called '**assertion**'. This is analogous to generalisation of findings in quantitative research.

However, case study research (just as experiments) provides '**analytic generalisability**' (theoretical generalisation) and not '**statistical generalisation**' (that is, findings applicable to those other than the cases examined the style of quantitative research).

Interpretation of findings   The researchers' interpretations of the case study must be plausible and probable within the context of the case or cases examined (Yin, 2003). These interpretations should be valid for the time (in history), the situation (under study) and context of the case examined.

EXAMPLE 13.11

Interpreting the observations within a specific context

In the Nirogee study on the limited adoption of the intranet, one must take into account that Guthrie is a rural town and that in 1998, the internet and computers were less widely diffused and affordable than today.

The work routines of the centre also revolve around taking care of the everyday functions of life of otherwise-healthy clients, who cannot attend to them on their own due to being intellectually disabled.

Therefore, the centre's work force were not into using highly sophisticated or computerised equipment in their day-to-day work, as would be the case in a hospital.

Researcher subjectivity   A researcher's subjectivity due to life experiences, biases and prejudices about issues under study may have a negative impact on the study's findings and interpretations.

Researcher subjectivity

EXAMPLE 13.12

Researchers who are believers in economic rationalism and/or technological determinism (which sees that when technology is available in society, they must be used) will see no problem with the head office unilaterally implementing intranet access only to some members of staff at Nirogee due to budgetary constraints.

They may see it as a positive step and not consider it necessary to examine its effects on staff morale and organisational communication.

They may assume the problems related to the intranet as caused by the indifference of direct care managers/deputy managers and the secretary who fail to pass the emails on.

REPORTING OF RESULTS

Writing a case study report   Case study research has a much wider audience than any other scholarly research report, due to their wider application in non-scholarly areas. Many public inquiries by parliamentary and Senate committees or Royal Commissions on specific issues of national and public interest are conducted as in-depth case studies, as all available sources of information are sought by the investigators. These include public submissions from state and federal agencies, corporations and non-governmental organisations (NGOs), research institutes and members of the public.

In recent times, Senate committee inquiries have reported on:

- information technologies (7 December 2000)
- privacy in the information age (9 November 2000)
- monitoring Australia's media (13 April 2000)
- online gambling in Australia (16 March 2000).

Senate inquiries in 2007 included:

- mental health services in Australia
- cost of living pressures on older Australians
- academic standards in school education
- the nature and conduct of Australia's public diplomacy
- the future impact of serious and organised crime on Australian society (www.aph. gov.au/senate/committee/inquiries, accessed 18 August 2007).

Writing style   The academic case study report does not have a standard format but may be written as a realist tale (analytic report) or confessional tale (reflective report) (van Maanen, 1988; also see Chapter 3). However, the style and language used in the report must fit its targeted audience (for example, policy makers, those from other academic fields or members of the public) and the descriptions provided in chronological order.

It also has to be written in a clear and interesting style and include sufficient evidence that supports as well as challenges the author's claims, interpretations, explanations and conclusions. It should be written in a neutral tone and include alternative explanations of findings (other reasons that may have led to the findings).

Reporting the findings   In a Parliamentary or Senate Inquiry or a Royal Commission, the boundaries of the study are indicated by the inquiry's 'terms of reference'. The topics listed in the case study protocol could serve as chapter or topic headings of the final report. Under each chapter, each of the themes and sub-themes identified with the data analysis can make up the headings and subheadings.

EXAMPLE
13.13

A case study report: *Netbets: A review of online gambling in Australia*

The topics and issues examined by the Senate Information Technologies Committee in this inquiry are used as chapter and section headings in the final report.

The headings and subheadings under each chapter are developed using data analysis and are based on the themes and sub-themes of data uncovered by the researchers. These topics (chapters), themes (issues) and sub-themes are listed as follows:

Introduction

Terms of reference of the Committee; its membership; table of contents; and the structure of the report and recommendations.

Chapter 1—Overview

Introduction; examination of terms used; online gaming; interactive wagering; online gambling in Australia; types of gambling activity; number of operators and players; the regulatory models; problem gambling; the potential for an increase in problem gambling; prohibition of internet gambling; harm minimisation; policies; additional improvements to the regulatory models; conclusion.

Chapter 2—Online gambling in Australia

Introduction; what is online gambling?; who are the online gambling operators in Australia?; numbers of internet gamblers; Lasseters online; Centrebet; Canbet; NetTab; under what regulatory schemes do they operate?; the power to regulate gambling in general and online gambling; the value of regulation; regulation in Australia of online gaming; the importance of cooperative approach; a standardised model for regulation; licensing; technical operations; audit and inspection; advertising; credit gambling; player protection; money laundering; privacy; taxation-sharing arrangements; interactive wagering; a national cooperative model; distinctions between online gaming and interactive wagering; conclusion.

Chapter 3—Problem gambling

Introduction; impact of online gambling on problem gambling; accessibility; links between online gambling, increased accessibility and problem gambling; evidence presented to the committee; independent research; measure of accessibility; other factors affecting the prevalence of problem gambling; profile of a problem gambler; access and availability; type of gambling product; demographic factors; other measures of health and well-being; summary; the challenges that are posed by online gambling; risk factors; policy options for addressing problem gambling; banning access to problem gambling; feasibility of a ban; technical aspects of prohibition; success of banning pornography on the internet; the consequences of a ban; other policy options; harm minimisation policies; player and third-party exclusions and the identification of problem gamblers; number of exclusions; effectiveness of player exclusions; time limits on gambling and the continuity of gaming activities; links to problem gambling information; advertising; warnings about the risks associated with gambling; player manipulation; improved customer information on the time taken, odds and financial records; clear statement of odds; financial records; time spent gambling; public education campaign; technology to implement harm minimisation policies; conclusion.

Chapter 4—Adequacy of regulations

Introduction; national cooperative model; Ministerial council on gambling; player protection; money laundering; privacy; security; access to minors; proof of identity; conclusion.

Chapter 5—International

Introduction; United States—overview, the *Wire Act 1961, Internet Gambling Prohibition Act 1997*; the effect of Wire Act; Senate 692—the 'Kyl bill'; progress of Kyl bill; South Africa—overview of South Africa policy, features proposed for South African model for regulation; national regulatory body; player protection; problem gambling; underage gambling; taxation; Europe— Gaming Regulators European Forum; Great Britain—online gaming, interactive wagering; the Caribbean; conclusion.

Appendices

The appendices include details on: how the inquiry was conducted; list of submissions; list of additional Information; witnesses at hearing; Productivity Commission—Report on Australia's gambling industries; draft regulatory Control model for new forms of interactive home gambling; *Internet Gambling Prohibition Act 1999*; and Internet gaming in South Africa: Implications, costs and opportunities.

Source: www.aph.gov.au/Senate/committee/ inquiry (accessed 18 August 2007).

Note how the appendices serve as 'maintaining a logical chain of evidence' discussed under 'Data collection' in case studies earlier in the chapter. The original written submissions and transcripts of witness statements made to the Committee hearing will make up the 'case study database'.

Other formats for case study reports   A case study report does not have to be a written one; for example, it can be an art or photographic exhibition or an oral presentation. If it is about a famous person, it can be a biographical case study presented as a feature film or TV or film documentary. Even museum exhibits such as on the Holocaust; the preserved homes of famous authors, artists or singers containing their memorabilia; US presidential libraries or museums devoted to past presidents are non-written forms of case study reports.

An alternative format of a case study report

EXAMPLE 13.14

Artist and refugee activist Kate Durham held an exhibition of paintings as she imagined the sinking of the refugee boat SIEV-X (Suspected Illegal Entry Vessel—Unrecorded) carrying 353 'boat people' or asylum seekers en route to Christmas Island from Indonesia in October 2001.

Only 45 passengers of the boat survived, and of the survivors, only seven were granted refugee status in Australia, while the rest were accepted for settlement in Canada, New Zealand and Scandinavia (Kizilos, 2007).

ADVANTAGES AND DISADVANTAGES OF CASE STUDY RESEARCH

The main advantages of the case study method are that it can provide a holistic view of the phenomenon under study, either as a cross-sectional or longitudinal examination. Due to theoretical, methodological and data source triangulation, it also provides rich data and views from several perspectives (Daymon & Holloway, 2002).

The main disadvantages of the case study method relate to their lack of generalisability, costs involved, issues of accessibility to settings and data, and problems related to defining the time and space boundaries for the case or cases examined (Daymon & Holloway, 2002).

APPLICATIONS OF THE CASE STUDY RESEARCH METHOD IN JOURNALISM, MEDIA AND COMMUNICATION, AND PUBLIC RELATIONS

The case study method is often used in practical applications in the disciplines of journalism, media and communication, and public relations.

JOURNALISM

Journalists often use the case study method of collecting information from several sources when investigating an issue for a feature or news story, and to verify information collected, while they seek to gain an in-depth understanding of a complex phenomenon within a broader context.

Journalistic reports such as news stories or features are similar to case study reports because they provide '**particularistic descriptions**' using quotes from interviewees and observations made in the field. The **interpretive commentary** of a journalist, such as opinions and editorials, provide the context to a story and is analogous to an explanatory case study that indicates the possible causes and effects of a phenomenon under examination (Hass, 2004).

A 'hard news' story written by a journalist is comparable to an analytic, realist tale while a feature article is comparable to a reflective, confessional tale, common in case study research reporting.

The Watergate scandal   The classic application of the case study research method in journalism relates to the investigative journalism efforts of Bob Woodward and Carl Bernstein that exposed the Watergate Scandal in June 1972. They were published in the *Washington Post* (Woodward & Bernstein, 1972) and led to the resignation of US President Richard Nixon in August 1974.

The two reporters won the Pulitzer Prize for their efforts and their book *All the president's men* (Woodward & Bernstein, 1974), which details how the Watergate story was put together, became a best seller. It was made into the Oscar-nominated film of the same name in 1975, starring Robert Redford (Woodward) and Dustin Hoffman (Bernstein) (*All the president's men*, 1975).

EXAMPLE 13.15

All the president's men

In the run-up to the 1972 US presidential election, where President Richard Nixon was seeking re-election, journalist Bob Woodward of the *Washington Post* was assigned to cover a minor break-in at Democratic Party Headquarters on the sixth floor of the Watergate building in Washington DC. Five well-dressed men wearing rubber surgical gloves had been arrested around 2.30 a.m. on Saturday 17 June 1972. They were in possession of extensive photographic equipment and some electronic surveillance instruments capable of intercepting both regular conversations and telephone communication. Two ceiling panels had been removed near party chairman Lawrence F. O'Brien's office, apparently to slip a bugging device.

The five arrested men had given false names to the police and two had the phone number of Howard Hunt, a White House aide and CIA consultant. One of the burglars was James W McCord Jr, a retired CIA employee and a security contractor to the Republican National Committee. Former Attorney General and then Head of the Committee for the Re-election of the President, John N Mitchell, said McCord was employed to help install that committee's own security system. Interviews with other White House aides and Cabinet members uncovered contradictory stories.

Woodward was surprised to find top lawyers already on the defence case and, along with Bernstein, found the trail leading high up on the Republican Party hierarchy and eventually to the White House and President Nixon. This led the two journalists to ask the questions 'Why?' and 'How?' (the burglars happened to have the phone number of a White House aide) and examine 'What is going on here?' (in terms of the cover up at high levels).

The reporters also interviewed neighbours of burglary suspects, Judy Hoback (the bookkeeper for the Committee for the Re-election of the President) and many others, including an anonymous source named 'Deep Throat'—who was only identified on 31 May 2005 by *Vanity Fair* magazine as Mark Felt, the second-highest ranking official of the FBI at the time. Felt had told the journalists to 'follow the money'. Woodward and Bernstein consulted Felt to confirm the accuracy of information they collected from other sources or for data triangulation.

Woodward and Bernstein maintained handwritten notes during their investigation, available on the newspaper's website, that served as their logical chain of evidence.

Source: Woodward & Bernstein (1972); www.washingtonpost.com; www.imdb.com.

MEDIA AND COMMUNICATION

The case study method is common in research related to writing and producing media content. Often, non-fiction books and films based on biographies are written with the help of research carried out as case studies. The SIEV-X tragedy was the subject of the book *A certain maritime incident: The sinking of SIEV-X* by Tony Kevin (2004).

The event was also examined by the (Parliamentary) Select Committee on the SIEV-X maritime incident and was reported as *Select Committee on a Certain Maritime Incident report* (2002).

Hope: a case study of SIEV-X and its survivors

EXAMPLE 13.16

The 2007 Melbourne Film Festival held the world premiere of the documentary film *Hope* on 10 August 2007. The film was a case study of SIEV-X and its survivors. The main informant of this study was Ms Amal Basry—one of the seven among the 45 survivors granted refugee status in Australia. Directed by Steve Thomas, the documentary is also the life story of Amal (which means 'hope').

Amal, her husband and her two sons left Iraq during Saddam Hussein's regime when her husband was arrested and tortured, and several male members of her family were murdered. They escaped to neighbouring Iran in 1997, but her sons were not allowed to attend school there.

EXAMPLE 13.16

Her husband had arrived in Australia earlier and was on a Temporary Protection Visa (TPV), which did not permit him to sponsor his family to Australia. Amal had paid for herself and her younger son to be taken to Australia from Indonesia in August 2001, but her older son stayed behind as she did not have enough funds for his passage as well.

The film presents the story from Amal's point of view. She is educated, eloquent and fluent in English and had met the film director when Amal gave a speech at the art exhibition about the SIEV-X by Kate Durham. The story explains 'why' Afghanis, Iraqis and Iranians (among others) embark on the dangerous and uncertain voyage in leaky boats organised by unscrupulous people.

It also tries to understand what happened to the SIEV-X on that fateful day, what produced the three lights they saw once the 19.5 m fishing boat carrying 353 'boat people' had sunk, and why no one came to rescue them for 22 hours (Indonesian fishermen picked up the survivors the next day). It is believed that the boat was under surveillance in Indonesia and during its ill-fated voyage (Kizilos, 2007; *Hope*, 2007).

PUBLIC RELATIONS

Case studies in public relations shed light on both good and bad episodes in professional practice. They examine what worked and did not work, lessons to be learned and what could be improved. These could be specific public relations campaigns, such as a state government initiative to improve crisis and issues management plans, and their execution.

EXAMPLE 13.17

Mayhem in the Magic City: lessons to be learned

On 18 January 2002 at 1.34 a.m., a Canadian Pacific train derailed pouring 250,000 gallons of anhydrous ammonia in Minot (also known as Magic City) in North Dakota. The chemical vaporised into a toxic 350-ft-tall cloud that covered about 40% of the city, killed one person, injured more than 1600 and affected about 15,000 people out of a total population of 35,000. The noxious cloud burned the eyes and throats of residents and kept them stranded for hours without any information, due to breakdowns in emergency communication. This included 911 calls being jammed due to overloads, warning sirens not sounding, and radio and TV emergency broadcasts unavailable, as local broadcasts were off air at the time. To make matters worse, at an early press conference, city officials announced the emergency response a success as the responders did what they were trained to do.

Veil (2007: 337–8) reports on a case study that examined what went wrong in Magic City that day, what the city and the profession learned from the experience, the corrective action that followed, the organisational learning that helped restore the city's image and rebuild its legitimacy, and what it taught everyone about preparing an organisation for future crises.

Bad public relations—the 'McLibel' case　The McLibel case of the 1990s is a good example of a case study dealing with an episode of bad public relations. See Ackland and Florence (1995) for details of this case and wwww.mcspotlight.org (accessed 9 January 2008) for an activist view of its history.

EXAMPLE
13.18

Case study of a 'bad' public relations episode: the 'McLibel' case

In the 1990s, the fast-food giant McDonald's brought defamation action against London Greenpeace, after two of its members circulated pamphlets in the United Kingdom, condemning the environmental policies of McDonald's. Unexpectedly, this turned out to be bad public relations and publicity for McDonald's, even though they won the 'McLibel' case, as it was seen as a David and Goliath-like legal battle (Breit, 2004: 77).

Summary

This chapter examined the difference between teaching and research case studies and the different types of research case studies such as exploratory, descriptive and explanatory, as well as single and multiple case studies. The chapter also detailed the different steps to be followed when conducting a case study, such as selecting a topic, research design, developing the case study protocol, carrying out a pilot study, collecting data including triangulation, analysing data and reporting of results. It also provided examples of case study research applied in public policy, journalism, media and communication, and public relations.

Try this …

1   Design a case study to examine the production and reception (viewing by audiences) processes of your favourite Australian drama, using multiple methods of data collection (for example, depth interviews, focus groups, field observations, documentary and archival data) and the relevant informants and participants (for example, writers; actors; technical crews; production staff such as directors, producers, production assistants and executive producers; industry union officials; agents and managers of actors; extras; and viewers and fans.)

   a   Prepare a list of research questions or hypotheses to be examined.

   b   Decide on the boundaries of the case study (for example, time and space).

   c   Examine what methods of data collection would be suitable for which population.

   d   How would you design the entire study? (The 'How?' and 'Why?' questions you need to ask.)

   e   What types and forms of triangulation can you use (for example, data sources, methodologies, theories and investigators)?

   f   How would you choose respondents from each group of people?

   g   How would you gain access to the case settings and respondents?

   h   Develop a list of interview questions to be posed to respondents from each group/ data collection method.

   i   How would you develop and conduct the pilot study? (What would be your study protocol?)

   j   Apart from respondents, what other sources of data would you use (for example, documents, archival materials and physical artefacts)? Give specifics.

k   How would you maintain a case study database and logical chain of evidence?

l   How would you analyse the data using 'progressive focusing' and 'assertion'?

m   Who would be the audience for your case study report?

n   Can you prepare the report in a non-written format?

2   List a few hypothetical case studies you can conduct that are based on topics or research questions of your choice that use:

a   a single case

b   multiple cases.

How would you obtain a diversity of cases?

3   Keep an eye out for any public notices of forthcoming Parliamentary, Senate or Royal Commission inquiries and their hearings, or reports of completed inquiries on public policy issues related to media and communication. Log on to the Australian Parliament House website (www.aph.gov.au/senate/committees) to read a few reports of, and submissions to, inquiries on topics of interest to you. Examine how they may have been carried out as case study research.

Further reading

Center, A H & Jackson, P 1995. *PR practices: Managerial case studies and problems,* 5th edn. Prentice Hall, Upper Saddle River, NJ.

Fensch, T 1990. *Associated Press coverage of a major disaster: The crash of Delta flight 1141.* Lawrence Erlbaum Associates, Mahwah, NJ.

Hirst, M & Patching, R 2007. *Journalism ethics: Arguments and cases.* Oxford University Press, South Melbourne.

Maclurcan, D 2006. *The sinking of the SIEV-X: A case study for secondary schools.* SIEV-X Secondary Schools Case Study Committee, Wollstonecraft, NSW.

Rosenstiel, T & Mitchell, A 2003. *Thinking clearly: Cases in journalistic decision-making,* Columbia University Press, New York.

Additional resources

Case studies in public relations:

Public Relations Institute of Australia (PRIA)—Golden Target Awards: Public Relations Case Studies (www.lib.uts.edu.au/gta, accessed 7 September, 2007).

Textual Analysis 14

In Chapter 9 (Content Analysis), we examined how media **texts** or messages are quantitatively analysed with respect to their manifest content (literal meanings). This chapter is devoted to the qualitative analysis of their latent content—how to interpret or 'read' the hidden or implied meanings of a message.

As implied meanings are linked to people's attitudes and are reader-orientated, they cannot be quantitatively 'counted' or measured. Therefore, we require a different system of 'measurement', and textual analysis is that system. This chapter examines:

- types of textual analysis
- semiotic analysis
- types of **signs**
- signs and their **conventions**
- **denotations** and **connotations**
- **codes**
- signs and meanings
- genre analysis

- **narrative analysis**
- **polysemy** or **multiple readings**
- discourse analysis
- **discourses** and their **framing**
- **intertextuality**
- applications of textual analysis in journalism, media and communication, and public relations

TYPES OF TEXTUAL ANALYSIS

Neuendorf (2002) categorised the various types of textual analyses as:

- rhetorical (Aristotelian)
- narrative
- discourse
- **structuralist** or semiotic

- interpretive
- conversation
- critical
- **normative**.

Let us briefly examine each of them.

RHETORICAL (ARISTOTELIAN) ANALYSIS

About 4000 years ago rhetoricians became the first practitioners of human communication as a discipline. **Rhetorical analysis** examines 'how' a message is presented to persuade the audience rather than 'what' the message is. Often used to analyse political speeches, advertising, public relations campaigns and news, it examines how a message is constructed using strategies such as specific **metaphors**, frames, **priming**, argumentation structures and choices (Neuendorf, 2002: 31).

Rhetorical analysis of political speeches

Kathleen Hall Jamieson (1988), in her book *Eloquence in an electronic age*, illustrated how former US President Ronald Reagan successfully used various rhetorical strategies in his speeches, even while presenting information and facts that were inaccurate or deliberately misleading.

NARRATIVE ANALYSIS

Narrative analysis describes the formal narrative (storytelling) structure of a message.

Narrative analysis: telling a dramatic story

The story-telling structure of a text includes the various stock characters such as hero/heroine, villain, narrator, supporting actors, extras, situations involving conflicts and complications, the **plot** (how the story is told), elements of mystery, the turning point, the climax (the high point of the story) and the denouement (the unravelling or resolution of the complications of the story that follows the climax). These aspects of 'drama' apply even to news and current affairs, as they are meant to entertain and create audience appeal (Turner, 2000). After all, journalism talks about news 'stories'!

Stories are made predictable so a wide audience can easily understand them and anticipate what happens next. In narrative analysis, the researcher looks at the characters that carry the **story** forward (Sillars, 1991).

DISCOURSE ANALYSIS

Discourse analysis examines the characteristics of language and word use in a message, highlighting how a topic or subject gets 'talked about' in media or other texts. It explores how the central themes of a text are linked to the ideologies and motivations of the creator of the message and the institutions they belong to (see Thwaites et al., 2002: 138–41).

Discourse analysis: 'torrents' of refugees 'invade' the Netherlands

In a study of the Dutch print media's coverage of the arrival of 3000 Tamil refugees in the Netherlands, van Dijk (1988) examined how the news described the phenomenon as an 'invasion', using metaphors of water such as 'torrent' and 'inundated' in a country historically threatened by water. Often, the mass media depict minorities, refugees or migrants as a 'problem' to the mainstream. These are considered to be racist discourses.

STRUCTURAL OR SEMIOTIC ANALYSIS

Semiotic analysis looks for 'deeper meanings' of messages through relationships between signs and meanings, and the use of binary oppositions (for example, good vs bad and tall vs short) to create specific meanings.

Semiotic analysis: the 'good' and 'bad' in black and white

EXAMPLE 14.4

In old Western films, the villain was dressed in dark clothing, a black hat and stubble (unshaven), while the hero was clean shaven, wore lighter clothing and a white hat.

INTERPRETIVE ANALYSIS

Using observation and coding of various messages, **interpretive analysis** develops theories about how people do something and what is achieved in the process. For example, looking at conspicuous consumption, interpretive analysis will theorise that 'McMansions'—large suburban homes of similar designs and layout built in new property developments—have become an expression of 'aspirational' people, indicating they have become economically successful or have 'made it'.

CONVERSATION ANALYSIS

Conversation analysis examines naturally occurring conversations. Using the inductive method, it examines and describes how ordinary people use various conversational strategies in various situations; for example, professional–client relationships; between romantic partners; between acquaintances when seeking or refusing a favour; and when trying to avoid 'losing face' or to 'save face'. Conversation analysis can examine media interviews with politicians, interactions between talk show hosts and their guests, and so on. This area of research is generally applied in linguistics and interpersonal communication.

CRITICAL ANALYSIS

Stemming from the cultural studies tradition (to be discussed later), **critical analysis** looks at media messages to highlight what may be wrong or unfair in them, how they are linked to **power** relations in society, and how and why they should be changed.

Critical analysis: sexuality, emotional intimacy and people of colour

EXAMPLE 14.5

Beeman (2007) examined institutional racism embedded in US films between 1980 and 2001 and found that they depict people of colour as emotional unequals or as not sharing the same emotions and experiences as whites. They also lacked portrayals of interracial intimacy, and carried negative stereotypes of relationships involving people of colour. Beeman argued that such depictions help to maintain the status quo of continued opposition to interracial intimacy—especially involving African-Americans.

NORMATIVE ANALYSIS

Some textual analyses lead to generalisations, meaning they are normative and pre-scriptive (giving rise to general rules—see Chapter 2 for nomothetic explanations.)

Normative analysis: stereotyping, mythmaking and 'best practice'

Normative analyses prescribe or define what a negative portrayal of minorities or other social group is and thereby tell us (prescribe) what to look for in media texts to detect instances of stereotyping and mythmaking (which are generalisations). Normative analyses specify the 'best practice' of a balanced or more representative portrayal of minorities or other marginalised groups; how to design a good website etc.

We now examine semiotic, narrative and discourse analyses in more detail, along with genre, **culture**, post-stucturalism and ideological analyses, as applied to media texts (textual analysis).

SEMIOTIC ANALYSIS OF TEXTS

Semiotics is the science of signs and how they create meanings. Sometimes regarded as synonymous with structuralism—and therefore called the structuralist approach to understanding meaning—semiotics was developed by the Swiss linguist Ferdinand de Saussure (1966) in his *Course in general linguistics*.

Semiotics revolves around three main concepts:

* signs
* codes
* culture.

SIGNS

A sign can be an object, a word, a picture or (a thing) that is physical and can be perceived through our senses; for example, rock or classical music, the Sydney Harbour Bridge or an Australian accent. Anything can be a sign provided someone recognises it as one. A sign refers to something other than itself, which has a particular meaning to a person or group.

The **signified**, or the meaning (or meanings), of a sign is not fixed, as it depends on the interpretations or 'readings' of it by the 'reader'. A given sign has multiple meanings (polysemy) depending on each reader and their readings.

A text   A text is a combination of signs such as a conversation, a media message, fashion, an art work, literature or music. Texts can be used by different people to convey different meanings and to distinguish themselves from others (for example, clothing or fashion) or to create group or personal identity (to stand out as different from others).

Types of signs

Signs or **signifiers** can be of three types (Berger, 1999):

1 **icon**
2 **index**
3 **symbol**

Handy Hint

The concept of a sign is linked to the concepts of signifier (the thing) and the signified (meaning). A sign is neither the signifier nor the signified but the two together. Note how this links with the epistemology of constructionism (Chapter 1) and the theoretical paradigm of interpretivism (Chapter 2).

Icon   An icon is a sign that is a **representation** of 'a thing' or object that resembles it in some way. These could be visual, verbal/auditory etc.

Iconic signs: visual and auditory

EXAMPLE 14.7

Visual signs or signifiers that are icons include photographs, portraits, paintings, cartoons or caricatures, maps and line drawings.

Verbal or auditory signs or signifiers that are icons include **onomatopoeia**—words that represent the particular sounds the sign refers to. For example, cock-a-doodle doo (sound made by a rooster), bow wow (bark of a dog), buzz (a bee), meow (a cat) and bang (a gun fired).

However, these visual and verbal or auditory icons can be culture-based. For example, for the above verbal or auditory icons, a Sinhalese speaker (of Sri Lanka) would say that a rooster goes 'cook cookoo koo', a dog barks as 'book-book', a bee goes 'hhmmmmm', a cat goes 'gnaaawu', and a gun goes 'doa-ung'.

VISUAL ICONS TO INDICATE MALE AND FEMALE

For visual icons, the male and female line drawings used on doors of toilets indicate the Western-style clothing of the two sexes—a triangle to indicate a short dress for a woman and a pair of pants for a male. These will not mean the same for cultures that dress differently and who do not know what the icons represent.

Index   An index is a sign (signifier) that points or directs us to its signified (the thing).

Indexical signs

EXAMPLE 14.8

The most commonly used examples for indexical signs are: smoke (signifier or index sign) pointing us to a fire (the signified or the thing); and symptoms as an index of a disease. A 'For Sale' sign on a car or house is also an indexical sign as are the words 'men/male/gentlemen' and 'women/female/ladies' written on the doors of public toilets.

However, note that the line drawing of a male or female figure on the door of a public toilet discussed in Example 14.7 can be both an icon and an index, as they direct us to male and female toilets.

Symbol   A symbol is a sign (signifier) that bears no relationship to the concept or object it represents ('the thing' or the signified). These signs are arbitrarily assigned based on social conventions. This makes symbols the most important type of sign as they are arbitrary, highly developed and less constrained by outside factors compared with icons and indexes. From the perspective of semiotics, symbols are the most important type of sign, as they are entirely shaped by social conventions (Berger, 1991b).

When using symbol signs, the parties using the sign need to negotiate and decide on how it will be used. For example, users of a given language or symbol sign agree on: the symbols used to signify various phenomena or words; their conventions such as spelling, grammar and pronunciation; and how they may be used in a particular context. In other words, if we take a traffic light as a symbol, we needed to agree on what colours to use, in which order, what they mean and how we should react to each of the colours, if the symbol is to work.

EXAMPLE 14.9

Symbol signs: the tale of the 'table'

Words in a language, numbers and names given to people, objects or places are chosen arbitrarily based on the culture they are used in and the particular time in history. There are conventions agreed upon by the users of that system as to which names or other symbol signs should be used to signify what, and how, the symbol sign system should be used in specific contexts such as in spoken or written language. These may be modified during various times in history to adapt to the changing realities of that context (for example, changes in slang terms or vocabulary over time).

We also give names to things in our own languages. As a result, the same 'thing', object or the signified can be called by different names in different languages or cultures. For example, the word 'table' in English—which signifies a (generally) wooden structure with a flat top and four legs, used to sit at, eat at or write on—will be pronounced differently in French, even though it is spelled the same. A table is called a 'mesaya' in Sinhalese, 'meja' in Indonesian, 'bord' in Danish and 'tēburu' or 'shokutaku' in Japanese, and are written in their own script. This indicates the arbitrary and subjective nature of symbol signs.

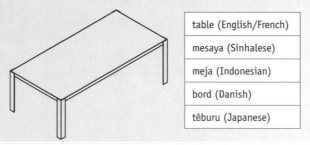

| table (English/French) |
| mesaya (Sinhalese) |
| meja (Indonesian) |
| bord (Danish) |
| tēburu (Japanese) |

Characteristics of signs   Signs, their meanings and the responses we are expected to make to them are invented by people; for example, 'Stop when a traffic sign turns red'.

- A sign is useful only to those who have learned to decipher, read, understand and/or interpret them; for example, a traffic light (or a written or spoken language) would mean nothing to someone who does not know what they mean.
- A sign's meaning is invented or learned though custom, continued use or legislation; for example, not stopping at a red traffic light can cause an accident or/and a traffic violation can attract a fine. We learn about it before we are able to drive.

Signs and their conventions   The above discussion indicates that all three types of signs and their meanings are governed by social conventions—some more than others. These conventions and the signs can change with the social situation or the group involved (Berger, 1999).

EXAMPLE 14.10

Social conventions: the 'Queen's English' and its variants

Even though based on the same origins (the language of English settlers), the English language used today by Americans, Canadians, Australians and New Zealanders indicate easily identifiable differences between each other in spelling, grammar, pronunciation, punctuation and accents. This also applies to the English language spoken in various other former British colonies, such as India, the West Indies, Singapore or Malaysia,

⌐⌐⌐⌐⌐⌐⌐>

where local social conventions and aspects of the users' mother tongue have caused modifications to how English is spoken, written and pronounced.

Even within a given nation, the same language may be used differently across ethnic, class, regional, geographic, gender and professional lines; for example, dialects (of, say, the Chinese language); different accents based on the person's socio-economic status (cockney vs 'posh' English); education (cultured language by the higher educated) or geographic region (Scottish, Irish or midlands accents in Britain or the southern, New York, mid-western, Californian and other accents in the United States).

From the point of semiotics, these various forms of the same language or sign systems are not considered hierarchical. Just like different cultures, they are just different.

Formal conventions in visual images There are several formal and informal conventions used with iconic signs with reference to camera shots in visual images. These relate to close-ups, medium shots, long or establishing shots, full shots, and high and low angle shots. Moving images will also include zoom in or out and fade in or out using the camera lens. Here, the camera shot used is the signifier while the signified is the meaning created (Berger, 1991), as listed in Table 14.1.

Conventions in camera angles used when representing a person

TABLE 14.1 Camera angles (denotations) and their meanings (connotations)

Signifier (the camera shot)	Definition (what is included)	Signified (meaning)
Close-up or CU	face only	highlights emotions or indicates intimacy
Medium shot or MS	most of upper body	indicates personal relationships
Long shot (establishing shot) or LS	**setting** and the character	provides context with reference to other characters or the setting
Full shot or FS	full body of person	indicates social relationships
High angle	camera looks down on person	makes person look smaller to indicate weakness and vulnerability
Low angle	camera looks up at the person	makes person look taller to indicate power and authority
Zoom in (ZI)	camera lens moved in from wider shot such as LS, FS or MS to CU	moves from context to close observation of emotions of person
Zoom out (ZO)	camera lens moved out from CU to a wider shot such as MS, FS or LS	moving from close details to context
Fade in (FI)	image gradually introduced moving from black screen	beginning of a visual segment or act
Fade out (FO)	screen gradually changes from image to black	conclusion imposed by creator of text

Source: Berger (2003: 39, 41).

Try this …

Take the courtroom scene of the popular film *A few good men* (1992), starring Tom Cruise, Jack Nicholson and Demi Moore, which included the famous phrase: 'You can't handle the truth.' Carry out a semiological analysis of this scene, examining how the various camera angles used by the film makers helped create specific meanings for the viewers.

Denotations and Connotations   The terms 'denotations' (signifier) and 'connotations' (signified or meaning) take the concept of meanings embedded in the latent content of a text even further, as denotations and connotations influence the meanings in a text (see Sillars, 1991: 109–27). Note that the denotation (or signifier) of a sign is related to the 'literal meaning' of the message in a text or message.

EXAMPLE 14.11

Denotations of our clothes

The clothes a person wears has the literal meaning that they protect the wearer from the elements of cold or heat (physical protection) or cover up the private body parts (psychological protection).

The connotation (or the signified) of a sign is related to the 'implied meaning' of a text or message. It could be what the sender or creator of the message wants to project to others (or the receivers) about themselves, or it could be what the others or receivers interpret from the message.

Naming things   Connotations are found in the language we use to name things; for example, the various words used to denote a 'group of people'—such as team, coalition, junta, gang, faction, group, committee, brood, posse and entourage—have different connotations: some positive, some negative and some neutral, and all are used in different contexts.

The words chosen by a user in a given situation lead to specific connotations. For example, the terms freedom fighter, militia, terrorist, insurgent, revolutionary and resistance fighter in news reports may denote the same group of people but mean different things.

Handy Hint

Connotations occur when the sign interacts with the feelings or emotions of the user, and the values of the culture within which it is 'read' or interpreted. Note how this links with the epistemology of constructionism (Chapter 1) and the theoretical paradigm of interpretivism (Chapter 2).

EXAMPLE 14.12

Connotations of our clothes

We sometimes intentionally dress to create a specific impression, such as dressing formally when going for an interview or expensively to indicate our high economic or social status. At other times, it may be to indicate a specific viewpoint; for example, to acknowledge his commitment to all groups, President Hamid Karzai of Afghanistan wears a mix of clothing and colours to depict the diversity of cultures and ethnicities of the Afghan people.

At other times, what a person wears may lead to others making assumptions or interpretations about, for example, the current weather or the season (wearing woollens in winter), the wearer's tastes (good or bad), culture (a sari by a South Asian woman or a hijab or head scarf by a Muslim woman), ethnicity, age, affluence (rich when wearing expensive or designer clothes or poor when wearing tattered or cheap clothes), profession (doctors in scrubs), attitudes (casual, carefree or serious), lifestyle (hippy or bohemian) or values (conservative or otherwise).

The readings made by receivers are not always what the senders intended. For example, the hijab is seen by the Western world as a symbol of female oppression and subjugation in Islamic countries, or as an act of defiance when worn in the West. However, many Muslim women living in the West or outside the Middle East claim they choose to wear it as an expression of their devotion to god. This also indicates that the same sign or denotation in a text may give rise to different connotations for different people and in different contexts.

Try this …

Select the main news story appearing on the front page of a newspaper that is accompanied by a photograph or cartoon. Examine the photograph to see how it has been selected by the newspaper to create specific meanings in the minds of the 'readers'. Write down what you think this photograph connotes to the reader.

For example, an unflattering photo of a politician might be used when something negative about or disadvantageous to them is being reported. You may remember seeing pictures of former Iraqi president Saddam Hussein with dishevelled hair and unkempt beard at the time of his capture by American troops, connoting or indicating a fugitive found in squalid conditions.

CODES

Codes are rules for interpreting relationships between the signifier and the signified, because a code interprets what signs mean. Signs cannot stand alone, so they are organised into codes. Codes are a system of meanings shared by members or a culture or subculture; for example, a language or traditions. These codes link signs together to reflect a particular interpretation of a culture's values, **myths**, ideologies and social realities (see Sillars, 1991: 118–20).

What do I call thee? Signs, codes and social realities

EXAMPLE **14.13**

The Sinhalese language (of Sri Lanka) has a large number of commonly used names indicating the various parts of the rice plant, unlike English, which has just two well-known words (rice and paddy). Some of these Sinhalese names refer to minute parts of the plant and grain— such as the broken grains of rice; the powdered residue; the various stages of the process of growing and harvesting the crop; the plant in its early, young, mature, harvested and dried stages; and the field and its different aspects. This is an indication of the role and importance of rice to the culture as its staple food.

The Sinhalese language also has many words that are synonymous with the term 'you', which should be carefully selected for use when addressing or referring to different people and in different contexts. The rules regarding their use are linked to the culture's traditional social hierarchies, the social and familial relationships, and the status differences between the communication partners in a given situation, which are clearly specified.

This indicates the highly stratified and traditional nature of that culture and its society.

Signs and meanings The ability to create signs, texts and their meanings is not innate, as we are not born with the ability to speak a specific language, but can learn any. Therefore, many factors influence how we learn to and do create signs and texts, as well as make meanings of them. These include:

- **subject position**
- subjectivity
- **negotiation**
- **self-reference**
- **self-reflexivity**.

Subject position Subject position refers to our place in society as members of powerful, privileged and dominant groups or powerless, marginalised and oppressed groups. This subject position varies with the context (where you are and who you are with).

Subject position and context

A poor, white woman may be marginalised and powerless when in the company of rich, white men and women, but may be in a dominant position when in the company of rich men and women of colour, depending on the situation. At the same time, a rich, coloured woman from a developing country could be in a more privileged position than a poor or even middle-class white man when both are in a developed country.

Handy Hint

Our life experiences are shaped by our social position as a member of a particular gender, age, race, ethnicity, nationality, class, education, profession etc. Most of all, our experiences are shaped by how the rest of the world treats us—which is based on our social position as being privileged or marginalised.

Subjectivity Subjectivity is where the same thing can be seen differently by different people, as a consequence of their individual life experiences. An individual will interpret or read signs based on, and shaped by, his or her gender, age, knowledge, ideology, ethical standards, religion, beliefs, attitudes, tastes, values, culture and social class.

Social position and subjectivity

Social positioning such as class, gender, occupation and ethnicity will give a person different life experiences and access to certain codes and ranges of connotations. A teenager from an affluent neighbourhood and family with no previous encounters with the police may refer to a police officer using the nickname 'cop', address his or her as 'officer' and have a neutral or positive interpretation of the police officer. However, a teenager from a depressed neighbourhood and previous negative encounters with the police may refer to them as 'pigs', use obscene language when confronted and see police as oppressors.

Negotiation   We use negotiation to overcome subjectivity by coming halfway to reach a middle ground. For signs to work, we must adjust and re-adjust our signs and texts and their meanings to reach a shared or common understanding (**intersubjectivity**).

Negotiation

A person highly proficient in the English language moves from one English-speaking country to another, and is surprised that she finds it difficult to understand what the locals speak. The locals, too, find it difficult to understand what she says, due to differences in pronunciation, vocabulary, slang, idiom and so on. After a while, however, the locals and the visitor learn to adapt to these differences and are able to interact without problems.

EXAMPLE 14.16

Self-reference (autobiography)   The meanings we make of signs or texts we create or use reflect our own experiences or autobiography.

Self-reference or autobiography

What we say about or do to others says more about us and our attitudes, values, beliefs, points of view, ideology, tastes, preferences and life experiences than it says about the other people or the topic of conversation.

EXAMPLE 14.17

Self-reflexivity   Self-reflexivity refers to looking at oneself through other people's eyes. Self-reflexivity influences how we read or interpret signs and texts or behave and act towards others.

Self-reflexivity

An upwardly mobile person will conspicuously consume or participate in activities seen as 'high culture' or expensive to appear sophisticated or rich.

EXAMPLE 14.18

CULTURE

Through participation in groups, organisations and societies, including professional or academic fields, we establish common experiences or common cultures with other people. This allows such individuals to create or read signs or texts similarly, and enjoy a shared reality or common culture of intersubjectivity.

Common culture: Hollywood goes global for directors

It is quite common for actors and directors who excel in films in their own countries—even in languages other than English—to be offered work in Hollywood films. Most live up to the challenge.

EXAMPLE 14.19

Director Ang Lee, who won an academy award for Best Director for the gay cowboy film *Brokeback mountain* (2005), is an ethnic Chinese from Taiwan who graduated in film from New York University. Previously, he was nominated as best director for *Sense and sensibility* (1995), which won several academy awards, based on the 1811 English novel by Jane Austen and using a predominantly British cast and crew on location in England.

SPECIAL STRATEGIES USED IN CREATING SIGNS AND TEXTS

Advertising and other texts use certain strategies in designing messages that create specific meanings for audiences. These include:

- **differentiation**
- **transference**
- metaphors

- myths
- the setting or **mise-en-scene**
- ideology (Williamson, 1978).

Differentiation An advertisement tries to create a differentiation between brands of a similar product of the same category, such as cereal or soap, so that the product being advertised will 'stand out from the crowd'. This is done by providing the product with an 'image' (Williamson, 1978). This differentiation may also be created by discussing its style, price and customer service.

Differentiation: vote for our experience

During the 2007 federal election campaign, Australian Prime Minister John Howard presented his incumbent coalition as 'experienced in managing the economy' in comparison to the opposition Labor Party, thereby differentiating itself.

Transference Transference refers to passing on the characteristics, qualities or image of one sign to another. As advertised products have no specific image, they need to get one from somewhere else. This is why celebrities are used to advertise or promote a product so that their qualities or 'image' may be passed on (transferred) to the product when persuading the consumer to purchase it (Williamson, 1978).

Transference: hanging with the 'cool' people

Transference is not limited to advertising or political campaigns. Many people will 'drop names' about their contacts or friendships with important people hoping to have these others' importance transferred on to themselves. In high school, many students like to hang out with the 'cool people' and avoid been seen with the 'uncool' ones.

Buying designer clothes or expensive products with popular brand names, marrying a 'trophy wife' or going out with a glamorous date are also based on the same principle, as they are considered indicators of the person being successful enough in life to afford the products or attract such desirable partners.

However, this strategy has backfired in the past when the celebrity used in an advertising campaign was involved in a controversy leading to the withdrawal of the advertising campaign, such as for Pepsi with Michael Jackson.

Metaphors   Metaphors use the strategy of having one sign or concept substitute for another to make comparisons and to create a new way of looking at the first sign or concept. Metaphors can be both verbal and visual (Lakoff & Johnson, 1980).

Metaphors from advertising and politics

In 2004, Mark Latham—the then leader of the Australian Labor Party—used the metaphor of 'ladder of opportunity' as the basis of his education and economic policies. US President George W Bush used the carved faces of the four great Presidents of the USA on Mount Rushmore as the backdrop, when giving a speech on homeland security after 11 September 2001, creating a powerful visual metaphor.

Nicknames such as Thorpedo (for swimmer Ian Thorpe) are also metaphors. Visually, in an advertisement for Tasmanian wines, they used the metaphor of Tasmania being the 'cellar of Australia' to evoke visions of the map of Australia.

EXAMPLE 14.22

Myths   A myth is a story that the members of a particular culture use to explain themselves (Sillars, 1991: 123). They are essential to a nation to define themselves as to who they are and who they want to be.

The best-known myths within Australian society are the ANZAC soldiers at Gallipoli in Turkey during the First World War and the story of Ned Kelly and his gang of bushrangers. The latter is about a group of poor and oppressed young Irish men ultimately executed by the authorities.

In the USA and other Western democracies, the most common myth appears to be that of a free and independent press, which is not real—as proven by the US media's collaboration with the US military in reporting the early stages of the Iraq War. Other myths include 'hard work is all you need to succeed', which invokes the connotation that those who are unsuccessful are so due to their own fault of being lazy or unmotivated, and do not deserve our help.

Myths, just like metaphors and **analogies**, can be used in politics, advertising, public relations and journalism to create specific meanings or connotations for 'readers' of texts. With time and continuous repetition, myths can also turn social signs into facts.

GEORGE W BUSH AND THE COWBOY MYTH   Case Study 14.1

Susan Faludi (2003) points out that US President George W Bush was presented to the world using the metaphor of a 'cowboy' (for example, 'smoke them out of their holes', 'hunt them down', 'go it alone', 'straight talking' and 'blunt') and invoked the 'cowboy myth' when going to war in Iraq.

Faludi argues that, according to writings of the late nineteenth century, cowboys were 'quiet, self-contained men' who did not fire first and used their guns only to protect themselves and the cattle in their charge. In other words, the 'pre-emptive war' practised by George W Bush did not agree with the 'cowboy myth'.

Try this …

Critically examine the ANZACs at Gallipoli, and Ned
Kelly and his gang, as popular Australian myths.

The setting or mise-en-scene   The concepts of staging, setting or mise-en-scene refer to
everything that is included in a visual text, and especially media texts. These include the
background in a specific scene, furniture, walls and their decorations, people, costumes,
make-up and props used, which connote a lot about the characters' nature, tastes, socio-
economic status, family situation, lifestyle, behaviour or even their functionality.

Case Study 14.2   THE SETTINGS IN *GILMORE GIRLS*: THIS IS HOW THE OTHER HALF LIVES

The TV series *Gilmore girls* (2000–) features
a single mother, Lorelai Gilmore, who left
her wealthy parents' home as a 16-year-old
unmarried mother to raise her daughter Rory
by herself. When Rory turns 16, Lorelai re-
establishes contact with her parents (Emily and
Richard) to ask for a loan so that Rory can attend
a prestigious private school. The parents agree
to help on the condition that Lorelai and Rory
attend regular Friday dinners with Emily and
Richard at their home.

Comparisons between the two households of
Lorelai and her parents, as well as their attitudes,
values and lifestyles, are made using staging
of the two settings. Lorelai's home furnishings
and furniture are basic, eclectic and quirky.
Her fridge is empty except for leftover Chinese
takeaways, as she never cooks. The house is
modest and located in the middle of a small
town, Star's Hollow, where everyone knows
everyone and their business.

In contrast, Emily and Richard's home
is large, luxurious and stylishly decorated
with expensive furniture, furnishings, crystal
chandeliers, fresh flower arrangements and
valuable ornaments tastefully displayed. Emily
has a maid who wears a uniform and they
serve drinks in crystal glasses, use expensive
china and formal table settings. The house is
located on a large and secluded estate.

When Rory's fellow Yale University student
and boyfriend Logan Huntzberger takes her
to his parents' home for dinner in his Porsche,
their house is shown as much grander than
Lorelai's parents, with high ceilings, expensive
paintings, and very large and luxuriously
furnished living and dining rooms. Rory
openly expresses her appreciation and awe
of this home.

With these settings or staging, the creators
of the TV program provided signs invoking
connotations to show the differences in
lifestyles and economic status of the three
households and families. It helps when Logan's
mother tells Rory that 'her background isn't
good enough to marry a Huntzberger'.

Ideology   Ideologies are specific beliefs in a culture, and are revealed in signs and texts
(Sillars, 1991: 123). Just like myths, an ideology helps a researcher to interpret a society
in which a text was created. Ideology is a representation of a specific political position.

The **dominant ideology** in a society is carried in media and other texts, which help
maintain the status quo. Therefore, taking the critical perspective, a researcher looks for
the ideologies embedded in texts to examine whose interests are served in the process
(see White, 1992).

For example, when current affairs programs cover stories about welfare recipients as too lazy to work and undeserving of state support, they connote that these people are in that position due to their own fault. It justifies the harsh policies imposed on the unemployed, even though the problems of unemployment for many may be due to a bad economy and a lack of skills, education, training and opportunities for the poor to improve themselves.

THE DOMINANT IDEOLOGY AND GAY THEMES ON *HOME AND AWAY*

Case Study 14.3

The popular Australian soap opera *Home and away* (1987–) once had a storyline involving a gay couple. Due to the G rating of the program and its family viewing time slot, the couple was discreetly presented as friends. The program had received a large number of letters from viewers praising their decision, but at the same time ratings for the program dropped by 20% during that period.

As the program earns a good chunk of Channel 7's advertising revenue, the network warned the creators of the program not to deal with such issues in the future, as they were alienating some conservative viewers.

This indicates how the media mirrors the conservative dominant ideologies in society and helps to maintain the status quo in their favour due to economic imperatives taking precedence over all others.

So far, we have examined individual texts and their meanings. Let us now look at how groups of texts may be analysed textually.

GENRE ANALYSIS

Texts are categorised into groups according to their distinct features. These categories are called 'genres', and the process is analogous to the classification of animals into mammals, birds, reptiles etc (Feuer, 1992). As a group, members of a genre indicate similar structures or subject matter. Conventions also exist for a particular genre that adjust and shape our expectations and interpretations of the texts. For example, in a musical, actors will suddenly break into a song and dance. Even if this does not happen in real life, the rules or conventions of the genre tell us to accept them. Similarly, in an action film, the hero will generally remain alive till the end of the story.

TYPES OF GENRE

All media forms have their texts classified into genres. The following list provides examples of the more commonly found genres:

- Newspapers—tabloids (for example, *Herald Sun*) and broadsheets (*The Age, The Australian*).
- Films—westerns (for example, *Wyatt Earp*), musicals (*Chicago, The sound of music*), screwball comedies (*Mr. Bean*), science fiction (*Star Wars*), fantasy (*The lord of the rings* series), action-adventure (*Die hard 4.0*), martial arts (*Crouching tiger, hidden dragon*), film noir (*Blade runner, LA confidential*), war films (*The thin red line*), anti-war films (*Born on the fourth of July*), road films (*Thelma and Louise*), epics (*Gladiator, Titanic*), animated films (*Shrek, The Simpsons movie*) and documentary (*An inconvenient truth*).

- TV—situation comedies (sitcoms; for example, *Ugly Betty, Desperate housewives*), cringe comedy (*Kath & Kim, Summer Heights High*), prison dramas (*Prison break, OZ*), crime shows (*CSI*), police dramas (*City homicide*), medical dramas (*All saints, Grey's anatomy*), soap operas (*Neighbours, The young and the restless*), game shows (*Deal or no deal*) and news and current affairs (*60 minutes*).

INTERCULTURAL GENRES

Just like language codes (for example, different forms of the English language) genres also indicate modifications across cultures.

Intercultural genres

Westerns can be produced in Hollywood, Spain, Italy (spaghetti westerns), Japan (noodle westerns) or India (curry westerns).

Some of these may indicate variations from the general conventions for the genre. For example:

- In his spaghetti westerns, Sergio Leone would present an immoral lead character, or allow the hero to die, violating the code of the genre (Gripsrud, 1999).
- Rap music can be from the US, Korea or Africa, and is sung in the local languages.
- On TV, modifications to the genre convention of a hero can be seen where the lead character, Michael Schofield (Wentworth Miller), in *Prison break* (2005–) is morally ambiguous as he lies to Dr Sarah Tancredi and uses her to get what he wants, even though they are in love with each other.

Some genres can also be entirely new and specific to certain cultures:

- The Masala films of India's Bollywood are a mix of several genres, such as action, crime, romance, musical and thriller.
- Manga cartoons and anime films (Japan and China) are culture specific.

RECOMBINANT GENRES

Recombinant genres are hybrids or re-mixes of existing genres in the same text. Film noir combines detective, gangster and thriller genres. Masala films are also a recombinant genre.

Recombinant genres on TV

Reality TV shows such as *Big brother* are a combination of a game show, soap opera, documentary, situation comedy and drama. *Grey's anatomy* is a romance, comedy, medical drama and soap opera.

In popular music, recombinant genres result when artists from different genres collaborate, such as Beyonce Knowles (rhythm and blues or R&B) with Shakira (Latin pop), or when Nellie Furtado (R&B) and Timberland (hip hop) sing 'Promiscuous Girl' together. Recombination of genres helps a text appeal to a wider audience by attracting fans from each genre recombined.

GENRE THEORY IN MEDIA RESEARCH

Genre theory makes genre divisions or classifications and justifies these classifications by explaining the criteria used. It looks at how a culture expresses its values in texts and genres. The current popularity of reality TV is read as due to their portrayal of average people enjoying adventures (for example, *Survivor*) or gaining fame, wealth and fortune (for example, *Big brother* and *Australian idol*) (see White, 1992). In the past, media exposure was generally given only to the privileged, unusual, exceptional, deviant or unique individuals or groups.

GENRE CONVENTIONS

Each genre has its own conventions. The opening credits, visuals and theme music indicate what the themes of the program will be like. Quirky characters, exaggerated behaviour, leading characters that are polar opposites, and stereotypes are common under the comedy genre.

TV'S *GILMORE GIRLS* AND ITS GENRE CONVENTIONS   Case Study 14.4

The TV romantic comedy-drama, *Gilmore girls* (2000–) displays the following conventions.

The theme song by Carole King says, 'Where you lead, I will follow, anywhere you tell me to …' indicating the relationship between Lorelai and her daughter Rory. Rory considers her mother as the most important influence in her life. The background visuals indicate the US New England region (Connecticut) as the setting in autumn, and a close relationship between the mother and daughter.

Comedies have 'quirky characters and weird people', with exaggerated behaviours, and *Gilmore girls* has several. Kirk, the town's odd-job guy who still lives with his mother; Luke, the temperamental diner owner; Miss Patty, the ballet teacher; Babette, the eccentric neighbour; and Taylor, the autocratic mayor and owner of most of the local businesses.

We are told that comedies are not to be taken seriously. This means that any representations considered unacceptable or unexpected elsewhere will be allowed in a comedy.

Comedies also present polar opposites in terms of character traits, which give meaning via contrasts. Oppositions can be also based on battles of the sexes, classes or generations.

For example, Lorelai and her mother Emily are polar opposites as Emily is conventional and Lorelai is not. Rory's first two boyfriends are opposites—Dean is loving, reliable, predictable, kind, considerate, obliging and honest but laid-back, while Jesse—for whom Rory leaves Dean—is unpredictable, unreliable, moody, not really honest, difficult and aimless. Logan, on the other hand, is the perfect 'good catch'.

In comedies, the lead does not get married, because it then changes the show into a domestic comedy. There will be romantic interests and sexual tensions between the lead and other characters from time to time and even engagements, but they do not marry or don't stay married for long.

Stereotyping is common in comedies. Good examples of this in *Gilmore girls* include Michel, the grumpy and rude French concierge at Lorelai's Dragonfly Inn, and Mrs Kim, Rory's Korean friend Lain's control-freak mother.

The show uses conventional and easily understood signifiers and codes, such as the above, to help audiences understand the characters easily. This is because TV programs do not have much time to develop characters, so they need to be simplistic (Gripsrud, 1999).

NARRATIVE ANALYSIS

A narrative is a story that has a beginning, middle and an end (**closure**). A story is what is told in a narrative (the signified), and the plot (signifier) is how the story is told (see Thwaites et al., 2002: 117–36).

URBAN MYTHS

It is often said that one way to understand a culture is to examine the stories it generates—be they true or fictional. These include the jokes or 'yarns' arising in a culture, as well as **urban legends**. Urban legends are stories spread around the world with minor variations—sometimes to fit local cultural or social realities. They reflect the times and what is important or problematic to the culture (see Sillars, 1991: 149–71).

Case Study 14.5   URBAN LEGENDS: THE MAFIA GOES 'HACKING'

In the late 1990s, a story went around about computer hackers messing up hospital records and changing dosages of patients' medications, resulting in patients dying and nursing staff getting blamed and punished for it. Some versions of this story had organised crime (the Mob, the Mafia etc) hiring the hackers to kill their enemies or targets. This indicated the rise of computer hacking as a problem and its potential for criminal activity. No one knows how these stories originated or if they were true. But they are used to warn society about the possible ramifications of new technology and to cause fear. This is an urban legend (also known as **urban myths**).

The aspects of any story indicate what was important to that culture at the time it was told, while what was excluded from the story says what may be taboo in that culture (Sillars, 1991).

Case Study 14.6   NARRATIVES AND WHAT THEY TELL US ABOUT OURSELVES

In some cultures, issues such as homosexuality will not be discussed in their popular culture or in society. In 2007, while visiting the US and addressing a gathering at New York University, President Ahmajinedad of Iran was posed the question of discrimination and oppression of gays in Iran. He replied that 'unlike in the US, there are no gays in Iran'.

Acclaimed Indian-Canadian film director Deepa Mehta faced opposition from the government and violent protests from conservatives in India during the filming of *Water* (2006), which addressed the mistreatment of widows. The story was set in pre-independence India, but dealt with a practice that continues even today. The critics' argument was, 'Why can't they talk about the good things about India?'

Both examples indicate the two societies' reluctance to change the status quo or openly discuss difficult issues. They try to eliminate these topics from their narratives instead.

Therefore, narrative analysis helps us read a culture through its stories, which are often repeated, as the morals embedded in it are bound to the culture's values. Narrative criticism tries to understand the culture in which the story was created (Sillars, 1991).

THEMES IN NARRATIVES

Most narratives carry themes such as 'good will triumph over evil', 'deviants in society such as adulterers will come to an unhappy or violent end' (for example, the title character in *Anna Karenina* commits suicide, and homosexuals are not shown as living happily ever after) and 'truth will prevail' (for example, the innocence of a person will be proven).

Bad guys in a story are also presented as exceptions within institutions, and generally they are caught and punished due to the checks and balances that already exist within the institutional structure. In other words, the system, institution or the status quo is fine as it is and need not be changed.

THE SYSTEM IS FINE: JUST A FEW BAD APPLES   Case Study 14.7

Many popular films depict injustices committed against individuals within an institution as unusual and the culprit as a single, exceptional, villainous individual who is responsible for the problem, and who must be caught and punished by the system itself.

In the film *The Bourne ultimatum* (2007), the senior female CIA officer Pamela Landy (Joan Allen) helps Jason Bourne (Matt Damon) and brings his former CIA colleagues—who were trying to kill him—to justice by taking the evidence to a Senate Committee appointed to examine it.

NARRATIVE STRUCTURE

The **narrative structure** of a text refers to where the beginning, middle and end of the story are located (Sillars, 1991). Is it over or still continuing? For example, the history of Australia can be presented to cover the period between Gondwana and today, European colonisation to federation, or federation to today. This includes and excludes various aspects of history based on the wishes of the storyteller and creates specific meanings for the reader.

However, the narrative structure of a popular text may be selected to create the highest possible audience appeal and to end the story on a high note.

The closure   The closure is the ending of the story, which carries particular cultural myths and positions the reader to accept them and the ideology embedded within them (Sillars, 1991). With the ending of 'They married and lived happily ever after', the myth perpetuated is that marriage is meant to be happy—and if it is not, then it must be the fault of the individuals.

DRAMATIC PERSONAE (CHARACTERS) IN NARRATIVES

Vladmir Propp (1968) examined Russian folk tales and found there was a set of 31 characters that appear in various combinations in most narratives, sometimes with minor modifications. These included the hero or heroine, villain or vamp, donor (who provides something to the hero), dispatcher (messenger), false hero (who makes others believe he or she is a good person for a while), helper, and the princess and her father (or father figure) (Sillars, 1991).

In a story, characters do things or have things happen to them that take the story forwards. Each genre has conventions about what each character is like and does.

For example, in the action genre, the lead does not get married, so that he will not be tied down and unable to take risks. These conventions provide predictability to narratives to make them easily understood by audiences as they can anticipate what will happen next.

So far, we have examined texts and their meanings without considering the differences between individual 'readers' or audience members who interpret these texts. This is addressed through polysemy and cultural studies.

POLYSEMY OR MULTIPLE READINGS OF A TEXT

As the audience to any media text is diverse and each person's interpretation of a given text or sign can be subjective, the narrative of a given text can give rise to multiple readings or interpretations. Cultural studies is interested in differences (such as the various ways in which we may 'read' the world or texts) and examines how it works and in what contexts. The central concept of cultural studies is representation—how meaning is given to things depicted in a text (Fiske, 1992).

Hall (1980) in his book *Encoding/decoding* argued that since texts—and especially TV—have to appeal to a large and heterogeneous (diverse) audience, they will be open to multiple readings. This means a text is 'polysemic'. These multiple readings fall into three categories: dominant (preferred), resistant (oppositional) and negotiated. He argued that there is a correlation between an individual's social situation or position (for example, class) and the meanings made from the text, as social position and a person's subjectivity are related.

Texts often bear the dominant ideology in society (or the ideology of the creator of the text). Generally, the dominant individuals and groups, such as media industries and powerful institutions, are in a better position to control the creation of media and other texts that are presented to wider audiences (Fiske, 1992).

At the same time, each reader has the power to actively make meanings of a text. This has given rise to the argument that it is the audience member who is the most powerful. However, one must note that an individual audience member can make meanings of a text only within the context of the message sent and received. In other words, a reader can make meaning only from what is presented in the text, rather than all else that could have been included in it from the entire universe.

This is analogous to going to an ethnic restaurant and choosing from the menu presented—which has been set by the restaurant—rather than the diner being able to ask for any dish from that culture.

Dominant (preferred) reading   When making a **dominant reading**, the reader reproduces the meaning intended by the sender, which is generally based on the dominant ideology in society at the time (Fiske, 1992).

Dominant or preferred reading: WorkChoices

The WorkChoices advertisements aired by the Australian Government in 2007 claimed that the new legislation benefited the employee, the employer and the Australian economy. This is the dominant ideology embedded in the text and, in a dominant reading, the 'reader' or audience member agrees with it.

Oppositional (resistant) reading   The **oppositional reading** challenges the connotations and codes of the **preferred reading** and comes up with a conflicting or alternative reading (Fiske, 1992).

Oppositional or resistant reading: WorkChoices

EXAMPLE 14.26

The reader making an oppositional reading of the WorkChoices advertisement would argue that the government passed this legislation at the behest of big businesses and wants to cover up its shortcomings. For example, many low-paid and young workers lost their entitlements, were exploited, received less than before, and have done worse since WorkChoices was introduced. The oppositional reader sees it as the government, fearing a voter backlash, trying to neutralise negative public opinion towards the legislation in an election year.

Negotiated reading   In a negotiated reading of a text, the reader does not accept the dominant reading but neither does she challenge the dominant ideology embedded in it. Here readers will pick and choose aspects of the dominant reading depending on their own experiences (Fiske, 1992).

Negotiated reading: WorkChoices

EXAMPLE 14.27

In making a **negotiated reading** of the WorkChoices advertisement, an audience member might argue that WorkChoices has been good for highly skilled workers in sectors facing staff shortages and where their skills are in high demand, such as in mining. It allows businesses to attract such workers by offering them individual contracts well above the award rates negotiated with unions. But for low-paid, young and causal workers and middle-level employees in other sectors, employers have been able to reduce staff costs by getting rid of workers and abolishing existing benefits and entitlements. The negotiated reader might point out that some employees have been pressured into signing individual contracts to get a job or to keep a job when their position has been redesigned or workplace restructured.

Cultural studies assume a negotiated reading because the heterogeneous audiences of a given popular text will have different life experiences and varying relationships to the dominant ideology (Fiske, 1992).

POLYSEMY OF THE FILM ROMPER STOMPER   Case Study 14.8

The Australian film *Romper stomper* (1992) with Russell Crowe (as Hando) and Jacqueline McKenzie (as Gabe) is about a neo-Nazi skinhead group terrorising Vietnamese youth in Footscray, Victoria, and how they treat women, gays and even Gabe's rich father with contempt and violence. They clash with the police and in the end Hando is killed by his best friend Davey, when Hando tries to kill Gabe for informing on the group to the police.

Neo-Nazi skinheads who saw this film read it as a celebration of them, while many

Case Study 14.8

groups and individuals (including the then Prime Minister Paul Keating) read it as a racist film. However, the film shows skinheads as self-destructive and leading aimless and miserable lives—with only the two 'good ones' (Davey and Gabe) remaining alive at the end. In contrast, the Vietnamese are portrayed as hardworking, motivated and upwardly mobile. Therefore, some readers saw it as an anti-racist, anti-sexist and anti-homophobic film.

CLASS IS NOT THE ONLY FACTOR

Although Hall (1980) theorised with reference to a reader's class affiliations affecting their readings of a text, others such as David Morley found cross-class similarities between the various readings, due to shared interests across different classes. Today we agree that gender, race, culture, ethnicity and sexual orientation can also influence the readings made of a given text. However, Morley (1980) based his theory of polysemy on discourse rather than on class.

DISCOURSE ANALYSIS

The term 'discourse' has several meanings. This chapter, however, defines it as the way a topic or subject gets 'talked about' in society at a given time and location in everyday conversations or in the media. Discourses are a society's or an institution's way of talking and thinking about a topic. They are shaped by culture and, in turn, shape culture (Dickens-Garcia, 1998). Any given subject or topic can be discussed using several different discourses or in different ways, all of which can be valid.

Case Study 14.9 THE MULTIPLE DISCOURSES OF MOBILE PHONES

The different discourses available on mobile phones (or any other technology for that matter) are the optimistic (gains), pessimistic (losses, costs or harms), pluralistic (technology per se is neutral but how it is used is what matters), historical development (importance and skills learned), futuristic predictions (promises and dangers), current uses (connectivity, convergence and interactivity) and the techno-realist view (as a mixed blessing).

But the discourses used in a discussion or debated in society are shaped and dominated by the agendas, interests, viewpoints, ideologies, subjectivity and subject position (of being dominant, privileged and powerful or oppressed, marginalised and powerless in society) of each of the individuals or groups participating in it.

This explains why any topic or subject can be debated or discussed using several different discourses and why some discourses dominate while more or equally valid, urgent or legitimate others get sidelined or ignored. For example, the perceived 'harms' of mobile phone content, which is of apparent concern to middle- and upper-class parents in Australia, dominate over the issue of high mobile phone costs, which research has found to negatively affect the less affluent and minority teenagers more than others (Weerakkody, 2007a).

DISCOURSES AND THEIR FRAMING

Framing or the frameworks used in a discourse involve selection (of certain aspects) and the salience (importance) given to the aspects included in the discourse. Frames diagnose (identify the sources causing the problem), evaluate (make moral judgments about causal agents and their effects), prescribe (suggest remedies and offer and justify treatments) and predict (their likely effects) for an issue or subject under discussion (Entman, 1993; Solomon, 1992).

In simple terms, one can 'frame' a glass that contains water as 'half full' or 'half empty'. Each discourse is shaped by the outlook of the person using the frame and, in turn, shapes how others are influenced to look at the situation (Dicken-Garcia, 1998).

Framing is the basis of advertising, marketing, political and public relations messages and campaigns. Media messages are framed—either consciously or otherwise—by journalists and other creators of messages in particular ways and carry particular discourses. They tell us 'what to think about and how to think about' an issue.

In journalism, framing is linked to the 'angle' used in a news story and choosing a 'lead' for it. The lead controls how one tells the rest of the story and what headlines may be used (Dicken-Garcia, 1998). Read the newspaper article (Example 14.28) on cyber bullying by Dubecki (2006) and its analysis (Case Study 14.10) in terms of its discourses and framing.

Technological trauma: cyber bullies more powerful than schoolyard thugs

EXAMPLE 14.28

Technology has turned the traditional image of the bully waiting at the school gates on its head. Now the 24-hour wireless, faceless, version 2.0 of the school bully hides behind text messages, MySpace, YouTube and social networking sites.

The perpetrator can choose to remain anonymous but the victim's humiliation is compounded by the often very public nature of the bullying. … The trouble is, the methods available to cyber bullies are as broad as technology and their imaginations allow. … Bullies use email, instant messaging, chat rooms, mobile phone cameras, text and websites. … Now treated as a form of social aggression, the consequences [of cyber bullying] include acute anxiety, depression, truancy, self-harm, eating disorders and, in extreme cases, suicide. It is a recent phenomenon that began with the widespread use of mobile phones by young people in Australia about five years ago.

In March [2006], some New Zealand teenagers were blamed for the suicide of a 12-year-old girl the day before the start of the school year after bombarding her with threatening text messages. Closer to home, five boys at Sydney's the King's School were expelled or suspended in August and last month for cyber bullying. … Melbourne's Methodist Ladies College, which has banned MySpace and YouTube, has recently updated its bullying policy to include cyber bullying. Principal Rosa Storelli said it was based on several incidents at the school. The policy was formulated with the help of students who were more tech-savvy than many teachers.

That fact—the difficulty parents have in monitoring their children's online behaviour—goes to the heart of the matter. … Psychologist Elaine Field, author of *Bully Busting*, says this new kind of bullying is a viral phenomenon. 'If they think they can get away with it, they will do it' she says. 'But let's not just blame the kids. Let's look at the families and their communities—where are the kids picking up these despicable habits?'

Nor should victims suffer in silence she says. 'There are always records on the hard drive that are traceable. Bullies can be caught and dealt with.'

Source: Dubecki (2006).

Case Study 14.10 DISCOURSES AND THEIR FRAMING: THE MOBILE PHONE AS 'VILLAIN'

The mobile phone (along with the internet) is framed as the 'villain' in cyber bullying in Example 14.28), taking the angle or discourse of 'harms'. The diagnosis of this frame is that bullying has become a twenty-four-hour, seven-day possibility that goes far beyond school boundaries. This is because bullies can use text messages and photos and videos captured by mobile phones, which can be uploaded to social networks such as YouTube and MySpace, anonymously and for anyone, anywhere to see.

Its evaluation is that this causes trauma and increases the humiliation and victimisation of those targeted by real-life bullying, leading to anxiety, depression, truancy, self-harm, eating disorders or even suicide. This is because the humiliation can reach a wider audience and go on for a longer period of time than when carried out face to face in the 'real' world.

It prescribes harsh punishments to perpetrators such as expulsion, citing the King's School in Sydney, and including cyber bullying in school anti-bullying policies drafted in consultation with students, citing Melbourne's Methodist Ladies College as an example.

However, it predicts that since cyber bullying leaves records on computer hard discs, culprits may be caught and all students will understand the inappropriateness of cyber bulling, and that redress and repercussions can be expected in future situations (Weerakkody, 2007a).

FRAMES AS RHETORICAL WEAPONS

By framing a discourse in a particular manner or direction, a sender of a message can place 'blinkers' or 'blinders' on the receiver, guiding their view or attention in a particular direction and away from alternative viewpoints. This guides the receiver to think only about the sender-highlighted aspects of an issue under consideration (Weerakkody, 1999). In other words, different discourses and frames (denotations or signifiers) can contribute towards creating specific connotations (implied meanings or the signified) for the receivers of such messages and/or make their minds unconsciously stick to a particular paradigm.

Case Study 14.11 STRATEGIES OF FRAMING: THE CASE OF THE MOBILE PHONE

Framing uses various strategies (Dicken-Garcia, 1998). These include:

o **adjectives**—describing words such as 'empowering'.
o metaphors—understanding one thing in terms of another (Lakoff & Johnson, 1980: 5), such as the mobile phone as a 'digital leash' of tying teens to their parents for control, or an 'umbilical cord' tying parents to their children providing 'sustenance', with both parties contactable at all times.
o analogies—drawing similarities between two things, such as comparing the changes

brought by driving a car and mobile phones for teenagers expressing their freedom and independence from adult supervision (Levinson, 2004).

o **euphemisms**—a strategy of using a neutral or 'fancy' term to cover up an unpleasant reality (Planalp, 1998: 69), such as using 'child protection' to hide the fact that the policy involves surveillance and control of teenagers and their movements via their mobile phones using GPS (Global Positioning Systems) and other 'spying products' (Spiked-debate, 2006). Another example is use of the

⌐⌐⌐⌐⌐⌐⌐⌐⌐⌐▷

term 'premium services' by mobile phone companies to downplay the fact that they are expensive and provided by subscription.

o **disphemisms**—the opposite of euphemisms, where exaggerated terms are used to make something sound more unpleasant than it really is (Planalp, 1998: 69). For example, those advocating surveillance of mobile phones argue about the 'risks' of 'child abuse' and its detractors refer to these arguments as 'manufactured hysteria' (Spiked-debate, 2006). Those seeking more controls on mobile phones by parents on children argue that 'paedophiles' may use the technology to lure children. They in turn are accused of creating 'moral panics' by detractors who argue that paedophiles are unlikely to use mobile phones, which are more easily traced than the internet—the more commonly used technology by paedophiles (Weerakkody, 2007a).

FUNCTIONS OF DISCOURSE

The discourses that prevail in society belong to the various powerful individuals, groups, organisations and institutions (such as politics, medicine, education, religion, family, marriage, military and corporations) in society or a given context. Analysing texts according to the discourses embedded in them sheds light on the power relations in society with respect to that institution, individual, organisation or group.

DISCOURSE AND POWER

A dominant discourse specifies what can be said and how it may be said, and by extension what can be done with respect to an area of concern to a culture. In 2006, the Australian Government specified marriage as 'a union between a man and a woman' in view of the Australian Capital Territory (ACT) passing laws to legalise same-sex unions. This discourse (of marriage) was political and was introduced on the insistence of then Prime Minister John Howard, who had the power to do so. In other words, what cannot be said or done in society is decided by the powerful.

DISCOURSE AND POWER: REPERCUSSION OF OPPOSITION TO THE POWERFUL   Case Study 14.12

In 2003, when a member of the popular country and western group Dixie Chicks said she was embarrassed to be from the same state (Texas) as US President George W Bush—in reference to his going to war in Iraq—their songs were boycotted by many radio stations nationwide.

Any debates on, and in opposition to, the US's war against the Taliban in Afghanistan in late 2001 were silenced by President Bush by saying to other countries and their leaders that 'You are either with us or with the terrorists'. Americans were labelled unpatriotic or pro-Taliban if they opposed the war.

These discourses removed the chance of any other discourse being raised, such as neutrality, the need to go to war under the UN banner or repercussions for the civilian population of Afghanistan.

CONTROL OF MEDIA DISCOURSES

Powerful individuals and groups often try to influence or control the discourses about themselves or institutions they belong to, in spite of the freedom of the press enjoyed by the Western media. This can be illustrated by two well-known examples.

Case Study 14.13   DISCOURSE AND POWER: US MEDICAL DRAMAS

Content of medical dramas on commercial TV in the US is controlled by the wealthy and powerful American Medical Association (AMA), which makes sure their profession is portrayed favourably in the media. The AMA also ensures that the contributions made in a hospital by other allied professions, such as nurses or psychologists, are not depicted in these dramas as considerable, often portraying nurses only as love interests for the doctors. The AMA can do so as the media are dependent on it for technical consultants to make sure the medical aspects depicted in the texts are accurate (Turow, 1989).

Case Study 14.14   DISCOURSE AND POWER: THE TOM CRUISE BIOGRAPHY AND THE CHURCH OF SCIENTOLOGY

On 15 January 2008, Andrew Morton's *Tom Cruise: An unauthorised biography* was released in the USA, and was expected to become a best seller. However, the book was seen by the Church of Scientology—a wealthy, powerful and extremely litigious religious group, of which actor Tom Cruise is a high-profile and loyal member—as an attack on its teachings. The church threatened legal action on the author.

Fearing similar threats, the book was not published in the UK. In Australia, the leading booksellers decided not to sell or stock it as they feared the church's accusations of defamation (Cumming, 2008). The Church of Scientology is seen as bent on intimidation through prolonged and expensive legal procedures on adversaries, rather than by winning the lawsuits against anyone who 'talks about' it in a negative way.

Case Studies 14.13 and 14.14 indicate how the powerful get to decide 'who talks about them and how they will be talked about'.

TEXTUAL ANALYSIS

All texts, be they media or otherwise, borrow from existing texts. Even when we use language to speak or write in everyday situations, we draw on an existing text: a language. It is the same with media texts. The following examples indicate some common applications of this intertextuality:

- In 2007 the popular Australian Broadcasting Corporation (ABC) TV satire *Chaser's war on everything* referred to current events.
- A media or our interpersonal texts (for example, a conversation) can refer to current affairs or media texts.
- Every time a novel is adapted as a film, or a screenplay is used as the basis for the film, the process of intertextuality results.
- Cover songs or new versions of popular songs, rap music using existing sound tracks or referring to the singer's life experiences, and films using existing songs in their soundtracks are all applications of intertextuality.

In other words, texts are not completely original. Therefore, the meanings embedded in the existing ones will be carried over to the new ones as well.

APPLICATIONS OF TEXTUAL ANALYSIS IN MEDIA AND COMMUNICATION

Media studies are about examining media texts. Therefore, textual analysis is often used as a research method to examine biases, dominant discourses and their framing, and representations of various groups and issues embedded in media texts.

APPLICATIONS OF TEXTUAL ANALYSIS IN JOURNALISM

Textual analysis is an attempt to understand how meaning moves from the author to the audience and how the text is related to other variables such as power, ideology and discourses that came before it (Frey et al., 1991). In journalism, programs such as *MediaWatch* (on the ABC) or organisations such as Fairness and Accuracy in Media, which critique the media's performance, do so via textual analyses. The research method is useful on a daily basis for reporters, editors, news directors, producers, media critics and researchers (Morris, 2004). It helps these professions to:

- evaluate a news story or feature they have written by using the aspects of a narrative, which has a description and a turning point, to write it in chronological order.
- consciously use specific connotations, analogies, myths, metaphors, euphemisms, disphemisms, induction and deduction (general to specifics) within news reports. They can use specific angles (analogous to frames in discourses) to enrich their stories or to create specific meanings. For example, they may choose among the synonyms 'refugees', 'illegal immigrants', 'asylum seekers' and 'unauthorised arrivals' based on the angle used in a news story.
- look for 'coded language' that refer to specific issues (Morris, 2004) when reading legal or political texts. For example, former US President Ronald Reagan used the code word 'unfair advantage' to refer to Affirmative Action policies benefiting minorities; former US President George Bush Snr used the code word 'family values' to refer to unmarried mothers stereotyped as black and on welfare (Weerakkody, 2001); and former Australian Prime Minister John Howard used the terms 'middle Australia' and 'aspirational voters' when referring to supporters of his Coalition, creating specific connotations.
- look for permissive language in legal and policy documents such as 'may' 'shall' and 'will' to examine how much latitude is available under these rules and legislation, in order to interpret them for their readers (Morris, 2004).
- use textual analysis to examine media bias based on the ideology embedded or 'spin' used in a news story (Frey et al., 1991).
- use news angles (framing) (Solomon, 1992) and specific images to create specific connotations (Frey et al., 1991).

APPLICATIONS OF TEXTUAL ANALYSIS IN PUBLIC RELATIONS

Public relations (PR) uses textual analysis in order to examine how its messages can be made more effective. This can be in terms of the layout, colours and other aspects of semiotics related to producing printed or audio-visual materials, or designing websites and signage.

EXAMPLE 14.29

Discourses of politics and campaign slogans

Discourses and their framing are the basis of PR messages. The most suitable slogans and metaphors or arguments used in political campaigns depend on the public making the dominant reading of PR messages.

In the 2004 Australian federal election campaign, the incumbent Coalition framed the discourse of interest rates by saying: 'Interests rates (on home loans) will go up under a [opposition] Labor government.'

During the 2001 federal election campaign after the refugees crisis, Australian Prime Minister John Howard used a specific discourse and framed the issue as, 'We decide who comes into our country and under what circumstances'. This eliminated from the discussion Australia's international responsibilities towards refugees and asylum seekers.

These discourses and their framings and slogans are developed by PR professionals, applying the concepts of denotations and connotations. Incidentally, on both occasions the party using these discourses and frames won the election.

Summary

We learned that there are several types of textual analysis and three types of signs—icon, index and symbol—used in semiotic analysis, which looks at signs and their meanings. Signs have their conventions, as well as denotations and the respective connotations they give rise to. We examined the concept of codes such as languages, before learning about genre and narrative analysis of texts. Polysemy or multiple readings of the same text is linked to our culture and shaped by our memberships in specific social groups in society.

Discourse analysis was discussed in terms of their frames and links to power relations in society. We looked at intertextuality (a text borrowing aspects from existing texts) and examined the use of textual analysis in journalism, media and communication, and public relations.

The next chapter examines the analysis of data collected from quantitative and qualitative research methods.

Try this ...

Choose your favourite TV program or film and look for examples within the text that illustrate the following concepts under each type of textual analysis discussed in the chapter:

- a semiological analysis—look for examples (specific scenes or segments) that illustrate the three different types of signs used, and the denotations and connotations arising from the techniques of film or video (such as camera angles, settings, costumes, props, music and sound effects), as well as the metaphors and myths, used in creating meanings. For example, what do the settings, costumes, props etc connote about the characters and their nature, lifestyles, affluence and socio-economic status?

- a genre analysis—examine what genre it belongs to and how it is different from any other genre based on its salient features; identify other texts that fall into the same genre and the type of audience it is aimed at; ascertain how its iconography (related to settings, mise-en-scene) creates specific meanings; and identify the conventions and functions of the genre the text belongs to.

- an examination of its use of recombinant genres—study a few mass media texts that can be described as belonging to recombinant genres. What genres have been combined to create each of these texts?
- narrative analysis—examine the themes embedded in the film or program, its narrative structure; the **dramatic personae** (or stock characters) present and the cultural myths embedded in its ending; what its functions in society are; and what the story, plot and the narrative itself says about the society and the times in which it is set. (For example, link it to any urban legends or myths included.)
- an examination of its use of multiple readings—identify the multiple readings (or the polysemic nature) of the text and the dominant, resistant and negotiated readings that can be made.
- a discourse analysis—identify whose individual, group, organisational or institutional discourses are embedded in it; whose interests are served in the process; the types of framing, adjectives, metaphors, analogies, adjectives, euphemisms and dysphemisms used; and what alternative discourses and frames that are possible.
- an examination of intertextuality—examine a text and identify which aspects of existing texts it has borrowed from.

Further reading

Allen, R C (ed.) 1992. *Channels of discourse reassembled*. University of North Carolina Press, Chapel Hill, NC.

Berger, A A 2005. *Media analysis techniques*, 3rd edn. Sage, London.

Burns, G & Thompson, R J 1989. *Television studies: Textual analysis*. Praeger, New York.

Fairclough, N 2003. *Analysing discourse: Textual analysis for social research*. Routledge, London.

Hansen, A, Cottle, S, Negrine, R & Newbold, C 1998. *Mass communication research methods*, Macmillan, London.

McKee, A 2003. *Textual analysis: A beginner's guide*. Sage, London.

Ruddock, A 2007. *Investigating audiences*. Sage, Newbury Park, CA.

Schirato, T & Yell, S 2000. *Communication and cultural literacy: An introduction*, 2nd edn. Allen & Unwin, Sydney.

Additional resources

Feature films

A few good men 1992. Writer Aaron Sorkin, Director Rob Reiner. Castle Rock Films.

The Bourne ultimatum 2007. Writers Tony Gilroy and Scott Z Burns, Director Paul Greengrass. Universal Pictures.

Brokeback mountain 2005. Writers Annie Proulx and Larry McMurtry, Director Ang Lee. Alberta Film Entertainment.

Romper stomper 1992. Director Geoffrey Wright. Australian Film Commission.

Sense and sensibility 1995. Writers Jane Austen (novel) and Emma Thompson (Screenplay), Director Ang Lee. Columbia Pictures Corporation.

Water 2006. Director Deepa Mehta. Mongrel Media.

Part

5

Analysis of Qualitative and Quantitative Data

15 Analysing Data

In previous chapters, we learned in depth about the quantitative research methods of surveys (Chapter 8) and content analysis (Chapter 9), and the qualitative research methods of research interviews (Chapter 10), focus groups (Chapter 11) and field studies (Chapter 12).

This chapter examines the various issues and steps related to analysing the data collected using these methods in a systematic and efficient manner, with reference to the basic principles of qualitative and quantitative data coding and analysis. Thereafter, you will be introduced to the most popular computer software used in analysing qualitative and quantitative data in research related to media and communication.

This chapter will introduce you to the steps related to coding and analysing qualitative data using:

o the 'grounded theory' or the constant comparative method

o applications of the grounded theory method

o cultural issues and the grounded theory method

o analysing qualitative data

o computers and qualitative data analysis

o using **NUD*IST** or **NVivo** software in qualitative data analysis.

With respect to quantitative data, the chapter will introduce you to:

o analysing quantitative data

o data coding and analysis using Excel and **SPSS** software.

Note that since teaching you how to use these software programs is beyond the scope of this book, the principles of coding and analysis will be discussed in this chapter using manual methods, so that they can be applied once you familiarise yourself with the relevant software. In other words, what this chapter will do is analogous to teaching you the principles of creative writing so that you can either write that best-selling novel with a pen and ink or a computer, once you have learned how to use it.

Check if your institution has subscribed to NUD*IST, NVivo or SPSS software programs so that you can access them free of charge. There are training modules on the internet and commercially published workbooks or manuals accompanied by CD-ROMs that provide step-by-step instructions to help you learn Excel (Rosenberg, 2007) or SPSS (Norusis, 2006) on your own. Some vendors such as NVivo offer free interactive e-seminars and 30-day free trial software. A student version of SPSS is also available at an affordable price. These resources are listed at the end of this chapter.

Let's begin by examining the manual data analysis method of grounded theory, as applied to qualitative data.

THE GROUNDED THEORY METHOD

Introduced by sociologists Glaser and Strauss (1967), and further developed by Strauss and Corbin (1990), the grounded theory method or approach to the analysis of qualitative data refers to a process of using a systematic set of procedures to code data into named categories to discover **patterns** among them.

The interpretations and comparisons researchers make using these categories help them to understand a specific real-world phenomenon, develop theories (about the rules or patterns that appear to govern that phenomenon or people's behaviour related to it) and suggest strategies that may help to design measures to provide some control over that phenomenon (Strauss & Corbin, 1990).

The method is called 'grounded theory' because the 'theory' developed is 'grounded' in data collected from real life and then systematically examined. In other words, it is a very scientific method of theory development that is also creative (as categories and themes need to be identified and labelled) and combines the research traditions of positivism and interactionism (from the naturalistic research approach) (see Chapter 2).

The grounded theory method (also known as the constant comparative method or pattern coding) of qualitative data analysis uses a systematic set of procedures to develop an inductively derived 'grounded' theory about a real-world phenomenon (Strauss & Corbin, 1990: 24).

Grounded theory is different from hypothesis testing, which is deductive. Hypothesis testing uses a theory to generate a hypothesis that is then tested through observations or data collection (Babbie, 2002: 443). In other words, they are opposites.

> **Handy Hint**
>
> The grounded theory method tries to develop or build theories to explain a specific real-life problem or phenomenon by systematically analysing the patterns, themes and common categories observed in qualitative data. In other words, it looks at the data to see 'What's going on here?' and comes up with a theory to explain it by asking questions and making comparisons.

APPLICATIONS OF THE GROUNDED THEORY METHOD

The grounded theory method (or constant comparison) can be applied to: qualitative data collected from field studies to analyse field notes, depth interviews, focus groups, surveys (answers to open-ended questions), content analysis and documentary analysis. It also can be used to analyse written texts as well as audio and visual content. However, this chapter will only examine how written forms of texts can be analysed using this method.

The grounded theory method is applied across many disciplines, including social sciences, behavioural sciences, ethnography, conversational analysis, life histories, management, business, market research, organisational communication, and media and communication.

ANALYSING QUALITATIVE DATA

When analysing qualitative data using the grounded theory method, several steps need to be followed:

1 Have the interview data transcribed so that you can read the transcripts and familiarise yourself with what is available. If the data to be analysed are written—

for example, responses to open-ended questions in surveys, field notes from participant observations or printed texts such as documents—read them carefully to give you insights on what is going on with the phenomenon under study. The transcripts can be uploaded as electronic files when using computer software to analyse qualitative data.

2   Determine a 'statement of the problem' or a few general research questions. This statement of the problem would mostly apply to field studies. For others, preliminary research questions already should have been designed. The research questions or statement of the problem will indicate what you will need to focus on during the data coding. For example, in examining why Australians have been slow to adopt digital TV, the researcher needed to examine and code interviewers' and survey respondents' opinions on why they had not done so, and what would make them adopt digital TV.

3   Maintaining theoretical sensitivity is necessary to reduce interviewer bias during the data coding and analysis of data, which helps maintain the validity and reliability of the findings. Theoretical sensitivity is maintained by using the existing literature, researcher experiences and knowledge in the area under study. In other words, see if the data coding and analysis, as well as your interpretations, can be linked to or benefit from what is already known in the field (through prior research and theorising). This will indicate if you are looking at something new and previously unexplained.

4   Coding the data means breaking down the data, conceptualising them and putting them back together in new ways, so that they can be compared and interpreted to develop theories that can explain some aspect of reality. You may need to decide on the individual concepts or the unit of analysis at this stage. A unit of analysis is the smallest piece of information that can stand by itself, such as a word, phrase or opinion; for example, in explaining why they have not adopted digital TV yet, a respondent may say 'It's too expensive', which would be coded as an opinion.

TYPES OF CODING

There are several types of qualitative coding. We examine the following in this chapter:

* open or pattern coding
* **axial coding**
* **selective coding** (Strauss & Corbin, 1990)
* **housekeeping coding** (Baxter & Babbie, 2004).

OPEN OR PATTERN CODING

Open coding breaks down data into non-overlapping or discrete parts. The researcher then examines each of these parts closely and groups them according to their similarities and differences to answer the research questions. This is also known as 'pattern coding' (Miles & Huberman, 1984, 1994; Weerakkody, 1999, 2001, 2004a, 2006a, 2007b). Although tedious and time consuming, this is a precise process that gives the grounded theory method its specificity and scientific rigour.

Open coding: 'What will improve digital TV uptake in Australia?'

EXAMPLE 15.1

In pattern coding the 49 submissions made by members of the public to the Department of Communication, Information Technology and the Arts (DCITA) inquiry on digital TV uptake in 2005, an opinion expressed by Mr John Smith was coded as:

'Reduced price of set-top boxes will increase uptake.'

Source: Weerakkody (2006a).

The constant comparison of data (for example, opinions expressed by respondents) undertaken when coding these segments of qualitative data allows the researcher to see patterns between them emerging. But open coding can only allow for descriptions of the data under various themes of opinions expressed by respondents or field observations made by the researcher.

Once all the data have been coded, they are grouped according to similarities and differences and given a label (or name of a theme) that explains the characteristics of the theme and indicate its sub-themes, which will also be given names or labels.

AXIAL CODING

Axial coding takes open coding a step further by allowing a researcher to specify the conditions that created the category or how that category or sub-theme is 'framed' (Gamson, 1992; Weerakkody, 2004a, 2006a, 2007b). In other words, the opinions falling under each sub-theme are summarised or 'framed' to indicate its collective meaning.

Axial coding the theme: 'Why consumers do not adopt digital TV'

EXAMPLE 15.2

The 49 submissions made by members of the public to the DCITA inquiry (mentioned in Example 15.1) were pattern coded and grouped or categorised under six main themes.
They were:

1   Why consumers do not adopt digital TV
2   What should be done to encourage digital TV adoption
3   Problems faced when adopting digital TV
4   Advantages of adopting digital TV
5   Costs involved in adopting digital TV
6   'Other' opinions.

The main theme of 'Why consumers do not adopt digital TV' had ninety-nine opinions falling under it and were further grouped into the nine sub-themes, listed below.

Axial coding was conducted when opinions falling under each sub-theme were summarised as frames using Gamson's method (1992). It indicated the composite opinions of the individual members of the public who made the submissions to the committee on that theme. When summarised, they were categorised under the sub-themes and framed as follows.

a   Too few incentives—the cost of the digital set-top box needed to upgrade to digital TV is not worth the better picture and wide screen provided by digital TV, as there is not much additional content or programming available. Change from analogue to digital is not as

EXAMPLE 15.2

marked as in the move from black and white to colour TV. We do not care for surround sound or electronic program guides.

b   Limited choice of equipment for purchase—such as for sets with inbuilt set-top boxes, or DVD recorders with digital tuners.

c   Confusion as to what to buy—from the range of flat, high definition, wide screen, pay TV, plasma, LCD and digital TV sets available.

d   Happy with the existing system (established base or the old technology the new one will replace) and its reception and not interested in sports and films—people get used to bad reception with analogue and do not bother to improve it with digital TV.

e   Too expensive to upgrade as cannot afford to upgrade—will stay with current set until time to replace it.

f   Limited promotion—digital TV is not promoted by dealers such as Harvey Norman or Good Guys. Dealers not knowledgeable about the technology and are therefore not actually selling it. Very little publicity is given overall to digital TV on free-to-air TV— especially in regional areas.

g   Moving cut-off dates a disincentive—changing the cut-off date for the analogue signal from 2005 to 2008 is a disincentive to upgrade.

h   Ageing population not interested in upgrading.

i   Multiple dwellings (apartment complexes) need to upgrade their relay systems to receive digital television—owners not keen on the investment.

Source: Weerakkody (2007b).

SELECTIVE CODING

Selective coding refers to indicating what is most important about your study (or its central phenomenon) and its findings. It is the 'story' a researcher would like to tell the world about it. In the digital television study, Weerakkody (2006a) reported on 'What should be done to encourage digital TV adoption' (in Australia), as the most important finding, as the study was titled *Examining measures to improve digital TV adoption in Australia*.

EXAMPLE 15.3

Selective coding: 'What should be done to encourage digital television adoption?

The 49 submissions from the members of the public collectively indicated their views on the following theme of 'What should be done to encourage digital TV adoption?', with 101 opinions. It consisted of the following sub-themes:

a   Lift restrictions on multicasting—multi-channelling or additional channels can cater to those not 'sports mad' with greater variety and interactivity

b   Provide tax and other incentives to manufacturers and importers of equipment that suit the Australian standard.

c   Require all local programming to be produced in wide-screen format.

d   Mandate built-in digital tuners to cut the cost of buying one separately.

e   Increase digital TV coverage and signal strength in all areas.

f   Publicise the free-to-air digital TV service and the cut-off date of analogue TV more actively—especially in regional areas.

⋯⋯⋯>⟩

g   Address issues related to multiple dwellings to receive digital TV signals.
h   Examine the experiences of the UK in their early stages of digital TV adoption.
i   Encourage development of high-quality content (drama, documentaries and education).
j   Lift restrictions on datacasting and information services to free-to-air broadcasters.
k   Ban sale of analogue receivers without digital converters or set-top boxes, and subsidise low-cost set-top boxes.
l   Address people's motivations to embrace the technology and take account of cultural and social factors as well as technology and economics, which are constrained by geography and history.

Source: Weerakkody (2006a).

HOUSEKEEPING CODING (COMBINED WITH OPEN OR PATTERN CODING AND AXIAL CODING)

Housekeeping coding relates to making notations or references to the sources of the units of analysis being coded, so that they may be easily located if the researcher needs to check anything later on. For example, when coding an opinion expressed by a subject (or a unit of analysis) during a depth interview, the researcher should make notations about the demographic details of the interviewee, the interview (depth or focus group), and the page and line number of the interview transcript. This is analogous to giving an ID number to each returned survey when entering their data before analysis.

Pattern coding and housekeeping   When open coding the qualitative data, the process of pattern coding suggests using 6″ × 4″ or 15 cm × 10 cm index cards to code each opinion. A good approach is to use different coloured paper of the same size, where each colour denotes a different interviewee, type of interview (depth or focus group or survey) or different type of interviewee (men vs women). In the digital TV interviews seven different types of stakeholders of digital TV were interviewed: end-users (audience members), broadcasters (free-to-air and pay TV companies), TV content producers, the government, telecommunications organisations, equipment manufacturers, and dealers. Each group was given a different colour for the 6″ × 4″ coloured paper on which the opinion was coded. This helped compare the opinions of each stakeholder group when they were grouped under different themes and sub-themes.

Each opinion (the coloured paper) is given a specific identification number assigned in order of coding the data in sequence, beginning with the first interview, participant or opinion expressed in the first transcript and continuing through the sequence until the coding of all data is complete.

The opinions coded can be handwritten or cut and pasted from the transcripts on to the 6″ × 4″ coloured papers or cards. An opinion is not listed alone, as its context is also noted in sufficient detail on the coloured paper so that the opinion may be understood better during the analysis, without having to go back to the full transcript. The context is invaluable to an opinion to retain the richness of the data being coded (Lincoln & Guba, 1985).

The context may include: any information the subject drew on when making that comment, such as responses to the stimulus materials during a focus group; what sort of topic or issue caused the opinion to be expressed; and personal experiences of the subject or of another mentioned or drawn on when discussing that topic. On the other side of the 6″ × 4″ paper, write some details about the subject who expressed this opinion, such as age, sex and profession, and some interesting information about the person such as a 'sports fan' or 'does not watch TV' that would provide insights to the analyst when making interpretations of the data.

Entry on an index card or coloured paper used in pattern coding

ID No.	IN/FG	No.	Name of subject	Page no.	Line no.
0025	IN	2	John Smith	18	03

Opinion: Better pictures alone won't encourage people to buy digital TV.
Context: What do you think will improve take up of digital TV?

[Overleaf] Male aged over 50 years, end-user, earning less than $40,000 a year who is 'not a sports fan'.

In Example 15.4, the notation reads as follows:

- ID No.—identification number assigned to the opinion coded
- IN—interview (FG if focus group)
- No.—number assigned to the interview or focus group
- Name of subject—the interviewee's name or pseudonym
- Page no.—page number of the transcript where the opinion appears
- Line no.—line number of the page on which the opinion appears.

RELIABILITY CHECKS

The coding is carried out and described in the research report in a way that allows anyone other than the original coder or analyst to comprehend and replicate it, once provided with the basic description of the coding system. This aspect is useful in terms of carrying out an intra-coder or inter-coder reliability check on the data coding.

CODE MORE RATHER THAN LESS

Lincoln and Guba (1985) suggest that during the open coding (or examining each unit of analysis or unitising) stage, it is better to include data in the coding that is less relevant—and may be discarded—than fail to capture relevant materials or opinions. Therefore, it's helpful to include extensive details under the 'context' on the coloured papers.

It is also very important not to code more than one opinion on each coloured paper as a precaution against creating ambiguity when categorising them under themes and sub-themes. (This is analogous to avoiding double-barrelled questions in surveys; see Chapter 8.)

DEVELOPING THEMES AND SUB-THEMES (AXIAL CODING)

Once the coding is complete, the analyst must read each of the coloured papers and group them according to their similarities and differences of the opinions expressed, using continuous comparison as the coding progresses, within and between the groups.

These groupings arise out of the data itself because the grounded theory method is an inductive process.

Once each grouping or pile of opinions has a sufficient number of coloured paper or index cards, go through each pile to see if they are similar to each other and come up with a 'rule' for it. Then create a title or name based on the common theme apparent in the group of opinions or data. For example, in the digital TV study, the six themes identified were:

- Why consumers do not adopt digital TV.
- What should be done to encourage digital TV adoption.
- Problems faced when adopting digital TV.
- Advantages of adopting digital TV.
- Costs involved with adopting digital TV.
- 'Other' opinions.

A theme's title or name is one that catches its essence or the 'rule' as much as possible. The rule describes the theme's properties, how it will be 'framed' (with axial coding) and defines the specifications that justify the inclusion of each opinion or data segment under that theme. This is the basis of pattern coding, which helps identify the emergent sub-themes, patterns, frames or explanations of a theme of opinions, and summarises the theme into a number of overarching sub-themes or constructs (Lincoln & Guba, 1985).

THEORY BUILDING AND INTERPRETATION OF FINDINGS

The themes and their sub-themes and frames developed using the grounded theory method (constant comparison method or pattern coding) help a researcher to examine the research questions posed in a study and develop a theory to explain the phenomenon; for example, 'Why have Australians not adopted digital TV and what factors may encourage them to do so?'

THE GROUNDED THEORY METHOD AND FIELD STUDIES

The above discussion on how to code and analyse qualitative data using the grounded theory method applies to depth and focus group interviews, written and printed texts and answers to open-ended questions of surveys. In addition, the grounded theory method can be applied to data coding and analysing of field notes made of a participant observation. We examine this using a case study of an overt participant observation at a 'two-dollar shop'.

USING THE GROUNDED THEORY METHOD IN A FIELD STUDY: Case Study 15.1
THE TALE OF A TWO-DOLLAR SHOP

Nancy carried out an overt participant observation of the two-dollar shop in her local mall, visiting and observing the shop in several two-hour stints on different days and times, such as on weekday mornings, evenings and on weekends, to obtain a variety of observations.

She sometimes sat outside the shop observing its entrance and how people appeared to decide whether to enter the shop or not. When Nancy was outside the shop she was able to take field notes. For observations made while inside the shop, she made the notes immediately

Case Study 15.1

after returning home. She also recorded any conversations she overheard between the staff and customers or between various customers.

Nancy carried out some preliminary research about the two-dollar shop phenomenon, which arose due to the closure of shops during a recession in the economy. Various entrepreneurs would buy up the stock from these shops in bulk and sell them in the two-dollar shop outlets. Therefore, the two-dollar shops generally sold small miscellaneous items. These items were stocked for sale on rows of shelves arranged against walls, as well as all over the room, with wide enough aisles for customers to walk through, which meant a customer could see and be seen only by those shopping on that aisle, providing him or her a certain level of privacy. Customers could also linger without being noticed by the staff or too many other customers.

On one of her observations on a weekend, she noticed a middle-aged mother and her daughter in her thirties taking a long time examining almost every item on the shelves of each aisle, with the daughter saying, 'Mum look, this is beautiful …', and picking up small individual items such as ornaments but not buying them. During one of her observations on a weekday afternoon, she observed a group of intellectually disabled individuals being brought to the shop by their carers and being helped to buy small items and pay for them, with the carers asking, 'Do you have enough money?' She also saw fathers coming with their kids to buy plastic toys etc and leave within a few minutes without looking at other shelves.

Nancy also recorded as 'encounters' some conversations between staff and customers, customers who arrived together, and customers who struck up brief conversations with strangers while shopping (see Chapter 12).

In her data analysis, she used the grounded theory method to examine the real-life phenomenon of 'Shopper behaviour' in two-dollar shops. She observed how different people passing the shop would look at the shop and its windows and walk on, or examine the goods kept on racks outside the entrance without coming in. She also observed the diverse behaviours of shoppers inside the shop as:

o walking around taking a good look at what's on sale
o coming in to check specific items and then buying them and going away
o browsing through casually
o browsing leisurely, touching everything but not buying
o browsing leisurely and buying a few items
o buying a lot of items
o interactions between customers and staff
o interactions between customers who come in together
o interactions between customers who were strangers to each other
o characteristics of the different types of customers who seem to be more commonly seen at the shop.

Nancy examined her field notes or data and developed several themes or categories of shoppers who came in to the two-dollar shop, using open and axial coding. They were labelled as:

1 Cursory shoppers—those who came in for a few minutes, looked around and left
2 Non-shoppers—those who passed the shop without stopping or looking
3 Window shoppers—those who looked at the windows and racks outside but did not buy or come inside
4 Serious browsers—who spent a long time looking at things but bought nothing
5 Serious shoppers—who came in and bought a significant number of items for everyday use
6 Marginalised or stigmatised people—those who would not be comfortable or welcome in fashionable or regular shops, such as the intellectually or physically disabled and elderly people coming alone

⌐········>

7   Those that appeared to be just 'killing time'.

She also categorised the types of conversations or 'encounters' between customers and staff, customers arriving together, and customers who are strangers to each other based on their subject matter

discussed—such as asking for clarifications or about additional items.

She summarised and described the characteristics and behaviours of each of these groups and developed theories related to each group's uses and gratifications of the shopping experience at the two-dollar shop.

CULTURAL ISSUES AND THE GROUNDED THEORY METHOD

Strauss and Corbin (1990) point out that just as in other research methods, grounded theory also can make use of labels, categories, themes and sub-themes used by other researchers in similar or comparable previous studies when coding data for a new study. This is similar to using survey questions or instruments, or coding manuals or content categories for content analyses from previous studies. However, one should be careful as these come with 'baggage' from the previous studies, such as researcher biases or shortcomings in the methodology used.

Cultural issues become relevant when coding and analysing qualitative data using the grounded theory method because what a researcher assumes to be the meaning of a phenomenon or observation may not be the same as what the subjects consider them to be. For example, in the two-dollar shop field study, differences in demographic memberships between the researcher and the research subjects observed may lead to discrepancies between the interpretations of the shoppers' behaviours when analysed by different researchers. The meanings made by a researcher, shoppers or staff may vastly differ between individuals and groups. Therefore, methodological triangulation such as carrying out interviews and focus groups with shoppers, and interviews with staff, may become necessary to maintain the validity and reliability of the findings.

So far we have examined the manual methods of qualitative data coding and analysis. Let us consider how it may be done using computer software.

COMPUTERS AND QUALITATIVE DATA ANALYSIS

Since the late 1980s, using computer software in qualitative data analysis has become much easier as the programs have become more user-friendly. Word processing has made it easy to mark or highlight—as well as cut and paste—segments of data from interview transcripts or electronic documents, as a means of coding them. These segments can be copied into separate data file folders and analysed.

Today, the most commonly used computer software in qualitative data analysis are QSR NUD*IST (Non-numerical Unstructured Data Indexing, Searching and Theory-building) (Richards & Richards, 1998) and NVivo (QSR NUD*IST Vivo)—both developed in Australia but used worldwide. However, these software use the same principles of pattern coding and can only help process the text by doing the more mechanical and routine aspects.

In other words, the thinking behind the data coding and analysis still has to come from the researcher, who gets help from the software to search for the occurrences of similar data such as looking for keywords and phrases, and then copy, cut and paste them in a separate file before the analysis. This makes the process faster and more efficient and is useful when analysing large amounts of data. For small projects with up to about twenty interviews, the manual pattern coding method may be used, if learning to use the software at short notice is not an option.

NVivo carries out the same functions as NUD*IST, but is more user-friendly. However, for large projects, NUD*IST would be more suitable. If your institution has a site licence for these software, try their tutorials to teach yourself.

COMPUTER-ASSISTED QUALITATIVE DATA ANALYSIS

There are three steps involved in qualitative data analysis using computer software (Baxter & Babbie, 2004):

1 preparing computer data files
2 preparing the data for analysis or coding
3 analysing the data

Preparing computer data files   This step involves entering the texts or documents to be coded and analysed into a computer. These include your word-processed field notes, interview transcripts, answers to open-ended questions of surveys, and electronic versions of documents such as newspaper articles on NexisLexis or Factiva that are to be coded and content analysed.

Preparing the data for analysis or coding   The next step is to organise and prepare the text available as computer data files for the coding and analysis. This is similar to combining the housekeeping and open coding steps of the data coding process, where text indexing and retrieval functions will help the researcher to keep track of where the data come from.

In other words, the software will search for the occurrences of specific data segments, note their locations and the context in the document, just as each 6″ × 4″ cards or coloured papers do but much faster and more conveniently and efficiently.

The 'keyword in context' function will search for a given word in the data file, as well as look for its synonyms. It can also look for word occurrences to search for a given sequence of letters that will identify different forms of a word; for example, the sequence 'happ' to find 'happy', 'happily' and 'happiness'.

'Boolean operators' (for example, 'and', 'or' and 'not') help to search for occurrences of words within a given context (as done when searching a library's catalogue or on Google). The researcher can ask the software to look for specific words located within a certain number of words within each other; for example, 'Tasmania' within ten words of 'protests', 'environment', 'pulp mill' or 'pollution' if examining the media coverage of the proposed Tasmanian pulp mill in late 2007.

Searching under 'vocabulary' or 'word frequency' for different words terms, and slang used when discussing a given topic, theme or issue helps to help identify the differences between respondents when discussing the same topic. (Note that most functions available with word-processing software, such as a thesaurus, have been included in this data analysis software.)

Analysing the data   The software can help examine 'co-occurrences' and 'associated words' within the text analysed that can identify the framing (selecting aspects and giving them salience) within a discourse or the ideology embedded in the message (see

Chapter 14). For example, it can examine the co-occurrence of the words 'refugees' with 'crime', 'integration', 'assimilation', 'illegal immigrants' or 'queue jumpers' (negatively) or with 'multiculturalism', 'humanitarian', 'migration' and 'diversity' (positively) to provide a context in which these discourses are framed.

Having examined the data analysis of qualitative data, we now briefly examine how quantitative data may be analysed.

Analysis of quantitative data   If the source of quantitative data comes from fewer than 200 surveys or units of analysis (texts) content analysed, and you are not familiar with the use of relevant computer software, the data analysis may be carried out manually without much difficulty using pen and paper. You will need an unused or 'blank' survey or content analysis coding sheet when manually coding the data. Use a slash (/) near the category of each variable on the 'blank' survey or coding sheet where a response has been recorded to indicate it has been selected by the respondent (in a survey) or coder (in a content analysis).

As you code each survey or coding sheet, you can indicate the selection as /, //, ///, //// and 7/// to indicate that one, two, three, four or five occurrences have been recorded, respectively. Remember to count incidents where there has been no response to each variable or question, so that the frequencies and percentages can be calculated accurately.

Once the data entry for all the surveys or coding sheets has been completed, add up the slashes under each category (for example, 7///7///// as 13) to indicate their frequencies (how many per category of the same variable) and calculate their percentages. You can also calculate the mean, median, mode, maximum, minimum and range the same way. However, if you need to calculate the cross-tabulations to compare between variables and their categories (for example, numbers and percentages of readers of newspaper A and B who are male and female) it will be more complicated and may require using software such as Excel.

Data analysis using Excel   Today, most computers will have Excel software as a matter of course, which means it will likely be more accessible to you than SPSS for analysing quantitative data. A manual and accompanying CDROM for using Excel (Rosenberg, 2007) allows you to learn and carryout a descriptive data analysis and the statistical tests discussed in Chapter 7.

A row in an Excel data file can be dedicated to one survey, case or unit of analysis (coding sheet), while each column can be devoted to one variable. You may be able to follow the Excel tutorial to teach yourself. Also note that Excel data files can be transferred to SPSS for analysis.

Data analysis using SPSS   SPSS (Statistical Package for the Social Sciences) was introduced in the 1960s and has gradually become more user-friendly. The latest version (16.0) uses Windows-like dialogue boxes that allows us to select the required function or statistical test that needs to be carried out (Hansen et al., 1998).

Just as with NUD*IST and NVivo, data analysis using SPSS involves three steps:

1   creating a data file
2   entering the data or coding
3   analysing the data.

Creating a data file   Once you open the SPSS program on your computer—assuming it has been downloaded from your organisation's website (which has a site licence) onto your desktop—open its data entry window. This will look similar to a blank data file in Excel. On the top row, columns are labelled 'var' while rows are numbered from 1 onwards. See the book's Online Resources Centre <www.oup.com.au/orc/weerakkody> for Figures 15.1 to 15.6, which explain the process for creating a datafile and data analysis on SPSS. (See Figure 15.1 SPSS Data entry window.)

Note that just as with Excel, each row in SPSS is devoted to each case (survey or content analysis coding sheet) and each column is devoted to one variable in the survey or coding sheet. Move the cursor to the first cell on the top left-hand corner of the data file and click it. Pull down the Data menu to open the dialogue box titled 'Define Variable'. This is where you name each variable for your data file. Each name or value can take up to eight characters and can be numeric (numbers), a date (10.12.07) or a string (words or phrases). (See Figure 15.2 'Define Variable' dialogue box.)

You will see that the 'Define Variable' dialogue has the 'Variable Name' VAR0001 (eight characters), which can be changed to any variable name of your choice. Let us say it is a name of a newspaper. So the variable can be named 'NEWSPAPR'. Click OK and you will see the dialogue box 'Define Variable Type'. (See Figure 15.3 Define Variable Type dialogue box.)

You will need to select the type of variable from the list (numeric, date, string, dollar etc) and indicate the 'width' of the variable (up to eight spaces) and the number of decimal places needed to code your data if it is a numerical value (for example, two decimals). Click 'Continue' to open the 'Define Labels' dialogue box. (See Figure 15.4 Define Labels dialogue box.)

When it asks for 'Variable Label', we can indicate 'Newspaper'. It is a good idea to use variable names that are easily linked to the actual variable to make the analysis and interpretation of data analysis easier to grasp. In other words, it is better to use NEWSPAPR than labelling your variables VAR 1, VAR 2 etc.

This dialogue box also asks for values (or categories of the variable). Looking at your survey or the content analysis coding sheet, you could list 'Value 1 for the 'Value Label' 'MelbAge' (*The Age*—Melbourne). Click 'Add' and enter the next one: 'Value 2' as 'AUSTRALN' (*The Australian* newspaper). Click 'add' again and continue until all the values for the variable have been entered. When it is done, click 'Continue'. Enter the next variable until completed.

Make sure you choose the correct 'variable type' for each variable and remember to save your data file.

Entering the data or coding   Take each survey (or content analysis coding sheet) and enter the corresponding data under each variable. Once all data have been entered, save the file. Now you are ready to carry out your data analysis.

Analysing the data   Examine the research questions (or hypotheses) to identify the independent and dependent variables involved and what types of statistical analyses are required to examine or test them. Identify the variables that need to be selected for calculating descriptive statistics, such as frequencies and statistics. Select the 'Frequencies' dialogue box for this purpose. (See Figure 15.5 'Frequencies' dialog box.)

Note that the list of your variables will appear on the left-hand side, from which you need to select the ones needed for the calculations. You will also be able to obtain the descriptive summaries for mean, median, mode, maximum, minimum and range.

Click the appropriate boxes such as 'Display Frequency Tables' and select the statistical tests you want and click OK. This will provide you with your 'output tables' that may be used as tables in your report. You may carry out 'Cross tabs' (cross tabulations) the same way. (See Figure 15.6 output window for 'Frequencies'.)

Summary

This chapter examined the grounded theory method, pattern coding and data analysis as applied to analysing qualitative data, collected from depth and focus group interviews, responses to open-ended questions in surveys, field notes from participant observations, and electronic and other texts. It outlined the different stages of the data coding and analysis process—such as open or pattern coding, axial coding, selective coding and housekeeping coding—required before qualitative data can be analysed.

It introduced the reader to using computer software such as NUD*IST or NVivo for analysing qualitative data and Excel and SPSS for analysing quantitative data.

Try this ...

To obtain hands-on experience in coding and analysing both qualitative and quantitative data, try the following exercises.

1 Use the list of survey responses to open-ended questions provided in this book's Online Resources Centre (www.oup.com.au/orc/weerakkody). Following the grounded theory method, carry out an open or pattern coding to develop a set of themes and sub-themes that arise from the qualitative data and summarise their frames. Develop a theory that can explain the real-life phenomenon examined with the survey.

2 Use the transcript of the depth interview provided in the online resources. Carry out a qualitative data analysis using the grounded theory method to identify the themes and sub-themes of opinions expressed and summarise their frames embedded in the data.

3 Use the field notes you made when carrying out the participant observation exercise in Chapter 12. (Alternatively, you may use the field notes provided in the online resources.) Carry out a qualitative data analysis using the grounded theory method to develop a few categories of behaviour indicated by the subjects observed in the setting. What kind of theory can you develop to explain this phenomenon?

4 Download the survey provided in the online resources. Make ten copies of it and ask your friends, family and acquaintances to complete it. Carry out a manual data analysis of this survey data to obtain frequencies and percentages, as well as descriptive statistics such as the mean, median, mode, maximum, minimum and range for your survey respondents and their responses. See if you can do the same using Excel and SPSS software.

Further reading

Bazeley, P 2007. *Qualitative data analysis with NVivo*. Sage, London.

Gahan, C & Hannibal, M 1998. *Doing qualitative research using QSR NUD*IST*. Sage, London.

Goulding, C 2002. *Grounded theory: A practical guide for management, business and market researchers*. Sage, London.

Hahn, C 2008. *Doing qualitative research using your computer: A practical guide*. Sage, Newbury Park, CA.

Additional resources

Software

QSR International free trial software NVivo 7—www.qsrinternational.com/products_free-trial-software.aspx (accessed 10 October 2007).

SPSS Student Version 15.0 for Windows, Prentice Hall—www.spss.com/vertical_markets/education/SPSS_student_versions.htm (accessed 10 October 2007).

References

Ackland, R & Florence, K 1995. More McCircus. *Gazette of Law and Journalism, 33*, (August), 18.

Adler, E S & Clark, R 2006. *How it is done: An invitation to social research*, 3rd edn. Thomson Higher Education, Belmont, CA.

Alexander, M 2001. Thirty years later, Stanford prison experiment lives on. *Stanford Report*, 22 August. Retrieved 23 February, 2007 from http://news-service.stanford.edu/news/august22/prison2-822.html.

All the president's men (1976). Alan J Pakula (Director), William Goldman (Screen writer), Bob Woodward & Carl Bernstein (Writers). Warner Brothers. Feature film.

Amatas, C 2003. *An introduction to survey design*. School of Psychology, Deakin University, Geelong, Vic.

American Psychological Association 2001. *Publication manual of the American Psychological Association*, 5th edn. American Psychological Association, Washington D.C.

Anonymous 1996. *Primary colors: A novel of politics*. (Author Joe Klein). Random House, New York.

APA 2003. *Publication manual of the American Psychological Association*, 5th edn. American Psychological Association, Washington D.C.

Asimov, I 1980. Science must be understood and understanding. *Evening Gazette* (Worcester, MA), 19 August, p. 19.

Atwater, T & Weerakkody, N D 1994. *A portrait of urban conflict: The* Los Angeles Times' *coverage of the Los Angeles riots*. Paper presented to the Association for the Education of Journalism and Mass Communication (AEJMC) Annual Conference, Atlanta, GA, USA. August (pp. 1–30 plus appendices).

Australian Broadcasting Corporation, 2006. *Answered by fire*. Accessed 12 December 2006 from www.abc.net.au/tv/guide/netw/200606/programs.

Australian Bureau of Statistics 2006. *Household form: August 8, 2006 census*. Australian Bureau of Statistics, Canberra, ACT.

Australian Bureau of Statistics 2007a. Collecting data using Live Audience Voting Technology. *Methodological News (Newsletter)*, June. Australian Bureau of Statistics, Canberra, ACT. Retrieved 7 June 2007 from www.abs.gov.au/ausstas/abs@.nfs.

Australian Bureau of Statistics 2007b. *2006 Census non-response rates fact sheets*. Australian Bureau of Statistics, Canberra, ACT. Retrieved 9 July 2007 from www.abs.gov.au/ausstas/abs@.nfs.

Australian Communications and Media Authority 2007. *Australian families with children are 'media-rich', research finds*. Media Release 148/2007, 17 December. Retrieved 25 February 2008 from www.acma.gov.au/WEB/STANDARD/pc=PC_310897.

Australian News Commentary 2008. www.australian-news.com.au/codethics.htm.

Awad, I 2006. Journalists and their sources: Lessons from anthropology. *Journalism Studies, 7*(6), 922–39.

Babbie, E 2002. *The basics of social research*, 2nd edn. Thomson-Wadsworth, Belmont, CA.

Bauer, R 1964. The obstinate audience, *American Psychologist, 19*, 319–28.

Baxter, L A & Babbie, E 2004. *The basics of communication research*, Wadsworth-Thomson Learning, Belmont, CA.

Beeman, A K 2007. Emotional segregation: A content analysis of institutional racism in US films, 1980–2001. *Ethnic and Racial Studies, 30*(5), September, 687–712.

Berger, A A 1991. *Media analysis techniques* (rev. edn). Sage, London.

Berger, A A 1999. *Signs in contemporary culture: an introduction to semiotics*, 2nd edn. Sheffield Publishing Company, Salem, WI.

Berger, A A 2003. *Media and society: A critical perspective*, Rowman & Littlefield Publishers Inc., London (pp. 39; 41).

Berkowitz, D & Hristodoulakis, I 1999. Practitioner roles, public relations education and professional socialization. *Journal of Public Relations Research, 11*(1), 91–103.

Blue heelers 1994–2006. Southern Star TV, Channel 7. TV drama series.

Blumer, H 1969. *Symbolic interactionism: Perspectives and method*. Prentice-Hall, Englewood Cliffs, NJ.

Blumler, J G & Katz, E (Eds) 1974. *The uses of mass communications: Current perspectives on gratifications research*. Sage, Beverly Hills, CA.

Boring, E G 1930, A new ambiguous figure. *American Journal of Psychology, 42*, 444–5.

Boyle, M P, McCluskey, M R, McLeod, D M & Stein, S E 2005. Newspapers and protest: An examination of protest coverage from 1960–1999. *Journalism and Mass Communication Quarterly*, 82(3), 638–53.

Breit, R 2004. The legal environment. In J Johnston & C Zawawi (eds). *Public relations: theory and practice*. Allen & Unwin, Crows Nest, NSW (pp. 75–8).

Butchart, G C 2006. On ethics and documentary: A real and actual truth. *Communication Theory*, 16(4), 427–52.

Campbell, G 2001. *The little black book*, 2nd edn. Victoria University, Footscray, Vic.

Carey, C 2007. Woomera: Victims of the war zone. *Sunday Age*, 25 February, 'News Extra', p. 11.

Carpenter, S, Lacy, S & Fico, F 2006. Network news coverage of high-profile crime during 2004: A study of source use and reporter context. *Journalism and Mass Communication Quarterly*, 83(4), 901–16.

Caterson, S 2004. A plagiarism on them all. *Age*, 20 November, p. 8.

Charters, M M 1933. *Motion pictures and youth: A summary*. Macmillan, New York.

Cho, S 2007. TV news coverage of plastic surgery, 1972–2004. *Journalism and Mass Communication Quarterly*, 84(1), 75–89.

Christians, C G, Rotzoll, K B, Fickler, M, McKee, K B & Woods, R H Jr. 2005. *Media ethics: Cases and moral reasoning* (7th edn). Pearson Education Inc., Boston.

Citing your sources, Harvard style 2006. Retrieved 20 December 2006 from www.library.uwa.edu.au/education_training_support/guides/how_to_cite_your_sources/citing_your_sources_-_harvard_style.

Cohen, S B (Writer), Hines, A (Writer) & Charles, L (Director) 2006. *Borat: Cultural learning of America for make benefit glorious nation of Kazakhstan*. One America (Productions). Feature film.

Coleman, R 2004. Oral and life histories: Giving voice to the voiceless. In S H Iorio (Ed.). *Qualitative research in journalism: Taking it to the streets*. Lawrence Erlbaum Associates, Mahwah, NJ (pp. 93–107).

Commonwealth of Australia 2007. *Media and communications in Australian families: Report of the Media and Society Research Project*. Australian Communications and Media Authority, Belconnen, ACT.

Commonwealth of Australia, 1999. *National statement on ethical conduct of research involving humans* (p. 68). Retrieved 24 February 2004 from www.nhmrc.gov.au/publciations/synopses/e35syn.htm.

Commonwealth of Australia, 2005. *Telecommunication services availability in Australia 2004–2005: A report on the availability of fixed voice, mobile and data services in Australia*. Australian Communications and Media Authority, Melbourne, Vic.

Comte, A 1896. *The passivist philosophy* (Vol. 2). Bell, London.

Conway, M 2006. The subjective precision of computers: A methodological comparison with human coding in content analysis. *Journalism and Mass Communication Quarterly*, 83(1), 186–200.

Cooper, D 2004. Uni in turmoil as head rolls. *Weekend Australian*, 10–11 April, p. 6.

Cooper, E & Johoda, M 1947. The evasion of propaganda: How prejudiced people respond to anti-prejudiced propaganda. In W Schramm & D F Roberts (Eds). *The process and effects of mass communication* (rev. edn). University or Illinois Press, Urbana, IL.

Crotty, M 1998. *The foundations of social research: Meaning and perspectives in the research process*. Allen & Unwin, Sydney.

Cumming, A 2008. Scientology holds sway in banning Cruise book. *Age*, January 13.

Cunningham, S & Sinclair, J (Ed) 2000. *Floating lives: The media and Asian diasporas*. University of Queensland Press, St Lucia, Qld.

Cuthbert, M, Kent, K & Evans, J 1987. A cross-sectional study of newspaper coverage of the invasion of Granada. *Studies in Latin American Popular Culture*, Vol. 6, Arizona University Press, Tucson, AZ.

Da Rin, J & Groves, J 1996. *What's on the Web now for Australian Farmers?: A content analysis of 206 World Wide Web sites for Australian farm businesses*. Rural Industries Research and Development Corporation, Barton, ACT.

Daymon, C & Holloway, I 2002. *Qualitative research methods in public relations and marketing communication*. Routledge, New York.

de Klerk, F W 1998. *The last trek—a new beginning: The autobiography*, Macmillan, London.

de Saussure, F 1966. *Course in general linguistics*. McGraw Hill, New York.

Della Vigna, S & Kaplan, E 2004. *The Fox News effect; Media bias and voter behavior*. University of California, Berkeley Working Paper, November 6.

Dicken-Garcia, H 1998. The Internet and continuing historical discourse. *Journalism and Mass Communication Quarterly*, 75 (Spring), 19–27.

Donny Brasco 1997. (Director) Mike Newell and (Writers) Joseph D Pistone and Richard Woodley (book). Baltimore Pictures. Feature Film.

Donohew, L & Palmgreen, P 2003. Constructing theory. In G H Stempel III & G C Wilhoit (Eds). *Mass communication research and theory*. Pearson Education Inc., New York (pp. 111–27).

Dubecki, L 2006. Technological trauma: Cyber bullies more powerful than schoolyard thugs. *Age*, October 28, p. 6.

Durkheim, E 1982. *The rules of sociological method*. Free Press, New York.

Educational Broadcasting Corporation 2004. *Constructivism as a paradigm for teaching and learning*. Retrieved on 14 January 2008 from www.thirteen.org/edonline/concept2class/constructivism/index.html .

Eisenberg, E M & Goodall Jr, H L 2004. *Organizational communication: Balancing creativity and constraint*, 3rd edn. Bedford/St Martins, Boston, MA.

Enker, D 2006. *Fire in their hearts (Answered by Fire). Selected postings from East Timor*. Accessed 20 December 2006 from www.etan.org/et2006/may13/18answer.htm.

Entman, R. M. 1993. Framing: Toward clarification of a fractured paradigm. *Journal of Communication*, 43(4), 51–8.

Errington, W & van Onselen, P 2007. *John Winston Howard—The biography*. Melbourne University Press, Melbourne, Vic.

Faludi, S 2003. Sun sets on cowboy myth. *Weekend Australian*, 5–6 December, p. 9.

Fearns-Banks, K 2006. *Crisis communication: A case book approach*, 3rd edn. Lawrence Erlbaum Associates, Mahwah, NJ.

Feil, M 2006. Census should tell everything. *The Age*, 31 August, 'Opinion', p. 1.

Feldshuh, D & Bernstein, W (Writers) & Sargent, J (Director) 1997. *Miss Evers' boys*. HBO. TV Movie.

Feuer, J 1992. Genre study and television. In Allen R C (Ed.) *Channels of discourse re-assembled: Television and contemporary criticism*, 2nd edn. Routledge, London (pp. 138–60).

Fico, F, Freedman, E & Love, B 2006. Partisan and structural balance in newspaper coverage of US Senate race in 2004 with female nominees. *Journalism and Mass Communication Quarterly*, 83(1), 43–57.

Field, A 2000. *Discovering statistics: Using SPSS for Windows*. Sage, London.

Fink, A 1995. *How to ask survey questions*. Sage, Thousand Oaks, CA.

Fiske, J 1992. British cultural studies and television. In R C Allen (Ed.). *Channels of discourse-re-assembled: Television and contemporary criticism*, 2nd edn. Routledge, London (pp. 284–326).

Foucault, M 1974. *The archaeology of knowledge*. Tavistock Publications, London.

Frey, L R, Botan, C H, Friedman, P G & Kreps, G L 1991. *Investigating communication: An introduction to research methods*. Prentice Hall, Englewood Cliffs, NJ (pp. 89–93).

Gadamer, H-G 1976. *Philosophical hermeneutics*. D E Linge (Trans.). University of California Press, Berkley, CA.

Gamson, W 1992. *Talking politics*. Cambridge University Press, Cambridge, UK.

Gerard, I & Dayton, L 2003. A shock to the system. *Weekend Australian*, 'Inquirer', 27–28 December, p. 17.

Gilroy, T, Burns S Z (Writers) & Greengrass, P (Director) 2007. *The Bourne ultimatum*. Universal Pictures. Feature film.

Glaser, B & Strauss, A 1967. *The discovery of grounded theory*. Aldine, Chicago, IL.

Goffman, I 1967. *Interaction ritual: Essays in face-to-face behaviour*. Pantheon, New York.

Gordon, W T 1997. *Marshall McLuhan: Escape to understanding*. Stoddart, Toronto.

Graeme-Evans, P (Writer-Producer) & Zwicky, C (Executive Producer) (2001–2008) *McLeod's daughters* (Television series). Millennium Television, Nine Films and TV and South Australian Film Corporation. Channel 9, Sydney.

Gripsrud, J 1999. *Understanding media culture*. Oxford University Press, New York.

Grossberg, L 1991. Strategies of Marxist cultural interpretation. In R K Avery & D Eason (Eds). *Critical perspectives in media and society*. Guildford Press, New York (pp. 126–59).

Habermas, J 1981. *The theory of communication action*. T. McCarthy (Ed. & Trans.), two vols. Beacon, Boston.

Hall, S 1980. Encoding/decoding. In S Hall et al. (Eds). *Culture, media and language*. Hutchinson, London, (pp. 128–39).

Hansen, A, Cottle, S, Negrine, R & Newbold, C 1998. *Mass communication research methods*. Routledge, London.

Hass, T 2004. Qualitative case study methods in newsroom research and reporting: The case of the Akron Beacon Journal. In S H Iorio (Ed.). *Qualitative research in journalism: Taking it to the streets*. Lawrence Erlbaum Associates, Mahwah, NJ (pp. 59–73).

Heath, R L & Bryant, J 2000. *Human communication theory and research: Concepts, contexts, challenges*, 2nd edn. Lawrence Erlbaum Associates, Mahwah, NJ.

Hendrix, J A & Hayes, D C 2007. *Public relations cases*. Wadsworth, Belmont, CA.

Henningham, J 1998. Australian journalists. In D H Weaver (Ed.). *The global journalist: News people around the world*. Hampton Press, Cresskill, NJ (pp. 91–107).

Hindman, D B 2006. Ethics and the use of student samples. *CT & M Concepts*, Spring, p. 3.

Hirschheim, R A 1985. *Office automation: A social and organizational perspective*. John Wiley, New York.

Hope (2007). Feature film/documentary, Steve Thomas (Director), Sue Brooks, Steve Thomas, Kim Anning (Producers). Flying Carpet Films, Australia. Retrieved 15 August 2007 from www.melbournefilmfestival.com.au/2007.

Horkheimer, M 1972. *Critical Theory: Selected essays of Max Horkheimer*. M J O'Connell and others (Trans.). Continuum, New York.

Horkheimer, M & Adorno, T W 1994. *Dialectic of enlightenment*. J Convoy (Trans.). Continuum, New York.

Hornig, S, Walters, L & Templin, J 1991. Voices in the news: Newspaper coverage of hurricane Hugo and the Loma Prieta earthquake. *Newspaper Research Journal*, 12, 32–45.

Iraq Diaries, 2003. *Salam Pax: News from the ground #1*, Salam Pax, Electronic Iraq, 20 May, retrieved 13 February 2006 from http://electroniciraq.net/news/iraqdiaries/Salam_Pax_-_news_from_the_grand_1_817–817.shtml.

Jamieson, K H 1988. *Eloquence in an electronic age: The transformation of political speech making*. Oxford University Press, New York.

Jha, S 2007. Exploring internet influence on the coverage of social protest: Content analysis comparing protest coverage in 1967 and 1999. *Journalism and Mass Communication Quarterly*, 84(1), 40–57.

Jhally, S & Lewis, J 1992. *Enlightened racism: The Cosby Show, audiences and the myth of the American Dream*. Westview Press, Boulder, CO.

Just, M, Crigler, N, Alger, D, Cook, T, Kern, M & West, D 1996. *Crosstalk*. University of Chicago Press, Chicago, IL.

Kagay, M 1999. A sample of a sample: How the 'typical' respondent is found. *New York Times, November 4*. Retrieved from www.nytimes.com/library/national/ Accessed on November 6, 1999.

Katz, E & Lazarsfeld, P F 1955. *Personal influence: The part played by people in the flow of mass communication*. Free Press, New York.

Kevin, T 2004. *A certain maritime incident: The sinking of SIEV-X*. Scribe Publications, Carlton North, Vic.

Keyton J & Shockley-Zalabak, P (eds) 2006. *Case studies for organizational communication: Understanding communication processes*, 2nd edn. Roxbury Publishing Company, Los Angeles, CA.

King, C & Lester, P M 2005. Photographic coverage during the Persian Gulf and Iraqi wars in three US newspapers. *Journalism and Mass Communication Quarterly*, 82(3), 623–37.

Kizilos, K 2007. Small dreams. *Age*, August 8, p. 16.

Klapper, J 1960. *The effects of mass communication*. Free Press, New York.

Knobloch-Westerwick, S & Coates, B 2006. Minority models in advertisements in magazines popular with minorities. *Journalism and Mass Communication Quarterly*, 83(3), 596–614.

Kristiansen, C M, Fowlie, G & Spencer, S J 1982. Britain's broadcast coverage of the Soviet invasion of Afghanistan. *Journalism Quarterly*, 59, 638–41.

Kuhn, T 1962. *The structure of scientific revolutions*, University of Chicago Press, Chicago, IL.

Kuiper, S 2007. *Contemporary business report writing*. Thomson-South Western, Mason, OH.

Lakoff, G & Johnson, M. 1980. *Metaphors we live by*. University of Chicago Press, Chicago, IL.

Larsen, J F 1986. TV and US foreign policy: The case of the Iran hostage crisis. *Journal of Communication*, 36, 108–30.

Lazarsfeld, P, Berelson, B & Gaudet, H 1948. *The people's choice*. Columbia University Press, New York.

Leach, M & Mansouri, F 2004. *Lives in limbo: Voices of refugees under temporary protection*. University of New South Wales Press, Sydney.

Lee, K-Y & Joo, S-H 2005. The portrait of Asian Americans in mainstream magazine ads: An update. *Journalism and Mass Communication Quarterly*, 82(3), 654–71.

Levinson, P 2004. *Cell phone: The story of the world's most mobile medium and how it had transformed everything*. Pelgrave-Macmillan, New York.

Lincoln, Y S & Guba, E G 1985. *Naturalistic inquiry*. Oxford University Press, Oxford, UK.

Littlejohn, S W 1989. *Theories of human communication*, 3rd edn. Wadsworth Publishing, Belmont, CA.

Livingston, S 1997. *Clarifying the CNN effect: An examination of media effects according to type of military intervention*. Research paper R-18, June, Harvard University John F Kennedy School of Government. Cambridge, MA.

Lofland, J & Lofland L H 1995. *Analysing social settings: A guide to qualitative observation and analysis*, 3rd edn. Wadsworth Publishing Company, Belmont, CA.

Lull, J (Ed.) 1988. *World families watch television*. Sage, Newbury Park, CA.

Lull, J 1990. *Inside family viewing: Ethnographic research on television's audiences*. Routledge, New York.

Maier, S R 2005. Accuracy matters: A cross-market assessment of newspaper error and credibility. *Journalism and Mass Communication Quarterly*, 82(3), 533–51.

Malinowski, B 1922/1961. *Argonauts of the Western Pacific*. E P Dutton, New York.

Malinowski, B 1948. *Magic, science and religion*. Beacon Press, Boston.

Marcellus, J 2006. Woman as machine: Representation of secretaries in interwar magazines. *Journalism and Mass Communication Quarterly*, 83(1), 101–15.

McCombs, M E & Shaw, D L 1972. The agenda setting function of the mass media. *Public Opinion Quarterly*, 36, 176–87.

McCracken, G 1988. *The long interview*. Sage, Newbury Park, CA.

McLuhan, E & Zingrone, E (Eds) 1995. *Essential McLuhan*. Basic Books, New York.

McLuhan, M 1964. *Understanding media: The extensions of man*. MIT Press, Cambridge, MA.

Mead, M 1943. *Coming of age in Samoa: A study of adolescence and sex in primitive societies*. Penguin, Hammondsworth.

Meadows, M 2002. 'Tell me what you want and I'll give you what you need': Perspectives on Indigenous media audience research. In M Balnaves, T O'Regan & J Sternberg (Eds). *Mobilising the audience*. University of Queensland Press, St Lucia, Qld (pp. 253–65).

Meeske, M D & Jevaheri, M H 1982. Network TV coverage of the Iranian hostage crisis. *Journalism Quarterly*, 59, 641–5.

Merrigan, G & Huston, C L 2004. *Communication research methods*. Wadsworth-Thomson Learning, Belmont, CA.

Meyrowitz, J 2003. Canonic anti-text: Marshall McLuhan's understanding media. In E Katz, J D Peters, T Liebes & A Orloff (Eds). *Canonic texts in media research: Are there any? Should there be? How about these?* Polity Press, Cambridge, UK (pp. 191–212).

Miles, M B & Huberman, A M 1984. *Qualitative data analysis: A source book of new methods*. Sage, Beverly Hills, CA.

Miles, M B & Huberman, A M 1994. *Qualitative data analysis: An expanded source book*. Sage, Thousand Oaks, CA.

Moody, J 2003. Public perceptions of biometric devices: The effects of misinformation on acceptance and use. *Proceedings of the Informing Science and IT Education Annual Conference (InSITE2003)*, Rockhampton, Qld, June (pp. 753–61).

Morley, D 1980. *The 'Nationwide' audience: Structure and decoding*. British Film Institute, London.

Morris, J L 2004. Textual analysis in journalism. In S H Iorio (Ed.). *Qualitative research in journalism: Taking it to the streets*. Lawrence Erlbaum Associates, Mahwah, NJ (pp. 163–74).

Moss, D, Warnaby, G & Newman, A. 2000. Public practitioners' role enactment at the senior management level within U.K. companies. *Journal of Public Relations Research*, 12(4), 277–308.

Murphy, K 2008. Research body given protection: Minister to name new advisory panel. *Age*, 7 January, p. 5.

Muschert, G W & Carr, D 2006. Media salience and frame changing across events: Coverage of school shootings, 1997–2001. *Journalism and Mass Communication Quarterly*, 83(4), 747–66.

Neuendorf, K A 2002. *The content analysis guidebook*. Sage, Thousand Oaks, CA.

Noble, T 2004. Bad blood over samples from newborns. *Age*, 'Insight', 10 July, p. 5.

Noelle-Neumann, E 1973. Return to the concept of a powerful mass media. In H Iguchi and K Sata (Eds). *Studies in broadcasting: An annual of international broadcasting science*. NHK, Tokyo (pp. 67–112).

Noelle-Neumann, E 1974. The spiral of silence: The theory of public opinion. *Journal of Communication*, 42, 43–51.

Noelle-Neumann, E 1984. *The spiral of silence: Public opinion—our social skin*. University of Chicago Press, Chicago, IL.

Noelle-Neumann, E & Mathes, R 1987. The 'event as event' and the 'event as news': The significance of 'consonance' for media effects research. *European Journal of Communication*, 2, 391–414.

Norusis, M 2006. SPSS 15.0 *Guide to data analysis*. SPSS, Chicago, IL.

Orwell, G 1949. *Nineteen eighty-four*. Penguin Books Limited, New York.

Pettigrew, A M 1972. Information control as a power source. *Sociology*, 6, 187–204.

Picoult, J 2007. *Nineteen minutes*. Astria Books, New York.

Planalp. S 1998. Current issues arising at the confluence of communication and emotion. *Australian Journal of Communication*, 25(3), 65–79.

Potter, W J & Riddle, K 2007. A content analysis of the media effects literature. *Journalism and Mass Communication Quarterly*, 84(1), 90–104.

Propp, V 1968. *Morphology of the folktale*. University of Texas Press, Austin, TX.

Putnis, P 1994. *Displaced, re-cut and recycled: File-tape in television news*. Centre for Journalism Research and Education, Bond University, Gold Coast, Qld.

Quinn, A 2004. Watching the watchdog: Investigating journalism. *Australian Journalism Review*, 26(2), 161–72.

Raboy, M & Dagenais, B (Eds) 1992. *Media, crisis and democracy*. Sage, Newbury Park, CA.

Radcliffe-Brown, A R 1935. On the concept of function in social science. *American Anthropologist*, 37 (July–September), 394–402.

Reich, Z 2005. New technologies, old practices: The conservative revolution in communication between reporters and news sources in the Israeli press. *Journalism and Mass Communication Quarterly*, 82(3), 552–70.

Reporter's guide to citizen journalism, 2006. *Press Gazette*, 24 March. Retrieved 25 May 2007 from www.pressgazette.com.uk.

Richards, T J & Richards, L 1998. Using computers in qualitative research. In N K Denzin and Y S Guba (Eds). *Collecting and interpreting qualitative methods*. Sage, London.

Robert, K 2006. *Guerrilla marketing research: Marketing research techniques that can help any business make money*. Keegan Page: Online Publishing.

Rohde, D 2007. Army enlists anthropology in war zones. *New York Times*, 5 October. Retrieved 7 October 2007 from www.nytimes.com/2007/10/05/world/asia/05adghan.htm?.

Rosenberg, K M 2007. *The Excel statistics companion—CD ROM and manual*. Thomson-Wadsworth, Belmont, CA.

Ryall, J 2008. Enter the sisterhood: Melbournian is first Western geisha in 400 years. *Age*, 8 January, pp. 1, 2.

Sales, L 2007. *Detainee 002*. Melbourne University Publishing, Melbourne, Vic.

Samuels, B, Bodle, J & Meek, S (Executive Producers) 2006. *Answered by fire*. Television mini-series. Australian Broadcasting Corporation, Sydney.

Sarantakos, S 2005. *Social research*, 3rd edn. Macmillan, New York (pp. 395–421).

Savage, D 2002. *Dancing with the devil: A personal account of policing the East Timor vote for independence*. Monash Asia Institute, Clayton, Vic.

Schiffer, A J 2006. Blogswarms and press norms: News coverage of the Downing Street memo controversy. *Journalism and Mass Communication Quarterly*, 83(3), 494–510.

Select Committee on a Certain Maritime Incident Report 2002. The Committee, Canberra, ACT.

Signorielli, N 2005. *Violence in the media: A reference handbook*. ABC-CLIO, eBooks Corporation.

Sillars, M O 1991. *Messages, meanings and culture: Approaches to communication*. HarperCollins, New York.

Singleton, F N, Straits, B C & Straits, M M 1993. *Approaches to social research*, 2nd edn. Oxford University Press, New York.

Skalski, P D 2002. Computer content analysis software. In K A Neuendorf. *The Content analysis guidebook*. Sage, Thousand Oaks, CA (pp. 225–239).

Slonim, M J 1960. *Sampling: A quick, reliable guide to practical statistics for layman, student or businessman*. Simon and Schuster, New York.

Smith, C 1992. Media and Apocalypse: News coverage of the Yellowstone forest fires, Exxon Valdez oil spill, and Loma Prieta earthquake. *Contribution to the study of mass media and communication*, 36, Greenwood Press, Westport, CT.

Smith, G 1988. *Statistical reasoning*, 2nd edn. Allyn & Bacon, Boston, MA.

Solomon, W S 1992. News frames and media packages: Covering El Salvador. *Critical Studies in Mass Communication*, 9, 54–74.

Spencer, H 1896. *The principles of sociology*. Appleton, New York.

Spiked-debate 2006. Mobile phones and child protection: How far should we go? *Spiked/O2*, April. Retrieved 28 July 2006 from www.spiked-online.com/childprotection.

Stake, R E 1995. *The art of case study research*. Sage, Thousand Oaks, CA.

Star wars (1977). George Lucas (Writer and Director). Motion picture. Lucasfilm and Twentieth Century Fox Film Corporation.

Stern, S R 2005. Self-absorbed, dangerous and disengaged: What popular films tell us about teenagers. *Mass Communication & Society*, 8(1), 23–38.

Stewart, D W & Shamdasani, P N 1990. *Focus groups: Theory and practice*. Sage, Thousand Oaks, CA.

Strauss, A & Corbin, J 1990. *Basics of qualitative research: Grounded theory procedures and techniques*. Sage, Newbury Park, CA.

Sue, V M & Ritter, L A 2007. *Conducting online surveys*. Sage, Thousand Oaks, CA.

The Cosby show 1984–1992. Marcy Carsey, Tom Werner, Caryn Sneider and Bill Cosby (Producers). NBC TV. Carsey-Werner Company. TV series.

Thompson, H S 1966. *Hell's Angels*. Penguin, Hammondsworth, UK.

Thwaites, T, Davis, L & Mules, W 2002. *Introducing cultural and media studies*. Pelgrave, New York.

Trammell, K D & Keshelashvili, A 2005. Examining the new influences: A self-presentation study of A-list blogs. *Journalism and Mass Communication Quarterly*, 82(4), 968–82.

Turner, G 2000. Television news and current affairs: 'Welcome to Frontline'. In Turner G & Cunningham, S (Eds). *The Australian TV book*, Allen & Unwin, St. Leonards, NSW (pp. 89–102).

Turow, J 1989. *Playing doctor: Television, story telling and medical power*. Oxford University Press, New York.

Turow, J 2006. *Prime time doctors: Why should you care? A multimedia essay on CD ROM for first year medical students*, 2nd edn. Robert Wood Johnson Federation, Princeton, NJ.

United States Census Bureau 2007. *Data Finder— Population clocks*. Retrieved 13 April 2007 from www.census.gov/main/www.popclock.html.

US Government Printing Service 1949. 'The Nuremberg Code'. *Trials of war criminals before the Nuremberg Military Tribunals under Control Council Law*, No. 10. Vol. 2, 181–2. Washington D C. Retrieved 25 February 2007 from www.hhs.gov/ohrp/references/nurcode.htm.

van Dijk, T 1988. Semantics of a press panic. The Tamil 'invasion'. *European Journal of Communication*, 3, 167–87.

van Maanen, J 1988. *Tales from the field: On writing ethnography*. University of Chicago Press, Chicago, IL.

Veil, S 2007. Mayhem in the magic city: rebuilding legitimacy in a communication train wreck. *Public Relations Review*, 33 (September), 337–9.

Vickers, B 2002. *'Counterfeiting' Shakespeare: Evidence, authorship and John Ford's 'Funerall Elegye'*. Cambridge University Press, Cambridge, UK.

von Bertalanffy, L 1968. *General systems theory: Foundations, development, applications*. George Braziller, New York.

Wall, M 2006. Blogging the Gulf War II. *Journalism Studies*, 7(1), 111–26.

Walter, M (Ed) 2006. *Social research methods: An Australian perspective*. Oxford University Press, South Melbourne, Vic.

Weaver, D H & Wilhoit, G C 1986. *The American journalist; A portrait of U.S. news people and their work*. Indiana University Press, Bloomington, IN.

Weaver, D H & Wilhoit, G C 1992. *The American journalist in the 1990s: A preliminary report of key findings from the 1992 national survey of US journalists*. The Freedom Forum, Arlington, VA.

Weaver, D H & Wilhoit, G C 1996. *The American journalist in the 1990s: U.S. news people at the end of an era*. Lawrence Erlbaum Associates, Mahwah, NJ.

Weaver, D H & Wilhoit, G C 2006. *The American journalist in the 21st century: U.S. news people at the dawn of a new millennium*. Lawrence Erlbaum Associates, Mahwah, NJ.

Weaver, D H (Ed.) 1998. *The global journalist: News people around the world*, Hampton Press, Cresskill, NJ.

Weerakkody, N D 1999. Media and the construction of public opinion about Affirmative Action, race and related issues: A case study of opinions expressed during the 1992 US Presidential campaign. Unpublished doctoral dissertation, Rutgers University, New Brunswick, NJ, USA.

Weerakkody, N D 2001. Race as political strategy by US presidential candidates: A case study. *Ecquid*

Novi—The Southern African Journal for Journalism Research, 22(1), 67–95.

Weerakkody, N D 2002. The effects of censoring and the 'spiral of silence' on focus group interviews: A case study of discussions on immigration. *Qualitative Research Journal*, 2(3), 45–61.

Weerakkody, N D 2004a. A preliminary examination of public opinion in Australia on the use of biometric devices or identifiers in everyday life. *Proceedings of the Politics of Information Systems: Technologies and Applications (PISTA04) Annual Conference*, July 21–25, Orlando, FL, USA. (pp. 118–123).

Weerakkody, N D 2004b. Technology and marginalisation: A case study of the limited adoption of the intranet at a state-owned organization in rural Australia. *Issues in Informing Science and Information Technology*, 1, 545–64.

Weerakkody, N D 2006a. *Are we there yet? The adoption and diffusion of digital TV in Australia since January 1, 2001*. Paper presented at the Australian and New Zealand Communication Association (ANZCA) Annual Conference, 5–7 August, Adelaide, SA.

Weerakkody, N D 2006b. Left out of the loop. In J Keyton & P Shockley-Zalabak (Eds). *Case studies for organizational communication: Understanding communication processes*, 2nd edn. Roxbury Publishing Company, Los Angeles, CA (pp.142–9).

Weerakkody, N D 2007a. *The discourses and realities of children and their use of mobile phones in Australia*. Paper presented at the Annual Conference of the Australian and New Zealand Communication Association (ANZCA), Melbourne, Vic, July.

Weerakkody, N D 2007b. *The present and the future of digital TV in Australia*. Paper presented at the Computer Science and Information Technology Education (CSITEd 2007) Conference, 16–18 November , Balaclava, Mauritius.

Weiss, P 1989. Masters of the Universe go to camp: Inside the Bohemian grove, *Spy, November*, 59–76.

White, M 1992. Ideological analysis. In Allen R C (Ed.) *Channels of discourse-re-assembled: Television and contemporary criticism*, 2nd edn. Routledge, London (pp. 161–202).

wikipedia 2008. www.en.wikipedia/org/wiki/It's_the_ economy_stupid. Retrieved 7 January 2008.

Wilcox, D L & Cameron, G T 2006. *Public relations strategies and tactics*, 8th edn. Pearson, Boston, MA.

Wilcox, D L, Cameron, G T, Ault, P & Agee, W 2009. *Public relations: Strategies and tactics*. 9th edn., Allyn & Bacon, Boston, MA.

Willey, S 2004. Focus groups newsroom style. In S H Iorio (Ed.). *Qualitative research in journalism: Taking it to the streets*. Lawrence Erlbaum Associates, Mahwah, NJ (pp. 75–92).

Williamson, J 1978. *Decoding advertisements: Ideology and meaning in advertising*. Marion Boyers, London.

Wimmer, R D & Dominick, J R 2006. *Mass media research: An introduction*, 8th edn. Thomson-Wadsworth, Belmont, CA (pp. 66–86).

Woodward, B & Bernstein, C 1972. GOP security aide among 5 arrested in bugging affair. *Washington Post*, June 19. Retrieved 8 August 2007 from www.washingtonpost.com.

Woodward, B & Bernstein, C 1974. *All the president's men*. Quartet Books, London.

Wrigley, B 2002. Glass ceiling? What glass ceiling? *Journal of Public Relations Research*, 14(1), 27–55.

Wynhausen, E 2005. *Dirt cheap: Life at the wrong end of the job market*. Macmillan, Sydney.

Yin, R 1994. *Case study research: Design and methods*, 2nd edn. Sage, Thousand Oaks, CA.

Yin, R 2003. *Applications of case study research*, 2nd edn. Sage, Thousand Oaks, CA.

Yunjuan, L & Xiaoming, H 2007. Media portrayal of women and social change: A case study of 'Women in China'. *Feminist Media Studies*, 7(3), 281–98.

Index